UNFAIR DISMISSAL: LAW, PRACTICE AND GUIDANCE

by Michael Duggan

 Employment Law, Practice and Precedents Series

General Editor, Michael Duggan

© Michael Duggan 1999

Published by
CLT Professional Publishing Ltd
Part of the Central Law Group
31–33 Stonehills House
Welwyn Garden City
Hertfordshire
AL8 6PU

ISBN 1 85811 231 1

Typeset by Jane Conway

Cover design by Jane Conway
Cover photography by Jon Adams

Printed in Great Britain by Antony Rowe

For my Wife, Michelle,
and children, Francis, Andrew and Thomas.

CONTENTS

PREFACE

This book on unfair dismissal aims to provide systematic law and guidance of the general principles relating to unfair dismissal. Where possible I have set out the book in alphabetical order in order to make it more accessible. 1999 was a momentous year for unfair dismissal law. It saw the (long overdue) raising of the compensatory limit to £50,000. The Employment Relations Act 1999 has also introduced important changes to important areas of employment law, in particular by introducing new maternity and paternity rights, dependancy rights, new rights in relation to industrial action and new rights to be represented at disciplinary hearings. There is a raft of new regulations that flesh out these areas and more is one the way. In particular a new ACAS Code in relation to Disciplinary Matters is expected in the Spring. The new 'whistleblowing' provisions are likely to have a substantial impact upon the law.

The Book has been written as though the provisions of the Employment Relations Act 1999 are in force as it would otherwise prove too cumbersome to relate the old law which will shortly be repealed or out of date. It should be noted that the dating of the provisions of the Act coming into force are (or are expected to be) as follows:

- The right to be represented at a disciplinary hearing is likely to come into force in Spring 2000 (see Chapter 6)
- Parental leave and maternal care leave came into force on 15th December 1999 (see Chapter 18).
- New Maternity rights apply where the expected week of childbirth is 30th April 2000 (see Chapter 18)
- Trade Union recognition is likely to come into force mid 2000 (see Chapter 24)
- Part time working provisions come into force on 20th April 2000.

- The increase in the compensatory award came into force on 25th October 1999. (see Chapter 28) The basic award and additional awards increased from 1st February 2000.
- Industrial action ballots and dismissals is likely to l come into force some time in Spring 2000 (see Chapter 29).
- The Human Rights Act 1998 will come into force on 2nd October 2000.

There has also been much case law with **Haddon** (See Chapter 4 having a potentially far reaching impact on the approach to be taken by Employment Tribunals). Due to space constraints certain areas where there are no real changes and which are well covered by other texts (such as continuity) have only been summarised but it is hoped that they will provide separate Chapters in the next edition.

This book has taken far longer than intended because of the scope of the changes it has sought to wrestle with. I think I would have given it up long ago were it not for the unfailing support of my wife Michelle whilst writing it. My love and thanks to her. My three sons, Francis, Andrew and Thomas have also had to put up with much with an absentee father struggling to write and maintain a busy practice. The book is dedicated to the four of them.

MICHAEL DUGGAN,
Littleton Chambers,
February 2000

TABLE OF CASES

TABLE OF STATUTES

PART ONE
GENERAL PRINCIPLES

CHAPTER ONE
THE RIGHT TO
CLAIM UNFAIR DISMISSAL

This chapter will first consider the prerequisites to being able to bring a claim for unfair dismissal and then consider particular exclusions that apply to prevent, or modify the rights of particular categories of workers from being able to bring a claim in the Tribunal. It will finally consider the compromise agreements which exclude the Tribunal's jurisdiction.

Part 1. Prerequisites to the Right to bring a Claim

In order for a complainant to be able to present a complaint of unfair dismissal it is necessary that:

(1) the complainant is an employee within the definition contained in section 230 of the ERA 1996, who has

(2) sufficient continuous service (one year after 1st June 1999) to bring a claim, save where the complaint is of a type that does not require a period of qualifying service or the period is shorter, and

(3) the claim has been presented in time.

Part 2. Exclusions from the Right to Claim

An individual will **not** have a right to bring a claim where:

(1) The **category** of worker is excluded;

(2) **Diplomatic** or state immunity applies;

(3) The contract of employment is tainted with **illegality**;

(4) The employee has reached **normal retiring age**;

(5) The employee **ordinarily works outside Great Britain**.

Part 3. Compromises

Four headings will be considered under this section:

(1) ACAS settlements;
(2) Compromise agreements;
(3) Settlements before the Tribunal;
(4) Dismissal procedures agreements where there has been collective contracting out.

Part 1.   Prerequisites

(1) The Complainant must be an Employee

By sections 230(1) and 230(2) of the Employment Rights Act 1996 (ERA):

> "(1) In this Act 'employee' means an individual who has entered into or works under (or, where the employment has ceased, worked under) a contract of employment.
>
> (2) In this Act 'contract of employment' means an individual who has entered into a contract of service or apprenticeship, whether express or implied, and (if it is express) whether orally or in writing."

Since section 94(1) of the ERA 1996 provides that it is an employee who has a right to bring a claim of unfair dismissal against an employer, where the individual works under a contract for services (i.e. is self employed) rather than under a contract of service, he will have no such right. The same applies in respect of a claim for unfair dismissal under the provisions of section 295, TULR(C)A subject to certain modifications. It is therefore necessary to consider:

- the tests that the Tribunal is likely t o apply in deciding whether the complainant is an employee.
- Particular types of work namely:
    i) Agency workers
    ii) Casual workers
    iii) Directors
    iv) Office holders
    v) Parliamentary staff and Crown Servants
    vi) Partners

vii) Self employed contractors

viii) Temporary Workers

ix)   Workers Co-operatives.

The test to be applied

It is a question of mixed fact and law as to whether or not the contract is for services or service. The Tribunal's decision is not one with which the higher courts will interfere unless there has been a misdirection in law or the weight given to a particular fact amounts to a self misdirection. It is for the Tribunal to evaluate the facts which is a question of degree and to this extent there may be mixed fact and law. However, if the conclusion turns purely on the construction of a document this will be a pure question of law.

If the question of whether or not an individual is an employee is a question of law it is possible for the Employment Appeals Tribunal (EAT) to substitute its view for the findings of the Tribunal. Since no appeal lies to the EAT on matters of fact, the Tribunal's decision will not be interfered with unless it misapplied or misunderstood the facts or its decision was perverse – tests which are difficult to satisfy before the Higher Courts. Unfortunately, the Courts have differed over time as to whether the issue of employee status is one of fact or law, though it now seems to be reasonably settled that the question is one of mixed fact and law, so that provided the law has been correctly applied to the facts, the Higher Courts will not interfere with the Tribunal's decision.

It was held by the Divisional Court in **Global Plant Limited v Secretary of State for Social Services** [1972] 1 QB 139 that, in the absence of a contract in written form, whether or not there is a contract for services is a matter of fact. In **Ahmet v Trusthouse Forte Catering Limited** [EAT 124/82] the contrary view was taken by the EAT, following a passage from Stephenson LJ in **Young and Woods Limited v West** [1980] IRLR 201, so that it could revisit the issue. There continued conflicting decisions as to the correct approach to adopt (See **Addison v London Philharmonic Orchestra Limited** [1981] IRLR 261; **Midland Sinfonia Concert Society Limited v Secretary of State for Social Services** [1981] ICR 454 and **WHPT Housing Association Limited v Secretary of State for Social Services** [1981] ICR 737).

The Court of Appeal reconsidered the matter in **O'Kelly v Trusthouse Forte Plc** [1983] ICR 728. The Tribunal held that a number of waiters engaged on a casual basis were not employees but were engaged on fresh contracts, as independent contractors, each time they attended a banquet. The Court of Appeal, by a majority, held that the question of whether there was a contract for services or of service was a question of law and that it was for the tribunal of fact to both find and assess the facts which would dictate the correct legal answer. Sir John Donaldson MR stated:

> "In reality every tribunal of fact will find and assess the factual circumstances in ways which differ to a greater or lesser extent and so can give rise to different conclusions, each of which is unassailable on appeal, in this sense, but in this sense alone, their conclusions are conclusions of fact. More accurately they are conclusions of law which are wholly dependent upon conclusions of fact.

> The test to be applied in identifying whether a contract of one of employment or for services is a pure question of law and so it its application to the facts. But it is for the tribunal of fact not only to find those facts but to assess them qualitatively and within limits, which are identifiable in the abstract; those findings and that assessment will dictate the correct legal answer. In the familiar phrase "it is all a question fact and degree".

> It is only if the weight given to a particular factor shows a self-misdirection in law that an appellate court with a limited jurisdiction can interfere."

In **Lee Ting Sang v Chung Chi-Keung** [1990] ICR 409 the Privy Council held that the question of employment status was of mixed fact and law but was not open to any appeal unless there was an error of law or the decision was one that no Tribunal could have reached. It was for the Tribunal to interpret the facts, which was a question of degree.

Where the question of contract status turns purely on the construction of a document it is a question of law as to the correct status (**BSM (1257) Limited v Secretary of State for Social Services** [1978] IRLR 894). In **Davies v Presbyterian Church of Wales** [1986] IRLR 194, ICR 280 the House of Lords considered the test to be applied in respect of a full time paid pastor, whose appointment turned upon the Church's Book of Rules. Lord Templeman stated that:

> "The question to be determined is a question of law, namely whether upon the true construction of the book of rules a pastor of the church is employed and is under a contract of service."

Although, on the face of it, the House of Lords appeared to state that the issue of employee status is one of law in **McLeod v Hellyer Brothers Limited**, Slade LJ did not see any inconsistency between *Davies* and the *O'Kelly* or *Nethermere* case, since *Davies* involved the construction of a written document which is a question of law. (See also **Clarke v Oxfordshire Health Authority** [1998] IRLR 125.)

The intention of the parties is a relevant factor that will be taken into consideration though it is not conclusive, as the parties cannot alter the nature of the relationship by putting the incorrect label on it.

The parties may have described their status in a document but, whilst this will be one factor that may be taken into account, the description given by the parties is unlikely to be conclusive, as the parties cannot change their status merely by adopting the wrong label (See **Ferguson v John Dawson & Partners (Contractors) Limited** [1976] 3 All ER 817). In **Young & Woods Limited v West** [1980] IRLR 201 a sheet metal worker agreed to be treated as self employed. To this end he paid his own taxes and did not receive holiday or sick pay. The Revenue accepted him as self employed. The Court of Appeal upheld the lower court decisions that he was in reality an employee. Stephenson LJ stated that the pointers were strong enough:

> "to show that the label was a false label and that, though the mutual intention of the parties was undoubtably to call the work which Mr West was going to do for them services under a contract for services, nevertheless it was in reality service rendered under a contract of service. There is no such ambiguity in the relationship between Mr West and the company as could make their declared intention as to what is should be decisive of it."

The EAT took a similar approach in **Davis v New England College** [1977] ICR 6 where it did not accept a statement in the contract of a college lecturer that he was self employed.

The earlier case of **Massey v Crown Life Insurance Co Limited** [1978] IRLR 31; ICR 595 was distinguished. In that case a branch manager's status was changed from employee to independent contractor though his duties did not change. The scheme was approved by the Revenue. It was held that he was employed under a contract for services. Lord Denning stated that:

> "if their relationship is ambiguous and is capable of being one or the other, then the parties can remove that ambiguity by the very agreement itself which they make with one another. The agreement itself then becomes the best material from which the gather the true legal relationship between them..."

The Court of Appeal held that there was a genuine intention to change the relationship. It is apparent that the Courts will be astute to avoid the wrong label being placed on the employment relationship where this would have the effect of ousting the statutory jurisdiction. However, in limited circumstances, such as where the relationship is ambiguous or there is a genuine intention on the part of both parties to dictate the relationship the parties' intentions will be of some weight.

Where the legal relationship is not direct but is between two companies then there may be no contract of service (**Winter v Westward TV** [EAT 589/77]).

Mutuality of obligation is an important factor in considering whether the complainant was an employee as if there is no irreducible minimum obligation on the employer or employee during a period when the individual was not working he will not be regarded as an employee during those periods.

Mutuality of obligation has always been regarded as an important factor in deciding the true employment relationship between the parties. It was regarded as an important pointer in O'Kelly in showing that there was no employment relationship between the casual staff and the hotel. The issue has recently been considered in two cases where individuals were asked to work on an 'as required' basis. In **Clark v Oxfordshire Area Health Authority** [1998] IRLR 125 a nurse was registered with the Health Authority's pool to fill temporary vacancies that occurred from time to time. Her contract contained grievance and disciplinary procedures and a procedure for dismissal, there was a confidentiality clause, but there was no provision for holiday or sick pay. There was no obligation to provide continuous work nor was she under any obligation to accept work. No mutuality of obligation existed during the time that she was not working.

The EAT, however, found by a majority that she was an employee who was employed at all times under a 'global contract'.

The Court followed *Nethermere* and *McLeod*, stating that there could be no global contract that covered the time she was not working as there was no irreducible minimum obligation. Sir Christopher Slade commented:

> "On the findings of the industrial tribunal, the authority was at no relevant time under any obligation to offer the applicant work nor was she under any obligation to accept it. I would, for my part, accept that the mutual obligations required to found a global contract of employment need not necessarily and in every case consist of obligations to provide and perform work. To take one obvious example, an obligation by the one party to accept and do work if offered and an obligation on the other party to pay a retainer during such periods as work was not offered would in my opinion, be likely to suffice. In my judgment, however, as I have already indicated, the authorities require us to hold that some mutuality of obligation is required to found a global contract of employment. In the present case I can find no such mutuality subsisting during the periods when the applicant was not occupied in a 'single engagement'. Any obligation of confidentiality binding her during such periods would have stemmed merely from previous single engagements. Apart from this, no continuing obligation whatever would have fallen on the authority during such periods."

This decision makes it clear that the absence of mutuality will prevent there from being the status of an employee during the period when there is no minimum mutuality of obligation and has an important impact on the question of 'global' contracts in relation to casual workers (as to which see page 17). It may be contrasted with

Carmichael v National Power PLC [1998] ICR 1167; IRLR 301. The Appellants worked as tour guides round power stations on a 'casual as required' basis as and when they were asked to do so and were only paid when they worked. Evidence was given at the Tribunal that they felt obliged to work when asked but the Tribunal and EAT took the view this was a moral obligation and there was no mutuality of obligation. The Court of Appeal decided by a majority that this was wrong. Although the company only made work available as and when required, the intermittent nature of the engagement meant that a term would be implied that each guide be provided with, and required to take, a reasonable amount of the work. The Tribunal failed to take this into account in considering mutuality of obligation and, as this was the only reason for their decision, the appeal was allowed. Ward LJ stated that:

> "There was mutuality because there was an obligation to accept and perform some reasonable amount of work for the power station who were to make reasonable allocation of the work between the guides whom they had engaged."

It was further held that the contract of employment was a global or umbrella contract.

However, the House of Lords took the view that the Court of Appeal had taken the wrong approach and reversed the decision (18th November 1999). The House held that the Tribunal were entitled to find that it was not only the contract that governed the relationship. Lord Irvine took the view that the words "employment will be on a casual as required basis" in the contract was not capable in any event of imposing an obligation to work and the majority of the Court of Appeal were wrong in so finding. Lord Hoffman stated that:

> "Putting the matter at its lowest, I think that it was open to the industrial tribunal to find, as a fact, that the parties did not intend the letter to be the sole record of their agreement but intended it should be contained partly in the letters, partly in oral exchanges at the interviews or elsewhere and partly left to evolve by conduct as time went on....On this basis the ascertainment of the agreement was a question of fact with which the Employment Appeal Tribunal were right not to interfere."

The Tribunal had decided as a matter of fact that there was no mutuality and this was a decision it was entitled to come to.

A number of possible tests may be applied in considering the true position of the complainant though no one test is necessarily conclusive. Over the years the Courts have applied a number of tests:

1) The control test
2) The business integration test
3) The multiple or mixed test
4) Other factors

Over the years the Courts have developed and applied a number of different tests in trying to decide how to approach the question of whether an individual is employed or self employed and even today this is an area that remains in flux. Indeed, the Court's recent emphasis on mutuality of obligation, as discussed above, had thrown the law into a state of some confusion in relation to the status of many casual workers and it is apparent that many contracts of employment relating to casual workers are likely to require redrafting. The decision of the House of Lords in *Carmichael* is of some assistance in this respect.

1) The control test

An early test propounded by the Courts was the control test under which the Court would consider to what extent the employer had the right to control the work to be done by the individual and the manner in which it was to be carried out. The test itself is more difficult to apply where the work requires some specialist skill, for example that of a surgeon or computer programmer. The question of control may remain of significance as a *factor* in deciding whether the individual was an employee and was approached in this way in **Ready Mixed Concrete (South East) Limited v Minister of Pensions and National Insurance** [1958] 2 QB 497.

In **Narich Proprietary Limited v Commissioners of Pay-Roll Tax** [1984] ICR 286 the Privy Council considered whether lecturers of an Australian franchise of weight watchers were employees. They were paid by the lecture but had extremely detailed handbooks that contained instructions on how the lectures were to be conducted. The Privy Council considered the multiple test (below) but found that:

"While all relevant terms of the contract must be regarded, the most important, and in most cases the decisive, criterion for determining the relationship between the parties is the extent to which the person, whose status as employee or independent contractor is in issue, is under the direction and control of the other party to the contract with regard to the manner in which he does the work under it."

The control test will continue to play a part in helping to decide whether an individual is an employee or not, at least as a factor.

2) The business integration test
A second approach taken by the authorities is to ask whether the work of the individual is done as part of the business or whether he is on business on his own account so that he is not integrated into the business. This was the approach taken by Denning LJ in **Stevenson, Jordan and Harrison v McDonald and Evans** [1952] 1 TLR 101, where he stated:

> One factor which seems to run through the instances is that under a contract of service a man is employed as part of the business and his work is done as part of the business whereas under a contract for services his work, although done for the business, is not integrated into it but is only accessory to it."

Whilst this test has been followed in a number of cases (see **Beloff v Pressdram Limited** ([1973] 1 All ER 241) and is of use where the individual is a professional whose manner of work is not controlled by the employer (as with surgeons: **Cassidy v Ministry of Health** [1951] 1 All ER 574) the test has not been follows with much frequency and it is the third test that seems to be currently in favour. Although in **Lee Ting Saang v Chung Ci-Keung** [1990] IRLR 236 Lord Griffiths, in the Privy Council, approved the test as stated by Cooke J in **Market Investigations Limited v Minister of Social Security** [1969] 2 QB as being whether "the individual is in business on his or her own account", doubt was thrown on whether the test is of any real assistance in the case of someone carrying on a profession or vocation in **Hall (Inspector of Taxes) v Lorimer** (See below.)

3) The multiple or mixed test
The most popular approach in recent years is to look at all the facets of the relationship between the parties and to consider whether the factors cumulatively point to the relationship of employer and

employee or of independent contractor. The starting point in considering this test is the dicta of MacKenna J in **Ready Mixed Concrete (South East) Limited v Minister of Pensions and National Insurance** [1958] 2 QB 497:

> "A contract of service exists if these three conditions are satisfied. (i) The servant agrees that, in consideration of a wage or other remuneration, he will provide his own work and skill in the performance of some service for his master. (ii) He agrees expressly or impliedly, that in the performance of that service he will be subject to the other's control in a sufficient degree to make that other master. (iii) The other provisions of the contract are consistent with it being a contract of service."

MacKenna J also looked at the economic reality of the situation and asked where the risk of profit or loss lay in deciding that a lorry driver was an independent contractor. He considered a number of factors that pointed one way or the other in respect of there being a service agreement and considered that an individual is not prevented from being an independent contractor merely because some level of control is exercised.

Ready Mixed Concrete was considered by the Court of Appeal in **Express and Echo Publications Limited v Tanton** [1999] IRLR 367. Mr Tanton was engaged as a driver on a self employed basis. He, however, refused to sign an agreement which stated that, in the event of him being unable or unwilling to provide services he would provide another suitable person at his own expense but, in fact, did provide a substitute from time to time. The Court of Appeal considered that the Tribunal was wrong to have concentrated on what actually occurred rather than seeking to determine the mutual obligations between the parties. The Court of Appeal considered that where a person who works for another is not required to perform his services personally, as a matter of law, the relationship between the worker and the person for whom he works is not that of employer and employee. A right to provide a substitute is inherently inconsistent with the existence of a contract of employment. A contract of employment must necessarily contain an obligation on the part of the employee to provide his services personally. Without such an irreducible minimum of obligation, it cannot be said that there is a contract of employment. The recognition that a contract of employment involves mutual trust and confidence is consistent with a requirement of personal service. The approach to be adopted is summed up in the headnote to the case as follows:

> "In determining whether an applicant was engaged under a contract of employment or was a self-employed contractor, the employment tribunal should first establish what were the terms of the agreement between the parties. It should then consider whether any of those terms are inherently inconsistent with the existence of a contract of employment. If there is an inherently inconsistent term, what actually occurred may not be decisive. If a term is not enforced, that does not justify a conclusion that it is not part of the agreement. The obligation could be temporarily waived. If there are no such inherently inconsistent terms, the tribunal should determine whether the contract is a contract of service or a contract for services, having regard to all the terms".

In the present case the Court took the view that the provision in the contract entitling the applicant not to perform any services personally was not a sham and the only conclusion which could properly be reached was that this was a contract for services given the existence of this clause. It is apparent from *Tanton* that, whilst all the terms are to be considered, there is considerable emphasis on mutuality of obligation which may be decisive one way or the other. (Cf *Carmichael*.)

The mixed test was considered by the Court of Appeal in **Hall (Inspector of Taxes) v Lorimer** [1994] ICR 218; IRLR 171. Mr Lorimer worked as a freelance vision mixer and had built up a list of 22 companies for whom he worked. He performed all the work himself, on a first come first served basis save for 6 of 580 engagements. He had an office at home but worked from companies' premises with their equipment. The Court of Appeal considered that the decision of the Special Commissioners that Mr Lorimer was self employed was not perverse or wrong in law. Nolan LJ approved the statement of Mummery J in the EAT where he stated:

> "'In order to decide whether a person carries on business on his own account it is necessary to consider many different aspects of that person's work activity. This is not a mechanical exercise of running through items on a check-list to see whether they are present in, or absent from, a given situation. The object of the exercise is to paint a picture from the accumulation of detail. The overall effect can only be appreciated by standing back from the

detailed picture which has been painted, by viewing it from a distance and by making an informed, considered, qualitative appreciation of the whole. It is a matter of evaluation of the overall effect of the detail, which is not necessarily the same as the sum total of the individual details. Not all details are of equal weight or importance in any given situation. The details may also vary in importance from one situation to another. The process involves painting a picture in each individual case."

There are a wide range of factors that may be relevant to whether an individual is an employee or not:

- Whether the individual is exclusively tied to the one organisation (See **Thames Television Limited v Wallis** [1979] IRLR 136.) The fact that the individual cannot work elsewhere is a pointer to employment.
- Whether the individual can provide a substitute (See *Tanton*). The fact that a substitute may be provided is a pointer against mutuality of obligation.
- Whether the individual takes the risk of loss and the benefit of profit (See *Ready Mixed Concrete*). The fact that the individual bears the risk is a pointer to self employment.
- Whether the individual provides the tools of the trade. However, there are some jobs where by custom the individual provides the tools but is still an employee (See **Challinor v Taylor** [1972] ICR 129).
- The manner in which wages are paid. Where payment is for a task this may point to self employment (see *O'Kelly*).
- Where there are disciplinary powers under the contract, including powers of dismissal on certain grounds, this may point to an employee/employer relationship and other terms of the contract may be more consistent with the individual being an employee.
- The deduction of PAYE is a pointer towards an employee/employer relationship. Conversely, an agreement that the individual will be paid gross may point to self employment, though if the individual is clearly not his own boss, running his own business, this factor cannot make the individual self employed (see **Withers v Flackwell Heath Football Supporters Club** [1981] IRLR 307).
- Some degree of control may not prevent the individual being self employed where other factors point to self employment (See **Hitchcock v Post Office** [1979] ICR 100).

- The intention of the parties may be relevant but not conclusive (see *Massey* and the cases cited above).
- Some cases have considered that the view of the ordinary person as to whether there was a contract of service is of relevance (see **Cassidy v Minister of Health** [1951] 23 KB 343; *Withers*).
- The lack of mutuality of obligation is likely to be conclusive and the recent cases have emphasised the importance of this factor (See *Nethermere*; *Clark*; *Carmichael*; *McMeechan* and *Tanton*).

Particular types of work

(i) Agency workers

Where temporary workers are supplied to a client by an agency two questions may arise: whether the temporary worker is an employee or self employed and, if he is an employee whether the agency or the client is the employer. It was held in **Tyne and Clyde Warehouses Limited v Hamerton** [1978] ICR 6661 that an agent who was expressly engaged as self employed and paid his own taxes was nevertheless an employee. Other decisions have held that individuals supplied on an agency basis were self employed (**Construction Industry Training Board v Labour Force Limited** [1970] 3 All ER 220) **Wickens v Champion Employment** [1984] ICR 365).

However, the Court of Appeal in **McMeechan v Secretary of State for Employment** [1997] ICR 549; IRLR 353) held that a temporary worker who was on the books of an employment agency could be an employee under a contract of employment between the agency and the employee during the time that he worked for a client of the agency. Thus in respect of each individual stint of work he will be regarded as employed. Whether he is employed for the whole of the time that he is on the books of the agency will very much depend upon the terms of the engagement.

It was held by the EAT in **Serco Limited v Blair** [EAT 345/98] that the arrangement between agency workers and the agency does not create a legal relationship between the client and the worker as the employment contract is personal since it requires mutual trust and confidence.

Schedule 7 of the Employment Relations Act 1999 (in force since 25.10.1999) provides that regulations may be made which may regulate the way in which and the terms on which services may be provided by persons carrying on agencies and businesses under the Employment Agencies Act 1973 and it may be, in due course, that such regulations will have an impact upon the manner in which agency workers' contracts of employment are regulated.

(ii) *Casual workers*

The central issue in relation to casual workers is likely to be whether they are under any obligation to accept worker or whether there is any otherwise irreducible minimum obligation. In **Ahmet v Trusthouse Forte Catering Limited** [EAT 124/82] and **O'Kelly v Trusthouse Forte PLC** [1983] ICR 728 the Courts found that there was no employment relationship where waiters were not obliged to take work and the company was not under any obligation to offer work. This may be contrasted with **Four Seasons (Inn on the Park) Limited v Hamarat** [EAT 369/84] where it was found that there was in reality a mutual obligation to provide and accept work. Indeed the company would not have offered more work if the individual had turned it down and Mr Hamarat would have gone elsewhere if he had not been offered work.

In **Nethermere (St Nests) Limited v Gardiner and Taverna** [1984] IRLR 240; ICR 612 it was stated by the Court of Appeal that the minimum requirement is that the employee should be obligated personally to accept and perform some work for the employer in return for payment. Homeworkers who had accepted work over a substantial period had reached the stage where the Tribunal were entitled to conclude that an employment contract had been created by the parties (See also **Orpheus Footwear Limtied v Cope** [1978] IRLR 396).

The two recent cases of **Clark v Oxfordshire Health Authority** and **Carmichael v National Power Plc** (considered above) emphasis the importance of mutuality in relation to casual workers.

(iii) *Directors*

A director of a company is an office holder in a company law capacity. However, it is possible for a director of a company to also be an employee (See **Adamson v Arthur M Smith (Hull) Limited** [1967] ITR 224 and **Nottingham Egg Packers & Distribution v Mccarthy and Haslket** [1967] ITR 224). Recent cases have considered the position where the individual is a director and is also a controlling shareholder in the company. In **Fleming v Secretary of State for Trade and Industry** [1997] IRLR 682 it was held that the fact that individual has a controlling interest in the company does not prevent him from being an employee. The Court of Appeal approved of this decision in **Secretary of State for Trade and Industry v Bottrill** [1998] IRLR 120 and disapproved of the decision to the opposite effect in **Buchan and Ivery v Secretary of State for Employment** [1997] IRLR 80. It stated, however, that it is a matter of fact for the Tribunal to decide. Morison P stated:

> "The higher courts have taken the view that the issue as to whether a person is or is not an employee is a pure question of fact. The shareholding of a person in the company by which he alleges he was employed is a factor to be taken into account, because it might tend to establish either that the company was a mere simulacrum or that the contract under scrutiny was a sham. In our judgment it would be wrong to say that a controlling shareholder who, as such, ultimately had the power to prevent his own dismissal by voting his shares to replace the board, was outside the class of persons given rights under the Act on an insolvency."

It is clear that the shareholding in the company will be one factor to be taken into account in deciding whether the director/shareholder was in reality running the business on his own account and therefore not an employee.

(iv) *Office holders*

It is possible for an office holder to also be an employee. This was the position in **102 Social Club and Institute Limited v Bickerton** [1977] ICR 911 where the club steward also held an office from which he could be removed by a two thirds' majority. The EAT stated that the following facts should be considered:

> "(1) The payment made to the secretary...was it an honorarium ...or was it a salary..
>
> (2) ...whether the payment was fixed in advance, possibly on a periodical basis, or whether it was voted at the end of the year in token of the member's work. The former arrangement would favour the view that it was a salary, the latter that it was not; though neither would be conclusive.

(3) It is material to see whether the arrangements confer upon the secretary a right payment or whether what is paid is a mere bounty.

(4) The size of the payment.

(5) Whether he is exercising the functions of an independent office (somewhat in the way that a curate or police officer does) or is subject to the control and orders of the club.

(6) The extent and weight of the duties performed; the smaller they are the less likely he is to be an employee.

(7) The description given to the payment in the minute or resolution authorising it, and its treatment in the accounts, and for tax and national insurance purposes."

The following office holders have been held not to be employees: A Justice of the Peace (**Knight v Attorney General** [1979] ICR 194; Ministers of Religion where no contractual duties were owed (**Davies v Presbyterian Church of Wales** [1986] IRLR 194 and **President of the Methodist Conference v Parfitt** [1984] IRLR 141). It was, however, considered in **R v Civil Service Appeal Board ex parte Bruce** [1988] ICR 649 that civil servants may be employees.

Where, an office is held, as in the case of a Chief Constable of Police the rules of natural justice will apply (**Ridge v Baldwin** [1963] 3 All ER 66; 2 WLR 935).

(v) *Parliamentary staff and Crown Servants*

By sections 194 and 195 of the ERA 1996 House of Commons and House of Lords staff have a right to claim under Part X save for sections 101 and 102.

(vi) *Partners*

A partner will normally not be an employee (**Cowell v Quilter Goodison Co Limited and QG Management Services Limited** [1989] IRLR 392) though a salaried partner may in reality be an employee.

(vii) *Self employed contractors*

As has been seen from the earlier discussion about the test to be applied, a contractor who is described as self employed may in reality be an employee (See *Ready Mixed Concrete*).

(viii)   *Workers co-operatives*

It was held in **Drym Fabricators Limited v Johnson** [1981] ICR 274 that members of a workers co-operative registered with the Registrar of Friendly Societies were employees with the ability to sue the co-operative as it had was able to employ and dismiss its workforce. The society was registered as a limited company. The EAT also took the view that an unregistered co-operative could have legal personality since it could, as a whole, employ and dismiss. In **Winfield v London Philharmonic Orchestra Limited** [1979] ICR 726, however, the EAT stated that the reality of the situation must be looked as. In this case musicians were self employed as the facts pointed to a co-operative association between artistes who must subject themselves to self discipline in order that the result of the operation can be achieved (see also **Addison v LPO** [1981] ICR 726).

Workers

The National Minimum Wage Act 1998, the Working Time Regulations, the Public Interest Disclosure Act 1998 as well as certain parts of the ERA 1996 (i.e. deductions from wages) give protection to workers in respect of the contents of those statutory provisions (as to which see the later Chapters). **However, the right to claim unfair dismissal does not apply to workers but only employees. It is likely that the Government will extend the unfair dismissal legislation to cover workers in the future.**

The definition of worker in the Employment Relations Act 1999 is similar to the discrimination statutes and the ERA 1996. Section 230(3) of the ERA 1996 defines a worker as someone working under a contract of employment or:

> Any other contract, whether express or implied and (if it is express) whether oral or in writing, whereby the individual undertakes to do or perform personally any work or services for another party to the contract whose status is not by virtue of the contract that of a client or customer or any profession or business undertaking carried on by the individual.

In **Loughran and Kelly v Northern Ireland Housing Executive** [1998] IRLR the Northern Ireland Court of Appeal held that a similar definition under the Fair Employment (Northern Ireland) Act could apply to include the engagement of a solicitor by a client so long as the personal service was provided by the contracting party, so that a sole practitioner could come within the definition but not a partnership.

Though not at present of great significance for unfair dismissal, it is possible that such rights will be extended to workers in due course.

Disciplinary and Grievance Proceedings

By sections 10 to 15 of the Employment Relations Act 1999 workers have a right to be accompanied at disciplinary and grievance proceedings (See Chapter 6 Conduct for the details). A worker who is dismissed because he exercised or sought to exercise the right to be accompanied or sought to accompany another worker is taken to be automatically unfairly dismissed (Section 12(3)). For these purposes a worker is defined as:

(a) a worker within the meaning of section 230(3) of the Employment Rights Act 1996;
(b) an agency worker,
(c) a home worker;
(d) a person in Crown employment within the meaning of section 191 of [the ERA]
(e) employed as a relevant member of the House of Lords staff or the House of Commons staff within the meaning of section 194(6) or 195(5) of [the ERA])

The provisions relating to the right not to be unfairly dismissed in this case therefore applies to a considerably wider category of individuals than employees.

Sufficient Continuous Service

Since 1st June 1999 an employee may bring a complaint of unfair dismissal where he has a minimum of one year's continuous service. Dismissals prior to this date required two years service. It remains to be seen whether the case of **R v Secretary of State for Employment ex parte Seymour Smith** which is currently on appeal to the House of Lords will affect the position of individuals who were dismissed before this date.

There are, however, a number of grounds of complaint for which a shorter period of continuous service applies. No period of continuous service is necessary in respect of the following (in Chapter order):

Chapter 15:   Health and Safety Dismissals
Chapter 16:   Occupational Pension Trustees
Chapter 17:   National Minimum wage
Chapter 18:   Pregnancy and Maternity and right to time off to care for dependants
Chapter 19:   Protected Disclosures
Chapter 20:   Redundancy for an inadmissible reason
Chapter 21:   Dismissal for asserting a statutory right
Chapter 22:   Sunday Working
Chapter 24:   Dismissal for trade union reasons
Chapter 25:   Working time.

No period of service is required where the dismissal is one under section 10(3) of the Employment Relations Act 1999, relating to right to be accompanied to a disciplinary or grievance hearing.

One month is required in respect of dismissals where the employee is dismissed in circumstances where he would qualify for paid suspension on medical grounds (ERA section 108(2)). There are also special rules relating to section 84 or 96 dismissals which are considered in Chapter 18.

Continuity

There are detailed rules for working out continuity of employment which are set out in Part XIV, Chapter I of the Employment Rights Act 1996 and the Transfer of Undertakings (Protection of Employment) Regulations 1981 provide that employment will transfer with continuity on certain transfers of undertakings. The following points arise from sections 210 to 219 of the Employment Rights Act 1996:

- By sections 210(2) continuous service is to be measured in calendar months or years.
- By section 210(3) in computing whether service is continuous this shall be determined week by week but where it is necessary to compute the period of continuous service this will be in months and years of 12 months.

- By section 210(4) a week that does not count in computing the length of a period of employment **breaks continuity of employment**.
- By section 211(1) the period of employment begins on the date when the employee started work and ends with the day by reference to which the length of the employee's period of continuous is to be ascertained by.
- By section 211(3) where the employee's period of continuous employment includes one or more periods which do not count for computing the period of continuity but do not break continuity the beginning of the period is treated as postponed by the number of days that do not count.

Weeks that Count

Under section 212 any weeks during which the employee's relations with his employer are governed by a contract of employment will count in computing employment. The test is not whether the hours were actually worked but what hours the contract normally involved (See **Harber v North London Polytechnic** [1990] IRLR 198).

However, where the employee is absent from work in the circumstances set out below continuity will be retained even if there is no contract of employment between the employer and the employee during that time (**Ford v Warwickshire County Council** [1983] IRLR 126). It must be shown that the reason for the absence was one of those set out in the statute if continuity is to be retained (**Pearson v Kent County Council** [1992] ICR 20).

Weeks that count in continuing the employment will include:

- any week during which the employee's period of absence from work is occasioned wholly or partly by pregnancy or childbirth after the employee returns to work (212(2)).
- any week when the employee is incapable of work in consequence of sickness or injury (212(3)(a)). Incapability in this context means not being capable of doing the work that the employee was engaged to perform and not an inability to do any work (**Donnelly v Kelvin International Services** [1991] IRLR 496).
- any week when the employee is absent from work on account of a temporary cessation of work (212(3)(b)). For the purpose of this subsection:

- A temporary cessation of work is a short term closure of the business for whatever reason (**Newsham v Dunlop Textiles Limited** (1969) 4 ITR 268; **Hanson v Fashion Industries (Hartlepool) Limited** [1980] IRLR 393).
- There may be a temporary cessation of work where there was no work for the employee even if the factory or business as a whole did not close (**Fitzgerald v Hall, Russell & Co Limited** [1970] AC 984) but if there is work available for the employee then there cannot be a temporary cessation of work (**Byrne v City of Birmingham MDC** [1988] ICR 480).
- Absence because the employer does not have the funds to pay the employee may be a temporary cessation of work (**University of Aston v Malik** [1984] ICR 492).
- Where the absences are foreseeable, predictable and regular there may be a temporary cessation, as in the case of supply teachers of seasonable works (**Ford v Warwickshire CC** [1983] IRLR 126).
- The employee may take another job during the temporary cessation without it affecting continuity (**Thomson v Bristol Channel Ship Repairers** (1969) 4 ITR 262).

- any week when the employee is absent from work in circumstances such that, by arrangement or custom, he is regarded as continuing in the employment of his employer for any purpose (212(3(c)). However, by section 212(4) not more than 26 weeks count. It is necessary that there is an agreement or undertaking that the employee will be absent by arrangement or custom at the time that he departs and if there is no such mutual arrangement then continuity will be broken (**Murphy v A Birrell & Sons Limited** [1978] IRLR 458. This is likely to be the position where an employee has been seconded (**Wishart v National Coal Board** [1974] ICR 460) or in cases where the employee is habitually re-engaged when the employer has an order, as in shipyard workers (**Puttick v John Wright & Sons (Blackwall) Limited** [1972] ICR 457) so that continuity in all these cases is preserved and counts in computing employment.
- any week when the employee is absent from work wholly or partly because of pregnancy or childbirth (212(3)(d)). By section 212(4) not more than 26 weeks count subject to the above provision of section 212(2) which provides that the exercise of statutory maternity leave will not break continuity.

Intervals in Employment that count

There are three situations where an interval in employment will nevertheless count for the purpose of reckoning service for unfair dismissal purposes:

1) Where the employer has not given statutory notice so that the date when statutory notice expires is later then the period to that date will count (213(1)).
2) Where the employee terminates the contract and the employer then terminates the contract by giving notice that should have expired on a later date under the statutory notice period requirements (213(1)).
3) Where the employee is reengaged or the contract is renewed under section 138 of the redundancy provisions (213(2)).

Weeks that do not count

There are three situations where weeks will not count:

1) Employment Aboard

By section 215(2) a week of employment does not count in computing the period of employment if the employee was employed outside Great Britain during the whole or the part of the week and was not an employed earner for the purpose of paying Class 1 contributions. Continuity is not broken (215(3)).

2) Industrial Disputes

By section 216(1) a week does not count in computing the period of employment if during that week, or any part of it, the employee was taking part in industrial action. Continuity is not broken by a strike or lock out and the number of days that will not count will be number between the last day before the strike or lock out and the day of the return to work (216((2)(3)).

3) Reinstatement after military service

By section 217 a person who is entitled to apply to his former employer under the Reserve Forces (Safeguard of Employment Act) 1985 and does so within six months after his period of service will not be regarded as having continuity broken but the days between being employed and returning to employment will not count for the purpose of calculating the period of continuity.

Change of Employer

By section 218(2) of the ERA 1996:

> If a trade or business, or an undertaking (whether or not established by or under an Act) is transferred from one person to another–
> (a) the period of employment of an employee in the trade or business or undertaking at the time of the transfer counts as a period of employment with the transferee, and
> (b) the transfer does not break the continuity of the period of employment.

The other areas where there will still be continuity on the change of the identity of employer are:

- where one body corporate is substituted by another body corporate under an Act of Parliament (218(3)).
- where the employer dies and the employee is kept on by his personal representative (218(4)).
- where there is a change in partners, personal representatives or trustees who employ any person (218(5)).
- where the employee goes to work for an associated employer (218(6)).

Claim in Time

By section 111(2)(a) of the ERA a Tribunal shall not consider a complaint unless it is presented within a period of three months beginning with the effective date of termination. However, by section 111(2)(b) time may be extended where it can be shown that it was not reasonably practicable for the complaint to be presented before the end of that period of two months. Reference should be made to books on procedure in this regard.

Effective date of termination (EDT)

For the purpose of deciding the date when the three month period began to run and for the purpose of determining the period of continuous employment it may be necessary to ascertain the effective date of termination of the contract of employment. Section 97 of the ERA sets out the principles for ascertaining the EDT.

- By section 97(1) the EDT is the date on which notice expires whether the contract is terminated by the employer or employee, or where no notice is given, the date that the termination takes effect.
- By section 97(1) where a fixed term contract expires without being renewed the date of termination is the date that it expires.
- By section 97(2)(3) where the employer does not give the statutory notice required by section 86 or the notice would expire on a later date then the EDT will be the date that would have expired by statutory notice for the purposes of calculating qualifying periods of employment, the basic award and weeks pay.

Section 86 provides that where an employee has been continuously employed for one month he is entitled to one week's notice up to two years and to an additional week up to each full year worked to 12 years. Any provisions for shorter notice is subject to section 86 but a party may waive its rights or agree a payment in lieu of notice.

In the case of fixed term contracts which are for a certain term of one month but where the employee has been continuously employed for three months the contract will be treated as for an indefinite term (86(4)) but the statutory notice periods will not apply to a contract for the performance of a specific task (86(5)).

The contract can be terminated by either party because of conduct (86(6)).

Sections 87 to 91 set out rights whereby the employee is entitled to be paid during the notice period notwithstanding absence due to sickness or injury or because of pregnancy or childbirth.

A clear notice of immediate dismissal will take effect at once (**Batchelor v British Airways Board** [1987] IRLR 36) subject to the statutory extension where notice should have been given though the right to notice can be waived (**Secretary of State for Employment v Staffordshire CC** [1989] IRLR 117). The EDT will not be extended where there is an internal appeal process if it is made clear that the employee has been dismissed (**J Sainsbury Limited v Savage** [1980] IRLR 109) even if the individual was paid whilst awaiting the appeal (**Board of Governors, National Heart and Chest Hospital v Nambiar** [1981] IRLR 196).

Where the employer sends a letter terminating the employment on a summary basis the effective date of termination will be the date that the employee receives the letter as it is the employee's knowledge that is the crucial factor (**McMaster v Manchester Airport Plc** [1998] IRLR).

Part 2.   Exclusions from the Right to Claim

Category of workers

There are a number of special categories of worker whose rights to claim unfair dismissal are specifically excluded by the legislation. These cover:

- *Armed forces*

   By section 192 of the ERA 1996 the right to claim unfair dismissal is currently excluded from the right to claim unfair dismissal, save for claims under sections 100 to 103 of the Act.

- *Mariners*

   By section 199(2) of the ERA 1996 Part X did not apply to the employment as a master and by section 196(5) a person employed to work on board a ship registered in the United Kingdom was regarded as someone who ordinarily works in Great Britain unless the ship is registered at a port outside Great Britain, the employment is wholly outside Great Britain and the person is not ordinarily resident in Great Britain (See **Royle v Globtik Management Limited** [1977] ICR 552). Section 196 has been repealed . However, by section 32(4) of the Employment Relations Act 1999 there is a new section 199(6) which provides unfair dismissal rights can be claimed where the ship's entry specifies a port in Great Britain to which the vessel is to be treated as belonging, the employee does not wholly work outside Great Britain and the person is ordinarily resident in Great Britain. The effect is to continue the exemption for vessels registered outside the United Kingdom where the employee does not work in the United Kingdom and is not ordinarily resident in this Country.

- ### *National Security*

  Unfair dismissal rights had been excluded save for claims under section 99, 100, and 103 of the ERA 1996. However, substantial amendments have been made by Schedule 8 of the Employment Relations Act 1999. A new section 10 of the Employment Tribunals Act 1996 provides that an action for unfair dismissal may be dismissed if it was taken for the purpose of safeguarding national security. Wide ranging powers are given to a Minister of the Crown to control the conduct of proceedings and regulations may be made to this effect. However, they take away the right of Ministers to certify conclusively certify that an act was done for national security. Instead procedures may be directed to conceal the identify of witnesses, exclude an applicant or direct that the decision or parts are kept secret. These procedures will be enacted by regulations. (See further Chapter 10.)

- ### *Police*

  Persons employed in the police service are excluded from unfair dismissal rights by section 200 of the ERA 1996. This does not, however, cover prison staff.

- ### *Share fishermen*

  The crew and the master of a fishing vessel who are paid from a share in the profits or gross earnings of the vessel on which they are employed are excluded from claiming unfair dismissal by section 199(2) of the ERA 1996 though this provision will not apply if the fisherman is paid from a share in the profits of the fleet of vessels owned by the employer (**Goodeve v Gilsons** [1985] ICR 401).

Diplomatic or state immunity applies

As a matter of principle foreign states and emanations of their government are entitled to immunity from civil action unless they waive immunity or their are engaged in commercial transactions. Until the State Immunity Act 1978 it was not therefore possible to claim unfair dismissal against Foreign States and their emanations in this Country. By sections 1 and 4 of the Act:

1(1) A state is immune from the jurisdiction of the courts of the United Kingdom except as provided in the following provisions of this Part of the Act...

4(1) A State is not immune as respects proceedings relating to a contract of employment between the State and an individual where the contract was made in the United Kingdom or the work is to be wholly or partly performed there.

However, the right to claim is subject to important exceptions:

(1) By section 4(2) the right under section 4(1) will not apply where the individual was a national of the state concerned or at the time that the contract was made the individual was not a national of the United Kingdom nor habitually resident there or it was agreed in writing. These provisions will not apply if the work was carried out for commercial purposes unless the individual was habitually resident in the foreign state at the time the contract was entered into (4(2)).

(2) By section 16 immunity under the Diplomatic Privileges Act 1964 or Consular Relations Act 1968 mean that a claim cannot be brought where Article 1 on the Vienna Convention on Diplomatic Relations 1961 is applicable. See **Arab Republic of Egypt v Gamal-Eldin** [1996] ICR 13 (driver excluded).

(3) Immunity may be waived by the state taking a step in the proceedings (**London Branch of the Nigerian Universities Commission v Bastians** [1995] ICR 358).

The contract of employment is tainted with *illegality*

Where the contract of employment is tainted with illegality it will be regarded as an unenforceable contract and there will be no right to claim unfair dismissal. Whether it is illegal depends upon the nature of the illegality and the intention of the employer and employee. The following principles apply:

(1) Where the employment is illegal by statute then it will be void and unenforceable by either party (**Miller v Karlinski** 1962 TLR 85. An alien working without permission will not be acting under a lawful contract and has no right to claim unfair dismissal (**Rastegarnia v Richmond Designs Limited** (COIT 764/38). A similar result was reached in **Bambghose v The Royal Star and Garter Home** [EAT 841/95] where an

individual did not have the requisite two years service because he had worked illegally for the first 14 months.

(2)   Where the object and intention of the contract is illegal because it involves criminal conduct or is regarded as immoral it will not be enforceable even if the parties do not believe that it involves any wrongdoing. This is a long standing principle in relation to contract law (See **J M Allan (Merchandising) Limited v Cloke** [1963] 2 WLR 899).

(3)   Where the employee is asked to carry out activities that are not part of the contract, such as securing prostitutes for clients, this may be extraneous to the contract of employment and the employee may still claim unfair dismissal if this had not been the purpose and intention behind the contract (**Coral Leisure Group Limited v Barnett** [1981] IRLR 204).

(4)   Where the contract is legal but is being performed in a way that is illegal then it may be unenforceable. The classic example in the employment context is where a contract of employment is carried out in a manner that is intended to defraud the Inland Revenue. If the parties knowingly carry out the contract in this way it will not be enforceable, as in **Tomlinson v Dick Evans U Drive Limited** [1978] IRLR 777 where the employee was paid sums in cash as expenses when she rendered false invoices.

(5)   It does not matter that the parties do not realise that what they are doing is illegal provided that they know of the arrangements that are being carried out. If the employee knows what is being done the contract will be illegal (**Salvesen v Simons** [1994] ICR 409; **Corby v Morrison t/a The Card Shop** [1980] ICR 564; IRLR 218). Even if the sums involved are small the contract will be illegal, as in **Horner v Rymer** [EAT 794/78] where the sum involved was only £1 bonus per week that was paid out of 'the employer's pocket'.

(6)   Nevertheless, where the employees do not benefit from the fraud and expose its existence even though they had assisted the employer in relation to it there may not necessarily be illegality. In **Hewcastle Catering Limited v Ahmed** [1991] IRLR 473 it was held by the Court of Appeal that the employer's behaviour may be so reprehensible that public policy does *not* dictate that a claim cannot be brought. In this case the employer's perpetrated a VAT fraud by instructing its employees to sign different invoices when paid in cash. The Court of Appeal identified a number of factors that lead to the conclusion that there was no basis of public policy that should prevent the employees from claiming. First, the employer

submitted the VAT returns and kept the records. Second, the contract of employment did not provide that the employees would assist in the fraud. Third, the employee did not benefit from the fraud. Fourth, the Commissioner's had a wide authority as to the way that they conducted an investigation. Fifth, denial of a remedy may discourage disclosure by an employee. Sixth, the scheme would have gone ahead even if the employee had not got the bill signed. Seventh, *if the public in its conscience weighed the effect of the respondent's conduct against that of the appellants who not only perpetrated the fraud but involved their employees in it and then sacked them for telling the truth to the Customs officers* this would be likely to lead to unfortunate results.

(7)   If the employee is unaware that the employer is acting in a manner that is illegal then he will still be able to claim unfair dismissal (**Newland v Simons & Wiler** [1981] IRLR 359; **Davidson v Pillay** [1979] IRLR 275).

(8)   If the employee has acted in a manner that could be fraudulent this may not amount to illegality between employer and employee as where the employee does not declare benefits to the Inland Revenue (**McConnell v Bolik** [1979] IRLR 422).

(9)   Where the contract becomes illegal then continuity will be broken so that even if the employee had been employed for some time the right to claim may be lost (**Attridge v Jayders Newsagents Limited** [EAT 603/79].

(10)   A claim for sex discrimination may be made even if the contract is illegal where this is not founded on the contract of employment (**Leighton v (1) Michael (2) Charalambous** [1995] ICR 1091; IRLR 67).

(11)   A fraud on the employer does not prevent a claim for wrongful or unfair dismissal but may have an effect on compensation (**Broaders v Kalkare Property Maintenance Limited** [1990] IRLR 421).

The employee has reached normal retiring age

Employees are excluded from the right to complain of dismissal when they have reached the normal retiring age, in relation to the position which the employee held, which in the absence of a contractual or normal retirement age will be 65 for men and women.

Under section 109(1) of the ERA 1996 the right to claim under section 94 will not apply where the normal retiring age has been reached which is the same in relation to a position held by a man or a woman or, in any other case, the age of 65.

Section 109(1) does not apply in a number of circumstances:

- Where there is an express contractual retirement age that applies to men and women this will be the normal retiring age.
- Where there is no express contractual age or it is not always rigidly adhered to so that employees retire at different ages, then the presumption that the contractual age is applicable may be rebutted. (See **Waite v Government Communications Headquarters** [1983] ICR 653.)
- Where the evidence is that employees are regularly retained beyond the contractual retirement age this may mean that the contractual retirement age has been displaced. If it has not been replaced by another contractual retirement age or normal retirement age then the statutory limit of 65 will apply (**Mauldon v British Telecommunctions Plc** [1987] ICR 450; **Secretary of State for Scotland v Meickle** [1986] IRLR 208).
- Where there is a contractual retirement age the employer will not be able to reduce retirement by introducing a lower normal retirement age without changing retirement by a lawful contractual change (**Brakton v Beloit Walmsley Limited** [1995] IRLR 629; **Patel v Nagesan** [1995] IRLR 370) .
- The retiring age must relate to the position which the employee held. This is further elucidated upon by section 235(1) of the ERA 1996 which states that the matters taken as a whole include (a) his status as an employee, (b) the nature of his work and (c) his terms and conditions of employment. The relevant date is the employees normal or contractual retirement date at the date of dismissal (**Hughes v DHSS** [1985] IRLR 419) and the relevant group will normally be all employees of all ages in that grade (**Brooks v British Telecommunications Plc** [1992] IRLR 66 and **Barclays Bank v O'Brien [1994]** [IRLR] 580 and ct. **Barber v Thames Television Limited** [1991] IRLR 410).
- The statutory limit will apply if there are no other employees in the same group so that there can be no normal retiring age (**Age Concern Scotland v Hines** [1983] IRLR 477).
- There are a number of areas where there is no upper age limit which mirror those provisions where there is no requirement for a period of continuous employment to make a claim (the automatically unfair dismissals). These are referred to in the relevant chapters.

The employee ordinarily works outside Great Britain

Until its repeal with effect from 25th October 1999, section 196 of the ERA 1996 operated to exclude unfair dismissal rights where under the contract of employment the employee ordinarily worked outside Great Britain. The most recent decision on this section was **Carver v Saudi Arabian Airlines** [1999] IRLR.

By section 32(3) of the Employment Relations Act 1999 section 196 of the ERA 1996 was repealed. This repeal took effect on October 25th 1999.

Part 3.   Compromises

By section 203(1) of ERA 1996 any provision in an agreement (whether in a contract of employment or not) is void insofar as it purports to exclude the operation of the Act. However, there are exceptions. For unfair dismissal purposes, there are four grounds on which compromises may exclude the right to bring a claim for unfair dismissal.

(1)   ACAS settlements

Under section 203(2)(e) the right to bring proceedings may be contracted out where a conciliation officer has taken action under section 18 of the Employment Tribunals Act 1996. Section 18 of that Act provides that the conciliation officer is to endeavour to promote a settlement of the proceedings without their being determined by the employment tribunal. Where there is a settlement by way of conciliation it will normally be signed on a COT3 form though this is not necessary if there has been an agreement (whether oral or written) in which the conciliation officer acted as an intermediary (**Gilbert v Kembridge Fibres Limited** [1984] ICR 188). It is important to note that section 203(2)(e) refers to action having been taken under section 18. The Courts have considered the nature of the *action* that should be taken.

1)   The signing of a COT3 form will normally prevent any complaint being made by the employee (**Moore v Duport Furniture Products Limited** [1982] ICR 84).
2)   The conciliation officer is under no duty to explain the rights of the parties but if he acts in bad faith or is not impartial this may

be a ground for setting aside the agreement (**Slack v Greenham (Plant Hire) Limited** [1983] ICR 617).

(2) Compromise agreements

By section 203(2)(f) of the ERA 1996 a compromise agreement that meets certain conditions will be effective to oust the right to bring a claim for unfair dismissal. Section 203(3) sets out the requirements as follows:

(a) the agreement must be in writing,

(b) the agreement must relate to the particular proceedings,

(c) the employee or worker must have received advice from a relevant independent adviser as to the terms and effect of the proposed agreement and, in particular, its effect on his ability to pursue his rights before an employment tribunal,

(d) there must be in force, when the adviser gives the advice, a contract of insurance, or an indemnity provided for members of a profession or professional body covering the risk of a claim by the employee or worker in respect of loss arising in consequence of the action,

(e) the agreement must identity the adviser,

(f) the agreement must state that the conditions regarding compromise agreements under this Act are satisfied.

The advice must have been given either by a lawyer who is not acting for the employer and who satisfies the criteria set out in section 203(4), who is an official, employer or member of an independent trade union certified as competent to give advice and is authorised, or a worker from an advice centre is who is certified by the advice centre. This is a substantial relaxation on the previous law that was introduced by the Employment Rights (Dispute Resolution) Act 1998.

Other Points

•   In **Lunt v Merseyside TEC Limited** [1999] ICR 17 it was held that a single compromise agreement was capable of settling all the disputes between the parties. However, the fact that a compromise agreement must relate to a complaint means that it is not possible to put in a blanket exclusion clause but that the compromise must relate to the particular complaint. The case has a significant effect upon the drafting of exclusion clauses.

- The Tribunal may be able to hear a claim for a breach of a compromise agreement under the Industrial Tribunals Extension of Jurisdiction (England and Wales) Order 1994 if it relates to a matter that arises or is outstanding on the termination of the employee's employment if the compromise agreement does concern the terms under which the employment was *to be* brought to an end (**Rock-It-Cargo Limited v Green** [1997] IRLR 581).

- Section 203(5) also provides that an agreement to submit a dispute to arbitration under the ACAS arbitration scheme may exclude the right to bring a claim for unfair dismissal.

(3) Settlements before the Tribunal

Where the case is settled before the tribunal and subject to an order there will no longer be a right to bring a claim. The case will be res judicata (See **Green v Hampshire County Council** [1979] ICR 861; **O'Laoire v Jackel International Limited** [1991] IRLR 70; [1990] ICR 197. However, where there has been no judicial decision, order or judgment a person may not be prevented from claiming unpaid wages in the County Court (**Dattani v Trio Supermarkets Limited** [1998] IRLR 240).

(4) Dismissal procedures agreements where there has been contracting out

Under section 110 of the ERA a dismissal procedures agreement may exclude the right to claim unfair dismissal where it has been approved by the Secretary of State. This will not, however, exclude claims in relation to pregnancy and maternity, Sunday working, dismissals for asserting a statutory right or dismissal for inadmissible redundancy reasons.

CHAPTER TWO
THE CONCEPT OF DISMISSAL

Before the employee may make a claim for unfair dismissal there must have been a dismissal within the statutory definition set out in the Employment Rights Act (ERA) 1996. This Chapter will first consider those circumstances in which there has been dismissal then those situations where although the employment relationship has terminated there has been no dismissal as a matter of law.

Circumstances in which there is a Dismissal

Section 95 of the ERA 1996 sets out the circumstances in which an employee is regarded as having been dismissed. By section 95 an employee is dismissed in circumstances where:

(a) the contract under which he is employed is terminated by the employer (with or without notice);
(b) he is employed under a contract for a fixed term and that term expires without being renewed under the same contract, or
(c) the employee terminates the contract under which he is employed (with or without notice) in circumstances in which he is entitled to terminate it without notice by reason of the employer's conduct.

In addition to the above three concepts of dismissal, there will also be a dismissal where:

(d) the employer gives notice to terminate the contract and within the period of that notice the employee gives notice to terminate at an earlier date than that on which the employer's notice is due to expire (*Section 95(2) ERA 1996*).

(e) An employee has exercised a right to return to work after maternity but is not permitted to return to work (*Section 96 ERA 1996*).

(f) There are certain special rules relating to redundancy.

It is thus necessary to consider:

(1) Termination with or without notice;

(2) Termination where a cross notice to terminate is given by the employee.

(3) Termination by expiry of a fixed term contract;

(4) Termination by way of constructive dismissal;

(5) Termination based upon refusal to permit return after maternity (see Chapter 18 in relation to this area of dismissal).

(6) Redundancy dismissals (see Chapter 20 in relation to this area of dismissal).

Termination with or without notice

There will be an express dismissal in circumstances where the employer by words or by conduct signifies to the employee that the contract of employment will terminate with or without notice on a date that can be positively ascertained.

The onus is on the employee to show that there has been a dismissal if the employer disputes that this has occurred. The dismissal may or may not be with notice. If the former it is possible that it will amount to a wrongful dismissal as well. However problems may arise where the words used or the conduct of the employer is ambiguous so that the employee may mistakenly believe that he has been dismissed. It is also possible that what on the face of it appears to have been an unambiguous dismissal is not taken to have been a dismissal because of the circumstances of the case. In particular a statement of intention on the part of the employer that he intends to dismiss cannot be regarded as a dismissal if no specific date is given. This was the position in **Morton Sundour Fabrics Limited v Shaw** [1967] ITR 84. The employee was entitled to 28 days' notice and was told that his department would have to close down so that his employment would cease but he was not given the date that his employment would terminate. He gave notice when he found another employer and claimed a redundancy payment. The Divisional Court held that he had not been dismissed. Widgery J stated:

> "As a matter of law an employer cannot dismiss his employee by saying "I intend to dispense with your services at some time in the coming months". In order to terminate the contract of employment the notice must either specify the date or contain material from which that date is positively ascertainable."

A statement that the employment will end no later than a certain date will not be sufficient to amount to a dismissal. In **Burton Group Limited v Smith** [1977] IRLR 351 the employee accepted voluntary redundancy under a scheme that provided for volunteers to have their contracts terminated by no later than 26th November. He was told that his actual date of termination would be notified and it was agreed by his union on 24th October that it would be the last day. He died before he was notified and the EAT held that the requirement that the date should be positively ascertainable is not met by a statement that the date of termination of the employment is to be some specific date or such earlier date as the employer may select because the available alternative was not positively ascertainable on the date of the receipt of the notice. This was also the position in **Devon County Council v Cook** [1977] IRLR 188 where the employer announced that the workplace would be closed in the long term and in **International Computers Limited v Kennedy** [1981] IRLR 28 where the employee was told that the factory would close within a year and advised to seek alternative employment. A redundancy payment was refused in both cases. In **Hasaltine Lake and Co v Dowlker** [1981] IRLR 25 there was no dismissal where the employee was told to find a job elsewhere or be dismissed as there was no ascertainable date.

The dismissal cannot take place until it had been communicated to the employee so that where the notice of dismissal is by letter it does not take place until the employee has had an opportunity of reading the letter (**Brown v Southall and Knight** [1980] IRLR 130).

Where the contract of employment is divisible it is possible for one part of the contract to be terminated without there being a dismissal in relation to the contract as a whole.

In **Land & Wilson v West Yorkshire Metropolitan County Council** [1981] ICR 334, IRLR 87 the employees were full time firemen employed at a fire station in Morley. When they were off duty they were retained on call for a station at Batley. The whole time retained duty system was abolished with the agreement of the union. The Court of Appeal held that there was one contract and the employer was entitled to terminate the on call duties on reasonable notice without there being a breach so that there was no dismissal. Lord Denning stated that *"...although there may well have been one contract, it was most certainly divisible into two distinct parts..."* so that one part could be terminated without there having been a dismissal. On the other hand, if the contracts are separate then there will be a dismissal as in **Throsby v Imperial College of Science and Technology** [1977] IRLR 337 where it was stated that there is no reason in principle why a employee cannot have two separate contracts and one be terminated but not the other.

> Once notice of dismissal or resignation has been given it cannot be withdrawn otherwise than with the consent of the other party.

It was recognised in **Riordan v The Home Office** [1959] 1 WLR 1046 that a notice of dismissal, once given, cannot be retracted. This principle was stated by the NIRC in **Harris & Russell Limited v Slingsby** [1973] ICR 454 that:

> "...in the case of a master and servant relationship, the court is satisfied that where one party to the contract gives a notice determining the contract he cannot thereafter unilaterally withdraw the notice. It will of course, always be open to the other party to agree to his withdrawing the notice, but in the absence of agreement the notice must stand and the contract will be terminated upon the effluxion of the period of notice."

(See also **Gallagher v Union Transit Co Limited** [1969] ITR 214 and **William Hill Organisation Limited v Rainbird** [EAT 1406/96].)

There may however, be an exception in the case where there is a right of appeal that can render the original notice of dismissal null and void (**Petch v Taunton Deane DC** (unreported)).

> Unambiguous words or conduct by the employer or employee terminating the contract of employment can normally be taken at face value save in exceptional circumstances where it is apparent that dismissal was not really intended.

Where the words or conduct are clear that the employer is dismissing the employee then such words or conduct will normally be taken at face value by the Tribunal and they will not have to analyse the surrounding circumstances as there is no ambiguity. This is also the position where there has been clear words of resignation. In **Sothern v Franks Charlesly & Co** [1981] IRLR 278 where the employee had told her employer that she was resigning, Fox LJ in the Court of Appeal stated, as a matter of principle, that:

> "...it seems to me that when the words used by a person are unambiguous words of resignation and so understood by her employers, the question of what a reasonable employer might have understood does not arise. The natural meaning of the words and the fact that the employer understood them to mean that the employee was resigning cannot be overridden by appeals to what a reasonable employer might have understood. The non-disclosed intention of a person using language as to his intended meaning is not properly to be taken into account in determining what the true meaning is..."

It is to be noted that in the case of resignations the Courts may be more prepared to apply qualifications in respect of what are apparently on their face unambiguous words. This qualification is likely to be rare in the face of unambiguous words of dismissal. However, the Court did apply a qualification to apparently unambiguous words in **Martin v Yeomen Aggregates Limited** [1983] ICR 314, IRLR 49. After an angry exchange Mr Martin was dismissed by a transport manager, who realised that he had acted in haste in breach of the disciplinary rules of the company. He then changed the penalty to two days' suspension without pay but the employee insisted that the had been sacked. The EAT held that there had been no dismissal. The words had been spoken in the heat of the moment and were immediately withdrawn. In **Tanner v D T Kean** [1978] IRLR 110 the employer spotted Mr Tanner using the company van despite the fact that he had loaned him £275 to stop this practice. He said "That's it, you're finished with me." The Tribunal held that he had not been dismissed. The EAT agreed and also stated that later events are relevant in considering the context of the words spoken.

> Where the employer uses words which are ambiguous or its conduct is ambiguous the tribunal will have to consider all the surrounding circumstances, including events before and after the alleged dismissal, and consider how a reasonable employer or employee would understand the words or conduct. The same applies where it is alleged that the employee has resigned in circumstances where the words or conduct is ambiguous.

There are many reported decisions which illustrate that words or conduct in the working environment whilst on the face of it appearing to terminate the contract of employment were not intended and did not, as a matter of law, have that effect. Where the employer tells the employee to 'go home', 'take his coat', 'get out of the premises' or uses more robust language such words do not expressly state that there has been a dismissal. Where the employee is sent his P45 or his clocking card is removed such conduct is not an express dismissal. The Courts have held that, in these situations, it is necessary to look at the whole of the surrounding circumstances and to construe how a reasonable employer or employee would interpret the words or conduct.

The cases illustrate that it is necessary to look at the particular circumstances and the context in which the language was used. In **Kendrick v Aerduct Productions** [1974] IRLR 322 an employee was dismissed when he was told to 'fuck off and play with your shop', when he told his employer that he was intending to take a tenancy of an off licence. In **King v Webbs Poultry Products (Bradford) Limited** [1975] IRLR it was said that such words would amount to words of dismissal. He had been told to 'fuck off' and 'piss off' and his employer had repeated these words when he collected his belongings as well as taking back the company car. The Tribunal took the view that it was clearly the employer who was telling the employee to go.

However, in **Davy v JE Collins Limited** [1974] IRLR 325 the Tribunal took the words "If you are not satisfied you can fuck off" to be the equivalent of 'if you don't like it you can lump it'. In **Futty v D and D Brekkes Limited** [1974] IRLR 130 the complainant's foreman stated, "If you do not like the job, fuck off". It was held by the Court that these words should be seen in the context of the shop floor of a fish filleting factory in Hull. Clearly, the context of the workplace is of some importance.

Where conduct is ambiguous the nature of the employer's conduct may amount to a constructive dismissal but it is also possible for conduct to amount to an express dismissal.

The leading case is **Hogg v Dover College** [1990] ICR 39. A teacher had his hours halved and accepted the new position under protest. The EAT held that he was entitled to treat the same as a repudiatory breach and claim constructive dismissal. However, where the offer of new terms was so different that it was tantamount to acceptance of new employment it was possible that there had been a dismissal in respect of the original contract. Garland J stated:

> "There was here a dismissal. If we are wrong in our view in that respect, there was clearly a constructive dismissal because the applicant accepted the employer's conduct as repudiatory and cannot, by his subsequent conduct be said to have affirmed the original contract or any original contract as varied."

The same approach was taken in **Alcan Extrusions v Yates** [1996] IRLR 327 where the employers sought to impose a new shift system. The employees sent a form stating that they regarded the changes as amounting to a dismissal. It was held that they had been dismissed as a result of the new system.

There is a danger that an employee may be mislead into believing he has been dismissed due to certain conduct and his failure to return to work may in fact amount to a resignation. The conduct must be sufficient to amount to a dismissal. In **Frederick Day Limited v Davidson** [EAT 678/79] the sending of a P45 did not amount to a dismissal in itself though in that case there were other factors that lead to the conclusion there had been a dismissal. The removal of a clock card was not sufficient to amount to a dismissal in **Leeman v Johnson Gibbons (Tools) Limited** [1976] IRLR 11 since it was equally consistent with the management wanting to speak to the employee.

> Where the words or conduct are ambiguous it is necessary to construe the words or conduct in all the circumstances of the case, taking account of conduct before and after. If after considering the words or conduct in their context they are still ambiguous the question is how any reasonable employer or employee would have understood the words.

This approach was taken in **J & J Stern v Simpson** [EAT 92/82] where the employee was told to get out and the locks to the premises were changed. Tudor Evans J stated the approach as being:

> "It is only if...there is...ambiguity after looking at the words in their context that then a further test must be applied, namely, whether any reasonable employer might have understood the words to be tantamount to dismissal or resignation. That is the test which we propose to adopt in this case; that is to say, we propose to look a the words in the context of the facts..."

See also **Gale (BG) Limited v Gilbert** [1978] ICR 1149 – a resignation case).

> Where the employee is told to resign by his employer or the resignation is induced by deception or dishonesty there may in reality be a dismissal, unless the resignation was or became a genuinely voluntary one.

In circumstances where the employee has been told to resign or be dismissed or has been induced to resign by some form of deception then it is likely the court will say that there has in fact been a dismissal. Pressure or heavy handed behaviour by an employer the Tribunal may find that there has been an enforced resignation that amounts to a dismissal. In **East Sussex County Council v Walker** [1972] ITR 280 a cook was told that her employment was to end because of declining pupils and was told that she should send a letter of resignation. The NIRC held that there had ben a dismissal, stating that *"if an employee is told that she is no longer required in her employment and is expressly invited to resign, a court of law is entitled to come to the conclusion that, as a matter of common sense the employee* *was dismissed"* (See also **Spencer Jones v Timmens Freeman** [1974] IRLR 325 and **Scott v Formica Limited** [1975] IRLR 104.)

A threat that a severance package will not be paid unless the employee resigns may lead to the conclusion that it was in reality the employer's decision to terminate and there was a dismissal (**Rentokil Limited v Morgan** [EAT 703/95). However, the negotiation of a satisfactory severance package may mean that there was no dismissal as in **Sheffield v Oxford Controls Limited** [1979] IRLR 133 where the EAT held that if the threat to resign or be dismissed had been superseded by satisfactory severance terms the contract may have been terminated by agreement. However, if there is in reality a take it or leave it situation there will probably have been a dismissal (See **Bickerton v Inver House Distillers Limited** [EAT 656/9]).

A second exception may apply where the employee resigns rather than being dismissed in the context of disciplinary proceedings as in **Staffordshire County Council v Donovan** [1981] IRLR 108. (See further below under **Termination by Agreement.**)

If the employee is induced to resign by a deception then the Tribunal will be entitled to find that there has in reality been a dismissal. This was the position in **Caledonian Mining Co Limited v Bassett** [1987] ICR 425. In this case the employers had dishonestly persuaded the employees to resign in order to avoid having to pay a redundancy payment. It was held that there had in reality been dismissals.

Termination where a cross notice is served by the employee

By section 95(2) of the ERA 1996 an employee which had been given notice to terminate his contract and who at a time within the period of that notice, gives notice to the employer to terminate the contract on a date earlier than the date on which the employer's notice is due to expire will be taken to have been dismissed and the reason will have been that for which the employer's notice was given. It is necessary for the the employee to give notice to expire on a date that is certain or from which it can be ascertained (**Walker v Cotswold Chine Home School** (1977) 12 ITR 342).

However, in the case of redundancy dismissals, under section 136(3) of the ERA such counter notice must be given within the 'obligatory period' which is defined in section 136(4) as the statutory notice period or the contractual notice period so that if the employer has given a longer notice period and the employee gives notice before the 'obligatory period' has commenced the there will not be a dismissal for redundancy.

Termination by expiry of a fixed term contract

> The expiry of a fixed term contract without renewal is deemed to be a dismissal unless in reality it was a contract that terminated by mutual consent, by performance or upon a future contingency.

Under section 95(1)(b) the non renewal of a fixed term contract is taken to be a dismissal. A fixed term contract is a contract that is expressed to come to an end after a certain time on a date that is specified. It is important to note that a contract may still be one for a fixed term even though it contains provision that it may come to an end on an earlier date. In **Dixon & Constanti v BBC** [1979] ICR 281; IRLR 114 the employees entered into contracts that were stated to be of two months' duration "unless previously determined by one week's prior notice in writing on either side." The Court of Appeal held that there was a fixed term contract where it was for a specified term even though it was determinable by notice within that term. (See also **Wiltshire County Council v NATFHE** [1980] ICR 455; IRLR 198.)

However, where the contract is expressed to determine on the happening of a future contingency there will not be a dismissal on this ground as in **Brown v Knowsley Borough Council** [1986] IRLR 102 where the contract came to an end in the absence of funding so that when funding ran out it terminated automatically.

Similarly, the non renewal of a fixed term contract by mutual consent will not amount to a dismissal as in **Manson v University of Strathclyde** [EAT 356/87] where lecturers did not have their contracts renewed because they wished to work elsewhere. (cf **Thames Television Limited v Wallis** [1979] IRLR 136 and **McAlwane v Boughton Estate Limited** [1973] 2 All ER 299; [1973] ICR 470.)

Termination by way of constructive dismissal

> There is a constructive dismissal where the employee terminates the contract, with or without notice, in circumstances where he is entitled to terminate by reason of the employer's conduct. In order to show a dismissal it is necessary for the employee to prove:
> (a) there was a fundamental breach of contract by the employer.
> (b) the employee terminated the contract, with or without notice, because of the breach.
> (c) the employee did not affirm or waive the breach by waiting too long before he resigned.

(a)   *Fundamental breach*

The leading case which sets out the test of whether there is a constructive dismissal is **Western Excavating (ECC) Limited v Sharp** [1978] ICR 221, in which Lord Denning MR set out the test as follows:

> "If the employer is guilty of conduct which is a significant breach going to the root of the contract of employment, or which shows that the employer no longer intends to be bound by one or more of the essential terms of the contract, then the employee is entitled to treat himself as discharged from any performance. If he does so, then he terminates the contract by reason of the employer's conduct. He is constructively dismissed. The employee is entitled in those circumstances to leave at the instant without giving any notice at all or, alternatively, he may give notice and say he is leaving at the end of the notice. But the conduct must in either case be sufficiently serious to entitle him to leave at once. Moreover, he must make up his mind soon after the conduct of which he complains for, if he continues for any length of time without leaving, he will lose his right to treat himself as discharged. He will be regarded as having elected to affirm the contract."

It is necessary for the breach to be fundamental (See **Pederson v London Borough of Camden** [1981] IRLR 173 and not minor or inconsequential (**Gillies v Richard Daniels & Co Limited** [1979] IRLR 457) and it is a mixed question of fact and law as to whether there has been a breach (**Woods v WM Car Services (Peterborough) Limited** [1982] IRLR 413.

The change in terms and conditions imposed by the employer must be sufficiently serious to amount to a fundamental breach of contract, but once this is proved the reasonableness of the employer's behaviour or the surrounding circumstances, are irrelevant in deciding whether there is a constructive dismissal. In **Wadham Stringer Commercials Limited v Brown** [EAT 322/82], for example, the applicant resigned after he was demoted and transferred to an office environment which was cramped and unpleasant. The employer argued that the economic circumstances which brought about this change should be taken into account. Browne-Wilkinson J rejected this argument stating that neither the circumstances which induced the fundamental breach nor the employees conduct in accepting the breach are relevant. The question of reasonableness only becomes relevant when one moves on to consider whether the dismissal was fair.

There are many reported cases which consider whether the particular facts amount to a fundamental breach entitling the employee to resign and claim constructive dismissal. The cases in one sense turn on their own facts but do provide some useful guidelines as to the approach to be adopted.

Examples

1. Job Content and Status

Where the employer changes the job content and status of the employee it is likely that this will amount to a repudiatory breach of contract. In **McNeill v Charles Crimm (Electrical Contractors) Limited** [1984] IRLR 179, Mr McNeill a foreman electrician was moved to a contract where he was instructed to work as an ordinary plumber on instruction from another electrician who was not a foreman. He resigned and claimed unfair constructive dismissal. The EAT held that there was a breach of contract entitling him to resign. Lord McDonald stated that:

"We are concerned with the interpretation of the terms and conditions of employment. If these require an employee to work in a certain place and in a certain capacity, it is in our view a breach of these conditions for the employer to seek to insist that he should work elsewhere and in a different capacity albeit on a temporary basis."

The change in the above case was temporary but still amounted to a sufficiently fundamental breach. However, some temporary changes may not amount to a repudiatory breach. In **Millbrook Furnishing Industries v McIntosh** [1981] IRLR 309 it was stated by the EAT that a temporary transfer to another department may not constitute a repudiatory breach if the period was specified, or a short fixed period or employees were left in no doubt that it would not affect their salary. Nevertheless, in the particular case both the duration of the transfer was unclear and it was unclear that wages would be maintained so that the EAT held that the Tribunal were entitled to decide that there had been a constructive dismissal. In **Milthorn Toleman Limited v Ford** [1978] IRLR 306 a change in job content and demotion during notice period amounted to a repudiatory breach since the nature of the changes amounted to a clear breach of contract. (see also **Managers (Holborn) Limited v Hohne** [1977] IRLR 230)

There are many examples of cases in which a change in job content or status has been held to be a repudiatory breach of contract See:

- **Coleman v S & W Baldwin (t/a Baldwins)** [1977] IRLR 342: Interesting duties as buyer taken away and humdrum duties left.
- **Pedersen v London Borough of Camden** [1981] IRLR 173: Change from bar steward duties to catering assistant.
- **Stephenson & Co (Oxford) Limited v Austin** [1990] IRLR 609: Change in status without other changes.
- **BBC v Beckett** [1983] IRLR 43: Unreasonable demotion.

2. 'Last Straw' Changes

A series of variations to employees' contracts arising out of re-organisations may not be sufficiently fundamental, individually, to amount to a repudiatory breach of contract but their cumulative effect may be that the employee is entitled to treat himself as dismissed. In **Lewis v Motorworld Garages Limited** [1986] ICR 157 an employee was demoted and his salary structure changed. A number of criticisms were made of him over a period of time, culminating in a final warning. The Court of Appeal held that the demotion and change in salary could be taken into account as part of the sequence of events, entitling him to resign, even though these breaches had been waived, by not acting on them, in deciding whether a 'last straw' position had been reached. In **Miller v**

Shanks & McEwen (Contractors) Limited [EAT 263/78] it was held that a gradual erosion of a contract manager's position could amount to a series of events entitling him to resign.

3. **Place of work**

A change in the place of work may be a repudiation where the change the change is fundamental and amounts to a repudiation (**Hawker Siddeley Power Engineering Limited v Rump** [1979] IRLR 425. Even if there is an express mobility clause it will be subject to implied terms of reasonableness (**White v Reflecting Roadstuds Limited** [1991] ICR 733). Where the contract is silent as to the place of work it will be covered by implied terms which will be ascertained from the surrounding circumstances (**Jones v Associated Tunnelling Co Limited** [1981] IRLR 477). However, it should be noted that employees who are required to move at short notice will not necessarily accept the change as they are entitled to have a reasonable period to consider their position (**Shields Furniture Limited v Goff** 1973] ICR 191; **Sheet Metal Components v Plumridge** [1974] ICR 73; IRLR 86; **Air Canada v Lee** [1978] IRLR 392).

Where the employer seeks to incorporate a mobility clause which has no immediate effect the court will exercise great caution before deciding that the employee has consented to the variation by continuing to work without objection **Aparau v Iceland Frozen Foods Plc** [1996] IRLR 119).

4. **Trust and confidence**

Whilst it is apparent from the *Western Excavating* case that in order to claim constructive dismissal there must be a breach of contract the Courts have overt recent years interpreted contracts in such a manner as to imply terms of mutual trust and confidence. In **Post Office v Roberts** [1980] IRLR 347 the Court refused to imply a term that the parties must behave towards each other in a manner that was reasonable on the ground that it is too vague a term to enforce. However, the implied term of trust and confidence has been recognised by the House of Lords in **Mahmud v BCCI SA** [1997] ICR 606, where it was defined as follows:

> "The employer shall not without reasonable and proper cause conduct itself in a manner calculated and likely to destroy or seriously damage the relationship of trust and confidence between the employer and employee."

There are in fact a vast amount of cases where the Courts have held that the duty of mutual trust and confidence has been considered. See:

- **Bracebridge Engineering v Darby** [1990] IRLR 3: failing to investigate allegations of sexual harassment.
- **British Aircraft Corporation v Austin** [1978] IRLR 332: failing to properly investigate complaints.
- **F C Gardener v Beresford** [1978] IRLR 63 and **Murco Petroleum Limited v Forge** [1987] IRLR 50: inferior treatment of employee compared to other employees by failing to give pay rises.
- **Hilton International Hotels (UK) Limited v Protopapa** [1990] IRLR 316: undermining a supervisor in front of subordinates.
- **Palamor Limited v Cedron** [1987] IRLR 3030; ICR 1008: unacceptable abuse or **Post Office v Roberts** [1980] IRLR 347: intolerable conduct by the employer.
- **Robinson v Crompton Parkinson Limited** [1978] IRLR 401: false accusations of theft.
- **Wigan Borough Council v Davies** [1979] IRLR 127: failure to support an employee against harassment from co employees.
- **Wood v Freeloader Limited** [1977] IRLR 455: seduction of a female employee into a lesbian relationship.
- **Woods v WM Car Services (Peterborough) Limited** [1981] IRLR: attempting to alter the terms of the employee's contract to to the employee's detriment.

5. Remuneration

Since the payment of remuneration is one of the fundamental terms of the contract of employment it is likely that a unilateral change in the amount of wages payable or the manner in which wages are calculated will be regarded as a breach going to the root of the contract. In **R F Hill v Mooney** [1981] IRLR 258 the employers changed the way in which the salary of a salesman was calculated by taking away 1% commission on all sales and making commission payable only after a target figure had been achieved. Mr Mooney resigned in protest at this new commission structure. It was argued by the company that the new method of calculation was not a fundamental breach of contract and that Mr Mooney was not in any event adversely affected by the scheme. The EAT held that all breaches of the contractual obligation to pay salary go to the root of the contract and that employers cannot alter the way in which salary is calculated and then argue that it would not have made any difference to the employees by using figures not made known to employees. Browne-Wilkinson J stated:

> "What the employers have sought to do in this case is to tear up the existing contractual obligation as to the computation of remuneration by reference to a given formula. In its place they have sought to impose a different formula, the exact operation of which at the date at which they attempted to impose it was incapable of assessment. The obligation on an employer to pay remuneration is one of the fundamental terms of a contract. In our view if an employer seeks to alter that contractual term in a fundamental way such as he sought to do in this case, such attempt is a breach going to the very root of the contract and is necessarily a repudiation. It is not open to him, subsequently, to come along and seek to show by detailed calculations, not capable of being made at the time, that in fact it would not have operated in a very seriously detrimental way. The obligation on the employer is to pay the contractual wages, and he is not entitled to alter the formula whereby those wages are calculated."

(See also **Industrial Rubber Products v Gillan** [1977] IRLR 389).

The above case is a strong statement of the likely effect of attempting to alter terms and conditions relating to remuneration, but in fact not every such alteration will necessarily amount to a fundamental breach. In **Ropaigealach v THF Hotels Limited** [EAT 180/180], employers withdrew free transport with a cost to the employee of £1 per week. The EAT did not think this amounted to a fundamental breach, though they were influenced by the fact that the applicant's main complaint was in fact that she had not been consulted prior to the change. Similarly, in **Gillies v Richard Daniels** [1979] IRLR 457 a reduction in bonus of £1.50 per week from a salary of £60 per week was not sufficient to amount to a repudiatory breach. It is really a question of degree as to whether the variation is sufficient to amount to a fundamental breach. In **Power Lines Pipes & Cables Limited v Penrice & Ors** (EAT) the Scottish EAT held that removal of free travel leading to a loss of up to £17.50 and additional hours spent in getting to work was sufficient to amount to a fundamental breach of contract. This was despite the fact that the free transport was not stated as being part of the contract and had been at the initiative of the employer, since the Tribunal found that it had become an essential term of the contract which bound the employer.

Where the employer deliberately withholds or reduces an employee's pay this will be a repudiatory breach of contract regardless of the amount of money involved or its effect on the employee's pay packet. However, in **Cantor Fitzgerald International Limited v Callaghan** [1999] ICR 639; IRLR 234 the Court of Appeal held that where the employer inadvertently fails or delays in making payment this may not amount to a breach but depends on all the circumstances.

Disputes and mistaken belief about the terms of the contract

One area of particular difficulty is where there is a genuine dispute over the interpretation of the contract so that the employer genuinely believes that he is acting in such manner that is not in breach of contract. The position was considered by the Court of Appeal in **Financial Techniques (Planning Services) Limited v Hughes** [1981] IRLR 32. The employee was entitled to the benefit of a profit sharing scheme which was expressed to be discretionary. When he gave notice the employer gave notice that they intended to offset any deficits before he left. He then resigned immediately and claimed constructive dismissal. The Court of Appeal held that the scheme was contractual. However, it held that where there was a genuine dispute over the terms of a contract one party is not necessarily in breach by stating that it intends to adopt the interpretation it has placed on the contract. Templeman LJ stated:

> "In my judgment repudiation or not repudiation depends on the facts and consequences of each action by the party who holds mistaken views. What he says may amount to an actual or anticipatory breach of a term of the contract which would make it unreasonable to force the other party to go on without knowing what he would get at the end of it."

In this case there was not an actual breach because there was merely a dispute about whether the monies were payable on the last day of the contract of not. Brandon LJ took the view that if the belief was not genuine it would be a different matter. The difficulty for the employee is that he will be at risk if he resigns in circumstances where there is a genuine dispute about the contract. Indeed it was stated by Sir John Donaldson MR in **Brigden v Lancashire County Council** [1987] IRLR 58 that:

> "The mere fact that a party to a contract takes a view of its construction which is ultimately shown to be wrong does not of

itself constitute repudiatory conduct. It has to be shown that he did not intend to be bound by the contract as properly construed."

This was followed by the EAT in **O'Kelly v GMBATU** [396/87].

In **Brown v JBD Engineering Limited** [1993] IRLR 568 the EAT held that a Tribunal was wrong to decide that facts decided in good faith and based upon a genuine belief could not amount to a repudiatory breach. The whole of the circumstances should be considered in deciding whether or not the employer's conduct went to the root of the contract.

Anticipatory Breach or Premature reaction?

There must be a breach of contract on the part of the employer in the sense of a clear intention on the part of the employer which has been expressed to the employee that the terms and conditions of his employment will be unilaterally changed regardless of the terms of the contract. If the employer has not evinced an intention to act in breach of contract the action of the employee in resigning where varied terms are merely proposed may be premature so that there is no dismissal within the meaning of section 95 of the Act and the employee therefore has no claim. In **Mercer-Browne v AUEW (Engineering Section)** [EAT 119/8], it was proposed that the appellant's job content be altered to cover working on a switchboard when the junior secretary was on day-release. There were considerable negotiations when the appellant objected, and a letter was written which stated that "the time has come for reasonable finality to be reached". The EAT agreed with the Tribunal that the letter amounted to no more than a request and did not evince an intention no longer to be bound by the terms of the contract. A majority of the EAT considered the letter to be a request.

There is a difference between a mere request as in the case above and a clear intention on the part of the employer to repudiate the terms and conditions of the contract of employment by evincing an intention to change the terms and conditions of employment. Where the employer makes it clear that he intends to unilaterally vary the contracts of employment at a particular point in time the employee may treat this as an anticipatory breach of contract entitling him to resign. However, a date need not be specified so long as the employer has made his intention clear. In **Maher v Fram Gerrard Limited** [1974] ICR 31 a company was taken over by the respondent and the respondent decided to close down its depot at Swinton and move it to Adlington. The appellant who was a foreman did not want to move to Adlington and resigned. He had been told of the move and of the travelling arrangements that were being made but no firm date for the move had been given. The NIRC held that there was an anticipatory breach of contract as the employer had made it clear they intended to insist on the transfer. By the time he had given his notice he had been faced with the choice of moving to Adlington or losing his job.

A similar result was reached in **Greenaway Harrison Limited v Wiles** [1994] IRLR 380 where it was found that the employer had made it clear that the employee's hours of work were to be changed and the fact that she had been told she could speak to the managing director did not change this position.

Where there is a repudiatory breach of contract on the part of the employer the employee must accept the breach by resigning. If he delays too long he may be taken to have affirmed the contract. Moreover, the breach must be the cause of the employee resigning. There is some degree of tolerance where the employee is making up his mind whether to go along with the change, particularly where the job is tried out for a trial period. Nevertheless, the employee who delays too long will lose his right to resign.

(b)   Acceptance of Breach of contract

If the employee is to claim constructive dismissal where there is a repudiatory breach of contract he must bring his contract to an end by accepting the breach. He does this by resigning. An act that is inconsistent with bringing the contract to an end will mean that the breach has not been accepted. As Bristow J stated in **Hunt v British Railways Board** [1979] IRLR 379, "...the law does not allow you to have your cake and eat it, and you must not go on acting as if you were employed when what you are trying to say is "I'm not"."

It is important that employees make it clear that they are accepting a repudiatory breach of contract. Simply failing to turn up to work when a change is proposed may not be sufficient. In **Vose v South Sefton Health Authority** [EAT 388/83] Vose did not turn up for work when she was demoted. She appealed against the demotion but this was rejected, the employers making it clear that the job was still available. She claimed unfair dismissal and would have been out of time if she was taken to have accepted the breach by not turning up to work. The EAT stated that "the mere fact that an employee does not comply with a wrongful demand which is the repudiatory conduct is not such an acceptance of the repudiation".

In **Wight v Blackstone Franks Smith & Co** [EAT 610/86] it was held that an application for unemployment benefit was sufficient to amount to an acceptance of the employer's breach of contract, particularly where the employee had stated on the form that he had ceased to be employed.

Nevertheless, it is necessary that the acceptance be communicated in some form, whether by words or conduct, to the employer before the breach is withdrawn by the employer. In the above case it was because the Department of Employment had notified the employer of the benefit claim. In **Norwest Holst Group Administration Limited v Harrison** [1985] ICR 668, the employers proposed transferring Mr Harrison to another office and taking away his directorship of a subsidiary company with effect from 30th June 1982. He wrote to them on a without prejudice basis stating that the proposal constituted a determination of his employment and written discussions thereafter followed with the employer agreeing that he would retain a directorship and his salary would not alter. However, he accepted a job with another firm. The Court of Appeal agreed with the EAT that the announcement, by the employer, of the intention to alter the terms and conditions amounted to a repudiation of the contract and gave Mr Harrison a choice whether to accept or not. Until he communicated this acceptance the contract continued to run and it was open to the employers to withdraw the threatened breach. This was done before he resigned. As Neill LJ stated:

> "In my judgment, subject to any question of estoppel, which has not been raised in this case, the repudiatory act was capable of being cured at any time before Mr Harrison accepted the repudiation as a termination of the contract. This is not a case where the letter was offensive or couched in such terms as to be by itself wholly destructive of the mutual trust between employer and employee."

Similarly where an employer remedies a breach before the resignation of the employee then it may be too late for the employee to resign (**Amery v Ministry of Defence** [EAT 353/80]).

The recent case of **Weathersfield Limited t/a Van & Truck Rentals v Sargent** [1999] IRLR 94 clarifies the stance that the employee should take in cases where there is a breach of contract which the employee wishes to accept. Mrs Weatherfield was told to operate a discriminatory policy and was so upset that she resigned without giving reasons. She gave the reasons a few days later. It was argued in the Court of Appeal that because she did not advise the Appellants of the reason for leaving at the time that she left it could not be said that she had accepted the repudiation. Pill LJ rejected the argument that there can be no acceptance of a repudiation unless the employee tells the employer at the time that he is leaving because of the employer's repudiatory conduct. Whilst the fact finding tribunal may more readily conclude that the conduct of the employer was not the reason for leaving if no reason is communicated at the time, this depends upon the evidence and, in this case, Mrs Sargent had been placed in an outrageous and embarrassing position so that it was understandable that she did not want to immediately confront her employers with the reasons for leaving. It is possible to accept a repudiatory breach of contract by giving notice in accordance with the contract of employment. (**Peterborough Regional Council v Gidney** [EAT 1270/97].) The employee must, however communicate by words or by conduct the he or she is resigning and a mere intention by, for example drafting a letter of resignation is not sufficient (**Edwards v Surrey Police** [1999] IRLR).

Causation

The reason for the employee's resignation must be the breach of contract on the part of the employer. It is not necessary for the employee to expressly state the reason that he is resigning provided that the plain inference is that the employee has left because of the breach (**Joseph Steinfeld v Reypert** [EAT 550/78]). In **Walker v Josiah Wedgwood & Sons Limited** [1978] ICR 744 a works manager resigned because of the intolerable conduct of his supervisor. The tribunal did not consider there to be breach of contract though the conduct was unreasonable. The EAT did not interfere with this judgment. However, they also stated that employees claiming constructive dismissal must indicate that it was the employer's conduct which brought about the dismissal. It does not matter that the employee may not realise that the employer is behaving in repudiatory breach provided that this is the reason for the resignation. In **Sword v Ashley Vinters and Bariltone** [EAT 731/81] the appellant resigned her position, at the behest of her employer, and went to work for an associated company. She was dismissed after a week as the sole purpose was to take away her employment rights. The EAT held that there had been a constructive dismissal. Lord MacDonald stated that when she signed the resignation she was unaware of the reason which motivated the employer but she was nevertheless entitled to rely on what had happened to show there was a constructive dismissal. It is necessary for the Tribunal to consider the effective cause of the resignation. The EAT held that a Tribunal had erred in **Jones v F Sirl & Son (Furnishers) Limited** [1997] IRLR 493 in failing to consider this point where the employee resigned in order to take a job and the employer had committed repudiatory breaches of contract. It stated:

> "Instead of asking themselves whether the breach was the effective cause of the resignation, they appeared to take the view that simply because the appellant's departure had been 'prompted by the offer of alternative employment' it therefore followed that she had not left in consequence of the fundamental breaches of contract. In our judgment, it is plain that had the industrial tribunal asked themselves the correct question, ie what was the effective cause of the appellant's resignation, they would have been bound to conclude, on the evidence before them given by the appellant, that the main operative cause of the appellant's resignation was the very serious and fundamental breach of her contract by the respondents."

(c) Affirmation of contract

Where the employer insists on a unilateral variation in the terms and conditions of employment the employee who carries on working, to the new terms, will not be taken to have affirmed the change if he carries on working under protest. In **Marriot v Oxford & District Co-Op Society Limited** [1969] 3 All ER 1126, an employee was held not to have affirmed a contract when he carried on working for four weeks after his pay had been reduced and he had been demoted. He had protested at the change and submitted temporarily as he did not want to be unemployed. (See also **Shields Furniture Limited v Goff** [1973] ICR 191 and **Sheet Metal Components v Plumridge** [1974] ICR 73.)

The employee will have a reasonable period to make up his mind whether he is prepared to accept the change in his contract. As Phillips J stated in **Air Canada v Lee** [1978] IRLR 392:

> "...the duration of the trial period was unspecified. That of course does not mean that it can last forever, but only for what is a reasonable period in all the circumstances. Amongst the circumstances will be included the steps the employers take, during a trial period the length of which is unspecified, to enquire how things are coming along and what the employee is going to do. If they make no such enquiries, and if it is only a comparatively short period, or a reasonable period, then it carries on until either the employee announces his decision, or a period of time has expired which is long enough for it to be said that it would be unreasonable to consider the trial period as still subsisting."

In that case, the employee resigned after two months of being moved to a new location because she was unhappy with the quality of the accommodation. She was held to have resigned before the trial period had extended beyond a reasonable period.

The employee does not invariably have to inform the employer that he is accepting the change only on a trial basis if the circumstances are such that the employer should have known it was only being accepted on a trial basis. In **Superest Upholstery Co Limited v Rowberry** [EAT 74/77] a factory was closed and employees were moved fifteen miles to another factory. The applicant did not state that he was accepting the move under protest but left after a short period for another job. He claimed a redundancy payment. The EAT held that the applicant had agreed to a change in workplace on the evidence as there was nothing whereby the employers ought to have known that the change of place of work was only being accepted on a trial basis and this was upheld by the Court of Appeal. Arnold J stated the test in the EAT as follows:

> "..if there is dictation, so that all that happens is a mute non-resistance by the employee to the purported dictation of the employer, there is no material upon which one should find a consensual acceptance of the proposed variation. The second is that if the circumstances are such that the proper inference is that the employers know or ought to have known that what was an apparent acceptance was indeed no more than an indication of willingness to give the new arrangement a trial, then again that will not amount to a consensual variation of the contract."

It is not the actual delay in accepting the repudiatory breach of contract that is crucial but the question of whether there has been express or implied affirmation of the contract. Continuing to work without protest may be taken to be an implied affirmation of the contract. As Browne-Wilkinson J stated in **W E Cox Toner (International) v Crook** [1981] ICR 823:

> "Affirmation of the contract can be implied. Thus, if the innocent party calls on the guilty party for further performance of the contract, he will normally be taken to have affirmed the contract since his conduct is only consistent with the continued existence of the contractual obligation. Moreover, if the innocent party himself does acts which are only consistent with the continued existence of the contract such acts normally show affirmation of the contract. However, if the innocent party further performs the contract to a limited extent but at the same time makes it clear that he is reserving his rights to accept the repudiation or is only continuing so as to allow the guilty party to remedy the breach such further performance does not prejudice his right subsequently to accept the repudiation."

The EAT held that he employee had affirmed the contract when he continued to work after an ultimatum he had given had not been accepted. In **Joseph Steinfield & Co v Reypert** [EAT 550/78] Mr Reypert was appointed as a sales manager but asked to do clerical work on a temporary basis. When attempts to fill this post were unsuccessful Mr Reypert stayed on for a further four months, making it clear he was not satisfied with the change in his position, before resigning. He was held not to have affirmed the contract and that "it should not be held against him that he went on helping out until eventually he came to the conclusion that enough was enough".

Where a breach is a continuing one, the fact that there has been delay on the part of an employee may not lead to a conclusion that the contract has been affirmed. In **D H Russell (London) Limited v Magee** [EAT 201/78] the employee should have been appointed a manager in January 1976 but he was strung along for a year, before he resigned because of the failure to appoint him manager. The EAT held that the company was in continuing breach of contract and Mr Magee had not accepted the breach. Similarly in **Reid v Camphill Engravers** [1990] ICR 435 an employee who was paid below the Wages Council Order minimum wage for three years had not affirmed the contract where there was a continuing breach.

It should be noted, also, that continuing to work is not the only means by which what would otherwise be a repudiatory breach may be affirmed. An employee who accepts wages after a fundamental breach may be taken to have affirmed the contract. In **Grant v Brown & Root Manpower Services Limited** [EAT 167/84], because of a dispute with his union, Brown, a rigger, was kept on shore leave at a holding rate of pay which was below the rate he would earn if he was working. He alleged he had been dismissed but continued to accept wages. The EAT held that the employee's acceptance of wages after the employer's alleged repudiation was wholly inconsistent with being able to claim constructive dismissal. Similarly, in **Hunt v British Railways Board** [1979] IRLR 379 where an employee resigned within three days of being informed that he was to be demoted and transferred, but then reported daily to the depot at which he had been employed it was held that this was inconsistent with there being a constructive dismissal.

Circumstances in which there is No Dismissal

There are certain circumstances in which the employee will not have been dismissed:

(1) **Agreement:** Where the contract of employment has terminated between the parties by agreement;
(2) **Frustration:** Where the contract of employment has been frustrated;
(3) **Operation of law:** Where the contract of employment has terminated by operation of law;
(4) **Performance:** Where the contract was for a purpose which has been performed;
(5) **Resignation:** Where the employee has resigned in circumstances where there is no constructive dismissal.

Agreement

The parties are free to agree that employment will terminate and if the agreement is genuine there will be no dismissal. However, there is likely to have been a dismissal in circumstances where there is an automatic termination clause in a contract or the employee agrees to take early retirement for redundancy.

It is always open to the parties to a contract to agree to terminate it by mutual agreement. In the employment field where the parties genuinely agree to terminate a contract in this way there will be no dismissal as both parties will be released from any further obligations by mutual consent. However, the Tribunal will wish to satisfy itself that the agreement to terminate the legal relationship was by agreement. Indeed this head of 'non-dismissal' overlaps with the section on enforced resignation (See page 73) and on genuine resignations (See page 70). The Tribunal will ask whether a genuine agreement was entered into on a voluntary basis and if it does not consider this to be the true position there will have been a dismissal. Where, for example, the employee wishes to be released from the notice period the contract may be terminated by mutual agreement. This was the position in **Somerset County Council v Oderfield** [EAT 511/76] where the employer accepted that a headmistress could resign with immediate effect when she wished to leave without notice after criticism about her performance. The EAT stated that the parties had arrived at a *"consensual agreement by which she was to stop work"*. Similarly, in **Lipton Limited v Marlborough** [1979] IRLR 180 an employee, knowing that his future with the company with in doubt, wished to be released from his notice period and the employer replied that "By mutual agreement your employment will terminate with effect from...". The EAT held that the contract had been terminated by agreement as the employee's request to be released was such that it was clear that there was no termination on the part of the employer. Bristow J stated:

> "The whole difference between termination by mutual agreement in this context and constructive dismissal, is that in the first case the employee says 'Please may I go? And the employer says 'Yes'. In the second case the employee says 'You have treated me in such a way as I'm going without a by your leave'.

If there is no pressure put on an employee but he decides to resign and leave and the employer agrees then it may be a termination by agreement. This was the position in **Hart v British Veterinary Association** [EAT 145/678] where it was suggested that an employee should resign but she in fact decided to leave when she found another job. The employee had agreed voluntarily to go and without pressure. (See also **Sheffield v Oxford Control Company Limited** [1978] IRLR 133, **Crowley v Ashland UK Chemical Limited** [EAT 31/79], **Staffordshire County Council v Donovan** [1981] IRLR 108). These cases may be compared with **Glencross v Dymoke** [1979]

ICR 136 where the employee was told that she would be made redundant in any event so that she had been dismissed.

There are two particular factual situations where the courts have been especially exercised as to whether or not there was a termination by mutual agreement rather than a dismissal. Where an employer asks for voluntary redundancies or for early retirement the Courts have distinguished between cases where there is a redundancy situation in any event and where no pressure has been placed on the employee. In **Fail v Northumberland County Council** [EAT 234/79] the employee offered to retire early and it was an important factor in the EAT upholding the Tribunal decisions that there was *"no question here of any pressure being put upon the appellant."*

Where the employer invites people to take advantage of an early retirement scheme without any pressure the termination may be by mutual agreement (**Birch v University of Liverpool** [1985] ICR 470) even if the employees were already under notice of dismissal (**Scott v Coalite Fuels & Chemical Limited** [1988] ICR 355) although if notice has already been given and is not withdrawn it is difficult to see how there is not a dismissal (See **Gateshead Metropolitan Borough Council v Mills** [EAT 610/92]). However, if persons are to be made redundant in any event the termination is likely to be a dismissal (**Burton Allton & Johnson Limited v Peck** [1975] ICR 193 even if the employee has sought to be made redundant (**Walley v Morgan** [1969] ITR 122).

The second situation is where the parties have agreed that the contract will come to an end by mutual agreement if the employee overstays his leave. The Court of Appeal ruled in **Igbo v Johnson Matthey Chemicals Limited** [1986] IRLR 215, ICR 505 that an agreement that the contract will terminate by agreement if the employee overstays its leave is not valid as it is contrary to section 203(1) of the ERA since it would limit the operation of the unfair dismissal provisions. However, it should be noted that not all agreements will be so regarded as a genuinely agreed severance can be a termination by agreement (**Logan Salton v Durham County Council** [1989] IRLR 99).

Frustration

> The contract of employment may terminate by reason of frustration rather than dismissal where, through no fault of either party, it becomes impossible of performance, illegal or radically different from the contract that was envisaged by the parties.

The doctrine of frustration is well known in contract law but raises particular difficulties in the employment field since it may often be difficult to state that the contract has become impossible of importance. In particular, the fact that an employee is going to be absent from work for a period of time does not necessarily render the contract frustrated by operation of law. While the doctrine of frustration is a technical one in **Marshall v Harland & Wolff Limited** [1972] ICR 101 it was stated by Sir John Donaldson that:

> "...there is nothing technical about the idea that a contract should, cease to bind the parties if, though no fault of either of them, unprovided for circumstances arise in which a contractual obligation becomes impossible of performance or in which performance of the obligation would be rendered a thing radically differed from that which was undertaken by the contract. Yet this is all that the lawyer means by 'frustration' of a contract..."

Where one party is responsible for the frustrating event that party will not be able to rely upon that event to assert that it is the other party that is in breach. This principle has been particularly relevant in the case where the employee has been convicted of a custodial sentence which means that he can longer work under the contract of employment. In **F C Shepherd v Jerrom** [1986] ICR 802, IRLR 358 an apprentice was sentenced for a period of n not less than six months and up to two years. The Court of Appeal held that the sentence had frustrated the apprenticeship. The contract was frustrated by imprisonment in **Harrington v Kent CC** [1980] IRLR 353, even though an appeal against sentence had been lodged. However, in **Mecca Limited v Shepherd** [EAT 379/78] a short sentence of 24 days, of which 20 were served, did not frustrate the contract.

The most difficult aspect of this area is where the employee is absent because of sickness of an indefinite duration. This was the position in *Marshall v Harland & Wolff Limited* where an employee was absent for a period of 18 months but expected to recover after an operation. The NIRC in its judgment considered that the following points should be taken into account:

"(a) The terms of the contract, including the provisions as to sickness pay

The whole basis of weekly employment may be destroyed more quickly than that of monthly employment and that in turn more quickly than annual employment. When the contract provides for sick pay, it is plain that the contract cannot be frustrated so long as the employee returns to work, or appears likely to return to work, within the period during which such sick pay is payable. But the converse is not necessarily true, for the right to sick pay may expire before the incapacity has gone on, or appears likely to go on, for so long as to make a return to work impossible or radically different from the obligations undertaken under the contract of employment.

(b) How long the employment was likely to last in the absence of sickness

The relationship is less likely to survive if the employment was inherently temporary in its nature or for the duration of a particular job, than if it was expected to be long term or even life long.

(c) The nature of the employment

Where the employee is one of many in the same category, the relationship is more likely to survive the period of incapacity than if he occupies a key post which must be filled and filled on a permanent basis if his absence is prolonged.

(d) The nature of the illness or injury and how long it has already continued and the prospects of recovery

The greater the degree of incapacity and the longer the period over which it has persisted and is likely to persist, the more likely it is that the relationship has been destroyed.

(e) The period of past employment

> A relationship which is of long standing is not so easily destroyed as one which has but a short history. This is good sense and, we think, no less good law, even if it involves some implied and scarcely detectable change in the contract of employment year by year as the duration of the relationship lengthens. The legal basis is that over a long period service the parties must be assumed to have contemplated a longer period or periods of sickness than over a shorter period.
>
> These factors are inter-related and cumulative, but are not necessarily exhaustive of those which have to be taken into account. The question is and remains, 'Was the employee's incapacity, looked at before the purported dismissal, of such a nature, or did it appear likely to continue for such a period, that further performance of his obligations in the future would either be impossible or would be a thing radically different from that undertaken by him and accepted by the employer under the agreed terms of his employment?' Any other factors which bear upon this issue must also be considered.
>
> The ending of the relationship of employer and employee by operation of law is, by definition, independent of the volition or intention of the parties. A tribunal is, however, entitled to treat the conduct of the parties as evidence to be considered in forming a judgment as to whether the changed circumstances were so fundamental as to strike at the root of the relationship."

The above principles encapsulate the factors that must be taken into account in considering long term sickness. However, it was said in **Williams v Watsons Luxury Coaches Limited** [1990] ICR 536, IRLR 164 that the Courts must be careful about too easy an application of the doctrine of frustration and that the employer should keep itself informed about the progress of the employee by making inquiries and not removing the employee from being a member of staff without some act of final consideration. It is apparent from the *Williams* case that the onus on the employer is to make inquiries to find out the true position, but it is submitted that this does not fit well with the traditional concept of frustration as terminating the contract by operation of law.

Further, helpful guidance as to frustration by reason of sickness was given by the EAT in **Egg Stores Limited v Leibovici** [1977] ICR 260. The employee was absent for three and a half months after fifteen years of service. When he became fit to return he was then told that he had been replaced. The case was remitted to the Tribunal because it had made an error of law in not recognising that the doctrine of frustration automatically terminates the contract of employment. However, Phillips J set out nine matters that he considered to be relevant.

> '... Among the matters to be taken into account in such a case in reaching a decision are these: (1) the length of the previous employment; (2) how long it had been expected that the employment would continue; (3) the nature of the job; (4) the nature, length and effect of the illness or disabling event; (5) the need of the employer for the work to be done, and the need for a replacement to do it; (6) the risk to the employer of acquiring obligations in respect of redundancy payments or compensation for unfair dismissal to the replacement employee; (7) whether wages have continued to be paid; (8) the acts and the statements of the employer in relation to the employment, including the dismissal of, or failure to dismiss, the employee; and (9) whether in all the circumstances a reasonable employer could be expected to wait any longer.'

In **Williams v Watson Luxury Coaches Limited** [1990] ICR 101, it was stated:

> "To these we would add the terms of the contract as to the provisions for sickness pay, if any, and also, a consideration of the prospects of recovery."

Whilst the principles have been clearly set out in the above cases it is difficult to apply the doctrine of frustration where it is envisaged that the employee may be absent for long periods of time (see **James v The Greytree Trust** [EAT 699/95]) though there will be grounds for arguing frustration if the employee is not likely to work again (**Notcutt v Universal Equipment Co (London) Limited** [1986] ICR 414; IRLR 218).

An important recent case looked at the position where the employee had been absent for some time but was kept 'on the books' in order to qualify for certain scheme benefits. In **G F Sharp & Co Limited**

v McMillan [1998] IRLR 632 it was held that the contract had been frustrated when an employee was kept on the books for this purpose and there was no continuing contractual relationship that would have entitled him to any payments in lieu. This case is likely to be of some impact where employers keep employees on their books who are unfit to work.

Operation of law

> There are a number of circumstances other than frustration where employment terminates by operation of law that do not amount to a dismissal.

- Appointment of a Court Receiver
- Compulsory winding up of a company
- Death of the employer if the contract is with the employer as an individual

  Where the contract is for personal services the death of either party will dissolve the contract. This was the position in **Farrow v Wilson** [1869] LR 4 CP 744 where the employee was a farm bailiff and the contract was dissolved on the death of the farmer employer, in the absence of any express or implied term to the contrary, so that the personal representative was not bound to pay six month's wages under the notice period in the contract. (See also **Graves v Cohen & Ors** (1930) 46 TLR 121).

- Dissolution of a partnership
- Statutory provisions that provide for the automatic termination of a contract

  Where there are statutory provisions or regulations which provide that individuals cannot hold appointments upon the happening of certain events there will be an automatic termination should the event occur. This was the position in **Tarnesbey v Kensington, Chelsea & Westminster AHA** [1981] IRLR 369; ICR 615 where a part time psychiatrist was found guilty of professional misconduct and it was ordered that his name be erased from the register by the General Medical Council. This decision was substituted for a 12 month suspension. It was held by the House of Lords that this suspension terminated the contract under section 28(1) of the Medical Act 1956.

• TUPE Objections

Under the Transfer of Undertakings (Protection of Employment) Regulations 1981 a contract of employment will not be automatically transferred where the employee objects to a transfer. By Regulation 5(4B) the rights, duties and liabilities under or in connection with the contract will not transfer to the transferee where the employee informs the transferor or the transferee that he objects to the transfer. In those circumstances, by Regulation 4B, where the employee so objects the transfer shall operate to as to terminate the contract of employment with the transferor but the employee shall not be treated for any purpose as having been dismissed by the transferor.

Performance

> The contract of employment may terminates upon the performance of a particular project or task and not be a dismissal where the employee had been engaged to carry out that task.

In some circumstances employees may be taken on to carry out a specific project or task. A distinction is clearly drawn in the authorities between the expiry of a fixed term contract and the conclusion of a task for which the employee was employed. In **Wiltshire County Council v NATFHE** [1980] ICR 455; IRLR 198 the claimant was employed as a part time teacher and was not paid when the courses on which she taught ended. The Court of Appeal held that she was employed on a fixed term contract as she was bound to serve the Council for the whole of the fixed term. It was stated that:

> "It seems to me that if there is a contract by which a man is to do a particular task or to carry out a particular purpose then when that task or purpose comes to an end the contract is discharged by performance. Instances may be taken of a seaman who is employed for the duration of a voyage – and it is completely uncertain how long the voyage will last. His engagement comes to an end on its completion. Also of a man who is engaged to cut down trees and, when all the trees have been cut down, his contract is discharged by performance. In neither of these cases is

> there a contract for a fixed term. It is a contract which is
> discharged by performance. There is no "dismissal". A contract for
> a particular purpose, which is fulfilled, is discharged by
> performance and does not amount to a dismissal."

In the instant case the contract was for a fixed term even though it
may have come to an end early where was no more work to be
carried out. In **Ryan v Shipboard Maintenance** [1980] ICR 88;
IRLR 16, on the other hand where Mr Ryan, was employed in the
ship repair industry on a job by job basis, it was held that the
contract was discharged by performance. Each contract was for the
duration of the job so that it was indeterminate as to termination.

Resignation

> If the employee terminates his employment, by words or conduct
> which are unambiguous and there is no constructive dismissal on
> the part of the employer or the employer does not give earlier
> notice the employee will not have been dismissed. Apparently
> unambiguous words or conduct of resignation can normally be
> taken at face value. However, there may not be a resignation in
> certain circumstances where the employee is acting under stress
> or words are spoken in the heat of the moment.

Since a resignation is a termination of the contract of employment
by the employer there will have been no dismissal by the employee.
Where the employee no longer turns up for work or makes it clear
that he has no intention of honouring the contract of employment
then it will usually be quite straightforward to recognise that there
has been a resignation. In **Gale (BG) Limited v Gilbert** [1978] ICR
1149 during a disagreement with his employer, Mr Gale stated "I am
leaving, I want my cards". It was held by the EAT that the Tribunal
was entitled to find that these words amounted to a resignation,
though they expressed regret at their decision as there appeared to be
commercial considerations in the case which made it convenient to
the employer that the employee terminate his contract at that stage.
The EAT also took this approach in **Kwik Fit (GB) Limited v
Lineham** [1992] IRLR 156. The employee threw down his keys and
left after an argument with a divisional manner about a potential
disciplinary matter and left the premises. It was said:

"If words of resignation are unambiguous then prima facie an employer is entitled to treat them as such, but in the field of employment, personalities constitute an important consideration. Words may be spoken or actions expressed in temper or in the heat of the moment or under extreme pressure ('being jostled into a decision') and indeed the intellectual make-up of an employee may be relevant. These we refer to as 'special circumstances'. Where 'special circumstances' arise it may be unreasonable for an employer to assume a resignation and to accept it forthwith. A reasonable period of time should be allowed to lapse and if circumstances arise during that period which put the employer on notice that further enquiry is desirable to see whether the resignation was really intended and can properly be assumed, then such enquiry is ignored at the employer's risk. He runs the risk that ultimately evidence may be forthcoming which indicates that in the 'special circumstances' the intention to resign was not the correct interpretation when the facts are judged objectively."

The EAT reaffirmed this principle in **Stuart Denham v United Glass Limited** [EAT 581/98].

Therefore, whilst the starting point will be that unambiguous words of resignation can be taken at face value (See the dicta from **Sothern v Franks Charlesly & Co** set out at page 41) it is clear that there are noted exceptions that may particularly apply in relation to words or conduct by an employee. Fox LJ noted in that case that there may be an exception in the case of an immature employee or of a decision taken in the heat of the moment or of an employee being jostled into a decision by the employer.

Indeed the Courts appear to have been astute over the years to consider whether there has truly been a resignation. In **ASTMS v Skidmore** [EAT 646/80] Phillips J noted that:

"...some words are so clear that they can only be regarded as being words of dismissal or resignation. No doubt that is so. It is desirable to keep such cases to the minimum. It would not be helpful in this jurisdiction, if there grew up a category of words which automatically constituted dismissal or resignation. Ordinarily speaking, at all events, except in exceptional circumstances, everything must depend upon the circumstances in the individual case."

The Courts have therefore been readily willing to apply the exceptions. This was so in **Barclay v City of Glasgow District Council** [1983] IRLR 313 where Mr Barclay, who was mentally defective, stated that he wanted his cards after an altercation with his foreman. The EAT held that the employer should have realised that words such as this spoken under moments of stress were not intended to be taken seriously. A similar approach was taken in **Greater Glasgow Health Authority v MacKay** [EAT 742/87] where an employee purported to write out a notice of resignation while suffering from stress when she was not behaving rationally.

Where an employee fails to attend work this may amount to a resignation by conduct, as in **Harrison v George Wimpey & Co Limited** [1972] ITR 188 where the employee did not attend work for four months. However, if the employee is not required to work, for example, because he has been suspended there will be no resignation where the employer purports to accept non attendance as a repudiatory breach (**Hassan v Odeon Cinemas Limited** [1988] ICR 127).

Where the employee's conduct could amount to a breach the contract will not come to an end until the breach is accepted (**London Transport Executive v Clarke** [1981] ICR 355; **Brockley v Hursthouse** [EAT 762/87]; **Thomas Marshall (Exports) Limited v Guinle** [1978] ICR 905).

Where the employee does resign and the employer then serves notice which reduces the notice period the resignation will then be converted into a dismissal. This was the position in **John Brignell & Co (Builders) Limited v Bishop** [1974] IRLR 157 where, when the employee gave one week's notice he was immediately given his cards. In **Lees v Arthur Greaves (Lees) Limited** [1974] ICR 501 there was a dismissal where an employee was requested to go at an earlier date than his notice period. However, if there is a provision in the contract which permits the employer to pay in lieu of notice and the employee has resigned it will be possible for the employer to exercise the option to pay in lieu of notice without there being a dismissal (**Marshall (Cambridge) Limited v Hamblin** [1994] ICR 362; IRLR 260).

Ambiguous words or conduct may not be a resignation and the Tribunal will look at the surrounding circumstances (as with ambiguous words or conduct by an employer which could be a dismissal).

As with ambiguous words or conduct of dismissal the words or conduct may not in reality amount to a resignation. The Tribunal will have regard to the surrounding circumstances. Indeed the employer may have queried the words or conduct of the employee which is an indication that what happened was not really regarded as a resignation. This was the position in **Tom Cobeigh Plc v Young** [EAT 292/97] where the employee left the workplace in such a way that indicated that she had no intention of returning. However, the employer wrote to her to ask her intentions but then purported to accept a resignation. It was held that she had been dismissed. This was also the position in **Peebles Publishing Group Limited v Black** [EAT 179/91] where the employee told the managing director that she was leaving and handed in her keys after being told that she owed the company money. She was suffering from stress because her husband was dying of cancer and the Tribunal found that the employer did not have any reasonable belief that she was resigning. (See also **Hogan v ACP Heavy Fabrications Limited** [EAT 340/92]; **Goodwill (Incorporated) Glasgow Limited v Ferrier** [EAT 157/89] – in the latter case the employer actually queried whether the employee really had the intention of resigning.)

CHAPTER THREE
THE REASON FOR THE DISMISSAL

The general principles that must be followed in considering whether an employer has acted fairly or unfairly in dismissing are contained in Part X the Employment Rights Act 1996 (ERA) and the guidance contained in the substantial body of case law as to the approach to be adopted under this and other related legislation. It is first necessary for an employer to show the reason for the dismissal before it can argue that the dismissal was fair. It will be seen that there are five potentially fair reasons for dismissal contained in section 98 of the ERA 1996 and that there are a larger number of dismissals that will be regarded as automatically fair and automatically unfair.

When a potentially fair reason for dismissal has been shown by the employer it is then for the Tribunal to consider whether the dismissal was fair applying the test set out in section 98(4) of the ERA 1996. It will be seen that Tribunals are not permitted to substitute their own views as to whether a dismissal was fair or unfair but must consider whether the employer acted as a reasonable employer in the particular circumstances of the case. Chapter 4 will consider general principles relating to reasonableness whilst subsequent chapters will consider specific areas. In this chapter we consider the reason for dismissal.

Automatically Fair and Unfair Dismissals

Where the employer succeeds in establishing that the reason for dismissal is one that it automatically fair or the employee establishes an automatically unfair reason the Tribunal will not go on to consider the question of reasonableness as it is an issue that simply does not arise. These dismissals will be considered in detail in the later chapters of this book.

Automatically fair dismissals

National Security

Prior to the Act being amended by the Employment Relations Act 1999, by section 10(4) of the Employment Tribunals Act 1996 where it is shown that the dismissal was for the *"purpose of safeguarding national security"* the Tribunal must dismiss the complaint and by section 10(5) a certificate signed by a Minister of the Crown certifying that the action was taken for the purposes of national security was deemed to be conclusive. The Employment Relations Act 1999 has relaxed the position in relation to security staff by Schedule 8 so that certificates are no longer conclusive and directions may be made for the conduct of cases. This is considered further in Chapter 10.

Industrial action

Prior to the Employment Relations Act 1999 there were two areas of industrial action where the dismissal of employees taking part in industrial action would not be adjudicated upon by the Tribunals:

1) By section 237 of TULR(C)A where the employee was taking part in unofficial industrial action, dismissal was automatically fair.
2) By section 238 of TULR(C)A where the employee was taking part in official industrial action or the employer was conducting a lock out and the employer dismissed all participating employees and did not selectively re-engage within three month then dismissal will be fair.

However, the Employment Relations Act 1999 adds a new relaxation in respect of striking employees have taken 'protected industrial action' whereby he shall be regarded as unfairly dismissed if the dismissal takes place within the period of eight weeks beginning with the protected industrial action. This is considered in the context of Chapter 11.

Automatically unfair dismissals

Convictions

Dismissal because of a conviction which is spent within the terms of the Rehabilitation of Offenders Act 1974. (See Chapter 13.)

Employee Representatives

Dismissal under section 103 ERA 1996 in connection with duties as an employee representative. (See Chapter 14.)

Health and Safety

Dismissal under section 100 ERA 1996 for a Health and Safety reason. (See Chapter 15.)

Occupational Pension Trustees

Dismissal under section 102 ERA 1996 in connection with duties as an occupational pension trustee. (See Chapter 16.)

National Minimum Wage

Dismissal under section 104A of the ERA 1996 in connection with the national minimum wage. (See Chapter 17.)

Pregnancy, maternity and dependants

By section 99 of the ERA 1996, dismissal for an inadmissible reason connected with pregnancy or maternity is automatically unfair. The Employment Relations Act 1999 introduces important amendments to the right to take maternity leave. In addition family friendly policies relating to paternity leave and the right to take time off to care for dependants are given. These are all considered in Chapter 18. Paragraph 16 of Part III of Schedule 4 to the Act amends section 99 to take into account the new maternity, parental leave and time off for dependants and these are fleshed out by the Maternity and Parental Leave Regulations etc 1999 laid before Parliament on 4th November 1999.

Protected Disclosures

By section 103A ERA 1996 dismissal for making a protected disclosure or 'whistleblowing' as it has come to be know will be unfair. (See Chapter 19.)

Redundancy

Section 105 of the ERA 1996 provides that a dismissal will be automatically unfair if the reason for selection for redundancy is one of those set out in sections 100 to 104A of the ERA. This section used to apply in relation to section 99 (by section 105(2). Section 105(2) has been repealed and there are now new provisions in this respect whcih are considered in this Chapter. (See Chapter 20.)

Statutory rights

By section 104 of the ERA 1996 dismissal because of a assertion of certain statutory rights will be unfair. (See Chapter 21.)

Sunday working

By section 101 of the ERA 1996 a dismissal in connection with Sunday working may be unfair. (See Chapter 22.)

Transfer of Undertakings

By Regulation 8(1) of the Transfer of Undertakings (Protection of Employment) Regulations 1981 (TUPE Regs) where there has been a transfer of an undertaking and the transfer, or a reasons connected with it, is the reason or principle reason for the dismissal the dismissal will be unfair unless it falls within certain exceptions. The general principle and the SOSR exceptions are considered in Chapter 23.

Union Membership or activities and union recognition

By section 152 of TULR(C)A a dismissal in connection with union membership or activities will be unfair. The Employment Relations Act 1999 introduces new provisions about trade union recognition. Whilst it is not possible to do more than summarise these provisions in this book it is to be noted that, by paragraph 161 of Schedule 1A, inserted into TUL(C)RA by the Employment Relations Act, dismissals will be unfair whilst by paragraph 162 selection for redundancy for a related reason will be unfair. (See further Chapter 24.)

Working Time

By section 101A of the Working Time Regulations dismissal in connection with those regulations will be unfair. (See Chapter 25.)

Disciplinary and Grievance Procedures

Further, a dismissal will be unfair where it relates to exercising or seeking to exercise a right to be accompanied by a companion in relation to a disciplinary or grievance procedure. There rights are introduced by sections 8 to 14 of the Employment Relations Act 1999 and are considered in Chapter 6 on Conduct. By section 15 they do not extend to the security services.

Potentially Fair Reasons for Dismissal

Section 98(1) and 98(2) of the ERA 1996 provide that:

(1) In determining for the purposes of this part whether the dismissal of an employee is fair or unfair, it is for the employer to show-
   (a) the reason (or, if more than one, the principal reason) for the dismissal, and
   (b) that it is either a reason falling within subsection (92) or some other substantial reason of a kind such as to justify the dismissal of an employee holding the position which the employee held.
(2) A reason falls within this subsection if it-
   (a) relates to the capability or qualifications of the employee for performing work of the kind which he was engaged by the employer to do',
   (b) relates to the conduct of the employee,
   (c) is that the employee was redundant, or
   (d) is that the employee could not continue to work in the position he held without contravention (either on his part or that of his employer) or a duty or restriction imposed by or under an enactment.

> It is for the employer to show the reason for dismissal as being capable of justifying the dismissal and once a reason is shown that is capable of justifying the dismissal it is then for the Tribunal to consider the reasonableness of the dismissal.

The burden of proof is on the employer to show the reason for dismissal. As stated in **Gilham & Ors v Kent County Council**

[1985] ICR 233:

> "The hurdle over which the employer has to jump at this stage of an inquiry into an unfair dismissal is designed to deter employers from dismissing employees for some trivial or unworthy reason. If he does so, the dismissal is deemed unfair without the need to look further into the merits. But if on the face of it the reason could justify the dismissal then it passes as a substantial reason and the inquiry moves on to [section 98(4)] and the question of reasonableness."

With capability and conduct dismissals the employer must show that he genuinely believed on reasonable grounds that these heads applied. With redundancy and statutory ban cases it is for the employer to show that these reasons in fact did apply. With the latter two, a genuine belief that there was a redundancy or statutory ban may amount to some other substantial reason.

The burden of proof in establishing the reasons for dismissal remains on the employer even if the employee alleges that an automatically unfair reason is applicable. It was stated by the Court of Appeal in **Maund v Penrith District Council** [1984] ICR 143 that provided the employee satisfies the evidential burden to warrant the Tribunal investigating the matter the burden remains on the employer. Griffiths LJ stated:

> "If an employer produces evidence to the tribunal that appears to show that the reason for dismissal is redundancy , as they undoubtedly did in this case then the burden passes to the employee to show that there is a real issue as to whether that was the true reason. The employee cannot do this merely by asserting in argument that it was not the true reason; an evidential burden rests upon him to produce some evidence that casts doubts upon the employer's reasons...But this burden is a lighter burden than that placed upon the employer; it is not for the employee to prove the reason for his dismissal, but merely to produce evidence sufficient to raise the issue, or to put it another way, that raises some doubt about the reason for the dismissal. Once this evidential burden is discharged, the onus remains upon the employer to prove the reason for dismissal."

The exception here is where the employee does not have sufficient qualifying service so that he can only succeed if the reason is one of the inadmissible ones where the qualifying service does not apply (**Smith v Hayle Town Council** [1984] ICR 143).

The Tribunal must identify the real reason for the dismissal by reference to the actual facts rather than the label that the employer applied to the dismissal.

It may be that the employer has mistakenly identified the reason for dismissal or has deliberately given the wrong reason for dismissal. It is incumbent upon the Tribunal to consider the real reasons for the dismissal. Where the employer has identified a set of facts or has a genuine belief that those facts exist and they have been fully considered it will not matter that the employer has applied the wrong label. In **Abernethy v Mott, Hay & Henderson** [1974] ICR 323 Mr Abernethy was dismissed for redundancy. At the Tribunal hearing it was argued that he was dismissed for redundancy or capability. It was held that he had been fairly dismissed on the ground of capability. The Court of Appeal held that there were no grounds for interfering with the decision. Lord Denning MR stated:

> "I do not think that the reason has got to be correctly labelled at the time of dismissal. It may be that the employer is wrong in law as labelling it as dismissal for redundancy. In that case the wrong label can be set aside. The employer can on rely on the reason in fact for which he dismissed the man, if the facts are sufficiently known or made known to the man. The reason in this case was – on the facts – already known or sufficiently known to Mr Abernethy."

Cairns LJ stated that the reason for the dismissal is a set of facts known to the employer, or it may be beliefs held by him, which cause him to dismiss the employee. However, where the employee has not been made aware of the facts so that he has not had an opportunity to make representations then this goes beyond merely putting the wrong label on the facts and the dismissal will be unfair if these facts are relied upon (see below). See further **Post Office v Wilson** [EAT 762/98] where the real reason was found to be for SOSR and not capability as the employer had asserted.

> The Tribunal may only take account of reasons for dismissal that existed at the time of the dismissal though where there is a notice period then events during the notice period may be relevant.

It was held by the House of Lords in **Devis (W) & Sons Limited v Atkins** [1977] AC 931 that a Tribunal cannot take account of matters that come to light after the dismissal in order to find that the dismissal was fair. The position here differs from wrongful dismissal cases where the employer may seek to justify the dismissal by reference to matters that it did not know of at the time of dismissal. Viscount Dilhorne stated that evidence of misconduct that comes to light after a dismissal was irrelevant and inadmissible on the issue of whether the employer had acted reasonably as it cannot have influenced the employer's action at that time.

In two recent decisions, events between the date of notice and the actual dismissal date were considered to be relevant in deciding whether the dismissal was fair. In **Parkinson v March Consulting Limited** [1997] IRLR, 308; [1998] ICR 276 the complainant was given six month's notice of dismissal because a re-organisation was proposed. The Tribunal found the reason for dismissal to be Some Other Substantial Reason (SOSR). It was argued in the Court of Appeal that there was no reason for dismissal at the time it had been confirmed as there had been no more than a proposal at the date notice was given. The employer argued that one had to look to the date when the employment terminates. The Court of Appeal held that the relevant date was the date when notice was given but that an employer's reason for dismissal must be determined not only by reference to the date notice is given but throughout the notice period. This case was followed in **Alboni v Ind Coope Retail Limited** [1998] IRLR 131 where the employer told a manageress that they were prepared to consider an application from her when she had been given notice after her co-manager of a joint contract had resigned. These subsequent events were relevant in determining whether the dismissal was fair. Similarly, a dismissal that is fair at the time notice is given may become unfair because of events during the notice period, as in **Stacey v Babcock Power Limited** [1986] ICR 221 where the employee was fairly given notice for redundancy but this became unfair when the employer got a new order but did not retain the complainant whilst taking on fresh staff.

See also **West Kent College v Richardson** [1998] ICR 511 where the employee was given notice of redundancy but was not redundant at the time his notice expired because the college had enough teaching hours for him.

Where the employee has not been given the full nature of the allegation so that the employee has not had an opportunity to answer the true facts the dismissal is likely to be unfair.

Even if the employer choses not to make the employee fully aware of the reasons for the dismissal because he wishes to spare the employees feelings so that the employee did not have an opportunity to answer them the dismissal will be unfair. The employer should ventilate the true reason for the dismissal. In **Hoton v Conservative Club** [1984] ICR 859 the employee was dismissed for inefficiency whereas the true reason was dishonesty. The dismissal was unfair as this had never been put to her. Similarly, in **Midland Bank Plc v Whittington** [EAT 453/94] the dismissal of two employees where the reason given was breakdown in trust and confidence was unfair when the true reason for the dismissal was suspected dishonesty of one or the other of them.

Where the employer choses at the time of dismissal not to rely upon a particular reason it cannot be used later as the reason for dismissal.

It was stated in **TricoFolberth Limited v Devonshire** [EAT 178/88] that where the employer choses to dismiss for a reason that is unfair then the fact that there was a fair reason that was not relied upon cannot later be relied upon as the reason for dismissal. In this case the employer's chose to dismiss for a medical reason when they could have dismissed fairly for absences after warnings.

Where there are several reasons for the dismissal the Tribunal should consider the principal reason for dismissal or the employer may argue that they are all of equal importance.

It is possible for the employer to put forward a number of alternative reasons for dismissal in the alternative, all of whcih may be potentially fair reasons. This was the position in **Carlin v St**

Cuthberts Co-op Association Limited [1974] IRLR 188 where the employer had put forward two reasons for the dismissal and the Tribunal found only one of them proven. The NIRC stated:

> "If an employer gives two reasons for dismissing an employee and only one is established by the evidence led before the tribunal and there is no evidence as to which reason, if either, was subordinate to the other, the employer's defence may fail upon the view that was in fact the principal reasons for dismissal has not been proved."

However, the NIRC made it clear that it is possible that there may be a number of reasons which are all of equal importance in the mind of the employer so that any one of the reasons could lead to a finding of fairness if that reason was made out. In **Smith v City of Glasgow Limited** [1987] ICR 796; IRLR 326 the complainant was dismissed for a number of reasons relating to his conduct including a failure to respond to requests for information and also for incompetence. The Tribunal found that he had been dismissed for conduct and capability but that the allegation about failure to respond to requests for information had not been made out. The House of Lords held that the need for the employer to establish the principal reason is important both in discharging the burden of showing the reason for dismissal and also in accordance with the reasonableness test whether the employer acted sufficiently in treating the principal reason as one to justify dismissal. The failure to establish the allegation with regard to information was vital as the employer's had not shown that it was not or did not form part of the principal reasons for dismissal. Lord Mackay stated:

> "To accept as a reasonably sufficient reason for dismissal a reason which, at least, in respect of an important part was neither established in fact nor believed to be true on reasonable grounds is, in my opinion, an error of law."

The danger is if the employer puts forward a number of reasons and one of them is not found to be made out, but is found to be part of the principal reaosn for dismissal then either the employer may not show an admissible reason for dismissal or be able to show that it acted fairly. However, where the reasons are so inextricably bound up so that "no distinct reason can be separated from ony other distinct reasons to as to establish a dichotomy" it may not matter that one of the elements was not a proper ground for dismissal (**Shakespeare**

and Henry v National Coal Board (CA unreported 30th March 1988).

> Where constructive dismissal is alleged but is denied, the Employer may still plead a reason for dismissal in the alternative.

Where it is in dispute that an employee has been constructively dismissed the employer is asserting that there has been no dismissal. If the Tribunal find that the employee has been constructively dismissed it is still possible for the employer to go on and assert a reason for the dismissal. This may typically be the case where the employer has acted in the mistaken belief that it may vary the contract of employment when it, as a matter of law and fact, the variation amounts to a fundamental breach or where a re-organisation is implemented. In such cases, Tribunals has been able to find that the reason for the dismissal was SOSR. In **Savoia v Chiltern Herb Farms Limited** [1982] IRLR 166 the Court of Appeal stated that although it will be more difficult for an employer to say that a constructive dismissal was fair, nevertheless there may be circumstances where it is perfectly possible to do so. The difficulty with the case was that the Court of Appeal appeared to import the notion of reasonableness into the first stage. Waller LJ stated that in establishing the reason for dismissal:

> "...this goes beyond the employer's conduct which amounted to dismissal and involves looking into the conduct of the employee and all the surrounding circumstances."

However, in **Berriman v Delabole Slate Limited** [1985] ICR 546 the approach to take was expressed as:

> "requiring the employers to show the reasons for their conduct which entitled the employee to terminate the contract thereby giving rise to a deemed dismissal by the employers..."

(See also **Crawford v Swinton Insurance Brokers** [1990] IRLR 42). This may be so even where the employer had not appreciated that its acts amounted to a dismissal (**Ely v YKK Fasteners (UK) Limited** [1993] IRLR 500) as where he believed that the employee had resigned.

No account may be taken of industrial pressure to dismiss.

By section 107(2) the ERA 1996:

> In determining the question [of the reason for dismissal] no account shall be taken of any pressure which by calling, organising, procuring or financing a strike or other industrial action, or threatening to do so, was exercised on the employer to dismiss the employee; and the question shall be determined as if no such pressure had been exercised.

The pressure need not be explicit pressure to dismiss, as for example applying pressure to move a worker where dismissal is a possible consequence if the worker refuses to move. It was said in **Ford Motor Co. Limited v Hudson** [1978] IRLR 66 that the test is:

> "Was the pressure exerted on the employers such that it could be foreseen that it would be likely to result in the dismissal of those employees in respect of whom the pressure was being brought."

Where the real reason is pressure as defined in this section the employer will be unable to put forward any admissible reason so that the dismissal will be unfair (**Hazells Offset Limited v Luckett** [1977] IRLR 430).

CHAPTER FOUR
THE REASONABLENESS
OF THE DISMISSAL

A number of factors that have been taken into account by the Higher Courts over the years in considering whether employers have acted reasonably will be considered. It cannot be overemphasised that the case law does not set out hard and fast rules but, rather, guidance as to the various matters that may be weighed in the balance in considering whether an employer acted fairly or not. The increased emphasis on adopting a fair procedure since the decision of the House of Lords in *Polkey* is exemplified by a body of case law that sets out guidance on those matters that are required if a fair procedure is to be followed and this will be considered in the final part of this chapter.

General Principles: Reasonableness

Where the Tribunal have identified a potentially fair reason for dismissal they must apply the test contained in section 98(4) ERA 1996 in considering the reasonableness of the dismissal:

> 98(4) ...the determination of the question whether the dismissal is fair or unfair (having regard to the reason shown by the employer –
>
> (a) depends on whether in the circumstances (including the size and administrative resources of the employer's undertaking the employer acted reasonably or unreasonably in treating it as a sufficient reason for dismissing the employee, and
> (b) shall be determined in accordance with equity and the substantial merits of the case.

> The Tribunal must ask whether the Employer acted reasonably in dismissing the employee considering the words of section 98(4). It should not simply ask: "what would I have done in the circumstances?" as there will be circumstances in which different employees could have taken a different approach and still have behaved reasonably. However, the test of whether the employer acted with a 'band or reasonable responses' introduces a perversity test into section 98(4) which is to be eschewed.

There has long been confusion as to the proper approach to section 98(4) with a well followed line of case law which decides that Tribunals should consider whether the dismissal fell within the band of reasonable responses that an employer could adopt so that different employers may adopt a different approach yet still act reasonably. The effect of this is that the Tribunal must ask whether the employer behaved within such a band taking into account all the circumstances and it must not substitute its own view for that of the employer by considering what they would have done if they had been in the same position. These cases added a gloss onto the wording of the section but it is submitted that a recent decision of the EAT is in accordance with the correct approach to be adopted.

Band of reasonable responses

In **British Leyland (UK) Limited v Swift** [1981] IRLR 91 the Court of Appeal set out the test as follows:

> "The correct test is: Was it reasonable for the employers to dismiss him? If no reasonable employer might reasonably have dismissed him then the dismissal was fair. But if a reasonable employer might reasonably have dismissed him then the dismissal was fair. It must be remembered that in all these cases there is a band of reasonableness, within which one employer might reasonably take one view; another quite reasonably take a different view. One would quite reasonably dismiss the man. The other quire reasonably keep him on. Both views might be quite reasonable. If it was quite reasonable to dismiss him,. Then the dismissal must be upheld as fair; even though some other employers might not have dismissed him."

Following this test the approach to section 98(4) was set out by Browne-Wilkinson J in the EAT as follows:

"We consider that the authorities establish that in law the correct approach for the Industrial Tribunal to adopt in answering the question posed by s.57(3) of the 1978 Act is as follows.

(1) the starting point should always be the words of s.57(3) themselves;

(2) in applying the section an Industrial Tribunal must consider the reasonableness of the employer's conduct, not simply whether they (the members of the Industrial Tribunal) consider the dismissal to be fair;

(3) in judging the reasonableness of the employer's conduct an Industrial Tribunal must not substitute its decision as to what was the right course to adopt for that of the employer;

(4) in many (though not all) cases there is a band of reasonable responses to the employee's conduct within which one employer might reasonably take one view, another quite reasonably take another;

(5) the function of the Industrial Tribunal, as an industrial jury, is to determine whether in the particular circumstances of each case the decision to dismiss the employee fell within the band of reasonable responses which a reasonable employer might have adopted. If the dismissal falls within the band the dismissal is fair: if the dismissal falls outside the band it is unfair."

There are many statements of this test in the authorities (See **Rolls Royce Limited v Walpole** [1980] IRLR 343; **Richmond Precision Engineering v Pearce** [1985] IRLR 179; the cases referred to in the above two authorities themselves and the cases referred to in the next section).

The Tribunal must not substitute its own views

Alongside the fact that the employer may act fairly if it acts within a band of reasonable responses is the principle that the Tribunal must be astute not to substitute its own views of whether dismissal was warranted in the circumstances even if it does not agree with the course that the employer took. In **Grundy (Teddington) Limited v Willlis** [1976] ICR 323 the test was expressed thus by Phillips J:

"It has to decide, not what it would have done if it had it been the management, but whether or not the dismissal was fair or unfair, which depends on whether the employer acted reasonably in treating it as a sufficient reason for dismissing the employee."

Similarly, in **NC Watling & Co Limited v Richardson** [1978] IRLR 255; ICR 1049 said that:

"For a tribunal to say it was unfair...merely because if they had been the employers that is what they would have done is to apply the test of what the particular tribunal would have done and not the test of what a reasonable employer would have done."

The 'Band of Reasonable Responses' is no longer good law?

Undoubtedly the test of the 'band of reasonable responses' is a gloss on the wording of section 98(4) of the ERA 1996 and commentators have argued for many years that it is an unwarranted gloss that detracts from the clear task that Parliament set Tribunals in the statutory wording. Indeed, in **Gilham and Others v Kent County Council (No 2)** [1985] IRLR 18, the Court of Appeal commented on the 'over sophistication' of the approach that was being taken by Tribunals because of the gloss on the statute. Griffiths L J stated:

"The wording of [s.98)(4)] is straightforward and easy to understand, and I do not myself think that it helps to try and analyse it further, save only this, that a tribunal in applying the section must not ask themselves what they would have done, but must ask themselves how a reasonable employer would have acted."

Dillon LJ stated:

"The reported decisions contain, as it seems to me, a good deal of what I would venture to call over sophistication as to the approach to be adopted by industrial tribunals to the question of reasonableness. In my judgment it is sufficient for the tribunal to answer directly the question posed by [s.98(3)]: "In all the circumstances, did the employer act reasonably or unreasonably in treating the reason in the particular case as a sufficient reason for dismissing the employee?" That is a question of fact and not a sophistication of law. A tribunal may in a particular case react to the facts by saying, "What the employer did is not what we ourselves would have done, but we cannot say that it was unreasonable." That again, however, is an answer on the facts to a question of fact, and not a guideline of law to be applied by all other tribunals in all other cases. Because the question is one of fact, and there are many different industrial tribunals, it is quite likely that different tribunals will reach different conclusions on the question of reasonableness on very similar facts. That is inherent in the system which Parliament has set up, and is no indication that any tribunal has misdirected itself or erred in law."

There is a clear distinction between the approach taken in the *Gilham* case and the earlier authorities cited above. The most recent case, which it is submitted gets this branch of the law back on track, is one of the last decisions of the outgoing President of the EAT, Morison J. In **Haddon v Van Den Bergh Foods Limited** [1999] IRLR 672 Mr Haddon attended a ceremony where he was presented with a good service award for 15 years' loyal service. He had been told by his manager that he would have to return to his shift after the ceremony, which included a buffet supper. However, as he had consumed alcohol he decided not to do so. He was dismissed for failing to follow an order, even though there had only been one and a half hours left of his shift to run and his absence had made no difference. The Employment Tribunal found that he had been dismissed for failing to follow a lawful order and that his employers had followed a fair procedure. Applying the range of reasonable responses, though many employers would not have dismissed, it could not be said that no reasonable employer would have dismissed. The EAT allowed an appeal.

The EAT stated that it was regrettable that so many judges had felt it necessary to interpret a section that was clear and unambiguous. However, at the end of the day the Courts were saying no more than two things:

The first point

"First, the question for the tribunal is the reasonableness of the decision to dismiss in the circumstances of the particular case having regard to equity and the substantial merits. Because the tribunal are applying an objective test, that is, a test of reasonableness, it is not sufficient for them simply to say 'well, we would not have dismissed in those circumstances'. They must recognise that, however improbable, their own personal views may not accord with reasonableness. Just asking 'what would I have done?' is not enough. However, it is neither reasonable nor realistic to expect the objective question to be asked and answered without the members of the tribunal having first asked 'what would we have done?' And provided that they do not stop there, we see nothing wrong with that approach."

Thus it is clear that Tribunals must not substitute their own view and ask: "What would I have done in these circumstances?" However:

"The mantra 'the tribunal must not substitute their own decision for that of the employer', is simply another way of saying that the tribunal must apply the reasonableness test by going somewhat further than simply asking what they themselves would have done. It is likely, however, that what the tribunal themselves would have done will often coincide with their judgment as to what a reasonable employer would have done. The tribunal is, after all, composed of people who are chosen to sit as an industrial jury applying their own good sense of judgment. The task of the tribunal is to pronounce judgment on the reasonableness of the employer's actions and whenever they uphold an employee's complaint they are in effect 'substituting their own judgment for that of the employer'. Providing they apply the test of reasonableness, it is their duty both to determine their own judgment and to substitute it where appropriate."

The test is and always remains that of reasonableness and it is for the tribunal to decide this applying the common sense of the industrial jury.

The second point

A second point was made by Mr Justice Morison:

"The second point simply recognises that there may be cases where a decision not to dismiss would be reasonable and a decision to dismiss would also be reasonable. This point is based upon logic. Because course A would have been reasonable, it does not follow that every other course is unreasonable. In other words, in some marginal cases, the tribunal might well consider that a dismissal by the particular employer was reasonable even though another reasonable employer might not have dismissed. The mantra 'the band or range of reasonable responses' is not helpful because it has led tribunals into applying what amounts to a perversity test, which, as is clear from Iceland itself, was not its purpose. The moment that one talks of a 'range' or 'band' of reasonable responses one is conjuring up the possibility of extreme views at either end of the band or range. In reality, it is most unlikely in an unfair dismissal case involving misconduct that the tribunal will need to concern itself with the question whether the deployment of each of the weapons in the employers' disciplinary armoury would have been reasonable. Dismissal is the ultimate sanction. There is, in reality, no range or band to be considered, only whether the employer acted reasonably in invoking that sanction. Further, the band has become a band or group of employers, with an extreme end. There is a danger of tribunals testing the fairness of the dismissal by reference to the extreme."

The 'band of reasonable responses' is thus an unhelpful test. Whilst recognising that different employers may take different views and be acting reasonably the test at the end of the day is that of reasonableness and *not* a perversity test of reasonableness.

Significance of Haddon

Haddon is an important decision since it re-emphasises that it is the wording of section 98(4) that is the appropriate test. The test is that of reasonableness not perversity. However, the many decisions that are mentioned in this book as to what would be expected of a reasonable employer are no less applicable. The caution that needs to be exercised when looking at the older authorities is that one does not fall into the trap of using cases that simply applied the 'band of reasonable responses test'. Cases that assist in telling us what a reasonable employer would have done in the circumstances are of no less validity.

The reasonableness test applies at the time of dismissal.

It has already been seen (see page 86) that the test of reasonableness must be applied at the time the dismissal takes place, though where there is a notice period events between the giving of notice and the termination of employment may be taken into account. Where there is an appeal process then evidence available at the internal appeal may also be taken into account **National Heart and Chest**

Hospitals v Nambiar [1981] ICR 441; IRLR 196). In **West Midlands Co-operative Society Limited v Tipton** [1986] ICR 192 the House of Lords pointed out that where there is an appeal process it will be artificial to separate out the process and only consider one part of it (see further Appeals at page 102).

It is the employer's conduct in dismissing that is relevant and not the effect on the employee.

It has repeatedly been pointed out that it is the reasonableness of the employer's conduct that the Tribunal is to focus on and not whether the employee acted reasonably or whether the decision to dismiss caused hardship or injustice to the employee, though it is apparent that the Tribunal will have to weigh in the balance factors relating to the employee, such as length of service, work record, possibility of improvement or the gravity of the employee's behaviour in the balance in deciding whether dismissal was an appropriate sanction. A summary of factors of this nature is contained in this Chapter and detailed consideration is given in the various relevant areas throughout this book. One area, in particular where both employer and employee may be acting perfectly reasonably relates to re-organisations that disadvantage the employee (see Chapter 8 at pages 267). The employee may be acting in a perfectly reasonable manner in refusing to accept such change yet it be held that it was reasonable to dismiss for such refusal. A leading example is **Chubb Fire Security Limited v Harper** [1983] IRLR 311 where the employee refused to accept a change that would involve a drop in remuneration. In the EAT, Balcombe J referred to **Evans v Elementa Holdings Limited** [1982] IRLR 143, stating:

> "....the President said: 'The question under s.98(4) is whether the employers' conduct in dismissing was reasonable. But, as the Industrial Tribunal recognised, that question necessarily required the Industrial Tribunal to find whether it was reasonable for Mr Evans to decline the new terms of the contract. If it was reasonable for him to decline these terms, then obviously it would have been unreasonable for the employers to dismiss him for such refusal.' We must respectfully disagree with that conclusion. It may be perfectly reasonable for an employee to decline to work extra overtime, having regard to his family commitments. Yet from the employer's point of view, having regard to his business

commitments, it may be perfectly reasonable to require an employee to work overtime. Indeed, in *Evans* v *Elemeta Holdings* the Employment Appeal Tribunal implicitly recognised that because, later in the same, passage, they say: 'If it had been shown in this case that there was some immediate need for the employers to increase the overtime worked or to require mandatory overtime as opposed to voluntary overtime, that might, have fundamentally altered the position.' Indeed it might, as regards the employers, although not necessarily as regards the employee. We agree with the comment on this decision in *Harvey on Industrial Relations and Labour Law*, Vol. 1, part II at paragraph 728: 'It does not follow that if one party is acting reasonably the other is acting unreasonably.'"

Whilst contractual rights and obligations may be relevant they are not determinative of the fairness of a dismissal.

Contractual rights may have some relevance in deciding whether or not the employer has acted reasonably but it has repeatedly been held that they are not decisive. Indeed, an employee may be wrongfully dismissed but it still be found that the dismissal was fair. In **Redbridge London BC v Fishman** [1978] ICR 569; IRLR 69, for example, a headmaster had a contractual right to require teachers to carry out work other than that for which they were engaged but the requirement of a particular teacher to carry out extra teaching was held to be unreasonable and dismissal unfair. Conversely, in **BSC Sports & Social Club v Morgan** [1987] IRLR 391 it was stated that the wrongful dismissal of an employee could still be fair where the employer was fully justified in dismissing for conduct/capability.

The Tribunal's approach to section 98(4) must be to apply the question of reasonableness in accordance with equity and the substantial merits of the case. The test is that of reasonableness taking into account all relevant circumstances. The Tribunal should consider the size and administrative resources of the employer's undertaking as part of the circumstances.

The statute particularly requires Tribunals to consider the size and administrative resources of the employer in deciding whether the dismissal is fair or unfair. The size and administrative resources of the employer may be relevant as follows, though every factual situation is bound to be different. By way of example:

Capability/sickness dismissals

- In considering the nature of the employee's incapacity and whether or not he could have been deployed elsewhere in the business.
- The length of time which it may be acceptable for a person to be absent may be governed by the size and needs of the business.
- Efforts to remedy before dismissal by supervision training and support.

See Chapter 5 for full consideration.

Conduct dismissals

- the nature of the disciplinary and appeal procedure may be governed by the size of the business. A more elaborate procedure may be expected in a large firm.
- the nature of the sanctions to be applied may be affected as demotion, alternative employment or some other sanction may be more appropriate in a large business.

See Chapter 6 for full consideration.

Redundancy dismissals

- The nature of the consultative process is likely to be affected since there may be more options in a large business and employees may be able to put forward alternatives to avoid dismissal or have representations to make about the pool of selection or need for redundancies. Note however, that the fact that the business is small is unlikely to excuse there being no consultation at all (**De Grasse v Stockwell Tools Limited** [1992] IRLR 269).
- The issue of alternative employment may be particularly affected by the size of the business.

See Chapter 7 for full consideration.

Dismissals for SOSR

- Where there is a pressing need for a business re-organisation the size of the business is likely to be relevant.
- The need to protect against competition may be greater in a small business.

See Chapter 8 for full consideration.

Having regard to the size and administrative resources the Tribunal must then decide whether the dismissal was fair having regard to equity and the substantial merits of the case. A wide range of factors are relevant here and they are considered in detail in the following Chapters. The following are some of the matters that have been taken into account in deciding, on the basis of equity and the substantial merits of the case, whether the dismissal is fair:

(1) Breach of rules and stated sanction

Where there is a detailed set of rules that relate to a particular set of circumstances then a reasonable employer will be expected to follow those rules (**Stoker v Lancashire County Council** [1992] IRLR 75). However, it was made clear in **Westminster City Council v Cabaj** [1996] IRLR 399 that not every breach of the rules will render a dismissal unfair. The Tribunal must still consider whether or not the employer acted reasonably and the dismissal was fair. Where a failure to follow the rules deprived the employee of a chance to make representations or state his case then it is likely that such breach will render the dismissal unfair (but see pages 102). Where there is a stated sanction of which the employee is fully aware for a particular act then employers can normally act in accordance with their rules. However, even here, caution must be exercised. It was said in **Ladbroke Racing Limited v Arnott, Paris and Stevenson** [1983] IRLR 154 that even where summary dismissal is the stated sanction for a particular act it is still necessary to consider all of the circumstances including the gravity of the behaviour and the culpability of the individual.

(2) Consistency of applying sanction of dismissal

As part of the principle of equity is the idea that employees who behave in much the same way will be treated in much the same way. This means that if the employer metes out different punishment in conduct cases or takes a different approach to employees in the other areas of potentially fair dismissals where employees could be treated the same i.e. sickness absences, any dismissal may be unfair due to inconsistency. This was the position in **Post Office v Fennell** [1981] IRLR 221 where the employee was dismissed despite other employees having behaved the same way in the past (see page XX on conduct). In **Hadjionnou v Coral Casinos Limited** [1981] IRLR 352 a casino inspector was dismissed for socialising in breach of company rules with clients with the permission or knowledge of management. At the Employment Tribunal hearing he referred to a number of other employees committing breaches from criminal offences to socialising and being treated more leniently. His complaint was dismissed and the EAT held that the Tribunal had taken proper account of inconstancy. The EAT accepted the arguments of Counsel for the Respondent that consistency arguments are limited to certain situations:

> "in broad terms, there are only three sets of circumstances in which such an argument may be relevant to a decision by an Industrial Tribunal under s.[98 the Act of 1996] Firstly, it may be relevant if there is evidence that employees have been led by an employer to believe that certain categories of conduct will be either overlooked, or at least will be not dealt with by the sanction of dismissal. Secondly, there may be cases in which evidence about decisions made in relation to other cases supports an inference that the purported reason stated by the employers is not the real or genuine reason for a dismissal. Mr Tabachnik illustrates that situation by the argument advanced in the present case on behalf of the appellant, that the general manager was determined to get rid of him and merely used the evidence about the incidents with customers as an occasion or excuse for dismissing him. If that had been the case, the Industrial Tribunal would have reached a different conclusion on the appellant's complaint but they considered the submissions about it and rejected them. Thirdly, Mr Tabachnik concedes that evidence as to decisions made by an employer in truly parallel circumstances may be sufficient to support an argument, in a particular case, that it was not reasonable on the part of the employer to visit the particular employee's conduct with the penalty of dismissal and that some lesser penalty would have been appropriate in the circumstances.

> We accept that analysis by counsel for the respondents of the potential relevance of arguments based on disparity. We should add, however, as counsel has urged upon us, that Industrial

> Tribunals would be wise to scrutinize arguments based upon disparity with particular care. It is only in the limited circumstances that we have indicated that the argument is likely to be relevant and there will not be many cases in which the evidence supports the proposition that there are other cases which are truly similar, or sufficiently similar, to afford an adequate basis for the argument."

The case was approved in **Paul v East Surrey District Council** [1995] IRLR 305.

In **Proctor v British Gypsum Limited** [EAT 535/89] it was stated that Tribunals must strike a fair balance and it will not be every case of leniency that will mean there has been inconsistency. Moreover, in **London Borough of Harrow v Cunningham** [1996] IRLR 256 the EAT held that even where the employees have committed the same offence it may be possible to take account of mitigation in relation to one that is not available to he other and so treat them differently and, indeed the individual circumstances of each employee should be looked at (see **Merseyside Passenger Transport Executive v Millington** [EAT 232/89]). Tribunals should hear evidence of dissimilar treatment but are entitled to limit it scope (**Clift v Smiths Flour Mills Limited** [EAT 232/81].)

(3) Employee's length of service, past record and position

The employee's length of service, unblemished record and position are likely to be highly relevant to the decision to dismiss (though they may be offset by the gravity of the reason for dismissal). Where the employee is long serving and has a good record the sanction of dismissal may be inappropriate even for an apparent offence of dishonesty. In **Johnson Matthey Metals Limited v Harding** [1978] IRLR 248 the employee was found wearing a colleague's watch which he admitted finding on the premises and was dismissed despite 15 years' service. The EAT held that the Tribunal was entitled to take his long service into account which called for a more careful consideration of the matter. However, an employee's conduct may be so grave that the length of service becomes irrelevant as where false receipts are put in for expenses (**AEI Cables Limited v McLay** [1980] IRLR 84).

(4) Nature of reason for dismissal

In **AEI Cables Limited v McLay** [1980] IRLR 84 the EAT stated:

"The length of service of an employee is in many cases a relevant consideration but in out judgment it would be wholly unreasonable to expect an employer who has been deceived by an employee in the way in which the respondent deceived the appellants, to have any further confidence in him and to continue him in his employ."

(5) Other sanctions that could have been applied

In certain cases alternative sanctions may be appropriate where the size and administrative resources of the employer so permit (See **P v Nottinghamshire County Council** [1992] ICR 706; IRLR 362). These alternatives are considered where relevant in the following Chapters.

(6) Steps taken to improve before dismissal

Where there is scope for improvement on the part of the employee or for rectifying the situation that has come to exist, the reasonable employer will consider whether training, supervision, support or other encouragement is appropriate and this may particularly apply with capability dismissals though it can also go to conduct matters. In **Turner v Vestric Limited** [1989] IRLR 528 there was a breakdown of communication and thereby trust and confidence between a branch manager and secretary. It was held that steps should have been taken to ascertain whether the position could have been improved before any dismissal.

(7) Warnings

There are many circumstances in which a warning is appropriate before the draconian sanction of dismissal is visited on an employee, especially where the individual needs to be made aware that his performance is unsatisfactory (**Laycock v Jones Buckie Shipyard Limited** [EAT 395/81]) though the managerial status of an employee may mean he should be aware so that no warning was necessary. It was stated in **A J Dunning & Sons (Shopfitters) Limited v Jacomb** [1973] ICR 448 that lack of warning is a substantive matter. Where an employee is aware that he is putting his job at risk but cannot or will not change a warning may not be necessary. Tribunals will take into account warnings that have been given, even if they do not relate to the same matters (**Auguste Noel Limited v Curtis** [1990] ICR 604; IRLR 326), but it should be noted that it is the final incident leading to dismissal which is the appropriate one in assessing reasonableness (**Distillers Company (Bottling Services) Limited v Gardner** [1982] IRLR 47).

Procedural Matters

> The dismissal may be unfair if the employer did not adopt a fair procedure before deciding to dismiss.

Up until *Polkey* the Courts approached procedural irregularities by holding that a dismissal would be fair if it could be shown that following a proper procedure would have made no difference, so that the very fairness of a dismissal would not be affected it this could be proven. However, with the landmark case of **Polkey v A E Dayton Services Limited** [1987] IRLR 503; 1988 ICR 142 the whole approach to procedural matters changed. The House of Lords held that a failure to adopt a fair procedure would render a dismissal unfair unless it could be shown that any procedure would have been futile. Mr Polkey was employed as one of four van drivers. The employer decided to replace them with three salesman and Mr Polkey was not regarded as suited to this task. He was dismissed without any consultation. The House of Lords considered whether, if there had been a procedural failing, the dismissal could still be regarded as fair where following a fair procedure would have made no difference. It held that there was no scope for this argument to be put forward. Lord MacKay in his speech, stated:

> "...the subject matter for the Tribunal's consideration is the employer's action in treating the reason as a sufficient reason for dismissing the employee. It is that action and that action only that the Tribunal is required to characterise as reasonable or unreasonable. That leaves no scope for the Tribunal considering whether, if the employer had acted differently, he might have dismissed the employee. It is what the employer did that is to be judged, not what he might have done. On the other hand, in judging whether what the employer did was reasonable it is right to consider what a reasonable employer would have had in mind at the time he decided to dismiss as the consequence of not consulting or not warning."

It was therefore not legitimate to consider what may have happened if a proper procedure had ben followed.

Note however, that there is no all or nothing answer since compensation may be affected if it can be shown the employee would have been dismissed or there was a chance of dismissal anyway (see Chapter 28).

> There is an exception to the general rule where adopting a proper procedure would have been utterly useless or futile.

In *Polkey*, Lord MacKay stated:

> "If the employer could reasonably have concluded in the light of the circumstances known to him at the time of dismissal that consultation or warning would be utterly useless he might well act reasonably even if he did not observe the provisions of the code. Failure to observe the requirement of the code relating to consultation or warning will not necessarily render a dismissal unfair. Whether in any particular case it did so is a matter for the Industrial Tribunal to consider in the light of the circumstances known to the employer at the time he dismissed the employee."

Lord Bridge echoed this view:

> "It is quite a different matter if the Tribunal is able to conclude that the employer himself, at the time of the dismissal, acted reasonably in taking the view that, in the exceptional circumstances of the particular case, the procedural steps normally appropriate would have been futile, could not have altered the decision to dismiss and therefore could be dispensed with. In such a case the test of reasonableness under s.57(3) may be satisfied."

The question then arises when it can be said that consultation was futile. In **Duncan v Marconi Command and Control Systems Limited** [EAT 309/88] the EAT thought that this may apply were redundant employees had to leave the premises immediately for security reasons so that individual consultation was not possible. In **Kidston v Static Systems Group** [EAT 368/87] the conduct of the employee rendered any consultation futile. In **MacLeod v Murray Quality Foods Limited** [EAT 290/90] although there had been no investigation a dismissal was fair where an employee ignored an instruction to work through tea breaks to meet an order on time. Although there had been no investigation he knew why he was dismissed and could have made representations. In **Ellis v**

Hammond [EAT 1257/95] a dismissal was fair where there had been no disciplinary hearing given the continued conduct of the employee where after several warnings she continued to be grossly insubordinate.

The Court of Appeal held in **Duffy v Yeomans & Partners Limited** [1994] IRLR 642 that the test is an objective one and is whether a reasonable employer could have concluded that consultation was futile. It is not necessary for the employer to have taken a conscious decision in this respect.

The following matters are of relevance in considering whether the employer adopted a fair procedure:

(1) The employer's agreed procedures
(2) The question of informants
(3) Consultation
(4) Proper investigation
(5) Proper notice of allegations or potential reason for dismissal
(6) Chance to state case
(7) Fair hearing
(8) Internal appeals

These matters are considered in the appropriate sections of the following chapters.

Appeals to the Higher Courts

An employer will not normally be permitted to put forward a different reason on an appeal where there has been no pleading or evidence putting forward that different reason.

This principle stems from **Nelson v BBC** [1977] ICR 649 in which it was held by the Court of Appeal that an employee will not be able to raise a quite different ground on appeal. The position may be different if it is simply a question of applying the wrong 'label'.

The Human Rights Act 1998 and The European Convention on Human Rights: A Note

The Human Rights Act 1998 incorporates into English law the European Convention on Human Rights with effect from 1 October 2000 although Courts have already started to take cognisance of the existence of the Act in arriving at their decisions. The detail is outside the scope of this book and this section will summarise briefly the effects of the Act and the potential impact upon unfair dismissal law of the Convention. It is anticipated that this section will become somewhat more lengthy should this book run into future editions as there is much scope for argument about the applicability of the Convention to unfair dismissal!

From the point of view of unfair dismissal law, three important points may be made:

(1) A Tribunal in determining a question which has arisen under the Act in accordance with a convention right must take into account European jurisprudence under the Convention whether from the European Court of Human Rights, the Commission or the Committee of Ministers (section 2).
(2) So far as possible to do so, primary and subordinate legislation must be read and given effect in a way that is compatible with convention rights (section 3(1)).
(3) A public authority cannot lawfully act in a way that is incompatible with a Convention right (section 6(1)).

It is clear that Tribunals can be asked to construe relevant legislation in accordance with the Convention and jurisprudence and consider the application of the same where it is a public authority that is before them.

Possible impact of the Convention

A number of areas of possible impact on unfair dismissal law (as opposed to other areas of employment law) are likely to include the following.

Article 6.   The right to a fair trial

By this article in the determination of civil right and obligations everyone is entitled to a fair and public hearing, within a reasonable time, by an independent and impartial tribunal established by law.

(1) The rights under a contract of employment are civil rights (**Darnell v UK** (1991) 69 D.R. 306),

(2) The EHHR decided in **Le Compte Van Leuven and De Meyere v Belgium** (1981) Series A No 43 E.H.H.R 1 that Article 6 applied to a disciplinary tribunal established by a medical association.

There is clearly scope for arguing that certain disciplinary hearings are covered by this Article.

Article 8.   Respect for private and family life

The right to respect for private and family life has been extended to the right to conversations on an internal office line and is likely to extend to other forms of monitoring (see **Halford v UK** (1997) 24 E.H.H.R. 525). The article is likely to have an impact in relation to discrimination but certain violations of privacy in a working environment (drug testing, monitoring conversations or asking about personal matters) are likely to be covered. Nevertheless, article 8.2. which limits the right in the interests of national security, public safety or the economic well being of the country, for the prevention of disorder or crime, for the protection of health or morals or for the protection of the rights and freedoms of others, means that there is wide ranging scope for justification of any such violations.

Article 9.   Freedom of thought, conscience and religion

The classic case in this respect is **Dawkins v Department of the Environment** [1993] IRLR 284 where a rastafarian was dismissed for wearing his hair according to his beliefs. Rastafarianism was not protected under the Race Relations Act. Mr Dawkins could now refer to Article 9. Note, however, where an employee is dismissed because he or she refuses to comply with the contract of employment, in accordance with religious beliefs, as in **Stedman v UK** (1997) 23 E.H.H.R 168 (where there was a refusal to work Sundays) the dismissal was because of breach of contract and not on the grounds of religious beliefs.

Article 10. Freedom of expression

This right includes freedom to hold opinions and to receive and impart information and ideas without interference by public authority. It is subject to limitations by Article 10.2, which include protection of reputation of others or preventing the disclosure of information received in confidence. A number of points may be made:

(1) Where the employee has views that conflict with the employer's right to manage and are dismissed the Article may not be applicable, as in **Kosiek v Germany** (1986) 9 E.H.H.R 328 where teachers, who were communists refused to swear allegiance to the constitution as was required by civil servants as they had a choice as to where to work and the Convention does not protect the right to work. (But cf **Vogt v Germany** (1995) 21 E.H.H.R 205).

(2) The convention may have an impact on dress codes where they cannot be shown to be necessary or reasonable.

(3) The restriction on the disclosure of confidential information may have an impact on 'whistleblowing' (But see the safeguards for employees set out in chapter 19).

Article 11. Freedom of Assemby and Association

The are most likely to be affected is that of trade unions (but see the protections set out in Chapter 24).

Clearly, when the Act comes into force there is going to be considerable scope for argument about the impact which it has on unfair dismissal rights.

PART TWO
POTENTIALLY FAIR DISMISSALS

CHAPTER FIVE
CAPABILITY AND QUALIFICATIONS

Definition

By section 98(2)(a) of the ERA 1996 a dismissal may be for a potentially fair reason where it:

> "relates to the capability or qualifications of the employee for performing work of the kind for which he was employed by the employer to do."

Section 98(3) further defines 'capability' and 'qualifications' for the purpose of the Act.

The definition of capability in relation to an employee *'means his capability assessed by reference to skill, aptitude, health or any other physical or mental quality.'* This definition encompasses dismissals for sickness or disability and such dismissals will be considered in this chapter.

The definition of qualifications in relation to an employee *'means any degree, diploma or other academic, technical or professional qualification relevant to the position which he held.'*

Capability

Definition of Capability

The definition of capability by reference to skill, aptitude, health or other physical or mental quality covers circumstances where an employee is not capable or is incompetent in carrying out the work of the kind that he was employed to do by reason of any of the factors enumerated in the definition.

There are many examples of dismissals for incapability falling within the definition of section 98(3) where the employee has fallen below the standard expected by the employer even if the standard is higher than other employers may have expected in similar circumstances. The test to be applied in considering whether dismissal for incapability is made out is whether the employer had an honest and reasonable belief that the employee was incapable or incompetent and that there were reasonable grounds for that belief. As was stated by Lord Denning MR in **Alidair Limited v Taylor** [1978] ICR 445:

> "Whenever a man is dismissed for incapacity or incompetence it is sufficient that the employer honestly believes on reasonable grounds that the man is incapable and incompetent. It is not necessary for the employer to prove that he is in fact incapable or incompetent."

Examples of cases where the Courts have found dismissals to be by reason of capability include employees who are inflexible and unadaptable (**Abernethy v Mott, Hay & Anderson** [1974] ICR 323); difficult and abrasive employees who affect work standards (**Bristow v ILEA** [EAT 602/79]) and employees who are unable to reach high or raised standards required by management (**Fletcher v St Leonards School** [EAT 25/87], **Godzik v Childema Carpet Co Limited** [EAT 598/78].)

The incapability must relate to the work of a kind that the employee was employed to carry out under the contract of employment of the employee, taking into account whether the contract permits any variation in the job functions of the individual. In **Plessey Military Communications v Brough** [EAT 518/84] an employee was employed as a miller to carry out wet work which caused him to develop dermatitis. He was transferred to dry work and when he was later retransferred to wet work he suffered a reoccurrence of the dermatitis so that he was again put on dry work. He was dismissed after a further eighteen months on the ground that he was incapable of carrying out wet work. The EAT held that his contract had been varied so that he had been permanently transferred to dry work and his capability had to be assessed in accordance with this change to his contract of employment.

Where the employee is only able to carry out some of the job functions required by the contract of employment then the dismissal will be for capability even though other functions can be carried out or the employee may be called upon to carry out other functions under the contract of employment, as in **Shook v London Borough of Ealing** [1986] IRLR 46 where the employee was unable to carry out her post as a social worker due to a back problem. Her contract permitted the authority to change her post and duties but the EAT held that the fact that the employee could potentially be called on to carry out functions for which she was capable did not prevent the dismissal being for incapability where her back problem related to the performance of some of her duties.

Capability and Misconduct

A dismissal for incapability may really be for misconduct where the failure to come up to the required standard is due to the employee's own attitude, negligence, laziness or carelessness and is not due to inherent capability or capacity on the part of the employee.

In **Sutton & Gates (Luton) Limited v Boxall** [1979] ICR 67 an electrician was dismissed after complaints from a number of customers about the standard of his work, which had hitherto been satisfactory. His dismissal was found to be unfair as there had been no hearing or opportunity to explain the reason for his poor work. The EAT commented that:

"We have had occasion to indicate more than once that it may not necessarily be that there is a wide range in the field of incapability but that incapability ought to be treated much more narrowly and strictly than has been done in the past and cases where a person has not come up to standard through his own carelessness, negligence or maybe idleness are much more appropriately dealt with as cases of conduct or misconduct rather than capability. It means of course that industrial tribunals, as argued in this instant case, may well be in danger of misdirecting themselves unless they clearly distinguish in their own minds how far it is a question of sheer incapability due to an inherent incapacity to function, compared with a failure to exercise to the full talent as is possessed."

The categories of reason for dismissal may overlap so that a dismissal may be for conduct and capability. Moreover, it does not matter that the wrong label was given as the reasons for dismissal provided that the facts relied upon are all there.

It was stated by the Kilner Brown J in **Hart v Sussex Group Training Association** [EAT 239/78] that there should not be an overrigid separation of the reasons for dismissal. In **Turner v Wadham Stringer Commercials** [1974] IRLR 83 an employee was dismissed after experiencing problems at work due to domestic problems so that he was failing to come up to the standard required by senior management. The NIRC held that this was a matter that related both to his capability and conduct.

In **Wood v Agnew Stores (Holdings) Limited** [EAT 582/85] Mr Wood was dismissed for misconduct due to large stock deficits. The Tribunal took the view that the dismissal was in reality for incapability but the EAT agreed that this was simply a matter of applying the wrong label and the mistake in name did not make the dismissal unfair.

General Principles: Capability and Reasonableness

In dismissals for incapacity it is necessary for the employer to show that he had an honest belief on reasonable grounds that the employee was incapable or incompetent.

It is already been noted that in **Alidair Limited v Taylor** [1978] ICR 445 Lord Denning MR pointed out that the employer does not have to establish the correctness of his belief in the employee's incompetence, only that he has a reasonable belief on reasonable grounds that the employee is incompetent. It is not the function of the Tribunal to substitute its own view of the employee's competence once the employer has established such reasonable belief. Therefore, where an employer has come to the conclusion over a reasonable period of time that an employee is incompetent this will be some evidence of incapacity although the view of management will have to be supported by some evidence. In **Cook v Thomas Linnell & Sons Limited** [1977] IRLR 132 a manager was dismissed after an 18 month period at a food depot but was offered an alternative post at a non food depot, where his previous experience had lain. The EAT upheld the IT's finding of fairness of dismissal and commented:

"When responsible employers have genuinely come to the conclusion over a reasonable period of time that a manager is incompetent we think that it is some evidence that he is incompetent. When one is dealing with routine operations which may be more precisely assessed there is no real problem. It is more difficult when one is dealing with such imponderables as the quality of management, which in the last resort can only be judged by those competent in the field. In such cases as this there may be two extremes. At one extreme is the case where it can be demonstrated, perhaps by reason of some calamitous performance, that the manager is incompetent. The other extreme is the case where no more can be said than that in the opinion of the employer the manager is incompetent, that opinion being expressed for the first time shortly before his dismissal. In between will be cases such as the present where it can be established that throughout the period of employment concerned the employers had progressively growing doubts about the ability of the manager to perform his task satisfactorily. If that can be shown, it is our judgment some evidence of his incapacity. It will then be necessary to look to see whether there is any other supporting evidence."

The case recognises that it may often be difficult to objectively quantify incompetence in certain jobs, for example in management, where any assessment turns on a subjective appraisal of the individuals ability in the job. It may be that falling orders or complaints from customers provides such evidence, as in **Fletcher v St Leonards School** [EAT 25/87] where the grades of pupils had fallen below what was acceptable. However, an employer will have to be cautious to ensure that complaints about competence are genuine as in **Kent County Council v Maidment** [EAT 3/87] where dismissal of a teacher by a disciplinary committee following complaints about competence by the head was not due to capability but to a personality clash between the individuals. No evidence of incompetence had been produced to the committee that took the decision.

It should be noted that it is for the employer to dictate the standard that is required of its employees (**Fletcher v St Leonards School** [EAT 25/87], though setting an unnecessarily high standard may be taken into account in considering the question of reasonableness.

A one off incident may establish incapability where the repercussions are potentially devastating, as in **Alidair Limited v Taylor** [1978]

ICR 445 where a pilot negligently landed an aircraft, putting lives at risk, whilst a series of small incidents over a period of time may lead to a conclusion that the employee is incapable (**Miller v Executors of John C Graham** [1978] IRLR 309).

More than one suspect

Where two or more employees are suspected of being responsible for acts or omissions that merit dismissal and the employer cannot, after a reasonable investigation, discover which one is responsible it may be reasonable to dismiss both. This principle has been applied on a number of occasions in relation to misconduct cases but has been held to be equally applicable to capability dismissals (**Guberman v Augustus Barnett (Scotland) Limited** [EAT 152/85]). The circumstances in which this exception to a genuine belief in the incompetence of *the* employee are limited in that suspicion between two or more employees should have been narrowed to the stage of certainty that it was one of the employees that was responsible for the act or omission meriting dismissal for incompetence (**Leyland Vehicles Limited v Wright** [EAT 712/81].

Reasonableness

Where the employer has shown that it has a genuine belief on reasonable grounds in the incapacity of the employee it is then necessary to determine whether the dismissal was reasonable within section 98(4) or the ERA 1996. In determining whether the employer has acted as a reasonably employer the Tribunal may take into account:

- The steps that the employer took to assist the employee in performing his job satisfactorily by supervision, training and support.
- The nature of the employee's job and the status of the employee;
- The service record of the employee.
- Whether the reason for incapability is due to a change in the employer's requirements.
- Alternative employment.
- Whether the employer adopted a fair procedure.

> It is necessary for the employer to extend proper supervision, training and encouragement, particularly to a new or a newly promoted employee and a failure to do so will be taken into account in deciding whether a dismissal was reasonable.

The leading case in this respect is **Mansfield Hosiery Mills Limited v Bromley** [1977[IRLR 301. Mr Bromley was employed as a boiler service fitter. He did not receive any training though the advertisement for the job stated that he would. He was promoted to plant maintenance supervisor but there were a number of complaints about his enthusiasm leading to warnings and eventual dismissal. A Tribunal found that he had been insufficiently supervised or warned of his shortcomings and had not been encouraged to improve. The EAT concluded that there was evidence on which the Tribunal could decided that the employer had failed to supervise and encourage to the extent that would be expected of a reasonable employer in the circumstances. (See also **Steelprint Limited v Haynes** [EAT 467/95] where there was a failure to train when the job requirements changed from proofreading to inputting orders requiring typing skills).

> The nature of the employee's job and status may affect the level of support that the employee is entitled to expect from his employer. Senior management may be aware of the standard that is required and what is expected of them whereas new or probationary employees may fairly expect support and training from the employer.

In **James v Waltham Cross UDC** [1973] IRLR 202 Mr James, a building maintenance officer, complained about the transfer of some of his work to another department and, despite the Council's attempt to deal with his grievance, he continued to refuse to particularise his complaints and was disrespectful to the Council members. He was dismissed on the ground that his conduct was not conducive to harmonious staff relations and because of his attitude. He had not been warned that his dismissal was under consideration, though the Tribunal took the view that this would not have made any difference. The NIRC stated that by the very nature of the job, senior managers may be fully aware of what it required of them and be able to judge whether they are falling below required standards. There was thus no need for a warning in such circumstances.

However, the approach taken in *James* has not been followed in other cases. It was stated in **McPhail v Gibson** [1977] ICR 42 that *"where you have a man, like a farm manager in a managerial capacity, there is a greater obligation on the employer to take preliminary steps to bring to the manager's notice that he, the employer, is dissatisfied and, in particular, he, the employer is contemplating a possible dismissal."* Ultimately, with senior management, it is submitted that the real issue is whether the employee was aware that his job was at risk and that his standard needed to improve if he was to retain his employment (see further the cases on warnings below).

The position is different with probationers as is clear from **Post Office v Mughal** [1977] ICR 763. Ms Mughal was appointed as a trainee clerical officer on one year's probation. She was warned that her clerical and telephone work was not satisfactory but after nine months was told her clerical work was satisfactory though her telephone work had to improve. There were no further complaints but she was dismissed at the end of the year by a manger who did not know that she had been told about the improvements in her work. The dismissal was held to be unfair as the improvements had not been taken into account and there had been a breakdown in communication between her supervisor and the person taking the decision to dismiss. The EAT stated:

> "The question for the Tribunal is: Has the employer shown that he took reasonable steps to maintain appraisal of the probationer throughout the period of probation, giving guidance by advice or warning when such is likely to be useful or fair; and that an appropriate officer made an honest effort to determine whether the probationer came up to the required standard, having informed himself of the appraisals made by supervising officers and any other facts recorded about the probationer? If this procedure is followed, it is only if the officer responsible for deciding upon selection of probationers then arrives at a decision which no reasonable assessment could dictate, that an Industrial Tribunal should hold the dismissal to be unfair."

Indeed in **Inner London Education Authority v Lloyd** [1981] IRLR 394 the Court of Appeal pointed out that employers who fail to recognise that they have a particular duty to guide and train probationers are likely to find any dismissal to be unfair.

Following on from *Mughal;*, it was argued in **White v London Transport Executive** [1981] IRLR 261 that there is an implied term in a probationer's contract of employment that the employer is bound to support, assist, offer guidance and train the probationary employee. This was rejected by the EAT who stated that the right term to imply is an obligation to take reasonable steps to maintain an appraisal of the employee during the trial period, giving guidance or warning where necessary. It may also be incumbent on the employer to consider whether the standard is likely to improve in the future, for example where there has been poor attendance during the probationary period (**Post Office v Stones** [EAT 390/80]).

Where the employee has given long service to the employer and has become incapable the test to be applied is whether the employer acted reasonably in all the circumstances, including the long service record in deciding to dismiss.

In **Mitchell v Old Hall Exchange and Palatine Club Limited** [1978] IRLR 160 an employee was dismissed for lack of capacity after 49 years' service. The Tribunal found the dismissal to be unfair, primarily on the basis of the sense of injustice felt by the employer. The EAT considered that the Tribunal had erred by considering the injustice to the employer when they should have considered whether there had been an injustice that created a situation of unreasonableness on the part of the employer.

A change in the employer's requirements may render an employee incapable of carrying out the job or highlight incapacity that was not hitherto revealed.

In **Godzik v Childema Carpet Co Limited** [EAT 598/78] the incapability of two employees was brought to light when a bonus scheme was introduced and they failed to improve despite warnings and training. The two workers were never fully capable in that they did not measure up to the other workers. When their incapability was highlighted by the new system, management were entitled to act upon it.

Where employees are incapable despite steps taken by the employer to train and encourage improvement the employer may need to consider alternative employment by way of re-deployment. Whether this is possible will depend on the size and administrative resources of the business.

Whether an employer should consider re-deploying staff who have proved to be incapable will depend on the nature of the business and the size and administrative resources. It is clear however, that the duty to consider alternative employment is not as onerous as that to be found in redundancy cases. It was said in **Bevan Harris Limited t/a Clyde Leather Co v Gair** [1981] IRLR 520 that every case must depend on its own circumstances and there is not necessarily an obligation upon every employer who dismisses an employee on the grounds of incapability to offer him employment in a subsidiary or other position. In *Bevan* the small size of the business and the circumstances in which the employee would be demoted were such that it would not be to the advantage of the business that the employee continue in it. However, a failure to make any effort on the part of the employer to consider whether there is an alternative job available may render the dismissal unfair, as in **Ladbroke Hotels Limited v Pickard** [EAT 93/85] where the employer failed to demote the employee to her former job when she proved incapable of carrying out a job after promotion.

Capability and Procedural Requirements

The procedural requirements that a reasonable employee may be expected to adopt in a case of incapacity differs from the approach that might be expected in misconduct cases where an employee may be facing a serious disciplinary charge. The 1998 ACAS Code on Disciplinary Practice and Procedure (soon to be updated) sets out detailed guidance for conduct cases and there is no similar provision for capability cases. In **The Littlewoods Organisation v Egenti** [1976] IRLR the EAT noted that the strict procedural requirements applicable to misconduct do not necessarily apply to incompetence cases so that where an employee is clearly incompetent no warning may be needed.

The essential requirements in a capability case if a reasonable procedure is to be followed will be:

- A full and proper investigation or appraisal of the performance of the employee entailing an identification of the reasons why the employee is not performing to the required standard.
- A warning or warnings to the employee that he is required to improve and of the likely consequences of a failure to improve.
- A reasonable opportunity for the employee to improve his performance given the provision of such assistance as is appropriate to the circumstances of the employer and employee.
- The provision of a procedure whereby the employee is able to appeal against any adverse finding against him.

Investigation and Appraisal

Since the onus is on the employer to show a potentially fair reason for dismissal it will be incumbent on the employer to carry out an investigation into the reasons for the employee's poor performance. It has already been noted that if the employer fails to carry out any proper investigation into whether or not the employee has acted in a manner that renders him incapable the employer is unlikely to be able to show a potentially fair reason for dismissal.

> The employee should be made aware of the allegations of poor performance that are being made against him and given an opportunity to make any representations that he may wish.

In accordance with the rules of natural justice an employee should be made aware of the complaints about the standard of his performance and given an opportunity to comment on such allegations subject to the *Polkey* argument that any procedure was pointless as it would have been futile. In **Barry v Turbo Flex Limited** [EAT 377/96] for example, the dismissal of an employee when he was out of the country and unable to answer any allegations was unfair. Indeed in **British Midland Airways v Gilmore** [EAT 173/81] the EAT made it clear that an employee is entitled to be made aware of the complaints being made against him, the scope and possible outcome of any inquiry and be placed in a position to deal with any facts that are alleged against him. Mr Gilmore captained an internal flight during which his relatively inexperienced co-pilot asked him to take over shortly before landing as he had not approached the airport in accordance with normal procedures. Gilmore landed the plane and four tyres were found to be damaged. An enquiry was launched which expanded its remit to the captaincy of the whole flight and decided that he had failed to exercise proper command. Mr Gilmore was not told the basis of the findings or the findings before his dismissal so that he was unable to challenge any findings of incompetence. The EAT agreed that the dismissal was unfair. Browne-Wilkinson J noted that Captain Gilmore had attended the inquiry to answer the allegations relating to the one incident and it was never indicated to him that he was facing a charge relating to the captaincy of the flight as a whole. The EAT distinguished the *Alidair* case on the ground that it was never self evident that the charge was to be put.

In capability cases it is likely to be appropriate to give a warning to the employee so that he has the chance to improve his performance. However, warnings may not be necessary where they would serve no purpose as the employee is unlikely to ever improve or the consequences of one mistake could be disastrous or where the position of the employee is such that, by the very nature of his job, he should be aware that his job is at risk if he does not improve his performance.

In **Polkey v Dayton Services Limited** (see 100) the House of Lords stated that warnings and a chance to improve will usually be a necessary part of procedure in capability cases. In **Winterhalter Gastronom Limited v Webb** [1973] ICR 245, Mr Webb was dismissed after the company experienced substantial losses which the directors thought were through Mr Webb's competence. He was given no warning about his capability. The NIRC held the dismissal to be unfair, rejecting the contention that warnings were not necessary in capability cases, stating that "there are many situations in which a man's apparent capabilities may be stretched when he knows what is demanded of him; many do not know they are capable of jumping the five-barred gate until the bull is close behind them."

However, a warning does not always have to be administered as in **James v Waltham Cross UDC** where the EAT stated that a warning may not be necessary where the employee has a senior position and should know the standard to be expected of him. In **McPhail v Gibson** [1977] ICR 42 the EAT considered that a warning may be particularly important for a senior employee so that they are aware of where they stand. Perhaps the better way of approaching the matter is that the employee, at whatever grade, should know that he is placing his job at risk by his incompetence so that he has a chance to improve. (**Laycock v Jones Buckie Shipyard Limited** [EAT 395/81] in which the emphasis was on the awareness of the employee of the employer's dissatisfaction with his work. Browne-Wilkinson J stated that:

> "...a tribunal will take into account, amongst other factors, whether or not the employee was aware that a continuation of his course of conduct might lead to his dismissal. In the ordinary case, such awareness will no doubt be brought home to him by formal warnings having been given. But if the tribunal is satisfied, as it was in this case, that the employee was aware that his conduct was failing to satisfy his employers it cannot be laid down as a hard and fast principle that the dismissal must be unfair unless a formal warning was given. As a matter of common sense, the higher someone is in the managerial scale the more likely it is that he will be conscious of the satisfaction or lack of satisfaction that his performance is giving..."

See also **Cook v Thomas Linnell and Sons Limited** [1977] IRLR 132.

Whilst a formal warning will make the position absolutely clear, in some circumstances a warning may be implied, as in **Judge International Limited v Moss** [1973] IRLR 208 where an employee's salary was not reviewed or **Brown v Hall Advertising Limited** [1978] IRLR 246 where a deterioration in the relationship between management and employee after an informal warning should have put the employee on notice that her performance was still not satisfactory, given the close working relationship between managing director and secretary.

Where a warning is given the employee should abide by the terms of the warning so that, for example if the employee is given a period of time to improve, it may be unfair to take any action before that time has elapsed (**Marks & Spencer Limited v Williams** [EAT 528/81].)

There are certain circumstances in which it is possible for an employer to dispense with a warning, as was recognised in *Polkey*. Where errors result in serious and costly losses a formal warning may be dispensed with as in **Lowndes v Specialist Heavy Engineering Limited** [1976] IRLR 246 or where one mistake could be disastrous dismissal without prior warning may be acceptable as in **Alidair Limited v Taylor** [1978] ICR 445. Moreover, the non-co-operative attitude of an employee may mean that a warning is not necessary where the employee is aware that his attitude is placing his job at risk (**A J Dunning & Sons (Shopfitters) Limited v Jacomb** [1973] ICR 448 see page 208).

Where the employee's continued employment is harming the interests of the business and there is little prospect that he will improve a formal warning may not be necessary. In **Littlewoods Organisation v Egenti** [1976] ICR 516 the EAT stated that there are circumstances where the person may be so incompetent that a warning is not necessary and it was obvious to the employee that he was at risk of dismissal for incompetence.

> The employee must be given an opportunity to improve his performance after having been warned that it is falling below standard. The requirements here are twofold; the employee should be given a reasonable period of time in which to demonstrate that his performance has improved and the employer should take such steps as are reasonable in assisting the employee to improve (whether by training or support and encouragement as is appropriate).

The period of time which should be given for the employee to demonstrate an improvement in his performance will vary depending on the circumstances of the case. In **Sibun v Modern Telephone Systems Limited** [1976] IRLR the Applicant had been employed as a salesman for many years and was dismissed when his targets fell during the twelve month period in the last fifteen months of his employment, during which he was given a number of warnings. The ET stated that:

> "We consider that before somebody of the long service and good conduct of the applicant can be dismissed on that ground, the capability perhaps falling off due to old age or illness, or some

reason of that sort, there should be a very great deal longer period. With the applicant coming within 25 or 30% of his target during the period in question, we would think that at least a three-year period of trial should have been given before it was fair to dismiss. It would be quite another matter if the applicant had only been there three or four years."

Length of service is thus an important factor in considering how long the period should be. The following are examples of periods that the Courts have considered appropriate:

- Five weeks' probation where there had been service of six years (**Evans v George Galloway & Co** [1974] IRLR 167).
- Three months for a sales' director with three years' service (**Winterhalter Gastronom Limited v Webb** [1973] ICR 245.

Where the employee has been promoted to a new job or has taken on different job functions it may be that the period should be extended.

As part of the normal procedural process a reasonable employer should consider the possibility of an internal appeal against a decision to dismiss for capability.

Whilst it will be seen that the ACAS Code states that there should be a right of appeal in disciplinary cases, a reasonable employer may allow a right of appeal though this will depend upon the circumstances and the size of the business. In **Sanderson v Hugh K Clarkson & Sons** [EAT 563/87] the EAT did not consider it fatal that there was no right of appeal in circumstances where it could only be to a director who had made the decision and where the employee had received full warnings about his performance. However, where there is a right of appeal the rules of natural justice will apply so that the appeal should if possible be heard by management that did not take the decision to dismiss. **Campion v Homeworthy Engineering Limited** [1987] ICR 966 illustrates a breach of natural justice where the person who took the decision to dismiss retired with the appellate panel (Cf **The Royal Navy School v Hughes** [1979] IRLR 383).

Sickness Dismissals as Incapability

> Dismissal for ill health may be a dismissal for capability where it affects the ability of the employee to carry out work of a kind for which the employee was employed.

Dismissal due to health is specifically referred to in the definition of capability as being a potentially fair reason for dismissal. The ill health must affect the ability of the employee to carry out the job in question. The case law shows that dismissal for incapability in the context of ill health arises in two particular set of circumstances; in relation to long term sickness and that of short term persistent absences due to health. These two areas will be considered separately. In addition there are particular kinds of sickness where the Courts have placed special emphasis on the approach to be adopted and these will be considered at the end of this section.

However, since December 1996 the Disability Discrimination Act 1995 (DDA) has been in force, which gives particular rights to disabled employees not to be discriminated against by less favourable treatment towards them because of their disability and which places on employers a duty to consider making reasonable adjustments in particular circumstances in order to obviate any substantial disadvantage that an employee may suffer by reason of his disability. It is therefore necessary to consider the definitions of disability and the concepts of discrimination under the DDA 1995 as there may be a potential overlap between the DDA and unfair dismissal legislation. It is then necessary to consider how the two interrelate. Adopting the alphabetical approach of this book we will therefore consider:

- Disability Discrimination and its interrelationship with capability dismissals.
- Long term sickness.
- Short term persistent absences.

Disability Discrimination Act 1995 and the concepts of disability and discrimination

It is clear that there is potential overlap between a claim under the DDA 1995 and a claim of unfair dismissal because of incapacity. The DDA 1995 imposes positive duties on the employer to consider whether reasonable adjustments may be made in order to enable a disabled person to work without being disadvantaged and it is clear that the provisions of this legislation will have a knock on effect in unfair dismissal cases. Before considering the overlap between unfair dismissal and disability discrimination, the following will be outlined:

- The definition of disability.
- The concept of discrimination based upon less favourable treatment where the disabled person is dismissed or claims constructive dismissal.
- The concept of discrimination based upon failure to carry out a reasonable adjustment where the disabled person is dismissed or claims constructive dismissal.

The provisions of the DDA 1995 are supplemented by secondary legislation and guidance:

(1) The Disability Discrimination (Meaning of Disability) Regulations 1996 (SI 1996/1455).
(2) The Disability Discrimination (Employment) Regulations 1996 (SI 1996/1456)
(3) The Guidance on Matters to be taken into account in determining questions relating to the definition of Disability.
(4) The Code of Practice for the elimination of discrimination in the field of employment against disabled persons or persons who have had a disability.

The definition of disability

Section 1 of the DDA 1995 provides that:

- a person has a disability for the purposes of the Act if he has
    - a physical or mental impairment
    - which has a substantial and long term adverse effect
    - on his ability to carry out normal day to day activities.
- a disabled person means a person who has a disability.

Physical or mental impairments

There is no definition within the Act but section 3 of the Act enabled the Secretary of State to issue Guidance. The following points emerge from the Guidance:

- Sensory impairments such as partial sight, deafness or other hearing loss are included (Para 12).
- Mental impairment includes a wide range of impairments relating to mental functioning including learning difficulties. (Para 13)
- Schedule 1 of the Act provides that mental impairment includes an impairment resulting from or consisting of a mental illness *only* if the illness is a clinically well recognised illness.

Schedule 1 para 1 permitted the Secretary of State to include or exclude conditions of a prescribed definition from the scope of the definition. The Disability Discrimination (Meaning of Employment Regulations 1996 (SI 1996/1455) list a number of matters that are excluded including:

- addiction of alcohol, nicotine or any other substance including a dependency. But note that i.e. liver damage as a result of alcohol would be included.
- a tendency to set fires, steal, to physical or sexual abuse of other persons, exhibitionism and voyeurism are not included unless it aggravates another condition (Regulation 4).

Substantial Adverse effect

The adverse effect must be substantial. The Guidance states that this requirement reflects the understanding as a disability going beyond normal difference in ability which may exist among people. The emphasis is on the effect that the impairment has, not on the severity of the impairment.

The Guidance at A2–10 sets out a number of factors to be taken into account:

- the time taken and the way in which an activity is carried out.
- the cumulative effects of an impairment.
- the effects of behaviour.
- environmental factors.

Schedule 1, para 8 of the schedule deems a person with a progressive condition to have a substantial adverse effect where it has an effect on his ability to carry out normal day to day activities event if the effect is not substantial. This means that as soon as a person with a progressive condition experiences symptoms which have any effect on his or her normal day to day activities he will fall in the definition of disability.

An impairment which consists of a severe disfigurement is deemed to have a substantial adverse effect on the ability of the person concerned to carry out normal day to day activities (Schedule 1, para 3(1) DDA 1995). Note that the Meaning of Disability Regulations exclude tattoos and body piercing for decorative or non medical purposes (Reg 5).

Long Term effect

The effect of an impairment must be long term. Schedule 1 para 2(1) provides that it is long term if:

- it has lasted 12 months, or
- the period for which it lasts is likely to be 12 months.
- it is likely to last for the rest of the life of the person affected.

Where the condition is likely to recur it is deemed to have long term effect. (Schedule 1 para 2(2) DDA 1995). The Guidance states that the likelihood of reoccurrence should be taken into account including what the person could do to seek to prevent such reoccurrence. The effect of medical treatment is only to be taken into account if it would cure the person without the need for further medical treatment.

Where a past disability reoccurs it is treated as having lasted through the period of good health (Schedule 2 para 5 DDA 1995).

Normal day to day activities

Normal day to day activities is not defined by the Act but Schedule 1 para 4 states that an impairment will only be taken to affect normal day to day activities if it affects one of the following:

- mobility
- manual dexterity
- physical co-ordination
- continence
- ability to lift carry or otherwise move every day objects
- memory or ability to concentrate learn or understand
- the perception of risk of physical danger.

It is not the person's ability to carry out the job but his ability to carry out day to day activities that is of relevance, so that the inability to carry out a job that, for example involves, heavy lifting will not necessarily make that person disabled within the meaning of the DDA 1995 (**Quinlan v B & Q Plc** [1999] Disc LR 76).

The concept of discrimination under the DDA 1995

Section 4 of the DDA 1995 sets out those areas in which it is unlawful to discriminate against applicants and employees.

The meaning of discrimination is contained in section 5. It can occur in *two* ways:

(1) Where for a reason connected with the disabled person's disability the Employer treats the disabled person less favourably than he treats or would treat others to whom the reason does not apply, and he cannot show that this treatment is justified (section 5(1) DDA 1995).

(2) Where the Employer fails to comply with a duty of reasonable adjustment imposed on him by section 6 of the DDA 1995 in relation to disabled persons, and he cannot show that this failure was justified (Section 5(2) DDA 1995).

The DDA 1995 allows an employer to justify disability related discrimination. This is in contrast to the direct discrimination provisions of the SDA and RRA. It means that an employer can take into account disability when making decisions about employment in a way not possible with race or sex. By section 5(3) treatment is justified if it is *both material to the circumstances of the particular case* and *substantial*.

Section 6 of the DDA 1995 contains provisions relating to the duty to make reasonable adjustments. This requires the employer in certain circumstances to take positive steps to accommodate the requirements of individual disabled persons. The duty to make reasonable adjustments is one of the central pivots of the *Act because the manner in which the non disabled world structures employment and the workplace* largely causes the difficulties that exist for disabled persons.

By section 6(1) where:

• any arrangements made by or on behalf of an employer, or

- any physical feature of premises occupied by the employer place the disabled person concerned at a substantial disadvantage in comparison with persons who are not disabled it is the duty of the employer to take such steps as it is reasonable in all the circumstances of the case for him to have to take in order to prevent the arrangements or feature having that effect.

A failure to comply with section 6 is not actionable in itself. The importance of section 6 is that it is unlawful discrimination to fail without justification to make a reasonable adjustment by section 5(2). This means that if there is a breach under section 4 and an employer has failed to make a reasonable adjustment then the employer will not be able to justify the discrimination. The disabled person must be placed at a *substantial* disadvantage before the duty may arise.

Arrangements means arrangements for:

- determining to whom employment should be offered.
- terms conditions or arrangements on which employment, promotion, transfer, training or any other benefit is offered or afforded.

Section 6(10) sets out a number of factors that will be taken into account in deciding whether it is necessary to take a particular step to comply:

(1) the extent to which taking the step would prevent the *effect* in question.
(2) the extent to which it is *practicable* to take the step.
(3) the *financial and other costs* which will be incurred by the employer and the extent to which it would *disrupt the employer's activities*.
(4) the *employer's financial and other resources*.
(5) the *availability* of financial or other assistance.

The Code also refers to some further factors:

- Effect on other employees.
- adjustments made for other disabled persons.
- extent to which the disabled person will co-operate.

It was made clear in **Morse v Wiltshire County Council** [1999] Disc LR 40 that the provisions apply to the case of dismissals and guidance is set out as to the steps to be taken in considering whether reasonable adjustments should have been made (a case of dismissal where the employee was no longer able to drive). (See also **Goodwin v The Patent Office** [1999] Disc LR 104.) It is necessary to consider what overlap there is between the concept of reasonableness under the ERA 1996 and the concepts of less favourable treatment and reasonable adjustments under the DDA 1995.

Less favourable treatment and reasonableness

The approach taken under the DDA 1995 and the ERA 1996 differ as the latter is concerned with reasonableness whilst the former is concerned with less favourable treatment which can be justified.

The Higher Courts have not considered the overlap between the two but there are a number of Employment Tribunal decisions, referred in to the IDS Study *Disability and Employment Law and Company Practice* (available from IDS; E mail ids@incomesdata.co.uk) which illustrate the problems. In **Mansoor v Secretary of State for Education & Employment** [ET No 1803409/97] a Tribunal took the view that where there is a discriminatory dismissal then such dismissal cannot be reasonable under section 96(4). The Applicant was unable to attend work at the employer's starting time because of his disability. Dismissal for poor timekeeping was discriminatory and was not justified, and, moreover, a reasonable adjustment could have been made. In **Samuels v Wesleyan Assurance Society** [ET 2100703/97] the Tribunal held that if a dismissal was unfair, because no reasonable employer would have dismissed, it would also be discriminatory because it could not be justified. However, in **Holmes v Whittingham & Porter Limited** [ET 1802799/97] where the employer had behaved reasonably in dismissing as a result of a medical report which stated that the employee should not be allowed to work, there was still discrimination as it had not been shown that dismissal was justified as being for a substantial and material reason. The Tribunal thought that justification had nothing to do with reasonableness but was a far more severe test. It is therefore clear that the statutory wording of the two tests should be approached separately.

Reasonable adjustments and reasonableness

Where a reasonable adjustment could have been made which would have meant that the employee would not have been dismissed and failure cannot be justified there will have been discrimination. However, the requirement to consider reasonable adjustments places a positive onus on the employer so that what may be reasonable for the purpose of considering alternative employment and consultation may not be sufficient in terms of the employer's duty under the DDA 1995 (**Ridley v Severn NHS Trust** [EAT 1400653/97). In **Clark v TDG Limited (t/a Novacold)** [1999] Disc LR 240 the Court of Appeal confirmed that the duty to make reasonable adjustments applies to pre-dismissal activities where, if a reasonable adjustment had been made dismissal may not have occurred, so as to found a claim for less favourable treatment under section 5(1) of the DDA 1995.

The moral of all of these cases is clear: where it appears that steps could have been taken to prevent dismissal a claim for less favourable treatment and failure to make reasonable adjustments should be made as well as a claim for unfair dismissal.

Long Term Sickness

In the case of absence because of long term sickness the employer is required to consult with the employee and discuss the position with him, to carry out a medical investigation so as to inform itself of the true medical position and, in certain cases, to consider whether an offer of alternative employment should be made to the employee.

In **Spencer v Paragon Wallpapers Limited** [1976] IRLR 373 the EAT commented that it is for management to decide how they wish to act in the case of absence due to chronic sickness. Where the employee has been absent for some time the question is whether the employer can be expected to wait any longer for the employee to return and if so, how long. Provided that the employer has carried out a proper review it is likely that the dismissal will be fair. The review may take into account the nature of the illness, the likely length of the continuing absence and the need of the employers to have the work done which the employee was engaged to carry out. In certain cases of long term sickness the contract may not come to an end by way of dismissal but may have been frustrated. These situations are considered in detail in Chapter 2 at page 64.

Consultation

> Discussion and consultation should take place between the employer and employee as this may bring to light facts and circumstances of which the employer was unaware and which throw new light on the problem. In certain circumstances consultation may not be necessary where it would be futile though such cases are likely to be exceptional in the context of long term sickness.

The leading case is **East Lindsey District Council v Daubney** [1977] IRLR 181. Mr Daubney suffered a mild stroke and was examined by a doctor at the request of the District Community Physician. As a result of the doctor's report the Community Physical reported that he felt Mr Daubney was unable to carry out his duties and should be retired on the grounds of permanent ill health. He was given notice of termination of his employment five days later. The dismissal was held to be unfair on the ground that no full medical report was obtained by the Council and there had been no consultation with Mr Daubney so that he never had an opportunity of stating his side of the case or seeking independent medical evidence. Phillips J stated:

> "Unless there are wholly exceptional circumstances, before an employee is dismissed on the ground of ill health it is necessary that he should be consulted and the matter discussed with him, and that in one way or another steps should be taken by the employer to discover the true medical position. We do not propose to lay down detailed principles to be applied in such cases, for what will be necessary in one case may not be appropriate in another. But if in every case employers take such steps as are sensible according to the circumstances to consult the employee and to discuss the matter with him, and to inform themselves upon the true medical position, it will be found in practice that all that is necessary has been done. Discussions and consultation will often bring to light facts and circumstances of which the employers were unaware, and which will throw new light on the problem. Or the employee may wish to seek medical advice on his own account, which, brought to the notice of the employers' medical advisers, will cause them to change their opinion. There are many possibilities. Only one thing is certain,

and that is that if the employee is not consulted, and given an opportunity to state his case, an injustice may be done."

The EAT took the view that the *Daubney* case was precisely the type of case where consultation may serve some purpose.

The rationale for and the exceptions to the duty to consult were considered in **Taylorplan Catering (Scotland) Limited v McNally** [1980] IRLR 53 in which a barman developed a depressive illness as a result of his work from which he was told he would not recover and which was causing behavioural difficulties. He was dismissed without consultation and the EAT agreed that it would have been pointless in the circumstances. Lord McDonald stated that consultation was necessary to ensure that the situation be weighted up 'balancing the employer's need for the work to be done on the one hand against the employee's need for time to recover his health on the other'. In the present case the employer needed someone of sufficiently robust health to withstand the stresses of employment in a worker's camp at Sullom Voe and the employee was aware of his permanent incapacity for the job. The fact that the employee is aware of his permanent incapacity was also taken as a reason for non consultation in **Nicol v John Paterson (Motors) Limited** [EAT 140/80] where the employee knew that he was unfit to drive.

It was held by the Court of Session in **Eclipse Blinds Limited v Wright** [1992] IRLR 133 that failure to consult may be reasonable where the employer did not want to divulge details to the employee about her health of which she was unaware.

Consultation in the circumstances of long term absence due to sickness will involve regular contact with the employee (**WM Computer Services v Passmore** [EAT 721/86]) which should involve personal contact with the employee rather than simply reviewing the matter on paper (**Post Office v Stones** [EAT 390/80].) (See also **MacDonald v Ayrshire & Arran Health Board** [EAT 465/80] where it was said that it is desirable that there be an interview before dismissal.)

Medical examination

> The employer should inform itself of the true medical position of
> the employee by seeking proper medical advice, where necessary
> consulting with doctors, and in some circumstances requiring
> specialist advice. However, the decision to dismiss is an
> employment one not a medical one so that employers are not
> under a duty to evaluate medical advice unless it is clearly wrong
> though where there is conflicting medical evidence the employer
> must have good reason to prefer one opinion rather than the other.

It is clear from the *Daubney* case that employers should inform
themselves of the true medical position of the employee so that it
can make an informed decision about dismissal. In **Patterson v
Messrs Bracketts** [1977] IRLR 137 the EAT stated that:

"..there should be an opportunity for the employer to inform
himself about the true situation of the employee's health; and
that should be arranged in such a way that the employee can
have an opportunity to contribute to it. What is required in a
particular case will, of course, depend on all the circumstances
but the principle is two-fold: first, that there should be
consultation or discussion with the employee; and secondly,
that such other steps as are necessary should be taken to enable
the employer to form a balanced view about the employee's
health. In some cases that will require consultation with the
doctors; in other cases it will not..."

Failure to obtain proper medical opinion will be likely to result in a
finding of unfair dismissal (**Parsons & Co Limited v Kidney** [EAT
788/87]). Employers will have to consider the nature of the medical
advice which they need in considering the true position of the
employee. The starting point is often to obtain the opinion of the
employee's G.P. with the employee's permission. The employer may
require the employee to undergo a medical examination though, if
there is no express power to so require in the contract of
employment, the employer may place itself at risk of a claim for
unfair constructive dismissal (**Bliss v South East Thames
Regional Health Authority** [1987] ICR 700). Where the
employee refuses to attend to a medical examination the employer is

entitled to rely on the medical information before it (**Macintosh v John Brown Engineering** [EAT 339/90].

A number of cases have considered whether an employer is under a duty to go further and commission a specialist report, depending on the nature of the illness, since it is the duty of the employer to obtain all facts that could reasonably be discovered at the time of the decision to dismiss. In **Crampton v Dacorum Motors Limited** [1975] IRLR 168 a Tribunal considered it unreasonable to rely upon the opinion of G.P in a case where the employee was diagnosed as suffering from angina and considered that the employee should have been examined by a specialist nominated by the employer.

It was made clear in **Liverpool Area Health Authority (Teaching) v Edward** [1977] IRLR 471 that employers are not under a duty to evaluate medical evidence. A report had advised that the Ms Edwards, a domestic worker, avoid lifting and bending and, when the employer could not find any alternative work, she was dismissed. She alleged that she should have been permitted to get her own report or a more detailed report have been obtained. On the issue of evaluation of medical evidence the EAT stated:

> "We do not think that an employer, faced with a medical opinion, unless it is plainly erroneous as to the facts in some way, or plainly contains an indication that no proper examination of any sort has taken place, is required to evaluate it as a layman in terms of medical expertise...Nor do we think that it is ever conceivably right, having had the opinion of a doctor, that it should be tested as to its validity by seeing if a nurse agrees with it. That is not the way the medical world works..."

Where there are conflicting medical reports it may be necessary for the employer to obtain a third opinion otherwise he will not have the material to reach an informed decision. It was stated in **British Gas Plc v Breeze** [EAT 503/87] that a dismissal will be unfair where the employer's own medical expert has suggested that an opinion be obtained from an independent consultant.

The employee must be given a chance to challenge the employer's medical evidence. This was not done in *Edward* and the case was remitted to another tribunal to consider whether, if a further medical report had been obtained, it would have affected the decision to dismiss. This requirement was also stated in **Herbert & Young Limited v Brain** [EAT 115/80].

Offers of alternative employment

Where the employee suffers from ill health in a particular job the employer should consider whether there is any alternative employment within the business which the employee could carry out although this duty does not extend to the creation of a post for the employee. This duty may overlap with the duty under the DDA 1995 to consider a reasonable adjustment in the case of disabled employees.

Where there is suitable alternative work that the employee could carry out then consideration should be given to offering this to the employee, even if it involves a demotion or a reduction in pay, as it is necessary for the employer to consider and discuss a solution of the problem with the employee. In **Rubery-Owen-Rockwell Limited v Goode** [EAT 112/80] there was work available which would not have involved the employee having contact with a substance to which he was allergic which would involve demotion but which the employee would have accepted. The employer did not consider offering the position and the dismissal was held to be unfair as there was certainly a job that the employee was willing and able to do and he was willing to accept downgrading if necessary. However, where the work cannot be carried out because of adverse reaction to the workplace environment and there is no other job it will be fair to dismiss (**Glitz v Watford Electric Co Limited** [1979] IRLR 89).

Employers are under no duty to create a job where none exists. For example in **Merseyside & North Wales Electricity Board v Taylor** [1975] ICR 185, Mr Taylor could only carry out sedentary work after heart trouble and there was no such post available. O'Connor J stated that "it cannot be right, that, in such circumstances, an employer can be called upon by the law to create a special job for an employee however long serving he may have been." (See also **Garricks (Caterers) Limited v Nolan** [1980] IRLR 259, where however, it was stated that some flexibility may be expected, for example some help in lifting.)

If the nature of the work is itself causing the ill health it may be incumbent upon the employer to consider whether it is possible to remove the conditions that are causing the problems (**Jagdeo v Smiths Industries Limited** [1982] ICR 47).

Under the DDA 1995 an employer may be under a duty to make reasonable adjustments to accommodate a disabled person in a job. As as been noted the Code sets out examples of such adjustments that may be made if an employer is to show that it has acted reasonably.

Short Term Persistent Sickness

> Where an employee is persistently absent due to sickness a medical examination may not serve any purpose as the symptoms and illness may not be manifest. In such circumstances, before considering dismissal, the employer should have carried out a fair review of the employee's record and reasons for illness, given the employee an opportunity to comment and issued proper warnings that there must be an improvement in the employee's attendance. If there is no improvement a time will come when the employer is entitled to say that 'enough is enough' and to dismiss the employee for capability.

The principles set out above were enunciated in **International Sports Company Limited v Thomson** [1980] IRLR 340. There was an agreement that an absence record of over 8% was unsatisfactory. The employee's record in the last 18 months of her employment was 22%. She had been counselled and warned but there was no decrease in absences and there was no discernible pattern to the absences. The EAT allowed an appeal against a finding of unfair dismissal. Waterhouse J stated:

> "... the employers did not purport to dismiss the employee on the ground of incapability. They were concerned with the impact of an unacceptable level of intermittent absences due to unconnected minor ailments.
>
> In such a case, it would be placing too heavy a burden on an employer to require him to carry out a formal medical investigation and, even if he did, such an investigation would

rarely be fruitful because of the transient nature of the employee's symptoms and complaints. What is required, in our judgment, is, firstly, that there should be a fair review by the employer of the attendance record and the reasons for it; and, secondly, appropriate warnings, after the employee has been given an opportunity to make representations. If then there is no adequate improvement in the attendance record, it is likely that in most cases the employer will be justified in treating the persistent absences as a sufficient reason for dismissing the employee."

Having carried out such a review the question, then, then is whether the dismissal was the response of a reasonable employer. Provided that the dismissal was reasonable a Tribunal will not interfere with the decision to dismiss. In **Rolls Royce Limited v Walpole** [1980] IRLR 343. The employee had an attendance record of about 50% in the three years before his dismissal. He was warned about his absences and the employer followed its own procedures. When they could see no improvement in sight he was eventually dismissed. The EAT held that this was a reasonable response in the circumstances of the case. The limbs of the approach to be adopted will be considered below, but it is necessary to consider first the true reason for the dismissal.

Incapability or Misconduct

Dismissal for a poor attendance record is likely to be a dismissal because of conduct (as to which see page 149) whilst dismissal for sickness will be for capability. In the case of persistent short term absences due to sickness there may be some overlap since it is likely to be the effect upon the employer's business of the repeated absences that is the cause of the employer's concern. Employers should be clear as to whether they are dismissing for conduct or capability. In **Trico-Folberth Limited v Devonshire** [1989] IRLR 396 the importance of the distinction was clearly illustrated. The employee was dismissed for her very poor attendance record. On an internal appeal, for compassionate reasons, her employment was treated as terminated on medical grounds. A Tribunal held that the dismissal was unfair as there had been no examination of the medical condition and insufficient consultation with the employee and her G.P. to justify dismissal on this ground, notwithstanding that, if she had been dismissed for poor attendance her record was so bad that the company could not be expected to tolerate it. The decision was upheld by the Court of Appeal.

It should also be noted that persistent absences because of sickness may amount to a dismissal for some other substantial reason (**Wharfedale Loudspeakers v Poynton** [EAT 82/92]).

> The employer should (1) carry out a fair review of the employee's absence record and the reasons for the absence and (2) permit the employee to make any appropriate representations or comments that he wishes.

A dismissal without a review of the medical record of the employee or permitting the employee to make such representations as he wishes is likely to be unfair. In respect of the latter an employee may be able to make representations as to the reasons for the absences and why his record will improve or, alternatively, it may come to light that the absences are symptomatic of an underlying medical condition so that the employee's condition should be approached on the basis of long term sickness rather than intermittent absences. A failure to carry out a review or warn the employee will make the dismissal unfair unless it can be shown that consultation and warning were futile (within the Polkey exception) or could have made no difference. In **Townson v Northgate Group Limited** [1981] IRLR 382 the employee was off work in excess of fifty days per year and was dismissed after an absence of $1^1/_2$ weeks for flu. His medical record was not reviewed and there was no warning that the absences could lead to dismissal. The dismissal was unfair but compensation of four weeks was ordered on the basis that consultation should have taken place though ultimately it would have made no difference. The EAT allowed the appeal on compensation. Similarly, in **Modern Methods & Materials Limited v Crabtree** [EAT 63/81] where the employee was dismissed for repeated absences amounting to 23% but was not interviewed before a final warning in accordance with company procedure, the dismissal was unfair as the employer did not persuade the tribunal that the interview would have served no purpose. As Browne Wilkinson J noted:

> "In the ordinary case, part of a fair procedure is to interview the employee to enable him or her to give any explanation there may be of his or her conduct or to draw attention to mitigating circumstances, and only in the light of such interview and what emerges at it does the employer take a decision to dismiss or No."

Although in *Trico-Folberth* the Court of Appeal considered that the employer should have consulted with the employee's G.P. this will not be necessary in every case of intermittent absence as it will depend upon whether it is necessary in the circumstances in order that the employer can consider the true picture, in particular whether there is an underlying medical reason for the absences **(London Borough of Tower Hamlets v Bull** [EAT 153/91].

The employee should have been warned about the likely consequences of continued unacceptable intermittent absences from work.

Whilst in the case of long term sickness a warning is unlikely to serve any purpose and to be inappropriate in the circumstances, in the case of intermittent absences a warning is likely to be of relevance to whether the employer acted reasonably. A warning was stated to be necessary in **Rolls-Royce v Walpole** and the significance of a warning was recognised by the EAT in **Lynock v Cereal Packaging Limited** [1988] ICR 670 where it was stated that a warning serves as notice to the employee that the stage has been reached where the employer may no longer be able to continue employment. The EAT commented:

"The approach of an employer in this situation is, in our view, one to be based on those three words which we used earlier in our judgment – sympathy, understanding and compassion. There is No principle that the mere fact that an employee is fit at the time of dismissal makes his dismissal unfair; one has to look at the whole history and the whole picture. Secondly, every case must depend upon its own fact, and provided that the approach is right, the factors which may prove important to an employer in reaching what must inevitably have been a difficult decision, include perhaps some of the following – the nature of the illness; the likelihood of recurring or some other illness arising; the length of the various absences and the spaces of good health between them; the need of the employer for the work done by the particular employee; the impact of the absences on others who work with the employee; the adoption and the exercise carrying out of the policy; the important emphasis on a personal assessment in the ultimate decision and of course, the extent to which the difficulty of the situation and the position of the employer has been made clear to the employee so that the employee realises that the point of no return, the moment when the decision was ultimately being made may be approaching. These, we emphasise, are not cases for disciplinary approaches; these are for approaches of understanding...."

Thus, whilst such cases are not to be treated as disciplinary matters, warnings do serve a useful purpose.

Other Relevant Factors

There are a number of other factors that may be relevant in considering whether an employer acted reasonably in deciding to dismiss for incapability arising out of ill health.

Factor 1:
Where the employer knew of the medical problem or disability on recruitment it may be taken to be aware that there may be particular problems and have to make allowances for them.

This factor is particularly affected by the duties now imposed by the DDA 1995, especially in relation to reasonable adjustments. However, even before the DDA the fact that an employer recruited an employee in full knowledge that a medical condition may cause particular problems was considered a relevant factor in deciding whether any dismissal was reasonable. In **Kerr v Atkinson Vehicles (Scotland) Limited** [1974] IRLR 36 the employer engaged an employee which it knew was 90% disabled. He was dismissed because of frequent absence despite the fact that they were below the employer's sick pay arrangements. The Tribunal held that the employer knew of the disability and a reasonable employer would have expected a higher level of absence. However, in **Witherton v Hammersley China Co** [EAT 609/77] a dismissal was held to be fair where a new management team expected higher standards of work and Mr Witherton who was mentally retarded but had worked for 13 years without complaint was unable to achieve the standard necessary.

Factor 2:

The employee's past service with the employer is a relevant factor as is the nature and effect of the illness and its likely duration.

It may be unfair to dismissal a long serving employee who has been off a few months in circumstances where dismissal my be justified if there is less service. Moreover, the length of the illness and the chance of it improving so that the employee's performance returns to standard are relevant considerations. In **Scott v Secretary of State for Scotland** [EAT 196/88] an improvement in the attendance record was considered to be a relevant factor. The employer must carry out a fair appraisal of the likely prognosis for the future.

Factor 3:

The effect of the employee's absence on the business or upon the employment conditions of other employees is a relevant factor where continued absence is likely to be detrimental.

If the continued absence of an employee is having a detrimental effect upon the profitability or sales of the business or on the smooth running of the business then it may be that dismissal will be fair. In such circumstances employers should consider whether there are any temporary measures that can be put into place, which may include the employment of temporary workers. The absence may have an effect on other employees, for example, where employees work as a team and their remuneration is dependant on team effort. This was the position in **Ali v Tillotsons Containers Limited** [1975] IRLR 272 where bonuses were dependant upon the outcome of a production team.

Factor 4:

If the continued employment of the employee is likely to endanger others due to the nature of the illness the employer may act reasonably in dismissing for incapability.

In **Harper v NCB** [1980] IRLR 260 an epileptic had three fits in which he was violent to other employees. He refused to take early retirement and was dismissed. Although a report suggested that other medication may lessen the risk there was no other work without close contact to vulnerable employees. The EAT agreed that the dismissal was for capability or some other substantial reason, though his ability to do the job was not affected, on the ground that if he became a danger to his fellow employees this affected his capability to do the job. Since the employer owed a duty to other employees for the safety the dismissal was fair. The same approach was taken in **Nicholl v Sir William Reardon Smith & Sons Limited** [EAT 463/81] where an employee was deemed permanently unfit after new standards were introduced though he had worked successfully for six years following a heart attack. He was held to be fairly dismissed having regarded to the accepted standards of the shipping industry.

Factor 5:
Where the nature of the employment calls for robust health or a certain level of attendance dismissal for incapability where the employee falls below such standard.

This was the position in **Taylorplan Catering (Scotland) Limited v McInally** [1980] IRLR 53 where the employee suffered stress given the conditions under which he worked. In **Leonard v Fergus & Haynes Civil Engineering Limited** [1979] IRLR 235 a North Sea oil rig engineer was fairly dismissed under an agreement whereby any worker who was absent for more than two shifts out of a 14 day period was regarded as unsuitable for work in the North Sea.

Factor 6:
The fact that the employer has a sick pay scheme which covers a specified period is not indicative of what period of absence will be regarded as acceptable or unacceptable.

It was held in **Coulson v Felixstowe Dock & Railway Co** [1975] IRLR 11 that the fact that there is a sick pay scheme does not indicate one way or the other that a certain period of absence will be acceptable or unacceptable so that it was wrong to find a dismissal unfair when the employee was dismissed within the period that the scheme was still running.

> **Factor 7:**
> The employer may be responsible for the employee's medical condition.

If the employer has actually caused the employee's medical condition this may be a factor to take into account where alternative methods could be employed that could mean the employee would have been able to continue to carry on the job. However, where it is apparent that the employer is exposing the employee to the risk of further injury by continuing to employ the individual in that position there may be no other alternative than dismissal.

> **Factor 8:**
> An employee who does not tell the truth about his health, who takes time off as holiday and claims sickness or who is malingering is likely to have been fairly dismissed.

However, if the employee has a sickness certificate the employer will need to satisfy himself as to the mala fides of the same before dismissing on the ground that the employee is malingering.

Sickness and Contributory Conduct

Where the dismissal was caused or contributed to by the employer compensation may be reduced to such extent as is just and equitable under section 123(6) of the ERA 1996. This principle can apply in capability cases (See Chapter 28 Compensatory Awards at page 426). An employee may contribute to his dismissal where he ignores medical advice that exacerbates his condition or fails to co-operate after an accident. Where the employee fails to respond to inquiries from his employer whilst off sick or absents himself so that his employer cannot ascertain the position this may be regarded as contributing to his dismissal (**Bham v CFM Group Limited** [1254/95]) though employers should be careful not to assume that because the employee is non-contactable or takes time to respond (especially in case of stress related illness) the employee may be misconducting himself (**McMaster v Manchester Airport Plc** [EAT 149/97]).

A to Z of Capability and Sickness

This section considers issues that have arisen in relation to particular areas of sickness.

Aids

Where an employee is diagnosed as being HIV positive or suffering from AIDS this is unlikely to justify dismissal unless the nature of the post is such that there is a risk to others (For example recent examples in the media of medical positions where there may be a risk of infecting patients). Where the illness renders the employee incapable of being able to carry out the job considerations of dismissal for incapability should be treated the same as other illnesses that may be terminal. Where it is apparent that the employee is not going to be fit to work in the same post again then the employer should still consider whether there are any adjustments that may be made under the DDA 1995 before dismissal is considered to be the only option. It should be noted that, in certain circumstances, dismissal may be for SOSR where pressure is brought to bear by a customer that the business will be boycotted unless the employee is dismissed. Where pressure is brought by fellow workers there remains a duty to render support to individuals employed in the business so that the employer may in fact be justified in dismissing those employees who refuse to co-operate with the infected employee. However, if this is likely to lead to widespread disruption of the employer's business it may be reasonable to take the course of dismissing the infected employee.

Whilst there have been a substantial number of tribunal decisions on this matter, each case turns on their own facts and have not been set out in detail for reasons for space, but it is believed that the above guidance reflects the approach that is being taken to this area.

Alcohol and Drugs

Where the employee's incapability to carry out his job arises from alcohol or drugs the starting question is whether or not the reason for dismissal is more appropriately dealt with as one of capability or whether it falls into the category of conduct (this is dealt with in detail in Chapter 6 Conduct at pages 00). Alcoholism and drug dependency should be dealt with as cases of sickness or, possibly being caused by some related illness, so that an employer may be under a duty to carry out medical and other investigations in considering how to deal with the problem (**Strathclyde Regional Council v Syme** [EAT 223/79]) though clear breaches of disciplinary rules (see **Walton v TAC Construction Materials** [EAT 526/80] and Chapter 6 on conduct) or unwarranted and unacceptable conduct at work (**Evans v Bass North Limited** [EAT 715/86]) or criminal behaviour arising out of the addiction (**Davis v British Airways Board** [EAT 139/80] may warrant dismissal for conduct.

Maternity and Pregnancy

See the chapter on Maternity and Pregnancy dismissals. Where dismissal is for a sickness that arises out of pregnancy or any reason that is connected the issue will then arise whether it is a dismissal that is automatically unfair or is a matter that is more appropriately treated as falling within the capability definition so that the usual standard of reasonableness apply. This is more properly considered in context and is therefore dealt with in Chapter 18.

Mental Illness

An employee who suffers from a mental illness may be incapable for a number of reasons of carrying out the job of the kind for which he was employed. His performance may be below standard, the illness may lead to periods of absence or his illness may affect his behaviour towards customers and employees with the consequent disruption to the employer's business. In such circumstances dismissal for incapability may be a reasonable sanction but it is necessary for the employer to follow the procedure or carrying out a proper appraisal of the employee's illness and obtaining medical evidence as necessary. Although mental illness is clearly a medical condition it is still an employment decision as to whether dismissal is an appropriate course. In **WM Computer Services Limited v Passmore** [EAT 721/86] the EAT emphasised that dismissal on the basis of mental illness is an employment matter not a medical decision and that, as with other areas of incapacity, it will only be in exceptional cases that there will be no necessity to consult the employee before terminating the contract of employment. Mr Passmore suffered from a prolonged period of depression which resulted in poor work and unstable conduct, including a suicide attempt. His own doctor and psychiatrist felt he was able to work but the company doctor was more pessimistic. It was decided to dismiss and the company doctor was consulted as to the best way to go about this. The Tribunal considered the dismissal to be unfair on the basis that the company doctor's report had been construed unreasonably and that Mr Passmore had not been consulted. It was apparent that the company had considered the question of dismissal as a medical matter. In the EAT it was stated that:

> "While, of course the medical evidence loomed large in the case, the continued employment or otherwise of the respondent was an employment decision and not a medical decision. The importance of consultation in situations such as the present has been discussed many times, and it is only in exceptional circumstances that it is not necessary to consult..."

Whilst, as Lord McDonald stated in **Thompson v Strathclyde Regional Council** [EAT 628/83] medical illness is an exceptionally delicate and sensitive field the employer remains under a duty to follow a full and proper procedure as for other areas of sickness, so that a failure to consult when a report was received that diagnosed paranoid schizophrenia rendered the dismissal unfair. Where there has been full consultation, as in **Wright v CIR** [EAT 385/79] dismissal for this reason may be fair.

Where an employee refuses to undergo a medical examination or investigation any decision will have to be made on the evidence that is available (**Petch v DHSS** [EAT 851/86]) and a dismissal may be fair where the employee refuses to accept medication or treatment that may assist (**Gillies v Scottish Equitable Life Assurance Society** [EAT 295/88]).

As with other areas of dismissal for incapacity a dismissal may be fair where the nature of the mental illness is such that it disrupts the employer's business (**Wright v Commissioners of Inland Revenue** [EAT 385/79]) or where one mistake can have disastrous consequences (**Singh-Due v Chloride Metals Limited** [1976] IRLR 56). Consideration may also need to be given to the question of alternative employment.

Qualifications

The definition of qualifications is intended to relate to qualifications that relate to the employee's ability or aptitude to carry out the job for which the employee is employed.

The second limb of section 98(2)(a) covers dismissal relating to qualifications (of the lack thereof) for work of the kind that the employee was employed to carry out. It is clear from the definition of qualifications that the qualification must relate to the ability or aptitude to carry out the job in question. This was made clear in **Blue Star Ship Management Limited v Williams** [1979] IRLR 16, where the employee was dismissed as a result of a question over his non union membership where a closed shop was in force. It was contended by the employer that he did not have the necessary qualification as he was not registered as a seafarer. The EAT held that qualification, as defined, had in mind matters relating to the aptitude or ability of the individual and that a mere licence, permit or authorisation was not such a qualification unless it was concerned with the aptitude or ability of the person to do the job.

It was held in **Blackman v The Post Office** [1974] IRLR 46 that the term qualification can include an examination or aptitude test set by the employer so that, even though an employee's work was satisfactory, dismissal could relate to capability where the employee failed to pass the test, where the aptitude test gives a technical or professional qualification relevant to the position. Moreover, certain jobs or advertisements may imply the requirement of a particular qualification, for example, a clean driving licence where driving is an essential part of the job (See **Tayside Regional Council v Macintosh** [1982] IRLR 272).

Where an employer's requirements change the employee may no longer possess the necessary qualifications for the post. In such circumstances it may be fair to dismiss but the employer must act reasonably towards such staff before dismissing (**Evans v Bury Football Club Co. Limited** [EAT 185/81]).

The loss of a qualification, for example a driving licence, may mean that the employee is no longer capable of carrying out the job so that dismissal is for capability (See **Tayside Regional Council v Macintosh**).

Where a disabled employee fails to pass an aptitude test due to his disability, and the test is not necessary for the job this may breach the DDA 1995.

CHAPTER SIX
CONDUCT

Definition

By section 98(2)(b) of the ERA 1996 a dismissal may be a potentially fair if the reason for it:

"relates to the conduct of the employee."

Whilst there are many different factual circumstances in which an employee may be dismissed for misconduct, a large body of case law has developed from which it is possible to distill general principles and guidance as to the approach that the Employment Tribunal should take in this area. ACAS has published a number of Code of Practice on Disciplinary Practice and Procedure. The current 1998 Code will be superseded by a new Code that ACAS is proposing to publish to take into account the effect of the Employment Relations Act 1999. The Code is of direct relevance and is a matter that Tribunals should take into account in their deliberations. By section 207 TULR(C)A 1992 such Code of Practice is admissible in any proceedings and where it is considered to be relevant to any question in the proceedings shall be taken into account in determining that question. In **Lock v Cardiff Railway Co Limited** [1998] IRLR 358, Morison J considered that a failure on the part of a Tribunal to examine an employer's disciplinary code by reference to the ACAS Code could be a misdirection in law. The employer's procedure failed to set out which offences could merit summary dismissal and this failure was held to have breached an essential term of the Code. Tribunals should take a breach of the Code into account in considering the fairness of a dismissal. Morison J stated:

"...tribunals should always have the Code of Practice to hand as a guide for themselves as to that is good sound industrial relations practice. In other words, this Code sets out the standards, as we see it, of sound industrial practice based upon a considerable body of experience..."

It is therefore important that Employment Tribunals consider the impact of whichever Code is in practice at the time when deciding issues relating to conduct. It will be seen that the vast majority of cases relate to the position where misconduct is *suspected* as opposed to where it is admitted. In the latter case different considerations may apply (i.e. the appropriateness of the sanction) and investigatory requirements may not be so rigid. In cases where misconduct is suspected the Courts have set out the approach to be adopted by Tribunals in some detail.

Harvey on Industrial Relations and Employment Law divides the categories of misconduct into three:

(1) Refusal to obey a lawful and reasonable order of the employer.
(2) An infringement of the Employer's disciplinary standards.
(3) Criminal offences committed outside the workplace.

These are convenient categories and most acts of misconduct can be pigeonholed into one of them. However, this Chapter will first of all consider the general principles to be applied in misconduct cases, in terms of reasonableness, investigation and the factors that may be considered in deciding the whether the sanction of dismissal is appropriate. It will then consider the areas of misconduct by reference to their factual content in alphabetical order.

General Principles: Conduct and Reasonableness

> In dismissals for suspected misconduct it is necessary for the employer to show that he had a genuine belief based upon reasonable grounds after a reasonable investigation of the guilt of the employee.

The general test was set out in **British Home Stores Limited v Burchell** [1978] ICR 303 in which an employee was dismissed for dishonesty over suspected financial irregularities. The Tribunal held that the employer had not proved the guilt of the employee. The EAT considered that this was too strict a standard to apply. Arnold J stated:

"What the tribunal have to decide every time is, broadly expressed, whether the employer who discharged the employee on the ground of the misconduct in question (usually though not necessarily, dishonest conduct) entertained a reasonable suspicion amounting to a belief in the guilt of the employee of that misconduct at that time. That is really stating shortly and compendiously what is in fact more than one element. First of all, there must be established by the employer the fact of that belief; that the employer did believe it. Secondly, that the employer had in his mind reasonable grounds upon which to sustain that belief. And thirdly, we think, that the employer at the stage at which he formed that belief on those grounds, at any rate at the final stage at which he formed that belief on those grounds, had carried out as much investigation into the matter as was reasonable in all the circumstances of the case. It is the employer who managed to discharge the onus of demonstrating those three matters, we think, who must not be examined further."

Whether the Tribunal would have formed the same view of the employee's guilt is irrelevant provided that the employer has satisfied the above test.

The approach adopted in *Burchell* was approved by the Court of Appeal in **W Weddel & Co v Tepper** [1980] IRLR 96, in which the employer's failure to give the employee a fair chance to refute the changes made the dismissal unfair. The test applies to all cases where employers do not have direct proof of the employee's guilt but only a suspicion and not just to cases of dishonesty (**Distiller's Company (Bottling Services) v Gardner** [1982] IRLR 47).

> Where the Tribunal consider the threefold *Burchell* test to be satisfied it must then go on to consider the test of reasonableness set out in section 98(4) ERA 1996.

Although some divisions of the EAT have considered that if the triple test is satisfied the dismissal will be fair, there is clear authority that a Tribunal should go on and consider the question of reasonableness. In **Secretary of State for Scotland v Campbell** [1992] IRLR 263,

Campbell, who had been the treasurer of an Officer's club was convicted of embezzlement. He was given an opportunity to explain the missing funds and argued that a change in the working of the club had made it difficult for him to control the finances and he argued that his conviction had been due to poor representation and the failure to call important witnesses. He was dismissed and his dismissal held to be unfair on the ground that the investigations were inadequate. The EAT allowed the appeal. It considered that:

> "..where the employer has been convicted in criminal court after a trial a guilty verdict might well suffice to form an adequate basis for dismissal."

The EAT considered that the employer had carried out sufficient investigation but stated that the reasonableness test must then further be considered:

> "The respondent in the present case was dismissed for dishonesty, and while the British Home Store's test can be regarded as a test of the adequacy or sufficiency of the employer's reason for dismissing, nevertheless the reasonableness of dismissing for that reason has still to be tested under section [98(4) of the ERA 1996]. The question may then be asked whether the dismissal was in the band of reasonable responses, having regard to the conduct of the employer.

The Tribunal may not, however, substitute its own decision for that of the employer as a reasonable employer may take the decision to dismiss in circumstances where a different approach view may be taken by another employer that could be equally reasonable. (See **Trust House Forte Leisure Limited v Aquilar** [1976] IRLR 251 and Chapter 4 at 86).

The overriding test of fairness is the reasonableness of the dismissal for misconduct and it is not necessary to show that the employee is guilty of 'gross misconduct' that would justify summary dismissal nor, in certain circumstances, is the blameworthiness of the conduct relevant. In **Jury v EEC Quarries Limited** [EAT 241/80] Mr Jury refused to retrain in order to obtain a class 2 HGV driving licence which was required in order to drive the Company's new fleet of vehicles. He was dismissed when the last of the lorries that he was qualified to drive went out of commission. The Tribunal considered the reason to be conduct and the dismissal to be fair. The EAT stated:

"It is not necessary at that stage [reason for dismissal] to consider whether the conduct is reprehensible, or blameworthy or to be described in any other way. The section simply refers to "Conduct"...It seems to use here, in the circumstances of this case, that the tribunal, having found that he had been inexplicably obdurate, were entitled to say that was conduct which was capable of being conduct for the purposes of subsection (2), and they were entitled to consider whether in all the circumstances it was fair to dismiss him because of it..."

The standard of proof is not beyond reasonable doubt or even on a balance of probabilities but is whether the employer had reasonable belief that the employee was guilty of the conduct complained of. The Courts have repeatedly emphasised that the standard of proof where misconduct is suspected is the reasonable belief of the employer (though compare this with the case where there are more than one suspects). Of course, where the balance of probabilities test is satisfied it will be a rare case indeed where the employer is taken to have acted unreasonably in deciding that the employee was guilty.

Where there is more than one company that is part of a group, then one company may rely upon the findings of the other in deciding that there has been misconduct (**Littlewoods Home Shopping Group Limited v Oliver** [EAT 685/97]).

Where the conduct is admitted or there can be no dispute about the facts the Burchell guidelines may be modified or inappropriate and a tribunal may only need consider the reasonableness of the dismissal.

The *Burchell* test is most appropriate where the conduct is suspected and the approach may not be as stringent where the conduct is admitted, although in *Campbell*, the EAT stated that there may still be circumstances in which the employer should carry out an investigation to satisfy itself as to the conduct of the employee: for example where the employee proffers a further explanation or new matters have come to light. Nevertheless, in **Royal Society for the Protection of Birds v Croucher** [1984] ICR 604 an employee admitted claiming fraudulent petrol expenses but claimed he was entitled to set off larger expenses to which he was entitled. The EAT held that the Tribunal was wrong to automatically apply the *Burchell* test, stating:

> "There was very little scope, therefore, for the kind of investigation to which this appeal tribunal was referring in Burchell's case; investigation, that is to say, designed to confirm suspicion or to clear up doubt whether or not a particular act of misconduct has occurred.

(See also **Boys and Girl's Welfare Society v McDonald** [1996] IRLR 129; **Scottish Daily Record and Sunday Mail (1986) Limited v Laird** [1996] IRLR 665).

Indeed in **P v Nottinghamshire County Council** [1992] ICR 706, where a groundsman of a girl's school had been convicted of indecent assault on his daughter, the school was entitled to believe that the offence had been committed. Balcombe LJ stated that any other conclusion 'would be ridiculous'.

Very rarely will the employer have to go beyond a guilty plea and to take it other than at face value. In **British Gas Plc v McCarrick** [1991] IRLR 305 the employee alleged that he had changed his plea to guilty to avoid a prison sentence. The Court of Appeal held that it was for the employers to satisfy themselves whether the guilty plea was a truthful admission of guilt or a false admission for the purpose of avoiding a prison sentence. To this extent it was necessary for them to carry out an investigation. On the basis of all the evidence they concluded that the employee was guilty and there were no grounds to interfere with that decision.

It should be noted that, despite a guilty plea, it may be necessary to investigate as to precisely what the employee pleaded guilty or where there is a dispute about what conduct was in fact admitted. In **McLaren v NCB** [1988] ICR 370 the Court of Appeal thought that an employee should have been allowed to explain the nature of his conduct where he admitted assault (threatened violence) but denied physical contact.

An employer may rely upon a confession that is not admissible in a criminal court as in **Morley's of Brixton Limited v Minott** [1982] ICR 444.

Where there is more than one suspect and it is not possible for the employer to identify the guilty individual the dismissal of all those suspected may be fair though it is impossible for the employer to have reasonable suspicion in the guilt of any one employee.

It may be impossible to apply the *Burchell* test where more than one employee could be guilty of the conduct in question but the employer cannot state that it has a genuine belief in the guilty of any individual employee. In such circumstances the test must be modified. It was held by the Court of Appeal in **Monie v Coral Racing Limited** [1981] ICR 109 that *"where there is a reasonable suspicion that one of two or possibly both employees must have acted dishonestly it is not necessary for the employer to believe that either of them acted dishonestly (Per Dunn LJ)"*. The employer considered that one of two employee's must have been guilty of theft but it was not possible to identify the culprit. The dismissal of both was fair.

It is not clear what standard is applicable to the level of the employer's belief that one or other must have committed the offence. Dunn LJ referred to "reasonable suspicion"; Sir David Cairn referred to a "case where it is virtually certain that a serious theft has been committed by one or both or two men and it is impossible to tell which…" and Stephenson LJ referred to reasonably believing in the guilt of one or more of two or more employees but unable in fairness to decide which of them is guilty. It is clear, however, that the employer must have carried out a reasonable investigation which left it unable to determine the guilt of any one individual in circumstances where the offence could have been committed by all those under suspicion. In **Leyland Vehicles v Wright** [EAT 712/81] the EAT referred to 'reasonably conclusive proof' that one of two employees may have been guilty of a theft.

The test applies in the case where more than two employees are under suspicion as having committed the offence and the employer decides on 'blanket dismissals'. In **Parr v Whitbread Plc t/a Threshers Wine Merchants** [1990] ICR 427 the EAT stated that a dismissal may be fair where on the evidence it could be found:

(1) that an act had been committed which if committed by an individual would justify dismissal; (2) that the employer had made a reasonable – a sufficiently thorough – investigation into

the matter and with appropriate procedures; (3) that as a result of that investigation the employer reasonably believed that more than one person could have committed the act; (4) that the employer had acted reasonably in identifying the group of employees who could have committed the act and that each member of the group was individually capable of so doing; (5) that as between the members of the group the employer could not reasonably identify the individual perpetrator...".

The dismissal of four employees was held to be fair in this case although it was noted that it would be in rare cases that the individual responsible cannot be identified after a proper investigation (See **Whitbread & Co t/a Ashe v Thomas** [EAT 403/86] and **Guberman v Augustus Barnett (Scotland) Limited** [EAT 152/85]. In the latter case it was stated that the employer should have taken all reasonable steps to identify the culprit and have failed before the *Monie* principle applied).

It should also be noted that there is authority that a dismissal will not necessarily be rendered unfair where one of a group under suspicion is not dismissed. In **Frames Snooker Centre v Boyce** [1991] IRLR 472, the EAT stated:

"As a general rule, if the circumstances of the members of the group in relation to the relevant offence are similar, it is likely to be unreasonable for the employer to dismiss one or more members of the group and not others, and those dismissed will thus succeed in a claim for unfair dismissal. But if the employer is able to show that he had solid and sensible grounds (which do not have to be related to the relevant offence) for differentiating between members of the group and not dismissing one or more of them, that will not of itself render the dismissal of the remainder unfair."

As with the *Burchell* test, the approach taken in *Monie* applies to cases other than dishonesty. In **McPhie v Wimpey Waste Management Limited** [1981] IRLR 316 it was applied to a case where it was not possible to identify which of two fitters had carried out a faulty inspection of a vehicle. In **British Aerospace v Mafe** [EAT 565/80] it was applied where it was not possible to identify which one of two employees had started a fight whilst in *Thomas* (above) it was applied where it was not possible to identify which supervisor was responsible for stock deficiencies.

Procedural Requirements

The increasing emphasis upon a fair procedure since the House of Lords decision in **Polkey v A E Dayton Services Limited** [1988] ICR 142 applies equally to misconduct cases. (See Chapter 4 for detailed consideration of fairness of procedures in the dismissal context). In *Polkey v Dayton Services Limited* it was emphasised that in cases of misconduct a full investigation of the conduct and a fair hearing to hear what the employee had to say in explanation or mitigation would usually be necessary if the procedure was to be fair. As Viscount Dilhorne stated in **W Devis & Sons Limited v Atkins** [1977] ICR 662 it cannot be said that an employer acted reasonably in dismissing if *"he only did so in consequence of ignoring matters which he ought reasonably to have known and which would have shown that the reason was insufficient."* The importance of procedural steps was also emphasised by the Court of Appeal in **W Weddell & Co Limited v Tepper** [1980] IRLR 96, in which Stephenson LJ stated:

> "That means that they (the employer) must act reasonably in all the circumstances, and must make reasonable inquiries appropriate to the circumstances. If they form their belief hastily and act hastily upon it, without making the appropriate inquiries or giving the employee a fair opportunity to explain himself, their belief is not based upon reasonable grounds and they are certainly not acting reasonably."

A reasonable investigation will include taking into account any mitigating circumstances and a dismissal may be unfair if an employee is not given an opportunity to make such representations (See below at 162).

The *ACAS 1998 Code of Practice on Disciplinary Practice and Procedures in Employment* which is presently in force, though soon to be superseded, helpfully sets out the appropriate procedural steps that may be taken in conduct cases. This is supplemented by the ACAS Advisory Handbook, 'Discipline at Work'. The Code sets out general guidance to be followed in drawing up disciplinary rules and sets out the essential features of disciplinary procedures (and see *Lock* referred to above as to its importance). At paragraph 9 it states:

> "Disciplinary Procedures *should not be viewed primarily as a means of imposing sanctions. They should also be designed to emphasise and encourage improvements in individual conduct."*

The clauses of the 1998 Code are likely to be replaced but provide useful guidance until the new Code comes into being.

Clause 10 provides that "Disciplinary procedures should:

(a) Be in writing.
(b) Specify to whom they apply.
(c) Provide for matters to be dealt with quickly.
(d) Indicate the disciplinary actions that may be taken.
(e) Specify the levels of management which have the authority to take the various forms of disciplinary action, ensuring that immediate superiors do not normally have the power to dismiss without reference to senior management.
(f) Provide for individuals to be informed of the complaints against them and to be given an opportunity to state their case before decisions are reached.
(g) Give individuals the right to be accompanied by a trade union representative or by a fellow employee of their choice.
(h) Ensure that, except for gross misconduct, no employees are dismissed for a first breach of discipline.
(I) Ensure that disciplinary action has not been taken until the case has been carefully investigated.
(j) Ensure that individuals are given an explanation for any penalty imposed.
(k) Provide a right of appeal and specify the procedures to be followed."

Although the Code provides very important guidance, the nature of the procedure that is required may differ depending upon the circumstances and the evidence that is available to the employer. Where the employee admits the offence or is caught red handed the degree of investigation required is likely to be less than where matters depend upon circumstantial evidence, inference and suspicion. The approach to be taken was set out by the Court of Appeal in **Clarke v Civil Aviation Authority** [1991] IRLR 412, as follows:

"Where something has occurred and where disciplinary proceedings may possibly be held, but where further investigation is thought to be necessary, the appropriate course for an employer is to suspend the employee on full pay and, if so desired, to require that employee to remain away from work.

After due investigation and before reaching any final decision, a disciplinary hearing is obviously necessary as are any appeal hearings. The practice at such hearings will follow the rules of natural justice, which are really matters of fairness and common sense.

As we have said the procedure may vary from one situation to another, but the industrial members would suggest a broad approach on the following lines: explain the purpose of the meeting; identify those present; if appropriate, arrange representation; inform the employee of the allegation or allegations being made; indicate the evidence whether in statement form or by the calling of witnesses allow the employee and representative to ask questions; ask whether the employee wishes any witnesses to be called; allow the employee or the representative to explain and argue the case; listen to argument from both sides upon the allegations and any possible consequence, including any mitigation; ask the employee whether there is any further evidence or enquiry which he considers could help his case. After due deliberation the decision will almost certainly be reduced into writing, whether or not an earlier oral indication has been given."

It is convenient to consider the nature of the disciplinary procedure for misconduct from the investigation, through to the disciplinary hearing through to the appeal stage, taking into account the types of issues that an employer and employee are likely to meet along the way.

Disciplinary procedures should be in writing and specify to whom they apply. The disciplinary procedures should indicate the disciplinary actions that may be taken.

This is a statement of requirement taken from the ACAS Code. There are a wide range of circumstances where employers may wish to regulate the conduct of their employees and treat certain matters as meriting certain disciplinary sanctions. This may not be apparent to employees so that it may be incumbent upon the employer to spell out in the disciplinary procedure the sanction that may be applicable for a first offence. For example, in **Aberdein v Robert L Fleming Limited** [EAT 1277/97], the employee was summarily dismissed when he absented himself from the employees premises during working hours. The EAT noted that the Employer's handbook did not state that this could result in summary dismissal and, as the employee was not aware that it was so categorised, dismissal was outside the band of ordinary responses and unfair. Some matters may, on the face of it, appear relatively unimportant and if an employer wishes to visit certain conduct with particular sanctions then this should be clearly spelt out.

The Disciplinary procedure will normally list a number of categories of offences that are regarded as misconduct meriting a warning and those that are regarded as gross misconduct which could lead to summary dismissal. It is important that procedures are flexible so that the categories of conduct are not closed.

> Where there is an agreed procedure then a failure to follow the procedure is likely to make a dismissal unfair, conversely it will usually be difficult for an employee to allege unreasonableness if the agreed procedure has been adhered to.

It may be the position, particularly with large organs where there is union representation, that a detailed procedure has been agreed and this may be regarded as the 'bible' governing the relationship between employer and employee. If there is such an agreed procedure then, provided the employer has followed its terms, it will be very difficult for an employer to argue that the investigation was not properly carried out or that the standards set out in the ACAS Code have not been complied with. The leading case in this respect is **East Hertfordshire District Council v Boyten** [1977] IRLR 347. Mr Boyten was involved in a fight with a fellow worker and suspended pending an investigation. Each blamed the other. The fellow worker also produced statements from two other employees stating that Mr Boyten had launched an unprovoked attack. Mr Boyten was dismissed. He exercised his right of appeal in accordance with the terms and conditions of service agreed with the unions and incorporated into his contract of employment. Each side had the right to call witnesses but the co worker and other employees were not called and the decision to dismiss was affirmed. Mr Boyten alleged that the employers acted unreasonably since the dismissing officer and appeal panel did not call these witnesses. The EAT reversed the Tribunal's decision that the dismissal was unfair. Forbes J stated:

"...this is not a case where the employer is following a code of procedure of his own devising or unassisted by others. This is a case where the employer was following a code of procedure laid down and agreed by both sides of the industry. It is in effect the bible on what should happen in these circumstances. As was pointed out in the course of the argument, it may be extremely difficult for an employer if he does not follow the agreed procedure laid down, because it may be said in those circumstances that in not following an agreed code of procedure he is in fact acting unreasonably because that code was one which in the context of industrial relations had been agreed between both sides of industry...The point is that there is a code, carefully agreed between the parties, and, in the way we look at it, it is not for an Industrial Tribunal or, indeed, this Appeal Tribunal to rewrite an agreed code of that kind which has been hammered out by both sides of industry. No employer, it seems to us, should be accused of acting unreasonably in those circumstances, if that employer follows a code which has been arrived at in that way. In our view the Industrial Tribunal wholly misdirected themselves about this. Had they directed their minds to the correct point they could not possibly have come to any other conclusion than that the employer was acting reasonably in this case. In those circumstances we are prepared to substitute our view for that of the Industrial Tribunal. We are of the opinion that the employers, on the material before us (as before the Tribunal), have made out their case that in the circumstances and having regard to equity and the substantial merits of the case they acted reasonably in treating the conduct of Mr Boyten as a sufficient reason for dismissal."

It was therefore not possible to reach any other conclusion than that the employer was acting reasonably. Similarly, in **Khanum v Mid-Glamorgan Area Health Authority** [1978] ICR 40, Bristow J stated that

"..it would be surprising to find that a hearing conducted, as the appeals panel hearing was expressly conducted, in accordance with agreed draft Whitley Council procedures turned out to have been conducted in breach of the rules of natural justice."

Where there is an agreed procedure, the employer will normally be expected to comply with it in full and a dismissal will be unfair if this is not done. In **Stoker v Lancashire County Council** [1992]

IRLR 75 an employee was only allowed to appeal on the issue of penalty whereas the procedure permitted him a full hearing as to his guilt. The Court of Appeal held that the employer had misinterpreted the procedure and that a reasonable employer could be expected to comply with the full requirements of the appeal procedure in its own disciplinary code.

However, it is open to a Tribunal to find that the dismissal was fair in all the circumstances notwithstanding the breach of procedure (See **Bailey v BP Oil Kent Refinery Limited** [1980] ICR 642). This point was made in **Westminster City Council v Cabaj** [1996] IRLR 399 where an appellate committee consisted of two rather than three councillors because one had failed to turn up. The EAT took the view that this affected the panel's jurisdiction to hear the appeal. The Court of Appeal were of the view that not every breach of procedure rendered a dismissal unfair and it was necessary for the Tribunal to consider whether the failure to convene a properly constituted appeal panel impeded the employee in demonstrating that the real reason for his dismissal was not sufficient.

There may be very rare circumstances where an agreed procedure is, in itself, so unreasonable that its application is still unfair. This was the position in **Vauxhall Motors Limited v Ghafoor** [1993] ICR 376 where an appeal could only be instituted with permission from the union convenor. The Court of Appeal took the view that this deprived the employee of his individual right to appeal.

The Investigation

> The disciplinary procedure should provide for matters to be dealt with quickly but at the same time disciplinary action should not be taken until the case has been fully investigated.

In cases where an employee is facing possible disciplinary sanctions it is incumbent on the employer to ensure that the matter is investigated as soon as possible and, if disciplinary procedures are to be involved, any procedures are not unduly delayed. In **RSPCA v Cruden** [1986] ICR 205 an RSPCA inspector was dismissed for gross misconduct in relation to allegations of conduct that had taken place seven months before an investigation had been implemented. The Tribunal rejected the reason given for the delay which was that other disciplinary matters were first being investigated. The EAT stated that:

> "...a Tribunal which finds that the employee merited dismissal and that prompt dismissal would not have been unfair may, it seems to us, perfectly reasonably reach the conclusion that postponement of that dismissal until the end of a lengthy period of unjustified delay makes the postponed dismissal unfair.

A delay of three weeks between discovering an act of misconduct and a hearing being held was criticised in **Sartor v P & O European Ferries (Felixstowe) Limited** [1992] IRLR 271.

Paragraph 11 of the ACAS Code provides that the superior or manager should take statements from witness before memories begin to fade.

The emphasis in *Burchell* and in the Code is upon a sufficiently detailed investigation being carried out. Where the facts are in dispute or unclear the employer must ensure that any investigation is sufficiently thorough or risk a finding that the dismissal is unfair. The employer must ensure that all witnesses that may be of importance have been interviewed as the process may be flawed if a material witness is omitted. It has already been noted that the scope of the investigation may differ depending go whether there is a factual issue to be determined or the employee has admitted the offence.

There may be particular difficulties in progressing an investigation where the police have become involved or criminal proceedings are pending. It may be that employers are hampered in investigating where police inquiries are being made or criminal proceedings are on foot. This is considered in more detail at pages 197 **Criminal Proceedings and Investigations**. Three points may be made at this stage. First, the employer cannot simply rely upon the police investigations but should carry out its own investigation unless the employee otherwise consents. In **Read v Phoenix Preservation Limited** [1985] ICR 164 the EAT considered that it was impossible to hold that an employee had an adequate opportunity to put his case where the disciplinary interview was in fact conducted by police officers under caution. Second, notwithstanding earlier authority to the contrary (**Carr v Alexander Russell Limited** [1976] ICR 469n) it was held in **Harris (Ipswich) Limited v Harrison** [1987] ICR 1256 that it may be appropriate to interview an employee where charges are pending to consider whether the employee wishes to admit the charge or the question of sanction. The employee should be given an opportunity to consider whether he wishes to make a voluntary statement. Third, if there is a real risk of prejudicing a pending trial or interfering with the course of justice then this may be a reason to delay investigating (*Carr*).

Where the evidence of informants, who wish to remain anonymous, is relied upon the employer should ensure that sufficient protections are built into the procedure so that it remains fair.

Particular difficulty may arise where the employer wishes to rely on the evidence of informants who wish to remain anonymous. The employer will have to consider what weight to give to such evidence since the employee may be particularly at a disadvantage by not being able to directly challenge the veracity of such evidence. The EAT set out extensive guidelines to be followed for cases concerning allegations made by informers in the case of **Linford Cash & Carry Limited v Thomson & Anor** [1989] ICR 518. The case concerned allegations made by an informant, who wished to remain anonymous because he feared physical reprisals, that two warehousemen had forged credit notes. A Tribunal held their dismissals unfair as it considered the employer should have made more stringent inquiries in the case of an informer to ensure that he had no ulterior motives. EAT upheld the finding and laid down guidelines to be followed:

"1. The information given by the informant should be reduced into writing in one or more statements. Initially these statements should be taken without regard to the fact that in those cases where anonymity is to be preserved, it may subsequently prove to be necessary to omit or erase certain parts of the statements before submission to others – in order to prevent identification.

2. In taking statements the following seem important: (a) date, time and place of each or any observation or incident; (b) the opportunity and ability to observe clearly and with accuracy; (c) the circumstantial evidence such as knowledge or a system or arrangement or the reason for the presence of the informer and why certain small details are memorable; (d) whether the informant has suffered at the hands of the

accused or has any other reason to fabricate, whether from personal grudge or any other reason or principle.

3.   Further investigation can then take place either to confirm or undermine the information given. Corroboration is clearly desirable.

4.   Tactful inquiries may well be thought suitable and advisable into the character and background of the informant or any other information which may tend to add or detract from the value of the information.

5.   If the informant is prepared to attend a disciplinary hearing no problem will arise, but if as in the present case, the employer is satisfied that the fear is genuine then a decision will need to be made whether or not to continue with the disciplinary process.

6.   If it is to continue, then it seems to us desirable that at each stage of those procedures the member of management responsible for that hearing should himself interview the informant and satisfy himself what weight is to be given to the information.

7.   The written statement of the informer – if necessary with omissions to avoid identification – should be made available to the employee and his representatives.

8.   If the employee or his representative raises any particular and relevant issue which should be put to the informant, then it may be desirable to adjourn for the chairman to make further inquires of that informant.

9.   Although it is always desirable for notes to be taken during disciplinary procedures, it seems to us to be particularly important that full and careful notes should be taken in these cases.

10.   Although not peculiar to case where informants have been the cause for the initiation of an investigation, it seems to us important that if evidence from an investigating officer is to be taken at a hearing it should, where possible, be prepared in a written form."

It was also noted by the EAT that the employer will have superior knowledge of its particular business and the workforce so that a tribunal should only interfere with a decision to keep anonymous the identification of informers if there are logical and substantial grounds for doing so. Since an employee does not necessarily have the right to cross examine witnesses as part of the process of natural justice during a disciplinary process there is no absolute right to insist on the identify of informants. The guidance set out in *Linford* need not be followed slavishly; in **Teven v Lynx Express Delivery Network Limited** [EAT 242/96] the employer did not take statements where three employees, who did not want to be identified, had related separate incidents of theft but the dismissal was fair on the ground that the employer had formed a reasonable belief.

There may be circumstances where the Court may order that the identify of informers be disclosed, so an employer cannot always guarantee anonymity to informers. In **A v Company B Limited** [1997] IRLR 405, A was dismissed in reliance on information provided by a third party alleging acts of misconduct in relation to external contractors. He was not told the nature of the information against him or who had made the allegations. The employer admitted the dismissal was unfair. A took the view that his reputation in the marketplace had been irredeemably harmed. A brought an action alleging breach of contract in the High Court and sought an order for discovery, as he wished to know whether he had an action for defamation or malicious falsehood. Scott VC ordered discovery stating that:

> "it would be intolerable that an individual in his position should be stained by serious allegations, the content of which he had no means of discovering and which he has no means of meeting otherwise than with the assistance of an order for discovery."

The Hearing

It is central tenet of cases where there are accusations of misconduct that the accused employee should be able to properly defend himself against the accusations that are made against him. The disciplinary procedure should provide for individuals to be informed of the complaints against them and given an opportunity to state their case before decisions are reached. The disciplinary procedure should specify the level of management who may take disciplinary action and it should ensure that there is a complete absence of apparent or actual bias in the conduct of the proceedings. A disciplinary proceeding should conform to the rules of natural justice since a man's job may often be at stake (See **Haddow v ILEA** [1979] ICR 202). It was made clear by the House of Lords in *Polkey* that the failure to operate a fair procedure will make a dismissal unfair except in the exceptional circumstances adverted to in the speeches of their Lordships.

However, a disciplinary panel is not sitting as a court of law and therefore the level of formality that is required and the nature and scope of the hearing may differ depending on the circumstances.

Requirements for a Fair Hearing

> The employee must be fully appraised of the allegations that are being made against him or her and should be informed in good time so that the employee has a proper opportunity to prepare any defence or mitigation.

It is a basic requirement of natural justice that the employee is made aware of the allegations that are being made against otherwise there is no chance to refute them. In **Bentley Engineering Co v Mistry** [1979] ICR 47, the employee was dismissed after fighting with another employee. He and other witnesses were interviewed and he was dismissed. He appealed and was allowed to give an explanation but not to question the other employee or witnesses. The dismissal was found to be unfair. On appeal it was held that, as he was not allowed to see the other employee's statement or hear other witnesses his dismissal was unfair. EAT stated:

> "...it is clear that in a matter of this kind, natural justice does require note merely that a man shall have a chance to state his won case in detail; he must know in one way or another sufficiently what is being said against him. If he does not know sufficiently what is being said against him he cannot properly put forward his own case. It may be, accordingly, to the facts, that what is being said against him can be communicated to him in writing, or it may be that it is sufficient if he hears what the other protagonist is saying, or it may be that, in an appropriate case, for matters which have been said by others to be put orally in sufficient detail is an adequate satisfaction of the requirements of natural justice.

The EAT stated that it is a question of degree depending on the particular case. What information must be given to the employee.

However, if the employee is not provided with the evidence before or at the outset the hearing, particularly that of witness statements it is likely that a dismissal will be unfair. In **Spink v Express Food**

Group Limited [1990] IRLR 320 a dismissal was unfair where a sales representative was not presented with details of the allegations made against him before the hearing which was such a fundamental procedural error to make the dismissal unfair. The charge was of falsifying reports and the employers deliberately did not make the employee aware of the seriousness of the changes before the hearing. Wood J stated:

> "Circumstances will inevitably vary. Management may be faced with an almost instant decision on the shop floor after violence or in the case of a dishonest act which is actually witnessed, whilst in other cases there may be and should be time for investigation and reflection; thus it is impossible – indeed unwise – to seek to lay down rules because the common law has given us sufficient guidance. However fairness surely requires in general terms that someone accused should know the case to be met; should hear or be told the important parts of the evidence in support of that case; should have an opportunity to criticise or dispute that evidence, and to adduce his own evidence and argue his case. How each such disciplinary hearing is handled will lie very much in the hands of management, there may be more than one hearing, there may be adjournments for one reason or another and outside the basic and fundamental principles of fairness to which we have eluded, there may be many variations. These were discussed in *Bentley Engineering Co Ltd* v *Mistry* [1978] IRLR 436 cited in Louies (supra) and indeed in other cases."

In the case of **Louies v Coventry Hood and Seating Co Limited** [1990] ICR 54 the EAT held that where the essence of the case against an employee is contained in written statements by witnesses, it is contrary to the rules of natural justice and prima facie unfair for an employer to refuse to let the employee see those statements. Thus where, in deciding to dismiss, an employer relies almost entirely on such written statements, it will be very rare for the procedures to be fair if the employee is not allowed to see the statements, or at least be told very clearly exactly what is in them. In this case the employer relied on two statements which stated Mr Louies had been involved in theft but he was not permitted to see the statements.

(See also **British Railways Board v Hammett** [EAT 139/89] where an expert's report was not provided and **London Borough of Camden v Edwards** [EAT 328/95] where a taped interview was not released in a case involving alleged sexual assault.)

However, in **Fuller v Lloyds Bank Plc** [1991] IRLR 336 dismissal
was fair even though the employee was not shown statements. The
employee was dismissed after attacking a work colleague with a
broken glass. He was not shown statements taken from those who
had witnessed the incident or a report on which the decision to
dismiss was based as a matter of policy. It was nevertheless, held that
the dismissal was fair as he knew the allegation against him, the
witness and had received copies of the police witness statements.
The EAT held that it could not be said that the Tribunal were
incorrect in saying that a reasonable investigation had been carried
out. Although it is normally desirable that material upon which a
disciplinary investigation is founded and on which any penalties
may be based should be made available to the person being
disciplined, failure to provide such material is not conclusive of
unfair dismissal. It commented that any defect in disciplinary
procedure has to be analysed in the context of what occurred. The
EAT stated that where there is a procedural defect, the question that
always remains to be answered is: did the employers' procedure
constitute a fair process? A dismissal will be held unfair either where
there was a defect of such seriousness that the procedure itself was
unfair or where the results of the defect taken overall were unfair.
The question does not alter because the procedural defect was based
on a policy adopted by the employers. The motivation of the
employers in adopting the policy which led to the procedural defect
is not a relevant subject of inquiry.

In **Hussain v Elonex Plc** the Court of Appeal were of the opinion
that a dismissal was fair where the employee was not shown witness
statements and they were not read out at the hearing. The employee
knew the case against him and was given a full opportunity to
respond to accusations of assault.

It is apparent that an employee must be given enough information
or sufficient detail to be able to make a proper response to the
allegations that are being made (See for example **Tesco Group of
Companies (Holdings) Limited v Hill** [1977] IRLR 63).

The employee must be given every opportunity to challenge the
evidence and to state his or her own case to the disciplinary panel.

It has been seen that the employee must know, in good time, the nature of the allegations against him. He must be given an opportunity to challenge the evidence. This will not necessarily entail the ability to cross examine witnesses (*Bentley Engineering v Mistry*).

It has been stated by the Court of Appeal that it is an essential procedural safeguard that an employee should have the right to state his or her own case and to put forward any mitigating circumstances. An extreme example of this is **McLaren v National Coal Board** [1988] ICR 370 which involved the dismissal of a striking minor convicted of assault on a working miner during the miner's strike. He was dismissed without any investigation or any opportunity to explain and in breach of the employer's procedures. Sir John Donaldson stated:

> "No amount of industrial warfare, and no amount of heat can of itself ever justify failing to give an employee an opportunity of giving an explanation of his conduct..."

It has been noted that in certain circumstances an employer may conclude after investigation that nothing the employee says will make any difference. Failure to give an opportunity to state the case may still render the dismissal unfair, for example because the employee cannot put forward any mitigation which could have had a different result on the decision to dismiss. (See **Performing Right Society Limited v Baig** [EAT 460/89].)

There is no set form of procedure that must be adopted by a panel though it was made clear in **Budgen & Co v Thomas** [1976] ICR 344 that a dismissal is likely to be unfair if the person who takes the decision to dismiss does not hear the individual's explanation. It may also be necessary to hear the employee's explanation even where the offence is admitted as there may be mitigating circumstances. AS Phillips J noted in *Budgen*:

> "Whatever the circumstances, whatever the employee is alleged to have done, and however, serious it may be, it is, in our judgment, always necessary that he should be afforded some opportunity of explaining himself to those persons in the management who will in the first instance take the decision whether or not he is to be dismissed...if, as here, the investigation of what happened is undertaken as a separate exercise then whatever the outcome of that investigation, and

however serious the offence disclosed, it is still necessary, when a decision is being taken whether dismissal is to follow, for the employee to have an opportunity to say whatever he or she wishes to the person who will take the decision."

Although in **Parker v Clifford Dunn Limited** [1979] ICR 463 another division of the EAT thought that *Budgen* had placed too high a significance on the right to a hearing it is submitted that *Budgen* is in line with the attitude of the House of Lords as exemplified in the *Polkey* decision.

There is no fixed rule as to when the employee should be entitled to make representations as to his or her case. In **ILEA v Gravett** [1988] IRLR 497 a swimming pool attendant was dismissed for alleged indecent exposure. After a second tribunal hearing it was found that the dismissal was unfair as there had not been sufficient investigation at the time when the employer formed the belief as to the guilt of the employee. The EAT noted however, that the time when the employee may state its case can vary from the investigatory stage to the initial disciplinary hearing depending upon the nature of the case.

Where an employee refuses to participate or choses not to state any case an employer may in certain circumstances consider that this reinforces the case against the employee since, as was stated in **Harris and Shepherd v Courage (Easter) Limited** [1982] IRLR 509, if evidence is produced that, in the absence of an investigation leads to an inference of guilt, the dismissal is likely to be fair.

Where an employee gives an explanation then the employer should ensure that it has been properly investigated (**Francis v Ford Motor Co** [1975] IRLR 25).

It has been held that cross examination is not necessary as part of the element of fairness (See **Ulsterbus Limited v Henderson** [1989] IRLR 251).

Representation at the Hearing

The Employment Relations Act 1999 gives workers the right to be accompanied to a disciplinary hearing by a single companion who may address the hearing but not answer questions on behalf of the worker. The hearing must be postponed for a period of five working days at the employee's request if the companion will not be available.

It has long been considered by ACAS to be good practice for an employee to be accompanied or represented at a disciplinary hearing. This right has now been enshrined in law by the Employment Relations Act 1999. By section 10(1) of the Employment Relations Act 1999 a worker has a right to be accompanied to a disciplinary or grievance hearing if he reasonably requests to be accompanied to the hearing. The employer must permit the worker to be accompanied by a single companion chosen by the worker.

The companion must be permitted to address the hearing but is not allowed to answer questions on behalf of the worker (10(2)(b)) (of course, if the employer is happy for the companion to answer questions then this procedure may be followed). The companion must be permitted to confer with the worker during the hearing. There is no definition of the extent to which the companion may confer but it would seem reasonable for the employer to permit adjournments of the hearing for short periods of time in order that the companion may properly confer. It is clear that the provisions give the right to be accompanied but not to be represented. Indeed the Minister of State for Trade and Industry stated that the provisions giver the companion the right to advise and support but not to intervene between the worker and the employer.

By sections 10(4) and 10(5) if the worker's chosen companion is not available at the time proposed for the hearing by the employer and the worker proposes an alterative time, which is reasonable and falls before the end of five working days beginning with the first working day proposed by the employer for the hearing, the employer must postpone the hearing to the time proposed by the worker. This period may give the worker and his companion the time for preparation of the case but the Act makes it clear that the trigger to postponing the hearing is the *unavailability* of the companion.

The companion is defined as a person employed by a trade union who is an official under sections 1 and 119 of TULC(R)A (i.e. an officer of the union or branch or section of the union or a person elected or appointed under the rules to represent members), an official of the trade union whom the union have reasonably certified as having experience or training as a worker's companion or another of the employer's workers.

The right to be accompanied applies to workers, which is a wider concept than employees. A worker is defined by section 13(1) of the ERA 1999 as:

> "(a) a worker within the meaning of section 230(3) of the Employment Rights Act 1996;
>
> (b) an agency worker (further defined in section 13(2) as being supplied by an agent to do work for a principal and who is not a party to the contract under which the work is to be carried out for a third party),
>
> (c) a home worker (further defined in section 13(3) as an individual who contracts for the purpose of the person's business to carry out work at premises that are not under the control or management of the person and who is not a party to the contract under which the work is to be carried out for a third party),
>
> (d) a person in Crown employment within the meaning of section 191 of the [ERA 1996] other than a member of the naval, military, air or reserve forces of the Crown, or
>
> (e) employed as a relevant member of the House of Lords staff of the House of Commons staff within the meaning of section 194(6) [of the ERA 1996]."

(See further Chapter 1 at page 20.)

It should be noted that earlier case stated that an employee may not need to be present in person provided his representative is present and has the opportunity of challenging witnesses (**Pirellis General Cable Works Limited v Murray** [1979] IRLR 190.

ACAS will in due course publish a new Code that takes into account the new provisions which give the right to be accompanied. It is also anticipated that the new Code will further attempt to define the role of the companion at the disciplinary or grievance hearing (i.e. as to note taking etc).

> The disciplinary panel should avoid the appearance of bias and, in particular, it will rarely be appropriate for the accuser or investigator to sit in judgment.

It has long been a fundamental principle of natural justice that the person conducting proceedings must not be a 'judge in his own cause'. In particular, supervisors who have carried out the investigation, the investigating officer or witnesses should not also sit on the decision making panel. In **Moyes v Hylton Castle Working Mens Club** [EAT 9/86], for example it was wrong for two witnesses to alleged misconduct to also sit on the investigative panel and then act as witnesses and decision makers at the full committee meeting! In some cases, particularly with small employers it may be impossible to delineate functions and, in such cases, it is a question whether the panel acted fairly in reaching its decision.

However, it will not be in all circumstances that it will be unfair for the same person to carry out the investigation and to conduct the hearing. In **Slater v Leicestershire Health Authority** [1989] IRLR 16 Mr Slater was dismissed after allegedly striking a patient. The Director of Nursing Services looked at the patient and considered that there were marks that were consistent with blows having been struck. He then held a disciplinary hearing at which he considered that Mr Slater had lost his temper and struck the patient. Mr Slater was dismissed and alleged that it was not open for the Director of Nursing to act as witness and to conduct the hearing. The Court of Appeal held that the ET and EAT had not erred by considering the dismissal was not rendered unfair for this reason. The Court stated that it could not be held that because the person conducting the disciplinary hearing had conducted the investigation, he was unable to conduct a fair inquiry. Whilst it is a general principle that a person who holds an inquiry must be seen to be impartial, the rules of natural justice do not form an independent ground upon which a decision to dismiss may be attacked. However, such a breach will clearly be an important matter when an Industrial Tribunal considers the question raised in s 98(4) ERA 1996.

It was further stated by Purchas LJ in *Sartor* that:

> "It *[the appeal process]* was a further step in the administrative enquiry. To the extent that each stage was an internal enquiry as

between employer and employee, there is nothing strange in the employer making his own enquiries and then reaching the decision whether or not he should dismiss."

Although desirable that the functions of investigator and judge are separated it is apparent from these two Court of Appeal decisions that this is not essential.

The Decision and the Sanction to be Imposed

Before arriving at its decision the disciplinary panel may wish to adjourn to consider all the circumstances of the case. In a case where the panel consider the allegations to have been proved it will wish to consider all the circumstances of the employee before arriving at its decision on sanction.

> Where the employee is dismissed the employment tribunal will not substitute its own opinion as to whether dismissal was a fair sanction in the circumstances but will ask whether the sanction of dismissal was that which a reasonable employer could have adopted.

It has already been noted in Chapter 4 that the Employment Tribunal will not substitute its own view as to whether dismissal was a fair sanction in the circumstances though the question at all times is reasonableness under section 98(4) as per *Haddon*. Indeed a number of the cases set out in that Chapter as to the general approach that should be adopted are misconduct cases. This is particularly so in relation to misconduct dismissals where there will be a measure of discretion on the part of the employer as to what sanction it considers to be appropriate. The Tribunal should consider whether the sanction of dismissal was reasonable in the circumstances. It is not a question of whether some other sanction would have been reasonable though this may be one factor that can be taken into account in considering the question of whether the employer acted as a 'reasonable employer'. As Lord Denning stated in **British Leyland v Swift** [1981] IRLR 91:

"The first question that arises is whether the Industrial Tribunal applied the wrong test. We have had considerable argument about it. They said: a reasonable employer would, in our opinion, have considered that a lesser penalty was appropriate'. I do not think that that is the right test. The correct test is: Was it reasonable for the employers to dismiss him? If no reasonable employer would have dismissed him, then the dismissal was unfair. But if a reasonable employer might reasonably have dismissed him, then the dismissal was fair. It must be remembered that in all these cases there is a band of reasonableness, within which one employer might reasonably take one view: another quite reasonably take a different view. One would quite reasonably dismiss the man. The other would quite reasonably keep him on. Both views may be quite reasonable. If it was quite reasonable to dismiss him, then the dismissal must be upheld as fair: even though some other employers may not have dismissed him."

(See also **Securicor Limited v Smith** [1989] IRLR 356). The Courts have particularly cautioned against the temptation for the Tribunal to substitute its own view in misconduct cases. In **City of Edinburgh District Council v Stephen** [1977] IRLR 135, in a case where a night watchman had absented himself from work the EAT were quite satisfied that the employers were entitled, if in their judgment they thought fit, to dismiss the employee and thought that the majority of the Industrial Tribunal must inadvertently have concentrated their attention not on what the employers could reasonably do, but on what they, the majority would have done had they been the employers which was not a permissible approach. (See also **Trust House Forte Leisure v Aquilar** [1976] IRLR 251 but see now *Haddon* in Chapter 4.)

Nevertheless, the Employment Tribunal is entitled to take into account a wide range of factors in deciding whether a reasonable employer would have dismissed as a fair sanction. The following section considers some of these factors in the context of this Chapter.

There are a range of factors that the Tribunal may consider in deciding whether dismissal fell within the bank of reasonable sanctions, which, in alphabetical order, may include:

(1) Consistency of treatment.
(2) Contents of the Rules including the sanctions that are set out.
(3) Effect of previous warnings.
(4) Employee's record.

(5) Gravity of the offence taking into account litigation.

(6) Other sanctions.

Each of these factors will be considered in turn.

Consistency of Treatment

> **Factor 1:**
> Where an employee is treated differently from other employees who have been guilty of the same or similar offences this inconsistency of treatment may render the dismissal unfair.

If the employer has in the past treated other employees more leniently and not dismissed them for the same or similar offences this inconsistent treatment may render the dismissal unfair unless the employer has intimated that there is a change of attitude to such conduct so that it is likely to be visited with the sanction of dismissal. This is illustrated by the case of **Post Office v Fennell** [1981] IRLR 221. Mr Fennell became involved in fight in the canteen with a co-worker and was dismissed for gross misconduct. The Tribunal considered that the employer had exaggerated the gravity of the offence and had acted out of line with their conduct in previous case. The Court of Appeal upheld the Tribunal. It considered that:

> "It seems to me that the expression 'equity' as there used comprehends the concept that employees who misbehave in much the same way should have meted out to them much the same punishment, and it seems to me that an Industrial Tribunal is entitled to say that, where that is not done, and one man is penalised much more heavily than others who have committed similar offences in the past, the employer has not acted reasonably in treating whatever the offence is as a sufficient reason for dismissal."

(See also *Hadjioannou* and the discussion at page 97).

Contents of the Rules, including the Sanctions that are set out

> **Factor 2:**
> Where the disciplinary rules spell out clearly the type of conduct that will warrant dismissal then a dismissal for this reason may be fair. Conversely, if the rules are silent or ambiguous as to whether particular conduct warrants dismissal a dismissal for a first offence may be unfair.

The Disciplinary Procedure should ensure that individuals are given an explanation for any penalty imposed.

This is a statement of good practice contained in the ACAS Code.

The ACAS Code recommends that the employer clearly sets out the type of conduct that may lead to dismissal. Failure to clearly spell this out is illustrated by **Trusthouse Forte (Catering) Limited v Adonis** [1984] IRLR 382 where a head waiter was dismissed when he was found smoking in the non smoking area of a restaurant. He admitted the offence and that he knew he should not have been smoking. Smoking was not described as warranting summary dismissal in the disciplinary rules. However, if the disciplinary rules provide that an employee may be dismissed after receiving warnings (i.e. final warning) and this is an agreed procedure then, on the basis of the approach taken in *Boyten*, a dismissal in accordance with the procedures is likely to be fair.

The disciplinary rules should state clearly what offences will merit dismissal so that employees are put on clear notice as to what conduct is likely to lead to their dismissal. In **Dalton v Burton's Gold Medal Biscuits Limited** [1974] IRLR 45 an employee, or over twenty year's service, was dismissed when he falsified a fellow employee's clocking card. The rules made it quite clear that such behaviour would warrant dismissal. The NIRC agreed that the dismissal was fair. Although dismissal was a severe punishment, one had to take into account (a) that ample warning of the consequences of this type of misconduct had been given and (b) the pernicious effect which laxity in enforcing these warnings may have upon practices which could develop all too quickly under factory conditions. (See also **Rowe v Radio Rentals Limited** [1982] IRLR 177.

Where the rules do not warn that dismissal will be the sanction for a first offence it may be that this will be too harsh a sanction, as in **Meyer Dunmore International Limited v Rogers** [1978] IRLR 167 where dismissal for fighting was held to be unfair since there was no reference in the rules to such conduct meriting summary dismissal.

However, the fact that disciplinary rules stipulate that certain conduct will lead to summary dismissal does not automatically mean that the employer will be acting reasonably if he dismisses for a first such offence, as in **Ladbroke Racing Limited v Arnott & Ors** [1983] IRLR 154 where there was a rigid rule against employees placing bets. Bets had been placed for relatives and old age pensioners with the permission of senior officials. The Court of Session agreed that the dismissals were unfair, taking the view that even if a rule expressly states that dismissal will follow any contravention that does not necessarily mean that all breaches of it will warrant dismissal and each case has to be looked at on its merits. The sentiments in *Arnott* echo the approach taken by the EAT in **Taylor v Parsons Peebles NEI Bruce Peebles Limited** [1981] IRLR 119 where an employee of over twenty years standing was dismissed after a fight as the disciplinary rules stated that any employee who deliberately struck another would be dismissed. The Court commented that it was not to the point whether the rules contained such provision since, no matter how expressed, it was always subject to how it would be applied by a reasonable employer having regard to equity and the substantial merits of the case.

Where there has been an inconsistent approach to the rules in the past or where a rule is relatively new so that an employee may not be aware of the sanction for breach or the gravity with which the employer regards the conduct dismissal without prior warnings is likely to be unfair.

The Effect of Previous Warnings

Factor 3:
As a general rule a person should not be dismissed for a first offence unless he has been previously warned that dismissal is likely to result.

The ACAS Code notes that dismissal should not normally follow for a first breach of discipline, echoing the sentiment of Lord Denning in **Retarded Children's Aid Society v Day** [1978] ICR 437 that it is

"good sense and reasonable that in the ordinary way for a first offence you should not dismiss a man on the instant without any warning or giving him a further chance."

The importance of previous warnings will be to put the employee on notice that he is at risk of dismissal if he commits a further offence. Previous warnings may relate to different conduct, but Tribunals may nevertheless take them into account in deciding the reasonableness of the employer's behaviour. In **Auguste Noel Limited v Curtis** [1990] IRLR 326 an employee was given two warnings for making racist remarks and for absenteeism. He was dismissed for failing to take care of company property and the warnings were taken into account. The EAT stated that it would be rare, if ever, that an employer contemplating dismissal could not take warnings into account even if the conduct was of a different kind. Wood J stated:

"The mere fact that the conduct was of a different kind on those occasions when warnings were given does not seem to us to render them irrelevant. It is essentially a matter of balance, of doing that which is fair and just in the circumstances and an employer is entitled to consider the existence of the warnings. He is entitled to look at the substance of the complaint on each of those occasions, how many warnings there have been, the dates and the period of time between those warnings and indeed all the circumstances of the case. It is quite impossible to lay down any rules nor is it desirable. However it does seem to us that those are matters which an employer is entitled to take into account and to look at."

See also **Stein v Associated Dairies Limited** [1982] IRLR 447.

However, where a warning has lapsed it may be unreasonable to take it into account. It is quite usual for disciplinary rules to state that certain types of warnings will lapse after a period of time (i.e. oral after three months, written after six months, final warning after twelve months). It would seem unfair on the employee if the warning was taken into account even though it was expressly stated as having lapsed. Indeed in **Charles v Science Research Council** [1977] ITR 208 the EAT were of the view that it was unreasonable to take account of incidents where it had been agreed that the slate would be wiped clean.

It should be noted however, that where a final warning in itself was unreasonable reliance upon it may make a dismissal unfair (**Co-operative Retail Services Limited v Lucas** [EAT 145/93]).

The Employee's Record

> ### Factor 4:
> A relevant factor in deciding the sanction to apply will be the employee's record, age and length and position of service.

Where the employee has given many years of loyal service dismissal for a first offence may be unfair even though the employee knows that he is acting in breach of the employer's disciplinary code. **Taylor v Parsons Peebles NEI Bruce Peebles Limited** [1981] 119 it was held unfair to dismiss an employee of over twenty years standing for fighting even though the disciplinary rules expressly stated that this was the sanction.

The Gravity of the Offence and Mitigation

> ### Factor 5:
> The gravity of the offence may be such that dismissal even for a first offence may be fair. The seriousness of the offence will be dependant on factors such as the impact on the employer's business, the effect upon safety of the employee and fellow workers or clients, whether the nature of the offence makes the employment relationship impossible and upon whether there are any mitigating factors which means that dismissal is not the appropriate sanction.

In some cases the gravity of the offence may be such that dismissal is the only appropriate sanction and nothing that the employee can say in mitigation can affect the decision to dismiss. Acts of theft, dishonesty, damaging company properly or of violence may be such that dismissal is an appropriate sanction even though the incident is a first act of misconduct. The ACAS Code recommends that, except for acts of gross misconduct, no employees should be dismissed for a first breach of discipline. The last section of this chapter, which sets out various area of misconduct contains many examples of when a first offence will or will not merit dismissal and reference should be made to this section. The distinction between gross misconduct for the purposes of wrongful dismissal and in the context of unfair dismissal has already been discussed (see Chapter 4).

Other Sanctions

> **Factor 6:**
> If the disciplinary rules themselves provide for alternative sanctions, such as transfer, demotion, alternative employment or suspension then failure to consider these alternatives may render the dismissal unfair. Even if the rules do not expressly set such alternatives out it may be necessary for the employer to consider them as a reasonable employer.

The circumstances of the offence may be such that a warning is appropriate rather than dismissal. Employers should define those circumstances in which oral, written or final written warnings may be issued (*See Duggan, Contracts of Employment* for appropriate employment terms). A Tribunal may consider the sanction of dismissal to have been excessive in the circumstances where a warning would have been sufficient.

Another sanction that may be considered appropriate is to move the employee from the post which he occupied to another post. The question of alternative employment in the area of conduct has been considered by the Court of Appeal in **P v Nottinghamshire County Council** [1992] ICR 706. An employee who worked at a girl's school was dismissed after pleading guilty to an offence of indecency with his daughter. The employer rejected the possibility of alternative work and a Tribunal considered that the employer had acted unfairly in failing to consider this possibility. The EAT reversed the decision and this was upheld by the Court of Appeal. Balcombe LJ stated that in some cases, taking into account the size and administrative resources of the employer, it may be appropriate for it to consider the question of alternative employment. The case was remitted to the Tribunal for consideration of the point.

Internal Appeals

> The disciplinary procedures should provide a right of appeal and
> specify the procedures to be followed.

The 1998 ACAS Code states that disciplinary procedures should
provide a right to appeal. Indeed it has been held by the House of
Lords in **West Midland Co-Operative Society v Tipton** [1986]
ICR 192 that a failure to provide a right of appeal may render a
dismissal unfair. The House of Lords considered that an appeal is part
of the whole dismissal process and is relevant in considered whether
a dismissal was reasonable within section 98(4). In particular new
matters may come to light during the course of an appeal that may
change matters. Moreover, an appeal may cure earlier procedural
defects in the disciplinary procedure. The existence of the right to an
appeal is therefore of some significance.

An appeal is part of the whole disciplinary process so that it will be
necessary for the Tribunal to consider the actions of the employer at
the appeal stage. Any argument to the contrary was rejected in
Tipton. This means that matters that come to light during the appeal
process should be taken into account so that an employer cannot act
unreasonably by ignoring new facts which have some bearing on the
decision to dismiss.

The following matters need to be considered in the context of the
appeal process:

(1) the scope of the appeal: rehearing or review?
(2) the effect of an appeal upon earlier procedural defects.
(3) procedural defects on appeal.
(4) the conduct of the appeal.
(5) the effect of a refusal to appeal.

The Scope of the Appeal: Rehearing or Review?

The appellate process may provide either for a complete rehearing or
for a review of the decision of the disciplinary panel. The distinction
is of some significance for several reasons. Firstly, where the appeal
process provides for a complete rehearing it is possible that earlier
procedural defects may be cured on appeal. Secondly, if the appeal

process is to be a complete rehearing then different considerations may apply to the way in which the appeal is to be conducted. The appeal process may of itself necessitate to right to a hearing, the right to call evidence and the right to state the case orally. The failure to carry out a reasonable and proper procedure at the appeal process may of itself render the dismissal unfair.

The Effect of an Appeal upon Earlier Procedural Defects

> Defects in the original disciplinary process may be rectified on appeal where the appeal is in the nature of a full rehearing as opposed to merely being a review of the disciplinary panel's decision to dismiss.

The fact that earlier procedural defects may be cured on appeal is illustrated by **Whitbread & Co Plc v Mills** [1988] IRLR 501; ICR 776. Mrs Mills sustained an injury at work and was required to be examined by a consultant. During the course of an appeal relating to her sick pay being stopped she made certain allegations about improper conduct on the part of the doctor. She was called to the Divisional Manager's office, ostensibly to be told the outcome of her appeal in relation to sick pay and to discuss the allegations she had made against the doctor. She was not told there was to be a disciplinary hearing. However, at the meeting she was told that in view of the scandalous and malicious allegations she had made against a senior medical practitioner she was dismissed with immediate effect. Her appeal was not successful. The Tribunal and EAT considered the dismissal to have been unfair and that any procedural defects had not been remedied at the appeal stage. However, it was said in **Adivihalli v Export Credits Guarantee Department** [EAT 917/97] that Tribunals should not get too bogged down with the definitions of a review or rehearing but look at all the facts of the case in deciding if the appeal did cure any earlier defects.

Wood J considered that the appeal in the present case was only by way of a review which did not remedy earlier procedural defects. In respect of the ability of an appeal to correct should defects if:

> "there is a rehearing de novo at first instance, the omission may be corrected, but it seems to us that if there is to be a correction

by the appeal then such an appeal must be of a comprehensive nature, in essence a rehearing and not a mere review.

This case may be contrasted with **Clarke v Civil Aviation Authority** [1991] IRLR 412 where the appeal process was a full and comprehensive hearing that cured earlier defects where the employee had been dismissed with no warning of the charges against him and no hearing. The EAT noted that it is a question of fact for the Tribunal as to whether the appeal cured the earlier defects.

However, if the decision to dismiss was in itself unreasonable an appeal cannot make an unreasonable decision to dismiss reasonable (**W Devis & Sons Ltd v Atkins** [1977] ICR 662).

Procedural Defects on Appeal

Procedural defects at the appeal stage may render a dismissal unfair where the disciplinary process had been carried out in a manner that was fair.

In **Stoker v Lancashire County Council** [1992] IRLR 75 the appeal process rendered the dismissal unfair where the employee was only allowed to appeal against penalty whilst the actual procedure should have permitted him to appeal against the reason for the decision to dismiss (See also **Westminster City Council v Cabaj** [1996] ICR 960).

Where the appeal hearing is itself defective it cannot cure earlier defects in the process. In **Byrne v BOC Limited** [1992] IRLR 505 the person hearing the appeal had already been involved in the disciplinary process and so was a judge in his own cause. The appeal could not therefore cure an earlier hastily convened and procedurally defective disciplinary hearing.

The Conduct of the Appeal

> As with the disciplinary hearing an appeal should be conducted in accordance with the rules of natural justice so far as is possible. This will entail, on a rehearing, handling the appeal in a similar manner to the disciplinary hearing and insofar as possible or practicable the appeal being heard by a panel that was not involved in the earlier disciplinary hearing.

Since, insofar as possible the rules of natural justice should be followed the appeal panel should not be 'tainted' by the earlier investigative process, disciplinary hearing or decision to dismiss. Three qualifications may however, be made in this respect. First, there is likely to be day to day contact between line management so that it is almost invariable that the person who made the decision to dismiss will have some contact with the person hearing the appeal. In **Rowe v Radio Rentals Limited** [1991] IRLR 412 Browne-Wilkinson J pointed out that there is no rule that the person making the decision to dismiss and the person hearing the appeal must be totally unconnected. At the appeal, Mr Rowe's superior, who had dismissed him, outlined the facts and stayed throughout the appeal. The dismissal was fair.

> "It is very important that internal appeals procedures run by commercial companies (which usually involve a consideration of the decision to dismiss by one person in line management by his superior) should not be cramped by legal requirements imposing impossible burdens on companies in the conduct of their personnel affairs.... But, in general, it is inevitable that those involved in the original dismissal must be in daily contact with their superiors who will be responsible for deciding the appeal: therefore the appearance of total disconnection between the two cannot be achieved. Moreover, at the so-called appeal hearing (which in this and many other cases is of a very informal nature) the initial dismissal is very often required to give information as to the facts to the person hearing the appeal. It is therefore obvious that rules about total separation of functions and lack of contact between the appellate court and those involved in the original decision simply cannot be applied in the majority of cases. "

Secondly, in small companies the person who made the decision to dismiss may be the only level of top management that there is to hear an appeal as in **Tiptools Limited v Curtis** [1976] IRLR 276.

Third, it should be noted that, whilst the person who took the decision to dismiss may properly be present at an appeal hearing he should not remain behind whilst the decision on the appeal is made as to do so gives an impression of bias (**Lawton v Park Cake Bakeries** (EAT 90/88]).

> Where the person who investigated and held the disciplinary hearing also hears the appeal the dismissal is likely to be unfair.

Where the investigating officer who conducted the 'prosecution' is also involved in the appeal he is likely to be regarded as a 'judge in his own cause'. This was the position in **Byrne v BOC Limited** [1992] IRLR 5050, where a manager carried out the investigation, consulted the personnel department about penalty then conducted the appeal hearing.

The Effect of a Refusal to Appeal

The fact that an employee choses not to appeal has been held not to be relevant to whether or not the employee has acquiesced in his dismissal (See **Chrystie v Rolls Royce (1971) Limited** [1976] IRLR 336, though it may go to the level of compensation payable (See 450).

Section 13 of the Employment Rights (Dispute Resolution) Act 1998 inserts a new section 127A ERA 1996 which provides that compensation may be reduced where a right of appeal is provided and the complainant did not appeal, unless the employer prevented him from doing so. The compensation may be reduced by such amount if any, as is considered just and equitable.

A–Z of Misconduct

This section will consider particular examples of misconduct and the application of the principles set out above to these particular cases. The categories of conduct are never closed. The Courts have, however, built up a large body of jurisprudence from which it is possible to set out guidance as to the approach to be taken in order for an employer to act fairly.

Absenteeism

Reasonableness of Dismissal

An employer is likely to have a standard as to when levels of absenteeism or lateness become unacceptable and dismissal the likely consequence. However, this is an area where it is important that the employee is made aware of the rules, is warned as to potential consequences and realises the potential consequences of continuing absences or lateness. The authorities may be divided into three areas:

(1) Persistent short term absenteeism or lateness.
(2) Overstaying or unauthorised leave.
(3) Long term absenteeism.

(1) Persistent short term absenteeism or lateness

Persistent short term absenteeism or lateness may be disruptive to the employer's business, particularly where the employer cannot rely upon the individual so that he cannot plan work with confidence. The reason for persistent intermittent absence may be an ongoing illness that necessitates sick leave or unauthorised absence without any good reason. The approach to be taken to persistent intermittent absences was set out in **International Sports Co v Thomson** [1980] IRLR 340. The Respondent had an absence record of over 25% is her third year of employment. The employer stipulated an absence record of 8% as being acceptable. He absences were mainly for minor ailments and were covered by medical certificates. She received four warnings and was absence for a month before being dismissed. The EAT held that the Tribunal was wrong to consider that there could only be a fair dismissal if there had first been an investigation into the authenticity of the medical certificates. Waterhouse J stated that what is required is:

> "a fair review by the employer of the attendance record and the reasons for it; and secondly, appropriate warnings, after the employee has been given an opportunity to make representations. If then there is no adequate improvement in the attendance record, it is likely that in most cases the employer

> will be justified in treating the persistent short terms absences as a sufficient reason for dismissing the employee."

The employer had given a number of warnings and reviewed the employee's record over a period of time. There reached a stage where they were entitled to say 'enough is enough'. The EAT emphasised that different considerations apply with persistent illness to that of long term absence.

(See also Short Term Persistent Absences in Chapter 5.)

In **British Coal Corporation v Bowers** [EAT 1021/93] the EAT held absences as a whole may be considered so that absences due to sickness may be considered together with unauthorised absences.

It should also be noted that persistent absences due to sickness may fall within the category of 'SOSR' (see **Wharfedale Loudspeakers Limited v Poynton** [EAT 82/92]).

The appropriate procedures that should be carried out are considered below.

(2) Overstaying or unauthorised leave

Where absences is unauthorised it be properly be regarded as misconduct (i.e. as opposed to persistent absences due to genuine sickness) and dismissal may be justified. For example, in **Rampart Engineering Limited v Henderson** [EAT 235/81], an employee took a two week holiday despite having been refused permission and having been warned that if he took the vacation he dismissal would be seriously considered. He was dismissed on his return from holiday. The EAT considered the dismissal to be fair. It may still be necessary to hold a disciplinary hearing and to await the employee's return from holiday before this is held (**Heskey v Adwest Reasby Limited** [EAT 158/97]) . Even if the employee is warned of dismissal should an unauthorised holiday be taken, the sanction of dismissal may still be unfair where the presence of the employee is not needed, as in **Charter Tea & Coffee Co Limited v McDonald** ([EAT 153/80]) where the employee had unexpectedly returned from sickness absence and was told she could not take a holiday that had already been booked. Nevertheless, any compensation is likely to be reduced by contributory conduct.

Where an employee has overstayed leave and has been warned about the possible consequences dismissal may be fair, as in **Ali v Joseph Dawson Limited** [EAT 43/89] where an employee was fairly dismissed, in the light of strict rules about extended absence, when he overstayed his leave by one week because of problems about his entry documents. (See also Chapter 2 on dismissals.)

(3)   Long term absenteeism

Where an employee is absent due to long term sickness, the dismissal may be for conduct, capacity or for SOSR. It is also possible that the absence may result in the contract being frustrated (See Chapter 2 at page 00). Dismissal due to imprisonment was held in **Kingston v British Railways Board** [1984] ICR 781 to be due to 'SOSR'. However, in that case, the Court of Appeal, in considering what factors could be taken into account, thought that the nature and the seriousness of the offence were relevant as well as the fact of and length of sentence.

Procedure

As stated in *International Sports Co v Thomson*, it is necessary for the employer to carry out a fair review of the reasons for absence and consider whether dismissal is appropriate in light of warnings administered and any opportunity to improve that was given. The ACAS handbook, 'Discipline at Work' states:

Review
The employer must be careful to ensure that a fair review has been carried out of the reason for absence or lateness.

This is illustrated by **Hallett & Want v MAT Transport Limited** [1976] IRLR 5 where the employer failed to draw a distinction between two employees who had been absent for different reasons. Mr Want was late on 12 out of 80 days following his second final warning. Mr Want was aware of the rules and aware of the sanctions likely to be invoked if he failed to substantially improve his time-keeping. His record of 12 days late out of 80 could not be said to constitute a substantial improvement. In Mr Hallett's case, however, his record following his second final warning of seven days late out of 77 was some improvement on his previous position. Moreover, of these seven days, three were days on which there was industrial action on the railways and, in respect of one other day, there was some conflict as to whether the applicant was in fact late.

It was held that it was fair to have dismissed Mr Want but the dismissal of Mr Hallett was unfair as the reasons for his lateness were not properly considered.

The employee should be given every opportunity to explain the reason for absence and failure to produce a satisfactory explanation may justify dismissal, as in **Solanke v Ford Motor Co Limited** [EAT 774/78] where the EAT commented that an employer is entitled to a reasonable and adequate explanation as to the reason for absence.

It is not necessary for an employer to hold a medical investigation as to the reasons for persistent absence. Where medical certificates are supplied, however, an employer is still entitled to go behind them in appropriate circumstances. In **Hutchinson v Enfield Rolling Mills Limited** [1981] IRLR 318, Mr Hutchinson was spotted at a demonstration when he had a medical certificate supporting his absence from work. He was dismissed and the EAT held that the employer was entitled to go behind the medical certificate. The EAT stated:

> "the Tribunal seems to have taken the view that since Mr Hutchinson had produced a sick note it was no concern of the employers to challenge whether or not he was in fact sick. They say 'it was not reasonable of the employer to go behind that sick note'. To make clear what they mean, they go on to say that the employers were not concerned with where he was or what he was doing. That, in our view, is a total misapprehension. The employer is concerned to see that his employees are working, when fit to do so; and if they are doing things away from their business which suggests that they are fit to work, then that is a matter that concerns them."

The employer should give the employee an opportunity to produce a medical certificate if there is a concern about the bona fides of the reason for absence (**Harrison Hire Co Limited v Jones** [EAT 638/81]).

Factors

(1) Absence Rules
Where the employer considers that lateness or absence above a specified limit will warrant dismissal this should be clearly stated. In *International Sports Co Limited* 8% was taken to be an

acceptable limit, whilst in **Post Office v Stones** [EAT 390/80], four separate absences or one absence over 14 days was regarded as not acceptable. The reasons for the absence must also be considered and whether the employee is on notice that his job is at risk, due to warnings, will be an important factor.

(2) Warnings

Employees should be warned where their absence record is unacceptable and given a chance to improve. Where an employee has been warned then the employer will be able to rely upon the earlier warnings and it may be that warnings will not 'lapse' in the same way as with other areas of conduct. In **Newalls Insulation Co Limited v Blakeman** [1976] ICR 543, the employee had received a number of oral warnings and eventually received a written warning that unless his record improved he would be dismissed. The employer relied on the earlier oral warnings as well as the written warning in dismissing. The EAT considered the Tribunal wrong to hold that the slate had been wiped clean because of the written warning. The dismissal was therefore fair. Kilner Brown J stated, as a matter of principle, that a man with a bad attendance record in a sense has the slate wiped clean was wrong and the time had come when the employer was entitled to say that it could not go on anymore.

(3) Future Record

An employer is entitled to take into account the employee's likely future attendance record, as in **Post Office v Stones** [EAT 390/80], in which Waterhouse J stated:

> "It was in our judgment open to the tribunal, on the facts of this particular case and the detail of the respondent's attendance record, to find that a mere paper consideration of the respondent's record was not satisfactory, and that any reasonable employer would hae examined the critical question about the respondent's likely future attendance record more closely."

It was therefore unfair to dismiss a probationary employee without consideration as to whether the record would improve.

Alcohol

Reasonableness of Dismissal

> It may be fair for an employer to dismiss an employee for alcohol abuse which affects the employee's performance at work or which leads to unacceptable behaviour although in the case of chronic abuse or alcoholism the problem may more appropriately be dealt with as one of sickness and capability.

Where the employee deliberately flouts company rules against drinking at work or during working hours then any dismissal is likely to be for gross misconduct and in the absence of mitigation or excuse will probably be fair. Where the employee is inebriated at work and this affects the way in which he carries out his job or may have an impact upon the employer's business or upon safety then this is likely to be gross misconduct even in the absence of any rules that prohibit drinking. This was the position in **Weir v Stephen Allen Jewellers** [EAT 550/97] where the manager of a jeweller's shop failed to secure the premises properly at the end of the day, having spent some time drinking at a local public house during the course of the day.

However, the employer should ensure that the alcohol problem properly falls into the category of misconduct rather than it being a 'sickness' problem. In **Strathclyde Regional Council v Syme** [EAT 233/79] the Tribunal and the EAT found that the dismissal of a school janitor was unfair in circumstances where he had agreed he would resign if he was found to be drunk, following several complaints about his drinking. The employee was suffering from manic depression and it was considered that the problem should have been treated as a medical one so that the Authority should have obtained independent medical evidence before it decided to dismiss.

Procedure

> The Employer must carry out a proper investigation into whether the Employee has in fact been drinking and whether that is in breach of the Rules or whether it affects performance or safety and this may mean waiting until the employee is sober before carrying out an interview. The employer should also consider whether the facts amount to 'misconduct' or are more appropriately dealt with as sickness or incapability matters.

There is a danger that an employer may dismiss unfairly if a full and proper investigation is not carried out as to whether the employee has in fact been drinking or, in cases where it appears that the employee is intoxicated, the reasons for the employee's condition. In **Martin v British Railways Board** [EAT 362/91] an employee was dismissed in circumstances where he was apparently drunk. However, on appeal he explained his condition as being due to hypertension. The appeal was dismissed and the EAT held that the employer should have further investigated to check whether the condition was in fact due to a medical reason. However, where the employee is in fact under the influence of drink and there is no dispute about this a dismissal may be fair, even if there is an underlying reason for the drinking. In **Forth Ports Authority v Lorimer** [Court of Session, 15.7.1992] a dismissal was held to be fair where the employee drove a crane whilst intoxicated, even though the reason for his drinking was depression. The essential consideration was that he was under the influence of alcohol whilst he was driving and any further investigation would not have changed this fact.

As with other misconduct cases, the employee should be given an opportunity to provide an explanation. In cases of misbehaviour due to the influence of alcohol it may be particularly appropriate for the employee to be given an opportunity to explain and apologise. This was the position in **Charles Letts & Co Limited v Howard** [1976] IRLR 248 where the EAT considered that the employer should have given the employee, who had lost his temper whilst under the influence of drink, the opportunity to 'climb off his high horse and apologise'.

Factors

(1) Consistency

Where drinking has been condoned in the past it is necessary for the employer to draw to the attention of its staff the fact that it will no longer be tolerated and dismissal may result. The employer failed to do this in **Sandon & N Co Limited v Lundin** [EAT 421/76] where the managing director had been in the habit of drinking at lunchtime and was dismissed for misconduct. The dismissal was unfair as he had not been warned about his drinking which the board had permitted to go on for years without comment.

(2) Content of the Rules, including the sanctions that are set out

It is good practice for an employer to have specific rules that set out the consequences of drinking at work or of alcohol abuse. Where employees are aware that alcohol abuse is likely to lead to dismissal so that they are on notice of the risk that they face by flouting such rules a Tribunal is more likely to find the dismissal to be fair. Strict and clear rules against being drunk at work will mean that any dismissal is likely to be fair for breach of the rules (**Gray Dunn & Co Limited v Edwards** [1980] IRLR 23). However, even if there is a rule against drinking or the possession of alcohol such rule must be applied in a way that is fair and reasonable. In **Scottish Grain Distillers Limited v McNee** [EAT 34/82] there was an absolute rule against unauthorised possession of alcohol and two employees were dismissed when ethyl alchohol was found in their lockers. It was held that, even if the liquid could be described as alcohol, which was dubious, the breach was so trivial that the dismissal was unfair.

The rules must be clear so that the employee knows what is prohibited. In **Dairy Product Packers Limited v Beverstock** [1981] IRLR 265 the employee was dismissed for drinking in a public house during working hours although others who had drank on the premises had not been dismissed in the past but only warned. The EAT held that if there was a distinction between these two situations it should have been made clear in the rules. In particular, where such conduct has been tolerated in the past the employer should draw the attention of the employee to any change in the rules if such conduct is no longer going to be tolerated (**Claypotts Construction Limited v McCallum**

[EAT 699/81]). However, where there is an aclohol policy the employer will act unfairly it it does not act in accordance with the terms of the policy (**Angus Council v Edgley** [EAT 1289/99]).

(3) Gravity of the offence, taking into account mitigation

Drinking at work will be regarded as a particularly serious offence where it may affect the health or safety or the employee or of fellow workers. Since the employer has a duty to ensure that the provisions of the Health and Safety at Work Act 1974, and all the associated legislation, is complied with the employer faces a risk of action against it if it does not ensure the safety of its workers. This will include ensuring that employees are not working whilst influenced by alcohol (or drugs) so that they may place themselves or others at risk. This was the case in **Connor v George Wimpey ME & C Limited** [EAT 387/82] where an oil rig worker was so drunk on his return to work that it was not safe to allow him on the return transport plane. Given the risks of working on an oil rig an absolute ban on alcohol was appropriate. Where the employer has a genuine concern that off duty alcohol abuse may have an impact on the workplace (because the employer is concerned that it may be repeated in the workplace) then dismissal may be fair (**McLean v McLane** [EAT 682/96]).

The offence may be more grave if it has an effect on the employer's reputation, for example, where the conduct of a representative means that the employer is likely to lose business. This is what happened in **Raylor v McArdle** [EAT 573/84] where the employee was drunk on a building site. Though off duty, the dismissal was fair as his conduct was likely to undermine the confidence of the site agent in the employer.

There may be mitigating circumstances which the employer should consider, as in **Hepwoth Pipe Co Limited v Chahal** [EAT 611/80] where the dismissal was unfair because the employer, who were aware that the employee was a diabetic, failed to carry out any medical examination in relation to the explanation that the employee's condition had been aggravated by lack of insulin.

It should be noted that even if the dismissal is unfair, in circumstances where the employee was admittedly drunk, there is likely to be a high degree of contributory conduct so as to reduce compensation or, alternatively, a Tribunal may find that the individual would have been dismissed in any event if a fair procedure had been followed (**Nairne v Highland and Islands Fire Brigade** [1989] IRLR 366).

Criminal Offences

Reasonableness

The test as to whether there are sufficient reasons to dismiss is whether the employer has a reasonable belief formed on reasonable grounds and not whether the employer believes that the employee is guilty on a balance of probabilities or beyond reasonable doubt (See the *Burchell* test set out at page 150). If the employer did have a reasonable belief after carrying out a proper investigation it will be entitled to dismiss (**Scottish Midland Co-operative Society Limited v Cullion** [1991] IRLR 161). Where there is more than one suspect it may be reasonable to dismiss all suspects (see page 114).

Where the criminal offence is committed outside work it may still be reasonable to dismiss if the nature of the offence is such that it has an impact upon the employer's business or reputation or means that the employer can no longer have trust and confidence in the employee. Dishonesty offences may mean that the employer can no longer tolerate the employee in the workplace. Other offences may, by their very nature (for example sexual offences) be incompatible with the employee's continued employment. Because the offence may be under investigation by the police, or be subject to criminal proceedings it is particularly important to consider what investigatory steps may be taken by the employer in these circumstances.

Even where it has been shown that there has been misconduct a dismissal will not necessarily be fair. It was held in **Johnson Matthey Metals Limited v Harding** [1978] IRLR 248 that the dismissal of an employee with 15 years' service was unfair where the offence committed was not in relation to the employer but was theft from a fellow employee.

Where the employee is in a position of trust a dismissal is likely to be fair even if the sums involved are minor. In **The Maintenance Co Limited v Dormer** [EAT 583/81] it was held to be fair to dismiss a managing director of a company that maintained a fleet of vehicles when he had covertly became involved in the sale of used vehicles with his brother. The EAT stated:

"Under the general law a director of a company is considered to be in many respects in a position similar to that of a trustee. It is his duty to safeguard the interests of the shareholders in the assets and, as such, he must be above reproach. Under the general law a director or a trustee dealing with the company's or the trust's assets in circumstances where his own personal interests and the interests of the company conflict cannot be allowed to retain or take any advantage from such a transaction."

(See also **John Lewis & Co Limited v Smith** [EAT 289/81] – falsification of expense claim by senior employee).

If the offence is deliberate it does not matter that the sums involved are small, so that dismissal was fair in **Trust House Forte Limited v Murphy** [1977] IRLR 186 where the sum involved was £8 and in **Tote Bookmakers v Glossop** [EAT 524/81] where it was only £1.84.

It was held in **Denco Limited v Joinson** [1991] ICR 172; IRLR 63 that the unauthorised use of a password to enter a computer which contained confidential information was gross misconduct which justified summary dismissal. Wood J stated:

"...in this modern industrial world, if an employee deliberately uses an unauthorised password in order to enter or to attempt to enter a computer known to contain information to which he is not entitled, then that of itself is gross misconduct which prima facie will attract summary dismissal, although there may be some exceptional circumstances in which such a response might be held unreasonable. Basically, this is a question of "absolutes" and can be compared with dishonesty. However, because of the importance of preserving the integrity of a computer with its information it is important that management should make it abundantly clear to its workforce that interfering with it will carry severe penalties."

Investigation

The employer may wish to suspend the employee pending the outcome of any investigation. If there is no contractual right of suspension the employee must be suspended on full pay or the employer will be in breach of contract. The employee must be given an opportunity to state his or her case and a failure to do so will render the dismissal unfair (**Lees v The Orchard** [1978] IRLR 20). Where the employer confronts an employee it should be aware that the employee may need time to answer the allegations because he or she may be too upset to respond or may need time to prepare any defence (**Tesco Limited v Hill** [1977] IRLR 63).

The employer will wish to approach the issue of criminal misconduct as an employment matter to decide what impact the offence has upon the future employment relationship. Any investigation is likely to be complicated by the fact that there is a police investigation or the employee is being prosecuted. It is therefore necessary to consider what impact criminal investigations should have upon the employer's investigation or decision to dismiss. There will be several stages in the criminal process that may be relevant:

- the police are making inquiries but there is no decision to prosecute;
- the employee admits his guilt or is caught 'red handed';
- the employee has been charged and a criminal trial is pending;
- the employee is acquitted;
- the employee is found guilty.

Police Inquiries

Where police inquiries are being made and a decision is being made as to whether the employee should or should not be prosecuted this may inhibit the employer's ability to carry out a full investigation into the alleged offence. Indeed, the employee may feel unable to comment about the alleged offence for fear of prejudicing the criminal investigation. The Court of Session took the view that it could be unfair for the employer to carry out an internal investigation where a criminal prosecution was pending in **Carr v Russell Limited** [1976] IRLR 220, though in **Harris (Ipswich) Limited v Harrison** [1978] ICR 1256 the EAT took the view that the employer should still discuss the alleged misconduct with the employee and given the employee an opportunity to provide an explanation if he so wished.

Admission of guilt

Where the employee admits his guilt or there can be no doubt that the employee has committed the offence, because for example, he has been caught red handed, the employer may not need to carry out as detailed an investigation as would otherwise have been warranted. There are many examples of this in the authorities. In **Scottish Special Housing Association v Linnen** [1979] IRLR 463 the dismissal was fair, without further investigation, where the police found stolen goods that belonged to the employer at the employee's home. It was said in **Parker v Clifford Dunn Limited** [1979] ICR 463 that a company is entitled to rely upon the confession of an employee to the police rather than having to intervene by independent inquiries.

Where, on the contrary, the employee refuses to speak or to take part in a disciplinary investigation the employer is still entitled to continue the investigation and to make a decision based upon the evidence which it has before it. Where the evidence leads to a reasonable belief that the employee is guilty of the offence then the employer will be entitled to act upon it (**Harris v Courage (Eastern) Limited** [1982] ICR 530). The employer can rely upon the fact that the employee did not protest his innocence or attempt to follow procedures that may have exonerated him (**Carr v Alexander Russell Limited**).

Where the employee has confessed to the employer, a later retraction is not likely to carry much weight, particularly if the retraction is in the context of criminal proceedings having been instituted (**University College at Buckingham v Phillips** [1982] ICR 318). Criminal principles do not apply to the admissibility of confessions in the employment field so that a confession excluded in a criminal trial may still be relied upon in disciplinary proceedings (**Morley's of Brixton Limited v Minott** [1982] ICR 444; IRLR 270).

Criminal Charges

The Courts have made it clear the mere fact that the employee has been charged with a criminal offence will not justify the employer in concluding that the offence has been committed. Indeed this approach has been described as a 'very dangerous doctrine' (**Scottish Special Housing Association v Cooke** [1979] IRLR 264). As with other offences, the employer must carry out a proper investigation to decide whether or not the employee is guilty of misconduct. The EAT stated:

"We have no hesitation in stating that the mere fact of a charge of theft being preferred, standing by itself and without any further information available to the employer, is not sufficient to constitute reasonable grounds. Moreover, although his investigation into the matter may be limited to the prospect of future criminal proceedings, we do not doubt that some inquiry at least might have disclosed the nature of the information upon which the police were proceeding."

Acquittal

Where the employer believes that there has been misconduct, it is not obliged to await the outcome of any criminal proceedings before carrying out its disciplinary process. Indeed, the employee may later be acquitted on a criminal prosecution but this will not affect the fairness of the employer's decision to dismiss if it had reasonable grounds at the time of dismissal (**Harris (Ipswich) Limited v Harrison** [1978] ICR 1256).

However, if the employer decides to await the outcome of the criminal trial and expressly or impliedly leads the employee to believe that this will be determinative of the outcome, a dismissal may be unfair. It is therefore sensible for the employer to make it clear that the result of the criminal trial will not affect the outcome of the disciplinary hearing. Indeed, even if the employee is acquitted of a criminal offence the facts that emerge at trial may justify dismissal. This was the position in **Greater Manchester Passenger Transport Executive v Sheikh** [EAT] where the employee was dismissed for breaches that became apparent at his trial.

Finding of Guilt

A finding of guilt will usually be sufficient ground for the employer to conclude that the employee is guilty of misconduct but the employer will still be required to carry out a proper investigation and form a view, on reasonable grounds, that the employee is guilty of misconduct. In **Secretary of State for Scotland v Campbell** [1992] IRLR 263 the EAT held that it may be necessary for the employer to carry out an investigation despite the fact that the employee was convicted of embezzlement. In that case sufficient inquiry had been carried out. The employer had monitored what happened at trial and, together with the guilty verdict for a serious offence, had carried out sufficient investigation. If the evidence is conclusive a Tribunal will act perversely if they disregard such evidence (**United Counties Omnibus v Amin** [CA unreported]). Where the employee is given a custodial sentence this may bring an end to the contract of employment by operation of law. (See Chapter 2 Frustration.)

Procedure

Where the matter is not complicated by criminal investigations it is important that the employer carries out any investigation with all due dispatch. This is especially so where the employee may be prejudiced by any delay because of difficulties of recollection of evidence. In **Marley Homecare Limited v Dutton** [1981] IRLR 380 a delay of one week was fatal in the case of a cashier who could not recollect the transaction in relation to which she was accused.

It was held in **Lovie Limited v Anderson** [1999] IRLR 164 that an employer has a duty to investigate depending on the circumstances of the case so that a dismissal which resulted from the employee being charged with offences of indecency was unfair. In the particular case the employee should have been given the opportunity of an interview to put his side of the case.

Factors

Contents of the rules, including the sanctions that are set out

Where the employer has set out clearly in its rules that particular conduct is likely to attract the sanction of dismissal and the employee is aware of the seriousness of the offence, then a dismissal is likely to be regarded as fair. This was the position in **Rotherham Engineering Services Limited v Harrison** [EAT 735/77] where a charge hand left work early and got his colleagues to clock him out. He was fully aware of the seriousness of what he was doing so the dismissal was fair. Where there are rules which are stringently applied a relatively minor breach (i.e. in terms of money) may justify dismissal if it breaks down trust and confidence between employer and employee (**Mecca Leisure Limited v Haggerty** [EAT 324/6/83] where the employee transferred floats cash to cover a temporary shortage).

Gravity of the offence, taking into account mitigation

The nature of the offence will affect the employer's view as to whether the employee can remain in employment. Dishonesty offences may be incompatible with the employee being able to remain in the job. Because of the nature of the job an offence committed outside work may mean that continued employment is not appropriate, in particular where the offence causes a breakdown in trust and confidence or makes the employee's position untenable (i.e. sexual offences).

If the employee is aware that he is behaving dishonestly then dismissal may be justified even though the offence is minor. Where the employee genuinely believes that he has committed no wrong the employer must consider whether the employee did or should have known that the behaviour amounted to misconduct and whether trust and confidence still exists. In **John Lewis & Co Limited v Smith** [EAT 289/81] the EAT accepted that an employee who submitted an expenses slip which she knew was over her entitlement had acted in a manner where she could not be trusted as her integrity was of paramount importance since she was responsible for the procedures in relation to others.

Where the offence if of dishonesty the courts have held that the fact that the amounts involved are trivial does not make an difference if the essential relationship of trust and confidence is undermined (**United Distillers v Conlin** [1992] IRLR 503; **Tote Bookmakers v Glossop** [EAT 524/81]) though there may be circumstances where the offences are so trivial that dismissal is not a reasonable sanction (**Secretary of State for Scotland v Campbell** [1992] IRLR 263).

In considering the gravity of the misconduct the nature of the employment and the effect that offence has on the possibility of continued employment are important factors that will be taken into account. Where the misconduct involves dishonesty, sexual activities or violence this may mean that the employment relationship cannot continue even thought the activity took place outside work. In **Moore v C & A Modes** [1981] IRLR 71, a senior employee was dismissed when she caught shoplifting from a neighbouring store. Despite her long service it was held reasonable to dismiss her. In **Richardson v City of Bradford** [1973] IRLR 296 the employee had been convicted of theft from his local rugby club. It was stated that:

> "It is only right when the integrity of a public servant who is employed in a position where integrity is of prime importance is found to be wanting, the local authority which employs him should take necessary action to remove him from public service."

(See also **Lloyds Bank Plc v Bardin** [EAT 38/89] – cleaner dismissed after being convicted of obtaining money by deception.)

Where the offence may have an impact upon the employer's reputation dismissal may be the appropriate sanction (**Gunn v**

British Waterways Board [EAT 138/81]). In **Baillie-Smith v Avon County Council** [EAT 436/79] it was held that the harmful effects of publicity about an allegation of incest meant that dismissal was fair, though the employee, a teacher, was acquitted on appeal because of doubts about his confession. However, the employer must have some basis for believing that it reputation will be affected. The dismissal of a security guard who had committed a number of sexual offences was held to be unfair in **Securicor Guarding Limited v R** [1994] IRLR 633 where the employee was dismissed because the company feared the reaction of a major customer to this information. No steps had been taken to ascertain the customer's views. The EAT stated that the employer had *"entirely neglected the obvious enquiry of the customer to see what they thought of the situation and how they would with it to be dealt with."*

The fact that the criminal offence has been committed outside work will not make any difference if the nature of the offence is such that it affects the integrity of the employment relationship. There are many examples of dismissal in these circumstances (and see the above cases already cited):

- In **Mercer v Commissioners of Inland Revenue** [EAT 324/78] it was held to be fair to dismiss a tax officer who assisted a friend in burying stolen goods. The EAT noted that *"Mr Mercer, being a tax officer, held a position in which honesty is essential, that his conduct in doing what he did was plainly dishonest and wholly inconsistent with the job that he had."*
- In **Nottinghamshire County Council v Bowly** [1978] IRLR 252 it was held to be fair to dismiss the head of an English department who was convicted of gross indecency and had homosexual inclinations. The EAT found that the majority of the Tribunal had erred in finding the dismissal unfair as they had substituted their decision for that of the employer. A similar approach was taken in **P v Nottinghamshire County Council** [1992] ICR 706; IRLR 262, where a groundsman was dismissed from a girls' school after being convicted of indecently assaulting his daughter.
- In **J Sainsbury Plc v Perry** [EAT 594/81] it was held fair to dismiss a senior manager for theft from neighbouring stores as there was more than a reasonable doubt regarding dishonesty. It did not make any difference that the employee was subsequently acquitted.

- In **Saunders v Scottish National Camps Limited** [1980] IRLR 174 it was fair to dismiss a maintenance handyman from a camp for young people when there were concerns about his homosexuality and he had been involved in an incident at the local town, even though a psychiatrist gave evidence that he represented no danger to young people. The EAT noted that *"a considerable proportion of employers would take the view that the employment of a homosexual should be restricted, particularly when required to work in proximity and in contact with children."*

Where the offence is of dishonesty then it is likely to be incompatible with the employment relationship. It was stated in **Rotherham Engineering Services Limited v Harrison** [EAT 735/77] that clocking offences must be regarded as serious offences which will normally warrant dismissal. Fiddling expenses will normally warrant dismissal even if the employee is a longstanding one (**Standard Telephones and Cables Limited v Burt** [EAT 496/77]) though the employer must still act fairly by permitting the employee a proper disciplinary hearing at which he may make representations (**Rank Xerox (UK) Limited v Goodchild** [EAT 487/78]). It does not matter that the employee makes no financial gain from the offence. Where the nature of the business calls for stringent rules regarding the use of money a breach of those rules may destroy the relationship of trust and confidence even if the employee has made no gain (**Mecca Leisure Limited v Haggerty & Ors** [EAT 324/83] and **AEI Cables Limited v McLay** [1980] IRLR 84).

Drug Abuse

Reasonableness

As with alcohol abuse it may be more appropriate to treat drug addiction as an illness. However, the use of controlled drugs will probably amount to a criminal offence and can more readily be treated as misconduct. Employers should have clear rules that prohibit the use of drugs at work and dismissal of an employee pursuant to such a policy is likely to be fair. It was held in **Walton v TAC Construction Materials Limited** [1981] IRLR 357 to be within the band of reasonable responses to dismiss an addict in line with the company policy against employing drug addicts. Nevertheless, many employers may seek to assist the employee if he is actively seeking a cure and the circumstances in which the drugs came to be taken should be considered. In **Davis v British**

Airways Board [EAT 139/80] it was held unfair to dismiss an airline steward who had taken amphetamines to counteract fatigue without any inquiry into the effect of the drugs on his capability to carry out his job.

Where the relationship of trust and confidence is destroyed because of drug taking dismissal may be fair, as in **Mathewson v B Wilson Dental Laboratory Limited** [EAT 144/88] where the employer had no trust in the employee's ability to carry on his job after his arrest for possession of cannabis.

If the conduct is off duty dismissal will only be a fair sanction where it affects the employment relationship. In **Norfolk County Council v Bernard** [1979] IRLR 220 a drama teacher was convicted of possession and cultivation of cannabis. His dismissal was held to be unfair. The EAT noted that in cases of this nature employees must be of the highest integrity. However, this alone did not make the dismissal fair. There is no automatic rule that the conviction of a teacher in such circumstances will automatically warrant dismissal (see also **Nottinghamshire County Council v Bowly** [1978] IRLR 252).

Procedure

Investigating Drug Abuse

It will usually be necessary for the employer to carry out an investigation even if there has been a conviction since there may be explanations or mitigation that was not relevant to the criminal offence. In some cases employers may carry out random drug testing, particularly in jobs where safety is an important factor. Where an employee has been tested positive, dismissal without a formal hearing can be fair if the employer reasonably forms the view that a hearing can serve no purpose, as in **Sutherland v Sonat Offshire (UK) Inc** [EAT 186/93] where an employee who worked on an offshore rig was positively tested.

Factors

Contents of the Rules, including the sanctions that are set out

It has already been seen that where there are clear rules against the possession of drugs or the use thereof, dismissal for breach of the rules will probably be fair provided that employees are made fully aware of the consequences of breach.

Gravity of the offence taking into account mitigation

There are a number of factors that may make the offence sufficiently grave to warrant dismissal, in particular, where safety is affected, where the employee holds a position of responsibility, the effect upon the reputation or business of the employer and where the employee's position brings the employee into contact with young or impressionable people (see *Bernard* referred to above). Clearly, safety is an important factor, as in *Sutherland* where it was not considered possible to allow someone onto an oil rig who had tested positively for drugs. If the employee holds a position of responsibility, as in **Stentiford v Goodalls Chemist** [COIT] where a trainee dispenser sought to obtain amphetamines when off duty, dismissal will be a fair sanction. If the misconduct affects the reputation or business of the employer dismissal may be fair as in **Gunn v British Waterways Board** [EAT 138/81] where an employee was convicted of drugs offences and the papers had mentioned the name of the employer. The main concern of the respondents was the effect which the history of the employee's conduct was having upon their reputation as a responsible body employing labour in the area.

Intransigent Attitude

Reasonableness

The attitude of an employee to the employer, the system of work, business re-organisations, customers, management or fellow employees may be such that it is no longer possible for the employee to remain employed. In the ordinary course of events investigation into the reasons for the conduct and warning may be appropriate before the employer takes the sanction of dismissal. However, as has been seen (See Chapter 4 at page 100) in *Polkey* the House of Lords recognised that there may be cases where the employer may reasonably take the view that consultation and warnings are futile. In **James v Waltham Holy Cross UDC** [1973] IRLR 202 the appellant asserted that the scope of his job had been reduced but refused to co-operate when his superiors sought to investigate and was disrespectful to the committee hearing the case. He was dismissed on the basis that his attitude and demeanour were not conducive to harmonious staff relations and his employers had lost confidence in his ability to maintain the relationship necessary for his job. The NIRC agreed with the Tribunal that the dismissal was fair, though no warning or opportunity to explain had been given. Sir John Donaldson commented that it may be reasonable to dismiss without giving an opportunity of an explanation where the employee:

"as part of the conduct complained of, states in terms why he is adopting that attitude. If it is clear that this is the employee's considered view and not merely the result of a passing emotion, there can be no point in giving him an opportunity of re-stating a view the expression of which led to the decision to dismiss him. But even so, an employer should be slow to conclude that an opportunity to reflect and a subsequent opportunity to explain could in no circumstances produce a changed situation in which dismissal would be unnecessary."

Where it is plain that the employee is never going to change his views then it may be fair to dismiss without further or any warning since any further period will not achieve any result (see **Mintoft v Armstrong Massey Limited** [EAT 516/80]). However, it is important that an employee is made aware that he is putting his job in jeopardy by continuing to adopt such an intransigent attitude (**Hart v Baxters (Butchers) Limited** [EAT 489/81]).

Attitude to working practices

There have been a number of cases where an employee's intractable opposition to a change in working practices has resulted in dismissal being fair, as happened in **Retarded Children's Aid Society v Day** [1978] ICR 437 where the employee stuck to his view that the employer's work methods were wrong. In the Court of Appeal, Lord Denning MR noted that an employee should not normally be dismissed for a first offence but in some cases it may be proper and reasonable to dismiss at once "especially with a man who is determined to go on his own way".

Attitude to customers

Where an employee is unable to change his attitude or his conduct has been such that he is no longer able to with customers it may be fair to dismiss without express warning, as in **A J Dunning & Sons (Shopfitters) Limited v Jacomb** [1973] IRLR 448 where the employee could no longer work for a major client and had "known over a relatively long period of time that his inability to get on with clients was placing his job in jeopardy."

Attitude to co-employees

Where a work situation has developed that employees will not co-operate with each other the employer should take steps to ascertain the cause and the possibility of improving the relationship. In **Turner v Vestric Limited** [1980] ICR 528, the EAT stated that the employer should satisfy itself that the position is irredeemable before dismissing.

Investigation

The reason for the attitude

As part of its duty to investigate the employer should seek to ascertain the reason for the employee's attitude as it may have been triggered by an extraneous factor of which the employer was not aware, as in **Mock v Glamorgan Aluminium Co** [EAT 493/80]) where the employee's behaviour was triggered by the fact that she had been assaulted by her manager.

Warnings

We have already seen that warnings may not be necessary in this context. What is necessary, however, is that the employee is made to realise the risk that continuance of the behaviour may have upon the contract of employment.

Loyalty

Reasonableness

All contracts of employment contain an implied term of fidelity and good faith (See Duggan, *Wrongful Dismissal: Law, Practice and Precedents*). The employment relationship is predicated upon a certain degree of loyalty from staff to their employer. However, there is a limit to what employers can expect in terms of loyalty, depending upon the nature of the employment contract and the nature and status of the work of the employee. In this situation the express terms of the contract may be of importance and this is considered further below. It is also important to consider whether the conduct complained of took place during or outside the working hours required by the contract of employment and, as with many conduct cases, the position in which the employer harbours a reasonable belief must be considered.

As with other conduct cases, it is necessary for the employer to show that there was a clear breach of the duty of fidelity or that the employer had a genuine and reasonable belief based upon reasonable investigation. In some cases the employer may only have suspicion as opposed to a reasonable belief. This was the position in **S & U Stores Limited v Bessant** [EAT 8/82] where the employer suspected a cashier at their Bridgend office of assisting an ex manager who had set up in competition. There was insufficient evidence to support a reasonable belief in guilt. The EAT commented;

> "We have sympathy with the employees in this case since there are cases where there is leakage of confidential information but it is very difficult to be reasonably satisfied that the employee in question is guilty of the conduct of which she is suspected. There may be cases where the nature of the leakage of information is such that the damage to the business of the employers would be so great that there would be "some other substantial reason" being the risk of damage to the company which would make dismissal for such a reason fair even though the matter had not progressed beyond grave suspicion. We would not rule out a case where, even though there was not reasonable belief in guilt, the suspicion was so great and the potential damage so great that dismissal might be justifiable on the ground of anticipated loss of a major nature to the company. But we think that would be an exceptional case."

It is possible to identify at least four factual situations where an employer may feel justified in dismissing on the ground that the employee has breached his duty of fidelity:

- Where the employee uses, proposes to use or passes on confidential information belonging to the employer whilst still employed.
- Where the employee is preparing to set up in competition with the employer whilst still employed.
- Where the employee acts in competition with the employer, whether by himself or through a third party whilst still employed.
- Where the employee has another job outside working hours i.e. 'moonlighting'.

Use of confidential information
Where the employee has access to confidential information there will be an implied term in the contract of employment that such

information will not be used other than for the purposes of the employer, without express permission. There will often be an express clause in the contract of employment to this effect. The information may not be used for any purposes, not just for the purposes of competition. In **Monk v Vine Products** [EAT 248/79], for example, a personnel manager was fairly dismissed when he disclosed information to shop stewards that placed his employer at a disadvantage in negotiations.

It is necessary for there to be a fair investigation and failure to carry out a proper procedure is likely to render the dismissal unfair (see below).

It is sometimes argued that disclosure of confidential information is in the public interest and the fairness of a dismissal may be open to challenge on this ground. In **Cornelius v London Borough of Hackney** [EAT 437/92] the employee sent copies of a confidential report to third parties where he was concerned about internal corruption. His dismissal was held to be unfair thought reduced for contribution. This may be contrasted with **Byford v Film Finances Limited** [EAT 804/86] in which it was held a dismissal was fair because the employee had gone behind the directors' backs, even though she suspected illegal activities.

Under the Public Interest Disclosure Act 1998 'whistleblowing' may, in certain circumstances, be protected. See Chapter 19.

In some situations an employer may fear that an employee may disclose confidential information; for example where a spouse, member of family or boyfriend or girlfriend works for a rival organisation. Dismissal may be fair on the basis of SOSR as in **Dyer v Inverclyde Taxis Limited** [EAT 462/87] where a husband went to work for a rival firm and the Tribunal accepted there was a risk of confidential information being passed on, despite the wife's assurances to the contrary. However, if there is no risk then an employer is likely to have acted unfairly if they have not fully investigated the matter (**Southwick v Linar Limited** [EAT 661/86]). It should also be noted that there may be a claim for sex discrimination where an employer dismisses a female in such circumstances. Moreover, there must be some basis for the belief that confidential information may be passed on or that the employer's business may be in some way affected. In **Blacks of Greenock v Hamer** [EAT 565/77] a dismissal was unfair where the employee's husband set up a rival business some 15 miles away. There could be no reasonable belief that confidential information would be passed on and any risk to the business was minimal. Moreover, there was no express prohibition in the contract of employment.

Setting up in competition during employment

Where an employee proposes to leave the employment of his employer to set up in competition, by himself or a third party, without more there will not usually be sufficient ground to dismiss the employee as he has not done anything to place himself in breach of the duty of fidelity. Merely proposing to set up in competition once the employment relationship has ended is not enough to amount to a breach of the duty of fidelity, though as will be seen, an employer is entitled to take steps to protect itself. That a mere intention to set up in competition is not enough is made clear by the EAT in **Laughton and Hawley v Bapp Industrial Supplies Limited** [1986] IRLR 245. Two employees who intended to set up in competition wrote to many of the employer's suppliers stating that they intended to start their own business. The employees were dismissed after the letter came to the attention of the managing director. In the Notice of Appearance it was alleged that they were guilty of gross misconduct/breach of trust. A Tribunal found the dismissals fair but this was reversed on appeal since the EAT considered that there had been no misuse of confidential information. An indication of an intention to set up in competition was not in itself a breach of the implied term and in the absence of an express term there must be some evidence of misconduct.:

> "The crucial question on this appeal is whether it is a breach of the term of loyalty for an employee whilst still in the employment of his employer to indicate an intention to set up in competition with the employer in the future. The employer and the Tribunal have assumed that it is. In our view, the Tribunal fell into error in accepting that the indication of such intention was in itself sufficient.

In *Harris and Russell Ltd v Slingsby* [1973] IRLR 221 Sir Hugh Griffiths, giving the judgment of the National Industrial Relations Court, said at p.222:

> 'This Court ... would regard it as a wholly insufficient reason to dismiss a man, that he was merely seeking employment with a competitor, unless it could be shown that there were reasonably solid grounds for supposing that he was doing so

in order to abuse his confidential position and information with his present employers. In the nature of things, when a man changes employment, it is more likely he will be seeking fresh employment with someone in the same line of business and therefore, a competitor of his present employers'."

Seeking work with a competitor will, likewise, not be a good reason for dismissal (as in *Harris & Russell Limited v Slingsby*) unless the employee is reasonably believed to be intending to misuse his position or confidential information that he possesses. Merely applying for other jobs is not sufficient for a reasonable belief that this is the position.

In some circumstances setting up in competition during employment may justify dismissal where the relationship of trust and confidence is broken, as in **Mansard Precision Engineering Co Limited v Taylor** [1978] ICR 44. However, certain positive steps may go beyond mere preparation and amount to a breach, as in **Adamson v B & L Cleaning Services Limited** [1995] IRLR 193, where the employee had asked a client if he could be put on the tender list. The employer is, however, entitled to protect himself and a refusal to transfer from a confidential position or co-operate with the employer may be a factor that justifies dismissal (see below).

Acting in competition during employment

Where the employee actively competes with the employer during employment this will be a clear breach of the employment relationship. Competition during working by using the employer's resources without express permission is the clearest possible breach. The EAT in **Golden Cross Hire Co v Lovell** [1979] IRLR 267 stated that where a senior employee has set out to assist his employer's potential competitor and to make use of his employer's premises for that purpose, and is later shown to have lied about it, that is misconduct of such gravity that no reasonable Tribunal ought to find that the dismissal was unfair.

The attempted solicitation of the employer's customers will almost certainly justify dismissal. In **Baxter v Wreyfield** [EAT 9/82] a customer complained that she had been approached to transfer her business to Mrs Baxter and her husband. The dismissal was held to be unfair as there was no proper investigation but no compensation was awarded as the evidence showed clear misconduct. Browne Wilkinson J noted that she only had herself to blame for her dismissal and that she had conducted an act of industrial misconduct of a very serious nature, that is, stealing customers from the employer.

Moonlighting

It is clear that merely taking up other employment outside working hours is not, without more, a breach of the duty of fidelity. It may even be legitimate for the other employment to be with a competition provided that it does not affect the interests of the employer. In the absence of an express term there is no breach of contract. The Court of Appeal made it clear in **Hivac Limited v Park Royal Scientific Instruments Limited** [1946] 1 Ch 169 that there is unlikely to be any breach in relation to out of hours activities if the employer's legitimate business interests are not interfered with.

However, the use of confidential information or certain skills or a real risk of harm to the employer's business by carrying out spare time work is likely to breach the implied term of fidelity. Employers should be careful not to overreact and not to apply any sanctions until they are clear that there is such a risk of harm.. In **EETPU v Parnham & Farnham** [EAT 378/78], a married couple worked as kitchen assistant and chef at a conference centre, their weekends being free. They were both dismissed when the wife got a weekend job at a 'Little Chef'. The action did nothing to harm the business and they had not been warned of the risk of dismissal if such outside hours employment was taken up. The EAT stated:

> "It would be deplorable if it were laid down that a workman could consistently with his duty to his employer, knowingly deliberately and secretly set himself to do in his spare time something which would inflict great harm on his employer's business...
>
> Nothing that Mr and Mrs Parnham did could ever be said to have inflicted great or any harm upon the appellant..."

A similar view was taken in **Novas Plastics Limited v Froggatt** [1982] IRLR 146 where an odd job man worked for a competitor in his spare time. The EAT thought that it was necessary to show great harm to the employer where the activities were in the employee's spare time before it could be said that there was a breach of trust.

The emphasis is on the fact that the spare time activities may cause serious harm to the employer and the employer must satisfy itself of this if the dismissal is to be fair. In **Scottish Daily Record &**

Sunday Mail (1986) Limited v Laird (see page 154) this argument failed where the editor of a newspaper was involved with two free regional papers in his spare time as his activities were minimal and could cause no harm to the employer.

Investigation

It is clear from the above that a reasonable employer should carry out an investigation to satisfy itself that the activities of the employee are in breach of the duty of fidelity and are likely to cause harm to the employer. The employee should be given a chance to put his case before dismissal as it may become apparent that the activities cause no harm to the employer. In **Ladbroke Racing Limited v Mason** [1978] ICR 49 it was also pointed out that an employee may choose to cease activities if faced with the threat of dismissal and that this is a reason that allegations should be put to the individual.

As with all cases of misconduct the employer should act promptly on discovering a breach so that he cannot be taken to have waived the breach or condoned the activities (**Thorn (UK) Limited v Little** [EAT 455/95]).

The employee should be given the chance to explain his activities and warned, though in cases where the employee has engaged in active steps during the employer's time, using the employer's resources dismissal without warning is likely to be fair. In **Coltman v Multilite (Rooflights) Limited** [EAT 585/79] the EAT said that where an employee sets up business in competition with his employer it is not reasonable to conclude that a prior warning would have made any difference.

Refusal to transfer/vary terms whilst still employed

When an employer discovers that an employee is intending to set up in competition it may seek to protect its business by transferring the employee to other duties, placing on garden leave or transferring to another place of work. If the contract does not contain such power there may be a breach of contract and the employee may resign and claim unfair constructive dismissal. On the other hand if the employer has properly consulted with the employee and explained the reasons for the variation in terms, any dismissal for refusal to agree the varied terms may be fair if there are sound reasons for the same (See **Ford v Milton Toleman Limited** [1980] IRLR 30). Moreover, a dismissal for a refusal to agree to varied terms may be for

'SOSR' and fair on this basis (See Chapter 8 and see **Davidson and Maillou v Comparisons** [1980] IRLR 360).

An employer may seek to impose restrictive covenants and a dismissal for refusal to accept such a covenant may be for 'SOSR'. In **R S Components Limited v Irwin** [1973] ICR 535 an employer sought to introduce restrictive covenants because of their experience of salesmen setting up in business and approaching customers. The EAT held that the employer was entitled to protect itself in this way and any dismissal was for 'SOSR' and, in the circumstances fair.

Factors

Contents of the Rules, including the sanctions that are set out

The terms of the contract of employment may expressly forbid the employee from working in any other business during the period of employment. In **Hughes v Christoe & Co** [EAT 21/77], the contract provided that the employee could not work 'in any other business not associated with the company' (insurance broking). The employee set up a newsagents/grocers with his wife and informed his employers who did not expressly disapprove. He was then dismissed because it was thought the venture would affect his ability to carry out work with the employer. The EAT took the view that the dismissal was unfair as there was no evidence of any deterioration in the quality of his work and there had been insufficient investigation, no warning and no chance for the employee to reconsider his position:

> "There appears to have been no very thorough investigation of the circumstances; there was no warning and there appears to have been little or no opportunity provided for an adequate statement of the case by the appellant...we consider it would have been reasonable for them in the first instance to have given him a warning and an opportunity of adjusting his arrangements in order to meet with the requirements of his contract."

In **Casson v John Lewis & Co Limited** [EAT 266/77], on the other hand, where a contract provided that the employee had to inform the employer of any outside business interests and the employee lied about the same, it was fair to dismiss as the relationship of confidence had broken down.

Language

Reasonableness

Whether dismissal may be fair for the use of abusive or bad language depends upon the nature of the workplace and the circumstances of the individual case. The type of language that may be acceptable on the shop floor may be different from what is acceptable in the Boardroom. In **Burnett v City of Glasgow** [EAT 491/76]. Mr Burnett, a baths attendant, was dismissed after refusing to move to another baths, using foul and abusive language to his departmental manager. He was held to be fairly dismissed, EAT commenting that in cases of this nature every situation must be assessed according to the individual facts. It is necessary to consider the context in which the language is used in deciding whether dismissal is a fair sanction for the conduct. It should be noted that some incidents may fit more appropriately under 'SOSR', for example where there is a personality clash that leads to a one off outburst (see **Lashirie v Brass & Alloy Pressings** [EAT 35/81]).

Factors

The Courts have identified a number of factors that are relevant:

The Employee's position

Language may not be acceptable from an employee who is a member of management and the language is directed at his superiors. In **Morris v Sperry Corporation** [EAT 51/81], Mr Morris, a senior legal executive, objected to a re-organisation that he considered to be a demotion in a series of abusive letters and telephone conversations. The EAT thought that he had behaved "in an irresponsible way quite out of keeping with the behaviour that any corporation would expect of a senior legal executive...". His dismissal was fair (See also **Snow v Wiltshire County Council** [EAT 215/80]).

It is clear that the employee's position is an important factor in considering whether the sanction of dismissal is fair.

The work environment

It has already been noted that the standard to be expected of an employee may to some extent depend upon the work environment. However, where the work of an employee entails contact with the public, different considerations may apply if the business of the employer may be affected (See **Sketchley v Kissoon** ([EAT] 514/79).

Effect on employer's business

As well as affecting the employer's business with customers, the use of bad or abusive language may have a detrimental effect on discipline if it undermines the authority of management as well as affecting the working environment if it causes disaffection amongst employees. It was made clear by the EAT in **MacIsaac v James Ferries & Co** [EAT 1442/96] that abusive language to a superior may cause an irreparable breach in the working relationship such that it becomes impossible of continuation.

Workplace abuse towards other employees may have the same effect, particularly where a difficult workplace situation is further exacerbated as in **Henry v National Coal Board** (Court of Appeal 30th March 1988) where returning miners abused those who had already returned to work some time earlier.

Mitigating Circumstances

In some cases the circumstances surrounding the incident may need to be considered, for example where the behaviour is out of character or is a one off act. This was the position in **Charles Letts & Co Limited v Howard** [1976] IRLR 248, where Mr Howard, whilst under the influence of drink, was abusive to a superior arising out of a re-organisation of the office layout. The Tribunal found that he had not been given a chance to explain his conduct or to apologise before he was dismissed. The EAT noted that the Tribunal had thought that there would have been a prospect that eventually the employee would have been brought to his senses and would have been persuaded to apologise so that the working relationship could be re-established, since:

> "...particularly in a case of what appears to have been a sudden explosion and loss of temper by a man who was under the influence of drink, it must be important for an officer, weighing the pros and cons of dismissal, or of lenience, to send for the man concerned and give him every opportunity and encouragement to climb off his high horse and to apologise so that maters can be put right before it is too late."

The desirability of a proper investigation and hearing, where the employee is given a chance to explain and, if appropriate, apologise is clear from this case.

Personal Hygiene and Appearance

Reasonableness

The nature of the employer's business may be such that it expects a certain standard of hygiene and appearance especially where the employee's job involves conduct with the public. In such circumstances a refusal to comply with dress or appearance policies may mean that a dismissal is fair. This was the position in **Boychuk v HJ Symons Holdings Limited** [1977] IRLR 395 where the employee, a ledger clerk in contact with the public, wore badges proclaiming the fact that she was a lesbian. She was given the choice of removing the badges or dismissal. The EAT stated that:

"...a reasonable employer, who after all is ultimately responsible for the interests of the business, can be allowed to decide what, upon reflection and mature consideration, could be offensive to the customers and to fellow-employees. We do not think that it can be said to be necessary for him to wait and see whether the business is damaged or what disruption is caused before he takes steps in those circumstances."

The employer has a large amount of discretion as to the image that it wishes to project for the business (**Schmidt v Austicks Bookshops Limited** [1977] IRLR 360; 1978 ICR 85) provided that it does not impose unnecessary or unreasonable requirements. It should however, be noted that in certain circumstances clothing requirements may be discriminatory if the requirements amount to indirect discrimination against a particular group (i.e. dress requirements in relation to a Sikh as in **Kaur v Kingston AHA** [1981] ICR 631 – though the result of this case was reversed by legislation).

The interests of hygeine may also dictate appearance as in **Singh v RHM Bakeries (Southern) Limited** [EAT 818/77] where it was held to be fair to dismiss a Sikh because there was a rule against beards imposed in the interests of hygiene.

Sleeping on Duty

Reasonableness

The employer should have a specific rule against sleeping on duty which spells out the consequences of such a breach though it was noted in **Ayub v Vauxhall Motors Limited** [1978] IRLR 428 that the absence of such a rule will not necessarily make a dismissal unfair. However, the offence of sleeping on duty is more likely to attract a warning in the first instance (see **McDonagh v Johnson & Nephew (Manchester) Limited** [EAT 140/78]). It will be important for employees to apply a rule against sleeping on duty consistently, taking into account the employee's length of service, work record and the effect on the employer's business and safety.

Third Parties

Reasonableness of Dismissal under Third Party Pressure

Where the employer is given an ultimatum by a customer that it is not prepared to allow the employee to carry out work for it anymore a dismissal may in these circumstances be fair. This was the position in **Scott Packing & Warehousing Limited v Paterson** [1978] IRLR 166 where the company's best customer stated that it would no longer place work with the employee. Dismissal without investigating the customer's reasons was found to be fair in **Dolphin Drilling Limited v Payne** [EAT 1060/97] in a case where the employee had already received two warnings about his conduct. Nevertheless, the employer should consider the question of whether the employee may be accomodated in another part of the workplace.

Refusal to Obey Instructions

Reasonableness

As its first category of misconduct, *Harvey* refers to a 'refusal to obey a lawful and reasonable order of the employer'. It is obvious that an employee cannot be expected to obey instructions from employers no matter how unreasonable or even unlawful. The test is ultimately that of reasonableness as with other areas of conduct.

Employees are under a duty to obey instructions that may be given within the legitimate scope of the contract of employment provided that they are lawful and reasonable. There may be certain circumstances in which it was reasonable for the employee to refuse to obey instructions even if that amounts to a breach of contract so that dismissal is unfair.

Even if there is not an express term, there will be an implied term in the contract of employment that the employee will obey the lawful and reasonable instructions of the employer. A refusal to obey instructions is likely to strike at the heart of the employment relationship and justify dismissal. However, the employee is not obliged to obey every instruction given by the employer. The Tribunal will ask itself the following questions:

- Could the instruction legitimately be given under the express or implied terms of the contact of employment?
- Was the instruction given to the employee a reasonable one in the circumstances?
- Even if the instruction was one that could lawfully be given under the contract did the employee act reasonably in refusing to obey the instruction?

Legitimate Instruction

Where the instruction is one that may be given to the employee under the express or implied terms of the contract of employment, a refusal to obey will amount to a breach of contract and is likely to amount to misconduct whereby the any dismissal will be fair. The starting point for the Tribunal will be to examine the express terms of the contract to ascertain the scope of the employee's duties and obligations. The employee will also be subject to implied terms, in particular that he obey the lawful and reasonable instructions of the employer in the performance of his job. The job description may be in sufficiently wide terms to encompass duties that the employee has not hitherto carried out (**Glitz v Watford Electric Co Limited** [1979] IRLR 89). The express or implied scope of the job functions will be of paramount importance since the employer is likely to act unfairly if he requires the employee to perform tasks that go beyond the basis on which he was recruited. This was the position in **Redbridge London Borough Council v Fishman** [1978] ICR 156 where a teacher had been employed to work in administration. A requirement that additional teaching duties were taken on was a breach of contract and was unfair. The employee had been assured that she was not being employed to teach so the imposition of teaching requirements was unreasonable. The EAT noted that the requirements of the contract are not conclusive in deciding whether a dismissal was unfair.

> "Many dismissals are unfair although the employer is contractually entitled to dismiss the employee. Contrariwise, some dismissals are not unfair although the employer was not contractually entitled to dismiss the employee. Although the contractual rights and duties are not irrelevant to the question posed by [section 98] they are not of the first importance."

In **Farrant v The Woodroffe School** [1998] ICR 184; IRLR 176 the employer sought to change the duties of a teacher in the mistaken but genuine belief that they had such a right. The dismissal was held to be fair. HHJ Peter Clark stated:

> "Where the claim is for unfair dismissal, and the employer relies upon a refusal to obey an instruction as the reason for dismissal, the lawfulness of the instruction will be central to any question of constructive dismissal, but of relevance to, not determinative of, the fairness of the dismissal."

Reasonable instruction

Since the Tribunal is looking at the reasonableness of the conduct of the employer, as stated in *Farrant*, the contractual position is not determinative and the Tribunal will go on to consider whether the instruction was reasonable in the circumstances. This can mean that an order which goes beyond the contract is nevertheless reasonable so that dismissal for refusal to obey is fair. This was the position in **Coward v John Menzies (Holdings) Limited** [1977] IRLR 428 where a branch manger refused to transfer from Leicester to Swansea to train as an assistant manager. There was no contractual entitlement to require such a transfer but the employers were found to have acted fairly in the interests of their business. On the other hand an unreasonable requirement to carry out an instruction that may be given within the terms of the contract will make a dismissal unfair, as in **Davies v Jack Troth t/a Richards Transport** [EAT 81/87] where the employee refused an overnight stay because he did not have any money or a change of clothes. The instruction was within the scope of the contract but the order given was not reasonable.

Reasonable refusal

An employee may act reasonably in refusing to obey an order and this is a matter that will be taken into account by the tribunal. This was the case in **UCATT v Brain** [1981] ICR 542 where the employee refused to sign an undertaking that could have exposed him to liability for libel claims. Although his refusal was a breach of contract it was reasonable in the circumstances. (See also **Osborn Transport Services v Chrissanthou** [EAT 412/77] – refusal to visit a customer when the employee had been told he would not have to go there again.) Where the employee is given an instruction that is contrary to the terms of his contract he may be acting reasonably in refusing to carry out that instruction (**Skelton v Biddles (Bookbinders) Limited** [EAT 332/86]).

A to Z of Specific Examples of Refusal to Obey Instructions

Company rules

Where there is a company rule which provides that breach of a particular requirement may mean the sanction of dismissal, the Tribunal will still consider whether the dismissal was reasonable in the circumstances. In **Scottish Grain Distillers Limited v McNee & Lennox** [EAT 34/82] there was an absolute rule against the possession of alcohol on the Company's premises. The two employees were dismissed when it was found that they had jars in their lockers which contained a fluid that had less than a 1% alcohol content. Despite the 'rigid regulations' the Tribunal found that the quantity of alcohol was so small that the de minimis rule applied so that the dismissals were unfair. It was made clear in **Ladbroke Racing Limited v Arnott & Ors** [1983] IRLR 154 that the existence of a rule which contains an absolute prohibition is still subject to the employer acting reasonably. The Court of Session stated:

"While the appropriate rule in each case specifically stated that a breach of the Rule would result in dismissal that cannot in itself necessarily meet the requirements of [section 98] which calls for the employer satisfying the tribunal that in the circumstances (having regard to equity and the substantial merits of the case) he acted reasonably in treating it as sufficient reason for dismissal. This seems to me to indicate that there may be different degrees of gravity in the admitted or proved offence, and, as each case has to be considered on its own facts, consideration has to be given, inter alia, to the degree of culpability involved."

Where the offence is minor dismissal may be unfair even it is clearly in breach of agreed rules (**Laws Stores Limited v Oliphant** [1978] IRLR 251) unless it can be shown that there is a need for absolute enforcement of the rules (**Ferguson v Stakis Casinos Limited** [EAT 223/81]). However, if the employee has made it clear that he is not prepared to abide by the rules so that there is a risk of a further breach then dismissal may be fair (**Retarded Children's Aid Society v Day** [1978] ICR 437; IRLR 128). Lord Denning stated that: *"It may be proper and reasonable to dismiss at once, especially with a man who is determined to go on in his own way"*. Moreover, a continual failure to obey instructions may justify dismissal (**Marshall v Alexander Sloan & Co Limited** [1981] IRLR 264).

Duties

The scope of the employer's duties will be contained in the express or implied terms or the contract of employment. The contract may also specify the sanctions that will be applied for breach of these duties and if the sanction of dismissal is not specified (i.e. because there is a process of warnings) any dismissal for breach will be unfair (**Wiggins Teape Fine Papers Limited v Murchison** [EAT 322/89]). However, a proposed change in the employee's duties may be reasonable and, thus dismissal for refusal to comply fair, even though the change is not stated as being permissible under the contract (see, in particular, the sections on overtime and emergencies below). A refusal to undertake a small increase in duties may warrant dismissal (**Bowater Containers Limited v McCormack** [1980] IRLR 50).

Emergencies

In some circumstances the employer may require the employee to carry out additional duties because of an emergency at work and refusal to comply may warrant dismissal. This was the position in **Martin v Solus Schall** [1979] IRLR 7 where an employee was fairly dismissed for refusing to work overtime in an emergency. Similarly, in **Grigg v Daylay Eggs Limited** [EAT 426/79] the EAT took the view that it was reasonable to require an employee to work away from home for one week and dismissal for refusal was fair. Talbot J stated:

> "In our view, when the tribunal found that the employers were entitled to look for, and receive, help from senior staff in times of crisis, they rightly stated the kind of obligation that an employer can look to in an employee and ask him to fulfill."

(See also **Tennant Caledonian Breweries Limited v McKiddie** [EAT 674/86]).

Health and safety

Where the employee refuses to obey an instruction because of health and safety reasons then an dismissal may be unfair under section 100 of the ERA 1996 (See Chapter 15). It should also be noted that the employer may be obliged to consider a reasonable adjustment under the DDA 1995 where work practices have an impact upon a disabled person. However, where an employee unreasonably refuses to work dismissal may be fair (**Lindsay v Dunlop Limited** [1980] IRLR 93). Moreover, if there is no alternative work for an employee who is adversely affected by the working environment dismissal may be fair, as in **Jagdeo v Smiths Industries Limited** [1982] ICR 47 where the employer had no alternative but to dismiss an employee who had an allergy to soldering fumes and there were no practical steps that could be taken to prevent this.

Hours of work

Where the employer finds it necessary to change the hours of work for the needs of the business a refusal to accept such change my justify dismissal. This will particularly be the case where a re-organisation has been carried out with proper consultation and the business may be otherwise brought to a standstill (**Ellis v Brighton Co-operative Society Limited** [1976] IRLR 419). However, employers should properly consult about proposed changes and it may be unreasonable to expect an employee to agree to blanket changes that will contractually oblige the employee to work whatever hours the employer requires (**Evans v Elementa Holdings** [1982] IRLR 143; ICR 323). The employer should be prepared to listen to, and take into account, any objections by employees as to why they are not prepared to agree a change in hours and consider whether any alternatives or exceptions are possible (**Martin v Automobile Proprietary Limited** [1979] IRLR 64) and should in any event ensure that any change in the hours of work is handled fairly and equitably within the workforce (**Dale v Lignacite Products Limited** [EAT 138/78]).

Overtime

Whilst the employee may not be contractually required to work overtime, a persistent refusal to work overtime where it is necessary for the needs of the business may justify dismissal (**Horrigan v Lewisham LBC** [1978] ICR 15 and see the cases in relation to changing hours or work).

Specific instructions

There are a vast number of cases which consider when it is reasonable for the employee to refuse to comply with specific instructions given by the employer. The following principles emerge:

- Deliberate refusal to rectify a mistake or poor work is likely to mean that dismissal is within the band of reasonable responses (**Hayden Nilos Conflos v Chapman** [EAT 415/80]).
- An express prohibition of which the employee is fully aware may justify dismissal even though the employer did not suffer any loss (**McCall v Castleton Crafts** [1979] IRLR 218) and deliberate refusal to comply with a specific instruction may justify dismissal without warning (**Courtney v Babcock & Wilcox (Operations) Limited** [1977] IRLR 30; **Kaye v Blackwell (Contracts) Limited** [EAT 765/78]).
- Where the employee refuses to comply with an instruction because of a mistaken belief that he was acting in his contractual rights a dismissal may be unfair if the employer has not given sufficient warning that the employee is mistaken and that certain consequences may follow (**Wallace v EJ Guy Limited** [1973] IRLR 175; ICR 117).
- Where the instruction given by the employer is unlawful, dismissal for refusal to carry it out will be unlawful (**Morrish v Henlys (Folkestone) Limited** [1977] ICR 482; IRLR 61).

Training

Where the employer forms the view that the employee is lacking in capability or qualifications it may reasonably require the employee to undergo training and a refusal to do so will probably result in a fair dismissal for misconduct even if there is no contractual right to require training (**Coward v John Menzies (Holdings) Limited** [1977] IRLR 428; **Minter v Wellingborough Foundries (BL) Cars Limited** [EAT 105/80]).

Transfers and mobility

Where there is an express mobility clause or the nature of the contract of employment leads to an implication that the employee be mobile, refusal to transfer the place of work may amount to misconduct and merit dismissal. However, the employer must act reasonably in requiring the employee to move so that failure to investigate the reasons for refusal (**Wilson v IDR Construction Limited** [1975] IRLR 260) or the unreasonable imposition of such an instruction (for example where it will cause the employee financial and personal loss **United Bank v Akhtar** [1989] IRLR 507) can make a dismissal unfair even if the employer is acting within the terms of the contract of employment.

Spent Convictions

Under the Rehabilitation of Offenders Act 1974 convictions become 'spent' provided that the convictions is not a custodial sentence of over thirty months. Tables A and B to the Act set out differing rehabilitation periods depending on the nature of the offence. Once a conviction is spent, by section 4(2), any question seeking information with respect to a person's previous convictions is to be treated as not relating to spent convictions. There are a number of excepted professions (i.e. teachers, social workers and certain regulation professions such as insurance managers – see the Rehabilitation of Offenders 1974 (Exceptions) Order 1975/1023 and 1986/1249). Dismissal for not disclosing a spent conviction is therefore likely to be unfair (**Property Guards Limited v Taylor** [1982] IRLR 175; **Hendry v Scottish Liberal Club** [1977] IRLR 5). However, deliberate concealment of a conviction that is not spent or concealment in a manner that forfeits the employer's trust and confidence may lead to a finding that it was reasonably to dismiss (**Torr v British Railways Board** [1977] ICR 785; IRLR 184).

(See also Chapter 13.)

Violence

Reasonableness

Violence at work will be regarded as misconduct. The Tribunal should consider the reasonableness of the employer's decision to dismiss and not become 'bogged down' with issues of whether the incident amounts to gross misconduct or breach of contract. This is what happened in **C A Parsons & Co Limited v McCoughlin** [1978] IRLR 65 where the Tribunal analysed whether a fight amounted to gross misconduct under the terms of the contract of employment. The EAT stated that:

> "..in these days it ought not be necessary for anybody, let alone a shop steward, to have in black and white in the form of a rule that a fight is something which is going to be regarded very gravely by management."

No every incident will merit summary dismissal even if this is stated in the company rules as being the sanction that will be applied (**Taylor Woodrow Construction Limited v Veale** [EAT 544/76]).

Where the assault takes place outside the workplace dismissal will be fair where the conduct has an impact on the work environment. In **Stevenson v Golden Wonder Limited** [1977] IRLR 474 it was stated that a serious assault on a fellow employee in the aggressor's "own time and outside factory premises" warranted dismissal whilst in **Malik v National Plastics Limited** [EAT 682/78] a dismissal was justified where it resulted in fear throughout the work premises. Moreover, where the employee is in a position of authority an assault outside the work premises may mean that it is not appropriate for the individual to continue in his position (**Rileys Potato Crisps Limited v Warden** [EAT 761/81]).

Investigation

Where it is not possible to identity the instigator of the fight an employer may be entitled to dismiss all of the employees who were involved in the incident. This was the position in **British Aerospace v Mafe** [EAT 565/80] where the employer was unable to identify the attacker as both employees gave a conflicting account as to what had happened.

The scope of any investigation will depend upon the circumstances (**Malik v National Plastics Limited** [EAT 682/78]) so that where a fight takes place openly and the facts are clear it may not be necessary to carry out an interview (**Reid v Giltspure Bullens Transport Services** [EAT 549/78]). As with other conduct cases it remains the position that the employee should be properly made aware of the allegations and be given a chance to state his case (**Bentley Engineering Co v Mistry** [1978] IRLR 436; 1979 ICR 47).

Factors

Consistency of treatment

Where employers have not treated violence at work as warranting summary dismissal but a warning, any departure from this practice without giving the workforce notice of the sanction is likely to result in a finding of unfair dismissal based upon inconsistent treatment with what has gone before (**Post Office v Fennell** [1981] IRLR 221).

Contents of the Rules including the sanctions that are set out

It was stated in **Meyer Dunmore International Limited v Rogers** [1978] IRLR 167 that any rules relating to violence should be made clear to the workforce where the conduct may result in summary dismissal. Although the employer's rules stated that any assault or violent act could result in dismissal the EAT found that this had not been sufficiently drawn to the attention of the workforce. Even if there are express rules prohibiting fighting they must be applied reasonably to the circumstances of the case. In **Taylor v Parsons Peebles NEI Bruce Peebles Limited** [1981] IRLR 119 an employee was dismissed after 20 years' unblemished service based upon a policy of summary dismissal for fighting. The EAT considered that the Tribunal were wrong to simply consider the policy and should have asked what the reaction would have been of a reasonable employer in the circumstances and any provision should be considered in this light. However, if there is a disciplinary procedure or code it will be difficult to fault an employer who follows the code and dismisses in accordance with it (**East Hertfordshire DC v Boyten** [1977] IRLR 347).

Gravity of the offence taking into account litigation

If the conduct of the employee puts his co-workers in continuing fear then a dismissal will be fair (**British Communications Corp v Smart** [EAT 227/79]).

Where the violence emanates from a superior or management the relationship of trust and confidence may be destroyed, even if the conduct is relatively minor so that employee may resign and claim unfair constructive dismissal (**Mock v Glamorgan Aluminium Co Limited** [EAT 493/80]).

In circumstances where violence puts the safety of employees risk, because of the nature of the premises or factory summary dismissal may be appropriate since, as was said in **Greenwood v HJ Heinz & Co Limited** [EAT 199/77], *"The potential for danger which any degree of violence involves in close proximity to machinery is blindingly obvious."*

CHAPTER SEVEN
REDUNDANCY

By section 98((2)(c) a dismissal may be potentially fair if the reason for it:

"is that the employee was redundant".

The Definition of Redundancy

The definition of redundancy is contained in section 139(1) of the Employment Rights Act 1996 (ERA):

"...an employee who is dismissed shall be taken to be dismissed by reason of redundancy if the dismissal is attributable wholly or mainly to-

(a) the fact that his employer has ceased, or intends to cease, to carry on the business for the purposes of which the employee was employed, or has ceased, or intends to cease, to carry on that business in the place where the employee was so employed, or

(b) the fact that the requirements of the business for employees to carry out work of a particular kind, or for employees to carry out work of a particular kind in the place where he was so employed have ceased or diminished or are expected to cease or diminish."

The definition is split into three limbs.

- First, there will be a redundancy if the business closes down altogether.
- Second, there will be a redundancy where the employee's workplace disappears. The employee's workplace will depend upon where he can be required to work under his contract of employment so that he may not be redundant where the place

he is physically working closes down but there is a mobility clause permitting the employer to move him elsewhere, as we shall see.

- The third situation is where the needs for employees to carry out work of a particular kind has ceased or diminished or is expected to cease or diminish. This may arise in two ways. The particular kind of work may have fallen off so that less employees are needed to carry out that kind of work. This may occur where the employer changes the type of work it carries out so that the specific kind of work the employee was carrying out has diminished. Or there may simply be a downturn in orders, for example, because of a recession. Alternatively, the business may need less employees to carry out that kind of work, though the work level remains constant. The common scenario here is where men are replaced with machines which require fewer employees to operate them.

The cause of the employee's dismissal must be one of the above reasons if the reason for the dismissal is to be redundancy. There is a vast amount of case law on the definition of redundancy which is beyond the scope of this book (It is anticipated that a further text: *Re-organisations, Redundancies and Transfers* will complement this series this Summer). However, the House of Lords have recently reviewed the appropriate way to construe section 13a(i). In **Murray v Foyles Meats Limited** [1999] IRLR 562 the Applicants were employed as meat plant operatives but could be required to work elsewhere in the factory and had done so. A decline in the business meant that there was a need to reduce the number of skilled slaughterers and the applicants were selected in consultation with the union. They alleged their dismissals were unfair. The employer argued that the dismissals were wholly attributable to the fact that the requirements of the business to carry out work of a particular kind had diminished and therefore fell within the definition of redundancy. On appeal to the House of Lords it was submitted for the Applicant's that the words "requirements for employees to carry out work of a particular kind" meant the requirements for which the employees were contractually engaged to carry out work. Since the employers chose to engage all of their employees on similar contractual terms there could be no distinction between those who were slaughterer's and those who had worked elsewhere so that it was wrong to select those who normally worked in the slaughter hall. The employer argued that the dismissals were wholly attributable to the fact that the requirements of the business for employees to carry out work of a particular kind, on the slaughtering line had ceased or diminished and there was therefore a redundancy situation. The House of Lords held that the definition of redundancy is simplicity itself and asks two questions of fact.

- The first is whether one or other of various states of economic affairs exists, in this case whether the requirements of the business for employees to carry out work of a particular kind have diminished.
- The second question is whether the applicant's dismissal was attributable, wholly or mainly, to that state of affairs. This is a question of causation and is for the Tribunal to determine.

Lord Irvine stated:

"The key word in the statute is 'attributable' and there is no reason in law why the dismissal of an employee should not be attributable to a diminution in the employer's need for employees irrespective of the terms of his contract or the function which he performed. Of course the dismissal of an employee who could perfectly well have been redeployed or who was doing work unaffected by the fall in demand may require some explanation to establish the necessary causal connection. But this is a question of fact, not law."

The case clears up the considerable confusion that has existed for some time about the approach to be adopted and gives welcome guidance.

Business

The statutory definition talks of a business ceasing to be carried on. Business is defined by section 235 ERA 1996 as "a trade or profession and includes any activity carried on by a body of persons, whether corporate or unincorporated". It is unnecessary that the business be carried out as a commercial enterprise. A private household is deemed to be a business for the purpose of an employee who is a domestic servant.

An employer may have several businesses and if one closes down, but the others continue, he will be entitled to a redundancy payment provided that he is employed in that part of the business that has closed down (**Babar Indian Restaurant v Rawat** [1985] IRLR 57).

Temporary recession

By section 139(6) "cease and diminish" also cover temporary cessation or diminution.

Economic decisions

> The Tribunal will not go into the rights and wrongs as to why a redundancy situation has arisen as this involves economic decisions on the part of management.

Where the reason for the dismissal is redundancy, it is not open to the employee to question the background reason for the redundancy dismissal. If there is not a redundancy so that the employer must rely upon 'some other substantial reason' to justify the dismissals the Tribunal will be able to question the need for the dismissals. In **Ladbroke Courage Holidays Limited v Asten** [1981] IRLR 59 a dismissal was found to be unfair as the employer had not produced evidence to justify a dismissal carried out in order to reduce the wages bill. Mr Asten was employed as a seasonal bar manager. At the end of the season he was kept on to do maintenance work and became a member of the permanent staff. He worked as a bar manager during the following season and then carried out maintenance work. He was dismissed with one month's notice. The employer argued that this was because the requirement for employees to carry out maintenance work had diminished. The Tribunal rejected this argument but found that the dismissal was for some other substantial reason, namely instructions to reduce the wages bill. The Tribunal found the dismissal unfair because there was no real need to reduce the wages bill and there had been no consultation or discussion with Mr Asten. If there had been he may not have been dismissed. Waterhouse J stated in the EAT that there was no error of law in the Tribunal's statement that if an employer seeks to rely on business re-organisation or economic necessity he should produce some evidence that there was some need for economy and that it was material for the Tribunal to know whether the company was making profits or losses. The Tribunal were also entitled to hold on the evidence that had such consultation taken place the appellants would have appreciated that their stance was not justified.

This may be compared with **J Moon v Homeworthy Furniture (Northern) Limited** [1976] IRLR 298. The appellants were dismissed for redundancy when their factory premises were closed following a series of disputes on the ground that it was not economically viable. They complained that their dismissal was unfair. The EAT held that the Tribunal had correctly refused to consider the question of the reasonableness of the employer's decision to close the factory on the ground it was not economically viable. Kilner Browne J stated that:

> "the applicants did not accept that it was justifiable to say that the factory was not economically viable...The employees, through the chosen applicants, were and are seeking to use the Industrial Tribunal and Employment Appeal Tribunal as a platform for an industrial dispute".

It is just this type of exercise that is not permitted if there is a redundancy situation. Nevertheless, in **Orr v Vaughan** [1998] IRLR 63 the EAT, while agreeing that it is for an employer to decide on a re-organisation and whether the requirements of the business have ceased or diminished, stated that the employer should act on reasonable information reasonably acquired. The employer had dismissed an employee and taken on her job because she was told the business was losing money. It is difficult to see why the principle in *Homeworthy* would not apply to such a situation (See also **Sutton v Revlon Overseas Corporation Limited** [1973] IRLR 173 which is to the same effect as *Homeworthy*).

Redundancy or Some Other Substantial Reason

> Where there was not a redundancy within the meaning of section 139 the dismissal may nevertheless be fair for some other substantial reason even if the employer treated the dismissals as redundancies.

If the definition is not satisfied the employer will not be able to point to redundancy as being the reason for the dismissals. This problem may occur particularly where the employer is seeking to change existing work patterns or job content because they are considered inefficient or uneconomic. Alternatively, in times of recession he may wish to reduce overheads by reducing the wages bill or taking away expensive perks or bonuses though he may not be able to point to any particular downturn in work. Since the requirements of the business for employees to carry out work of a particular kind have not ceased or diminished there will not be a redundancy situation. This was what happened in **Chapman v Goonvean and Rostowrack China Clay Co Limited** [1973] 2 All ER 310, where the employer withdrew transport facilities as being uneconomic, having made three men out of ten redundant. There was a constructive dismissal of the other seven men but this was not for redundancy. The seven jobs continued to be the same as before the transport facilities were withdrawn.

The test is always whether the cause of the dismissal comes within the definition of redundancy set out above. As Lord Denning MR said in **Johnson v Nottingham Police Authority** [1974] ICR 170:

> "It is settled that an employer is entitled to reorganise his business so as to improve its efficiency and, in so doing, to propose to his staff a change in the terms and conditions of their employment; and to dispense with their services if they do not agree. Such a change does not automatically give the staff a right to redundancy payments. It only does so if the change in terms and conditions is due to a redundancy situation. The question in every case is: was the change due to a redundancy situation or not? If the change is due to a redundancy situation, he is entitled to a redundancy payment. If it is not due to it, he is not".

Examples of cases where there was no redundancy situation giving rise to the dismissal, but where a decision to dismiss was made as a result of the re-organisation are **Banerjee v City of East London Area Health Authority** [1979] IRLR 147 and **Davey v Daybern Co Limited** [EAT 710/81]. In *Banerjee* two part time posts, one of three sessions and one of six sessions, were amalgamated into one when the surgeon who took the six sessions retired. Dr Banerjee, who took the three sessions, was therefore dismissed. The EAT held that this could amount to 'some other substantial reason' for the dismissal. However, the employer was unable to show any reason for the re-organisation and there was no material on which a tribunal could decide there was 'some other substantial reason for the dismissal'. Arnold J stated:

> "If an employer comes along and says "We have evolved such and such a policy" and either "we regard it as a matter of

importance" or "the advantages which are to be discerned from this policy are so and so", subject to there being any effective cross examination, it seems to us that it must inevitably follow that evaluation by the employer of the policy as a matter of importance, a matter in which substantial advantage is discerned, if it is properly the subject matter of another reason, can be seen to be the subject of a substantial other reason. But in this case what is the state of the evidence? One knows that there was the policy...a policy of rationalising and appointing one person, to fill separate part time employments. We know that it was logical to do this from a consultant's point of view...We know that it was the custom and practice to amalgamate part time posts. And that is all we know. We do not have the least idea, and the tribunal had not the least idea. what advantages this policy was supposed, or thought likely, or hoped to bring..."

Thus, it is essential that the employer can show some reason for the dismissal due to re-organisation, some advantage to the employer resulting from it. In *Davey* the appellant was employed on a sweet kiosk in the morning during the week. When sales declined the employer wanted to cut staff and re-organise hours so that Mrs Davey would have to work evenings. Due to family commitments she could not do this and was dismissed. The dismissal was fair. There were clearly commercial requirements for the re-organisation and Mrs Davey was unable to conform to the change. This amounted to 'some other substantial reason'.

See further, chapter 8 on SOSR.

Reasonableness

Assuming that a redundancy situation has arisen, as set out in earlier chapters, it will be incumbent on the employer to carry out the redundancies in a manner which is fair. The requirements here are twofold. He must show that the procedure was fair in terms of the pool of employees to whom the selection process was applied, the criteria that were used for selection, the application of that criteria and the consultative process that was followed before selections were made. Secondly, if there is a possibility of alternative employment for the particular employee then that offer must be made. Failure to consider alternative employment may result in a dismissal, although for redundancy, being unfair.

As part of the consultative process it will be necessary to consult with the individuals who are affected by the redundancy and, where there is a recognised trade union, there are statutory requirements with regard to trade union consultation though these are beyond the scope of this book. (*Reorganisations, Redundancies and Transfers* within this series will cover this.)

Dismissal for redundancy is a potentially fair reason under section 98 of the ERA 1996. However, section 105 of the Act provides that in certain circumstances dismissals for redundancy will be automatically unfair: See Chapter 20.

Reviewing the Employer's Conduct

> The Employer must show that he acted as a reasonable employer in relation to the selection process, consultative process and in considering alternative employment.

The employer will need to show in general terms that the procedure he followed was the type of procedure that would have been followed by a reasonable employer. It is not the function of the Employment Tribunal to substitute its own decision as to whether it would have taken the same approach. As Phillips J stated in **NC Watling & Co Limited v Richardson** [1978] IRLR 255:

> "in answering that question the industrial tribunal, while using its own collective wisdom is to apply the standard of the reasonable employer; that is to say, the fairness or unfairness of the dismissal is to be judged not by the hunch of the particular industrial tribunal, which (though rarely), may be whimsical or eccentric, but by the objective standard of the way in which a reasonable employer would have behaved. It has to be recognised that there are circumstances where more than one course of action may be reasonable. In the case of redundancy, for example, and where selection of one or two employees to be dismissed for redundancy from a larger number is in issue, there may well be and often are cases where equally reasonable, fair, sensible and prudent employers would take a different course, one choosing A, another B and another C."

The same point was made in **Grundy (Teddington) Limited v Willis** [1976] ICR 323. The employee worked for the employer for over a year. Another employee had worked for the employer for considerably longer though he had left for some time and only returned a few weeks previously. The employers decided to create a post of finishing controller which meant that one job was redundant. The employee was already carrying out many of these functions but the employer thought that the other employee could to the job better and so retained him. A Tribunal found the dismissal unfair on the basis that many of the duties were already being carried out by the applicant. The EAT reversed this decision on the ground that the test was not what the Tribunal would have done if it had the choice but whether the employer had acted unreasonably. Phillips J stated:

> "...it is quite obvious that the tribunal...had found that this was a case where the candidates were almost indistinguishably matched. In a situation like that it seems to me that, provided the employers have applied their mind to the problem and acted from genuine motives, they cannot really be faulted, or be said to have acted unreasonably in preferring one to another."

In **Bristol Channel Ship Repairers Limited v O'Keefe** [1978] ICR 691 the EAT, however, made it clear that there was an onus on the employer to show:

> "how the employee came to be dismissed, and who, or what body of, and in what circumstances took, the decision to dismiss him."

This was a case decided when the burden of proof was on the employee, but the above factors are matters that an employer will still need to show if the Tribunal is to have evidence on which it can decide a dismissal is fair.

(See the important decision of *Haddon* in Chapter 4. Some of the statements by judges as to the approach to be adopted must now be viewed with caution.)

Evidence of unfair conduct on the employer's part

> If the employee does not have any specific complaints about the employer's actions the employer needs only show in general terms that a fair process was carried out.

A Tribunal will not substitute its decision for that of the employer but, as was stated above, needs some evidence on which it can decide whether the employer's conduct was fair. However, unless the employee has specific complaints about the employer's actions, all the employer needs to do is show in general terms what approach was adopted, as is illustrated by **Buchanan v Tilcom Limited** [1983] IRLR 417. Mr Buchanan was selected for redundancy, the selection being made by the area contracts manager on the basis of factors such as skills, ability, length of service and the maintenance of a balanced labour force. The reason he was selected was that he had a history of absenteeism, no particular skill, no experience of heavy rollers which was required for the retained workforce and his supervisors were unhappy with him. Seven employees who were retained had shorter service than he did. However, two had been previously employed by the employer and five were considered key operators. A Tribunal found the dismissal unfair on the basis that the employer had not proved by direct evidence that retained employees did not have the same absenteeism rate as Mr Buchanan. The Court of Session held that this was the wrong approach. It stated that:

> "In the event the appellant apart from throwing out the suggestion that he might have been victimised because of dislike, merely expressed his concern that others, with even less seniority than he and employed in the same work (labouring) had been kept on. In this situation where no other complaints were made by the appellant all that the respondents had to do was prove that their method of selection was fair in general terms and that it had been applied reasonably in the case of the appellant by the senior official responsible for taking the decision."

In **Cox v Wildt Mellor Bromley Limited** [1978] ICR 736 Phillips J, expanding on what he had stated in *Bristol Channel Ship Repairers Limited*, above, said:

"In a case such as the present when no particular complaint has been made of the failure by the employer to fit the employee elsewhere into his organisation – all that was said in the notice of application was that the dismissal was 'vindictive' it seems to us to be sufficient if the employer calls witnesses of reasonable seniority to explain the circumstances in which the redundancy came about and, in general, what was done or contemplated for the employee... and it is not necessary to anticipate every possible complaint which may be made."

However, a Tribunal will look with a critical eye at what was done as is shown by **Thomas & Betts Manufacturing Limited v Harding** [1980] IRLR 255. The employee was engaged as a packer. Later she worked quite substantially on fittings rather than packing. When the demand for fittings decreased she was dismissed as redundant. A Tribunal found the decision unfair as she could have been offered alterative work as a packer thought this would have meant dismissing a more recently employed packer. The Court of Appeal considered that steps should have been taken to see if alternative employment in some other section could have been found and this should have included consideration of whether she could have been found work as a packer.

Union agreement to the process supports fairness but is not conclusive.

Even, though an employee's trade union agrees with the selection this will not be conclusive of whether the selection must be regarded as fair or not (See *T & E Neville Limited v Johnson*, above). In **Bristow & Roberts v Pinewood Studios Limited** [EAT 600/81] the employer chose two drivers for redundancy on the basis of LIFO but, with the approval of the union, limited the selection to the commercial section of the business. The drivers who were selected had longer service than drivers in other areas. Waterhouse J in the EAT, who upheld the Tribunal's finding that the dismissals were fair, stated:

"In all these selection for redundancy cases, agreement with the union is a matter of very considerable importance but it is not conclusive because it is always possible, at least theoretically, that an agreement genuinely negotiated between employers and a trade union may be unfair in relation to an individual employee within the meaning of the relevant statutory provisions."

The agreement of the union will carry considerable weight (**Hills v Lindsay Engineering** [EAT 187/79]) and a selection procedure may be fair where it has been agreed with the union, even though it other circumstances it may be regarded as unfair (Compare the last mentioned case with **NC Watling v Richardson** at page 237).

Procedure

It is for the employer to adopt a procedure that in all the circumstances will be regarded as fair. The leading case on the approach expected of employers when deciding to make redundancies is **Williams & Others v Compair Maxim Limited** [1982] ICR 156. Browne-Wilkinson J, in the EAT, set out five 'guidelines' which an employer should take into account in deciding who to dismiss:

> "...the fair conduct of dismissals for redundancy must depend on the circumstances of each case. But in their experience, [the lay members of the EAT) there is a generally accepted view in industrial relations that, in cases where the employees are represented by an independent trade union recognised by the employer, reasonable employers will seek to act in accordance with the following principles:
>
> 1. The employer will seek to give as much warning as possible of impending redundancies so as to enable the union and employees who may be affected to take early steps to inform themselves of the relevant facts, consider possible alternative employment in the undertaking or elsewhere.
> 2. The employer will consult the union as to the best means by which the desired management result can be achieved fairly and with as little hardship to the employees as possible. In particular, the employer will seek to agree with the union the criteria to be applied in selecting the employees to be made redundant. When a selection has been made, the employer will consider with the union whether the selection has been made in accordance with those criteria.
> 3. Whether or not an agreement as to the criteria to be adopted has been agreed with the union, the employer will seek to establish criteria for selection which so far as possible do not

depend solely do not depend solely upon the opinion of the person making the selection but can be objectively checked against such things as attendance record, efficiency at the job, experience or length of service.

4. The employer will seek to ensure that the selection is made fairly in accordance with these criteria and will consider any representations the union may make as to such selection.

5. The employer will seek to see whether instead of dismissing an employee he could offer him alternative employment...

That these are broad principles currently adopted by reasonable employers is supported by the practice of the industrial tribunals and to an extent by statute..."

Although this case is one of the classic statements of the approach to be adopted on a redundancy dismissal it has to be approached with some caution, since the Court of Appeal have eschewed any attempt to lay down over rigid guidelines, stating that each case must turn on its own facts (**Bailey v BP Oil Kent Refinery**) and the approach is not appropriate where there are small scale redundancies and the workforce is not unionised.

The guidelines were not considered appropriate in **Simpson & Sons (Motor) v Reid** [1983] IRLR 401. The respondents were two forecourt attendants who had started work in 1978 with a third attendant, although he started later that year. In 1982 due to a deteriation in business they decided to reduce the staff to one forecourt employee and use part time staff. The third attendant was retained after a great deal of thought by the employer and the other two made redundant. A Tribunal found that the dismissal were unfair as the guidelines in *Compair Maxim* had not been followed. The EAT reversed this decision, stating that the guidelines did not embody standards of behaviour and were only appropriate where substantial redundancies arise in enterprises where there is an independent recognised union. They do not apply in the case of a small business faced with selection of two out of three employees. The guidelines should not be used as thought they were a shopping list to be ticked off. It was not disputed that the appellants had exercised great care in deciding who had to go. Lord MacDonald said that it:

"is enough to say that if these guidelines are considered, it is clear that they can have no content in the situation of a small business like this faced with the selection of two out of three people for redundancy where no trade union is involved and where, if applied, the consequence would be illogical".

Neverthless, the guidelines were approved in **Robinson v Carrickfergus Borough Council** [1983] IRLR 122. It must be recognised that they are only guidelines and there mere fact that they are not followed will not create an unfair dismissal (**Rolls Royce Motors Limited v Dewhurst** [1985] ICR 869). The approach adopted by the guidelines were however approved in **Polkey v AE Dayton Services Limited** [1988] ICR 142.

Selection

(1) Selection Criteria: the pool of selection

The starting point for the employer considering redundancies is to ascertain the pool of selection from which employees are to be chosen. In the absence of an agreed procedure it is for the employer to decide on the pool of selection, subject to the issue of reasonableness. Employers may find themselves in difficulty if they unreasonably limit the pool of selection. An unreasonably limited pool of selection, particularly where there are unskilled employees, that could have been included in the pool may lead to a finding of unfair dismissal. In **Trusthouse Forte Supplies Services v Brown** [EAT 396/80] the employer decided redundancies on the basis of LIFO among a group of employees comprising cleaners and porters, but did not include meat porters though their work was unskilled. The Tribunal found the dismissal unfair. The EAT said:

> "We are unable to say that the tribunal erred in law in treating all those who were unskilled as doing similar work for this purpose, in particular cleaner/porters and meat porters. The actual difference in function between the two classes is not made clear in the evidence. It is not clear that there was hard and fast distinction between them. Indeed, the evidence was that there had been substantial transfers between departments in the past..."

It was accepted by the Tribunal in **Hassall v Fusion Welding Construction Limited** [1979] IRLR 12 that there was a material distinction between welders and platers so that the two jobs could be considered separately, although there had been flexibility in the past between the two trades.

We have already seen that one factor in deciding whether the employer was reasonable will be the extent to which there was union agreement regarding the pool from which workers will be chosen (*Watling; Hills* above). Nevertheless, if the pool does not include workers who are comparable so that it operates to the disadvantage of those selected where there is no reason why there should be a distinction, a tribunal is entitled to find that the pool was unreasonably small. Two cases illustrating the difference are **Guy v Delanair** [1975] IRLR 73 where it was reasonable for the pool of workers to be day shift workers and the night shift workers to be excluded as the shifts were clearly separate, and **Calvert v Allisons** [1975] IRLR 71 where it was unreasonable to restrict the pool to employees who worked on one shift as the workforce in fact worked alternate shifts.

The following are factors that an employer should bear in mind in deciding on the pool of workers from whom selection is to be made:

(i)   Is the business clearly compartmentalised so that it is possible to devise the pool by reference to one department, depot, factory, office or site? Is it possible for employees to be moved without any difficulty. In **Highland Fish Farmers Limited v Thorburn** [EAT 1094/94] it was unreasonable to treat two sites separately whilst in **Clews v Liverpool City Council** [EAT 463/93] it was reasonable to treat two groups of workers separately where they had refused to mix and, indeed, threatened industrial action when the employers sought to amalgamate the groups.

(ii) Are the skills or job content of employees the same or such that there is no difficulty in employees interchanging jobs? If so, then it is likely that the employer should take consider all those employees of commensurate skill as being within the pool. (**Trusthouse Forte Supplies Services v Brown; Hassall; British Steel Plc (Seamless Tubes) v Robertson** [EAT 601/94].)

(iii) Even if there are apparent differences in skill or job content, did employees as a matter of fact change between jobs so that they were regarded as able or liable to be called on to carry out jobs that were apparently outside their job title or content? If so, the pool is likely to be all of the employees who are in a position to carry out the particular work. Moreover, this will be reinforced if the employer is able, by the contract to move workers from job to job, since, though there may be an overall redundancy situation it should be the case that the pool of workers to be selected will include all those who could be required to carry out the job. (See **Blundell Permoglaze Limited v O'Hagen** [EAT 540/84] **British Flowplant Group Limited v Grimshaw** [EAT 41/94].)

(iv) Was the pool agreed with a trade union or after individual consultation and negotiation with employees?

(2)   Criteria used on selection

Having chosen the 'pool' from which employees are to be selected, it is then necessary for the employer to decide on who will be selected for redundancy by the use of appropriate selection criteria. The EAT have emphasised on more than one occasion the need for clear and objective criteria. Where selection criteria are too vague or subjective there is a possibility that a tribunal may decide a reasonable employer would not have used such criteria. This was in fact the case in *Williams v Compair Maxim* where the criteria adopted involved keeping on those employees "who, in the opinion of the managers concerned, would be able to keep the company viable". Similarly, in **Sun Printers Limited v Hampton** [EAT 776/86] operating a LIFO procedure with the proviso that a "balance of skills" would be retained was too vague. It was said in **Graham v ABF Limited** [1986] IRLR 90 that the more vague the criteria the more important it would be for employees to be consulted, if dismissals were not to be found unfair, though then EAT refused to interfere with a tribunal decision that "quality of work, efficiency in carrying it out and the attitude of the persons evaluated to their work" was a fair criteria. (See also **KGB Micros Limited v Lewis** [EAT 573/90] where criteria based on cost savings was held to lack objectivity. Selection based on LIFO subject to retention of balance of skills was held to be unreasonable in **Sun Printers Limited v Hampton** [EAT 776/86] though the result in that case was that the dismissals was fair as LIFO had in fact been applied.

The person who made the decision to dismiss will be expected to give evidence as to the criteria he used and how it was applied.

The following selection criteria have been used.

Ability and performance

Although ability and performance are legitimate matters to be taken into account in selecting employees, an employer must be careful to ensure that ability is merely criteria for selection and not the reason for the dismissal, since the reality may be that it was a capability dismissal as in **Timex Corporation v Thomson** [1981] IRLR 522. Mr Thomson was dismissed when the company decided to reorganise three managers' jobs into two. He was selected because he did not have the engineering qualifications that were required without any prior warning. At the Tribunal hearing the company also said that his performance had not been satisfactory. The Tribunal decided the manner of dismissal was unfair as the company had not convinced them whether it was for redundancy or incapability and that the manner of the dismissal was unfair given his 14 years' service. The EAT held that the Tribunal had not erred in stating that the company had not proven the reason for dismissal even though there was a redundancy situation. Even where there is a redundancy situation it is possible for an employer to use it as a pretext for getting rid of someone and the Tribunal are entitled to find that this is the real reason.

It may be fair to retain a person who has greater expertise or skills on particular tasks that are required (**Abbotts v Wesson-Glynwed Steels Limited** [1982] IRLR 51, though where employees are comparable in ability, length of service may be the overriding factor (**Farthing v Midland Household Stores Limited** [1974] IRLR 354).

Age
Where the employer has reached the normal retiring age the selection for redundancy cannot be challenged (section 109 ERA 1996) unless there is no normal retiring age, the age is discriminatory or is over 65 in which case the age will be 65 at which unfair dismissal cannot be claimed. Even where there is a normal retiring age and an agreement that persons will be retired at that age selection may be unfair if there is no consultation and there are special reasons why the employee should be retained (**East of Scotland College of Agriculture v Purves** [EAT 455/88]).

Attendance
Whilst an employee's attendance record may be a justifiable factor to be applied, especially where sporadic absences cause the employer's business difficulties, the employer must be careful how he applies such criteria. It may be necessary for the employer to go beyond merely looking at the absenteeism record and to inquire into the reasons for absences. This was the view of the EAT in **Paine and Moore v Grundy (Teddington) Limited** [1981] IRLR 267. The

respondent company selected those to be dismissed for redundancy from its night shift based on length of service, attendance record and whether the employee has an alternative source of income. The two appellants were selected on the basis of their attendance records. The employees appealed to the EAT on the basis that the company should have looked at the reasons for the absence rather than just at the periods of absence. Mr Justice May stated:

> "In general terms if employers are going to rely upon what we will describe briefly as an 'attendance record criterion' in redundancy cases, we think it is desirable that they should seek to ascertain the reasons for the absences which made up the attendance record of the particular employees concerned and, for instance, if an employee happens still to be absent at the time that the redundancies have to be put into effect, that they should try to find out when that employee is likely to return to work. We think that this is merely a particular application of the much more general principle that employers should do all that is reasonable to ensure that they have in their possession as full information as is reasonable about their employers and the relevant situation before coming to any decision."

A rather different approach was taken by the Court of Session in **Dooley v Leyland Vehicles Limited** (Unreported 17th June 1986) where it was said that "it is understandable that all that has to be considered is absence and not the cause of the absence nor the reason for it. Whether or not absence is due to fault on the part of the employee is neither here not there...". Furthermore, in **Gray v Shetland Norse Preserving Co Limited** [1985] IRLR 53 the EAT took the view that it is not necessary to warn an employee about his poor attendance record for the purposes of selection for redundancy, though a warning may be necessary where misconduct is being alleged.

Nevertheless, employers must be careful that they do not achieve unfair results in the application of this criteria. In **Eurocasters Limited v Greene** [EAT 475/88] where absenteeism over a two year period was one of the factors that were considered in deciding who to choose, and the applicant had been absent for nearly a year of that period due to maternity leave, it was unfair for the employer not to take account of the reason for the absence, especially when the employee had previously had a good attendance record.

In **Byrne v Castrol (UK) Limited** [EAT 429/96] it was stated that absenteeism should be one factor to be taken into account and not determinative.

Fitness

Whilst age and fitness may be factors to be taken into account, it may be incumbent on an employer to consult to ensure that there is no alternative employment for an employee who is otherwise regarded as not being sufficiently fit. Again, an employer must be careful to ask himself whether this factor is being applied as part of the criteria or whether the real reason for the dismissal is sickness or capability. In **Porter v Streets Transport Limited** [EAT 274/86] where an employee with an ulcer was selected, and this was a reasonable factor to be considered, the dismissal was unfair because of insufficient consultation about the possibility of alternative employment. Selection criteria that discriminate against disabled persons may be unlawful under the Disability Discrimination Act 1995 unless they can be justified and a reasonable adjustment is not possible (see Chapter 5).

Last in, first out (LIFO)

A last in, first out procedure has the obvious advantage of certainty, but it may prevent an employer from retaining those workers whom it is considered are best suited to the needs of the re-organised business. We have already discussed a number of cases where length of service was considered and regarded as important (*Bessenden Properties Limited v Corness; N C Wailing & Co Limited v Richardson; Thomas & Betts Manufacturing Co Limited v Harding*). However, an employer is entitled, and it is prudent for him to, take into account criteria in addition to length of service, as was the case in **BL Cars Limited v Lewis** [1983] IRLR 58. Mr Lewis was employed as an industrial engineer at the employer's Longbridge plant from 1959. He became a senior shop steward and spent 50% of his time on trade union duties. In 1980 a need for redundancies arose and the company issued a statement stating that the company would aim at ensuring a balanced workforce and account would be taken of service, occupation and skills but considered within the need for efficient operational requirements and strategic objectives. Mr Lewis was made redundant despite his service being substantially longer than other engineers who were retained. The EAT held that a tribunal in finding the dismissal unfair because insufficient weight had been given to his length of service had erred by substituting its own view of the proper way of making the necessary selection and in so doing had misapplied the criteria. Mr Justice Browne-Wilkinson stated:

> "The overriding factor was the need to retain a balanced workforce. In making the selection for that purpose there were to be taken into account (so far as we can see, on an equal basis) length of service, occupation and skill. There is no warrant for the approach of the majority that in making the selection in accordance with those criteria a long serving employee is to be treated as having some priority' by reason of length of service."

Accordingly, other factors may be considered in order for the employer to achieve his objective of keeping the best employees for the business. In **Westland Helecopters v Nott** [EAT 342/88] it was unreasonable not to give due weight to length of service.

Loyalty
It has been held that loyalty to the employer is a matter that an employer is entitled to rely on as a factor in deciding who to choose. In **Cruickshank v Hobbs** [EAT 229/76] loyalty to an employer during a strike was held to be something that the employer could take into account (see also **Laffin v Fashion Industries (Hartlepool) Limited** [1978] IRLR 448).

Personal Circumstances
The personal circumstances of the employee often fall to be taken into account. In **Forman Construction Limited v R Kelly** [1977] ICR 468, Mr Kelly was employed as a general labourer and was a registered disabled worker. He was working in the Dundee area when he was made redundant as a member of a particular squad of workers whose work had run out. There was no procedure for selection. The EAT stated that in the absence of a procedure or practice the personal circumstances of an employee who is proposed to make redundant should be taken into account. As the employer was a registered disabled worker who had longer employment with the company than some who were not dismissed, a Tribunal was entitled to find the dismissal unfair. (See also **Calvert v Allisons (Gravel Pits) Limited** [1975 IRLR 71). Nevertheless, there is no rule that disablement warrants preferential treatment (**Wellworthy Limited v Singh** [EAT 79/88]).

Pregnancy

The House of Lords has made it clear that the selection of a woman for redundancy because she is pregnant will constitute automatic unfair dismissal under section 60 of the Employment Protection (Consolidation Act 1978 (EP(C)A) (**Brown v Stockton on Tees Borough Council** [1988] ICR 410). See now sections 99 and 105 of the ERA 1996.

Skills

Skills may be an important factor where the employer has particular needs. It is necessary for the employer to clearly define the skills that are needed. In **Graham v ABF Limited** [1986] IRLR 90 selection was on the basis of "quality of work, efficiency in carrying it out and the attitude of the persons evaluated to their work". The complainant was selected mainly on the basis of his attitude to his work, including a number of abusive incidents. The EAT held that notwithstanding that "attitude to work" as a criterion for redundancy selection is a highly relative term involving personal and subjective judgments and is dangerously ambiguous and vague, the Tribunal were entitled to find that the selection was fair though the dismsisal was unfair for lack of consultation. (See also *Sun Printers* above)

Discrimination

In certain circumstances redundancy criteria may be discriminatory. The leading case is **Clark v Ely (IMI) Kynoch Limited** [1983] ICR 165. The employers had a full time labour force of men and women and some part time employees who were women. It was agreed with the union that part timers should be made redundant first and subject to this, last in first out would operate. The part time women workers who were dismissed for redundancy complained of discrimination under section 1(1)(b) of the Sex Discrimination Act. The EAT held the following:

a) that the applicants' inability to comply with a requirement or condition had to be looked at the time it was applied and since the applicant could not have transferred to full time work at the time of dismissal the requirements of section 1(1)(b) were satisfied;
b) a 'requirement or condition' in section 1(1)(b) included the implementation of a part time workers first agreement;
c) in order to show that the requirement or condition was justifiable the employers had to show that it was acceptable to right thinking persons as sound and tolerable.

Browne-Wilkinson J expressed the view that it was most undesirable that there should be any uncertainty about whether the application of last in first out principles was discriminatory and that it would be right for tribunals to take the view that the adoption of last in first out principles was a necessary means viewed in a reasonable and objective sense of achieving a necessary objective, that is agreed criteria for selection.

The EAT also expressed the view that in certain circumstances a dismissal that is discriminatory may still be fair within section 98 of ERA 1996. However, since in this case the applicants had made clear their view that they considered the selection criteria to be discriminatory the dismissal was unfair. Nevertheless, if the discriminatory criteria can shown to be justifiable the employer may have a defence to the Sex Discrimination Act 1975 to an allegation of sex discrimination, as happened in **Kidd v DRG (UK) Limited** [1985] ICR 405. The applicant was a part time employee at the employer's factory where the all female workforce consisted or 19 part time and 57 full time employees working shifts. A shortage of work led to a redundancy situation and since it was agreed that the full time shift was marginally more efficient, part time workers were selected and then last in first out applied. The applicant complained of indirect discrimination. The Tribunal considered that the pool of comparison was households where there was a need to provide home care to an extent normally incompatible with full time employment and that it should not be assumed that a greater proportion of women than men or of married rather than of unmarried women normally took on a child caring role in the absence of specific evidence. In any event the Tribunal considered the criteria that had been applied to be justifiable. The EAT considered that this was a conclusion that could be reached on the facts. The Tribunal had been correct in limiting the pool to that section of the community that needed to provide care for children. On the evidence the Tribunal was entitled to find that it had not been shown a considerably smaller proportion of women than men could comply and that in any event the criteria was justified.

Application of the Selection Criteria

> The selection criteria must be applied in a manner that is fair and objective.

The selection criteria may be fair, but it must also be applied in a manner that is fair. In *Paine* above that dismissal was unfair because of the manner in which it was applied by the employer. Similarly, in *Eurocasters* the criteria was potentially fair but applied in a manner which led to an absurd result. A selection based on the merit of the respective employees will be unfair if the employer cannot point to how the criterion was applied on an objective basis, as happened in **Alexanders of Edinburgh Limited v Maxwell** [EAT 796/86] where the selection was based on merit but there was no guidance as to how this was applied.

In **Boulton & Paul Limited v Arnold** [1994] IRLR 532 by agreement with the union, selection for redundancy would be made on an assessment under four equal criteria being performance, discipline, length of continuous service and attendance (regular unapproved short-term absences or lateness). However, the employers took every absence into account, including a half hour visit to the doctor so that Mrs Arnold only scored three points out of ten even though there was no unapproved absences. It was held that the criteria had been applied unfairly.

It has already been noted that the employee should be specific if it has complaints about the selection process and a general complaint means that the employer needs only show, in general terms, that the process was fair (*Buchanan* and see page 239). There have been a number of cases in which the employee has sought to challenge the accuracy or fairness of the way assessments have been carried out where there has been a grading process and the following guidance emerges:

(1) Where there is only a general complaint the person doing the grading only needs to show that he has carried out a fair assessment on information that is, on the face of it, accurate (*Buchanan*);
(2) The person who takes the decision is entitled to rely upon information provided to him by other persons who carry out the assessments (i.e. managers may rely on information provided by their subordinates).

In **Eaton v King** [1995] IRLR 75 selection of four employees for redundancy was based on the operational needs of the business and involved assessment of individual employees on the basis of commitment, flexibility, receptiveness to training, quality of performance, use of initiative, length of service with the company, qualifications, specific skills, efficiency, attendance record and disciplinary record. The assessment of each employee was made by a departmental supervisor and reviewed by the manager of the plant and the manufacturing manager and selection was based on those who scored the lowest points. Two of the employees demanded to see their marks. They were shown their own marks but the employer refused to show them the marks of those who were retained. At the hearing the manager who gave evidence was unable to explain discrepancies in the marks as he had not carried out the assessments and the dismissal was held unfair. The EAT reversed the decision, holding that a senior manager is entitled to rely on assessments of employees made by those having direct knowledge of their work. There is no material difference between the position of a senior manager who relies on such assessments and that of one who relies on information in company records. A good system of selection had been set up and there was nothing to indicate that the assessment process was not carried out honestly and reasonably.

(3) Assessments should not be subject to an over minute analysis. In **British Aerospace Plc v Green** [1995] IRLR 433, Waite LJ stated:

> "Employment law recognises, pragmatically, that an over minute investigation of the selection process by the tribunal members may run the risk of defeating the purpose which the tribunals were called into being to discharge – namely a swift, informal disposal of disputes arising from redundancy in the workplace. So in general the employer who sets up a system of selection which can reasonably be described as fair and applies it without any overt sign of conduct which mars its fairness will have done all that the law requires of him"

(4) It was held in **British Sugar v Kirker** [1988] IRLR 624 that where an employee alleges his disability was taken into account or influenced the selection for redundancy then employees are entitled to require the employer to provide evidence as to how the criteria were applied in the absence of a disability factor. The Tribunal was entitled to consider how the employee had been treated in the past and it was noted that he had scored nil in relation to promotion prospects based upon his poor eyesight which was a disability.

Discovery of assessments

Discovery of assessments of others will generally not be ordered. The reason for this was explained in *Green* as being that discovery will only be given in relation to relevant documents and except in exceptional cases the assessments of retained employees are not likely to be relevant as the Tribunal should not embark on a reassessment exercise. The applicant should specify why the documents are alleged to be relevant otherwise he will be embarking on a fishing expedition (cf **FDR Limited v Holloway** [1995] IRLR 400 which is probably wrong).

Bumping

An issue that often arises as the fairness of the way in which criteria was applied is where employee A is dismissed, so that employee B whose job is in fact redundant can replace him; the so called 'bumping' redundancy.

Although there was initially some doubt about whether an employee was redundant when he was replaced by another employee whose job was redundant this was confirmed as a true redundancy in **Gimber & Sons Limited v Spurrett** [1967] ITR 308. Lord Parker confirmed that:

> "If there is a reduction in the requirements for employees in one section of an employer's business and an employee who becomes surplus or redundant is transferred to another section of that business, an employee who is displaced by the transfer of the first employee and is dismissed by reason of that displacement is dismissed by reason of redundancy."

In **Gordon v Adams (Dalkeith) Limited** [1972] ITR 81 the appellant was given notice terminating his employment when it was decided that he would be replaced by someone who had carried out the job of chauffeur to the managing director. He claimed a redundancy payment. At the hearing it was argued that he was replaced because he was unsuitable. The Tribunal dismissed his application and he appealed contending that where an employee is displaced by the transfer of an employee who would have been dismissed for redundancy that must be a redundancy situation. The EAT held that the Tribunal could look at the reason for dismissal and accept the evidence which "indicates that the dismissal was wholly or mainly attributable to the unsuitability of the applicant for the new post and not to any cessation or diminution in the respondents requirements for employees to carry out work of a particular kind".

Gimber was stated as correct in **Elliot Turbomachinery Limited v Bates** [1981] ICR 218 where, as Kilner-Browne J said:

> "Shortly put and in broad and general terms, the employers, in order to reorganise their management structure, as they were fully and properly entitled to do, terminated one man's job and moved that man into the employee's job and then declared that employee redundant."

Consultation with Individuals

> As part of a fair process the employer should consult with individuals and allow them to make such representations as are appropriate.

As part and parcel of the redundancy procedure, the employer should consult with employees about the redundancies, warn the employees of impending redundancies, consider the representations of employees and where possible take account of them, and offer help to employees in finding alternative employment. The fact that an employee is represented by a trade union does not do away with the necessity for individual consultation (**Atkinson v George Lindsay & Co** [1980] IRLR 196). The EAT has said that employees should not assume that individual employees are privy to discussions with unions over redundancy (**Huddersfield Parcels Limited v Sykes** [1981] IRLR 115).

Consultation has taken on a more important relevance since the decision of the House of Lords in **Polkey v A E Dayton Services Limited** [1988] ICR 142. This is dealt with in the Chapter on Reasonableness at page 86.

The reasoning of the House of Lords in *Polkey* makes it essential for the employer to consult with employees before dismissals for redundancy him. The reasons why consultation is a necessary part of the process were well set out in **Freud v Bentalls** [1983] ICR 77 where Browne-Wilkinson J said :

> "Turning now to consideration of industrial relations practice, consultation (as opposed (to unilateral action by the employer) is one of the foundation stones of modern industrial relations practice. The statutory Code of Practice emphasises its importance in every aspect of industrial relations. In the particular sphere of redundancy good industrial relations practice in the ordinary case requires consultation with the redundant employee so that the employer may find out whether the needs of the business can be met in some way other than by dismissal and, if not, what other steps the employer can take to ameliorate the blow to the employer. In some cases ...the employee may be able to suggest some reorganisation which will obviate the need for dismissal; in virtually all cases the employer if he consults will find out what steps he can take to find the employee alternative employment either within the company or outside it. For example in present day conditions when so many people are unemployed many employees facing redundancy by reason of the disappearance of their existing job are prepared to take other jobs of lower status and commanding less pay. Only by consulting the employee can the employer discover whether such an option is open in any given case. Therefore good industrial relations practice requires that unless there are special circumstances which render such consultation impossible or unnecessary a fair employer will consult with the employee before dismissing him."

Scope of the duty to consult

There was held to be insufficient consultation in **Huddersfield Parcels Limited v Sykes** [1981] IRLR 115. Mr Sykes was a night driver/warehouseman. He was made redundant when his employers decided to reduce numbers. There were negotiations with the trade union and the basis for selection was agreed. Mr Sykes was not consulted before he was dismissed. He complained of unfair dismissal. The Tribunal found that there had been no diminution in the requirements of the employer for a class 1 lorry driver and that the job was now simply being done by one man where it had previously been shared with Mr Sykes. The EAT held that this was the wrong approach since the overall requirements of the employer had to be looked at and the requirements for the services provided as warehouseman had diminished. However, the EAT stated that the Tribunal were entitled to find the dismissal unfair as the company did not offer or even discuss the possibility of alternative employment with him. It could not be said that the employer was entitled to infer that he was privy to the communications with the trade union and therefore aware that there was a possibility of alternative employment.

The scope of consultation may vary depending on the case and the employees' attitudes to consultation. In **Hilton v BAT Building Products Limited** [EAT] an employee was dismissed after only one and a half days consultation, but since he had made is clear he would not accept another job which was a demotion the EAT held that a tribunal was entitled to find that this was sufficient.

In **Abbotts v Wesson-Glywed Steels Limited** [1982] IRLR 51 a failure to consult rendered a dismissal unfair because the employer had not sought to find out whether the employee would accept a demotion. Since it was likely that he would have been dismissed in any event compensation was awarded for 14 days which was the period that the Tribunal thought consultation would have taken.

The fact that the employer is a very small business may affect the formality of the process but it does not do away with the obligation to consult where it may have made some difference (**De Grasse v Stockwell Tools Limited** [1992] IRLR 269: see page 95, **Milne v Distillers Company (Cereals) Limited** [EAT 692/87]).

The scope of consultation was set out in **R v British Coal Corporation and Secretary of State for Trade and Industry ex parte Price** [1994] IRLR 72 by Vinelott LJ:

"Fair consultation means:

(a) consultation when the proposals are still at a formative stage;
(b) adequate information on which to respond;
(c) adequate time in which to respond;
(d) conscientious consideration by an authority of the response to consultation.

Another way of putting the point more shortly is that fair consultation involves giving the body consulted a fair and proper opportunity to understand fully the matters about which it is being consulted, and to express its views on those subjects, with the consultor thereafter considering those views properly and genuinely."

A letter advising the employee that she had been selected for redundancy and giving her an opportunity to discuss any matters arising from the letter was held to be insufficient consultation in **Rowell v Hubbard Group Services** [1995] IRLR 195.

It will be an error of law for a tribunal to fail to consider the issue of consultation (**Langston v Cranfield University** [1998] IRLR 172).

The Polkey Exception

There is an exception to the requirement for consultation and this is where it would have been futile. In **Duffy v Yeomans & Partners Limited** [1994] IRLR 642 the Court of Appeal stated that, in determining whether an employee made redundant without prior consultation was nevertheless fairly dismissed, the test is whether an employer acting reasonably could have failed to consult in the given circumstances and that it is not necessary that there must be a deliberate decision by the employer that consultation would be useless. The test is therefore an objective one.

A number of examples of whether consultation was futile:

- In **Oakes v Pentland Industries Limited** [EAT 343/87] a dismissal was unfair where an employee was selected because of his poor work performance as it could not be said that consultation would have made no difference.
- In **Poat v Holiday Inn Worldwide** [EAT 883/93] the EAT considered that it would have been "courteous and humane" to consult with a secretary before redundancy even though there were no other jobs.
- In **Saunders v Ecobic Foundry** [EAT 358/87] an employee was dismissed with no consultation. The only alternative to dismissal was demotion which he would have refused. However, the EAT held that it could not be said that consultation would have been futile.
- In **Duncan v Marconi Command & Control** [EAT 309/88] consultation with the union was held to be sufficient where the work was of a security nature, so that dismissed employees were ordered off site immediately. The EAT felt that the applicant could have been kept fully informed through union branch meetings.

See also *Mugford* referred to below.

Consultation with Trade Unions

Where there is a recognised trade union, there is a statutory duty on the part of an employer to consult with the union. The fact that this has not been carried out will not necessarily make the dismissal unfair. In **Atkinson v George Lindsay & Co** [1980] IRLR 196 the EAT considered that the Tribunal were wrong to award compensation on the basis that if a union had been consulted alternative jobs would probably have been found for the employee. The union had not complained about lack of consultation under the Employment Protection Act 1975 and the mere lack of consultation could not in itself be regarded as an unreasonable act. This was also emphasised in **Forman Construction Limited v R Kelly** [1977] IRLR 468. Mr Kelly was employed as a general labourer had was a registered disabled worker. He was made redundant when there was no work for the squad in which he worked. As part of its decision the EAT found that the Tribunal erred in considering that the dismissal was unfair because of failure to consult the union. The only remedy in respect of failure to consult was for the union to seek a protective award.

Nevertheless, in **Hough and APEX v Leyland DAF Limited** [1991] IRLR 194 the EAT held that a Tribunal was entitled to take into account the fact that there had been no consultation with the union about alternative employment or any alternative to redundancy. This must surely be the situation where the union is acting as the employees' representative so that individual consultation is minimal or non existent. In this situation the union should be consulted to the same extent that it would be expected that individual consultation will take place.

Consultation with the trade union will not normally excuse the need for individual consultation (**Walls Meat Co v Selby** [1989] ICR 601; **Alexanders of Edinburgh v Maxwell** [EAT 796/86]). However, it was held in **Mugford v Midland Bank Plc** [1997] IRLR 90 that where there had been full consultation with the union throughout and consultation was available to the individual after his selection the Tribunal was entitled to find the dismissal fair as a matter of fact. The EAT stated:

> "Having considered the authorities we would summarise the position as follows:

(1) Where no consultation about redundancy has taken place with either the trade union or the employee the dismissal will normally be unfair, unless the industrial tribunal finds that a reasonable employer would have concluded that consultation would be an utterly futile exercise in the particular circumstances of the case.

(2) Consultation with the trade union over selection criteria does not of itself release the employer from considering with the employee individually his being identified for redundancy.

(3) It will be a question of fact and degree for the industrial tribunal to consider whether consultation with the individual and/or his union was so inadequate as to render the dismissal unfair. A lack of consultation in any particular respect will not automatically lead to that result. The overall picture must be viewed by the tribunal up to the date of termination to ascertain whether the employer has or has not acted reasonably in dismissing the employee on the grounds of redundancy."

Alternative Employment

As part of a fair process the employer should consider whether there is any alternative employment available for the employee.

It has long been recognised that, as part of its duty as a reasonable employer, where redundancies are proposed the employee should take steps to find alternative employment in the business for otherwise redundant employees. (See **Thomas & Betts Manufacturing Limited v Harding** [1980] IRLR 255.) This principle was set out in the 1972 Code of Practice Relating to Redundancies which provided that an employer was obligated to consider transferring workers to other work or establishments within the undertaking. The Code has been repealed but the principle is still a sound one and the cases decided when the Code was in existence are still of relevance as is clear from decisions given after the repeal of the Code.

The starting point in considering the scope of the employer's duty is **Vokes v Bear** [1974] ICR 1. This was a case in which no attempt was made to look for alternative employment for a manager who had been employed for two years with an employer who was taken over by the Tilling group of companies which consisted of over 300 companies. He was dismissed shortly after the takeover on the ground of redundancy. The EAT agreed with the Industrial Tribunal that enquiries could have been made in the group of companies as to whether there was any alternative employment. Sir Hugh Griffiths stated:

> "The employer had not yet done that which in all fairness and reason he should do, namely, to make the obvious attempt to see if B could be placed somewhere else within this large group."

The Tribunal did not accept that it was not practicable for the employer to make such inquiries. The company was part of a massive group and it was considered that there were several vacancies within the group which were of the standard that the employee had previously held and he could have been considered for.

Reasonable steps

The employer is only expected to take such steps as would be considered reasonable. The EAT in **Quinton Hazell Limited v Earl** [1976] IRLR 296 pointed out that in *Vokes* not a single step had been taken by the employer. In *Quinton* a search was not made among low paid jobs which would have been a substantial demotion. EAT did not think that this, in itself, meant that the employer had acted unreasonably.

The scope of the obligation was considered in **Modern Injection Moulds Limited v Price** [1976] ICR 370. It is clear that if an alternative job is going to be offered to the employee he should be offered sufficient information on which to make up his mind. The case involved a re-organisation of a business. Mr Price, who was a manager was offered a demotion to shop foreman with fewer responsibilities and reduced wages. Mr Price turned down this offer and was dismissed. The EAT upheld the Tribunal's finding that the dismissal was unfair on the ground that Mr Price was not given sufficient information about the alternative job offer. Mr Justice Phillips stated:

> "In those circumstances there was an obligation on the employers to do their best, before actually dismissing him on the ground of redundancy (albeit there was a redundancy situation) to find him suitable alternative employment with the employers.

That statement of the law is taken from the decision of the National Industrial Relations Court in *Vokes v Bear* [1974] ICR 1. We adopt the statement of the law in that case, which in our view is correct. In our judgment it can be said that inasmuch as there is this obligation on the part of the employers to try to find suitable alternative employment within the firm, it must follow that, if they are in a position, pursuant to their obligation, to make an offer to the employee of suitable alternative employment they must give him sufficient information on the basis of which the employee can make a realistic decision whether to take the new job. It will, of course, depend upon the circumstances of every case how much information, and information upon what subjects must be given. Normally at all events, and certainly in this case, it is necessary for the employers to inform the employee of the financial prospects of the new job. The test must always be (it has to be looked at from the point of view of the employer): has he been given sufficient information upon which he can make a realistic decision whether to take the job and stay, or whether to reject it and leave?"

In **Cox v Wildt Mellor Bromley Limited** [1978] ICR 736 the EAT considered the steps that an employer should take in looking for alternative employment, though this was a case where the employee did not make any specific complaints about the procedures that had been followed but was alleging that the employer had been vindicative. Phillips J stated:

"it seems to us to be sufficient if the employer calls witnesses of reasonable seniority to explain the circumstances in which the redundancy came about and, in general, what was done or contemplated for the employee..."

Even where there is a dismissal which is in breach of contract, it may not be unfair if every effort is made to find alternative employment. In **Holliday Concrete (Testing) Limited v Woods** [1979] IRLR 30 the applicant's job was prematurely brought to an end. The EAT stated that the Industrial Tribunal must be "satisfied by evidence brought forward by the employer" who must show that "there was no possibility of any other work being found for the person in question". For the employer to fail to take proper steps to look for alternative employment will almost certainly make the dismissal unfair. In **Avonmouth Construction Co Limited v Shipway** [1979] IRLR 14 the employee's job as a senior agent had become redundant but the employer did not offer him the job of site agent as it was thought that this was a demotion which would not be accepted. The Employment Appeal Tribunal upheld the Tribunal's finding that the dismissal was unfair because the offer had not been made. Mr Justice Bristow stated that the company had a duty to consider carefully whether he could be transferred to another vacancy within the respondent company especially when there was no allegation of incapability. Similarly in **Thomas & Betts Manufacturing Limited v Harding** [1980] IRLR 255 a dismissal was unfair where the employee who was working on fittings could have been transferred to a job as a packer, a job she had previously carried out, when her post became redundant, though the transfer would have involved making a packer redundant. The Court of Appeal held that the Tribunal had not erred in law in deciding that the employee's dismissal on the grounds of redundancy was unfair because she should have been offered a job as a packer even if it meant dismissing someone else.

Nature of alternative employment

The question of whether someone will accept a subordinate role was against considered in **Barratt Construction Limited v Dalrymple** [1984] IRLR 385. In this case Mr Dalrymple was dismissed from his job as site agent because he was redundant.

The Tribunal accepted that it was a proper redundancy but considered that he should have been considered for alternative employment in a subordinate capacity and since the appellants were part of a larger group enquiries should have been made to see whether there were vacancies for him in any of the other companies. The Employment Appeal Tribunal considered that the Tribunal had erred since there was no evidence to show that if an enquiry had been made it would have been fruitless and the employee was therefore entitled to the benefit of the doubt. The employee had not suggested that he would be interested in a more junior capacity.

If there is a possibility of alternative employment on a subordinate basis, the employer must not offer the alternative employment on grounds that are unreasonable, for example, by insisting that the employee must accept the employment before he has had a chance to try out the job by way of a trial period. In **Elliot v Richard Stump Limited** [1987] IRLR 579 Elliot was offered a job which was demotion at another factory when his factory closed down, which would have involved him answering to someone who held the same job as he had held in the closed factory. He was told by ACAS that he had a right to a trial period but the company did not consider a trial period to be appropriate so he refused the employment. The EAT stated that the terms of the offer of alternative employment were crucial and that by refusing to allow the employee a trial period it had acted unreasonably. The fact that there *would* be a trial period did not prevent the offer being unreasonable as an unreasonable term was included in it. The fact that the term may have been ineffective did not prevent the offer as framed from being unreasonable. Consideration of alternative employment may invoice looking at other companies within the group (**Euroguard Limited v Rycroft** [EAT 842/92]).

The fact that the employer's business picks up *after* the dismissal so that there may be alternative employment because of the increased business does not mean that the employer will have to offer alternative employment to an employee who has already been dismissed in order to make the redundancy selection process fair. In **Stewart v Connal & Co Limited** [EAT 315/81] the employer obtained a contract the day after an employee had been dismissed for redundancy. The dismissal was still fair as there was no alternative employment at the time of dismissal and the employer was not under a duty to offer renewed employment. (See also **Octavius Atkinson & Sons v Morris** [1989] IRLR 158.)

Appeals

It was stated in **Robinson v Ulster Carpet Mills Limited** [1991] IRLR 348 that a dismissal was not unfair where there was no right to an appeal.

CHAPTER EIGHT
SOME OTHER SUBSTANTIAL REASON

Definition

By section 98(1)(b) of the ERA 1996 a dismissal may be potentially fair if the reason for it is:

> "that it is either a person falling within subsection (2) or some other substantial reason of a kind such s to justify the dismissal of an employee holding the position which the employee held."

> SOSR is a catch all provision that will cover areas that are not covered by the other four potentially fair reasons.

The provision relating to Some Other Substantial Reason (SOSR) is a residual catch all section that covers those areas not contained in subsection 98(2) since it is self evident that Parliament could not cover all of the areas where a dismissal may be potentially fair. By way of example, in **R S Components Limited v Irwin** [1974] ICR 535 a number of salesmen refused to sign a restrictive covenant as a result of which they were dismissed. It was held that they were dismissed for SOSR. The NIRC held that the concept was *not* to be construed ejusdem generis with the other reasons specified in the Act. The Court stated that the words must be construed according to the ordinary canons of construction and consistently with the manifest intention of the Act. It is for the employer to show that there was a substantial reason for dismissal and once this is shown, the Tribunal then must assess the question of reasonableness.

The reason is one that may justify dismissal

It was stated in **Mercia Rubber Mouldings Limited v Lingwood** [1974] ICR 256 that the reason for dismissal has to be a reason that can justify dismissal, not one that *does* justify dismissal otherwise the reasonableness test would have no application where the employer showed SOSR. This point was also made in **Gilham v Kent County Council** [1985] ICR 233 in which Griffiths LJ stated:

> "The hurdle over which the employer has to jump at this stage of an enquiry into an unfair dismissal complaint is designed to deter employers from dismissing employees for some trivial or unworthy reason. If he does so, the dismissal is deemed unfair without the need to look further into its merits. But if on the face of it the reason could justify the dismissal then it passes as a substantial reason and the enquiry moves on to section 98(4), and the question of reasonableness."

It is clearly necessary for the reason to be genuine and if it is so, it may be substantial, even if a body of evidence may be produced to show that the reason has no scientific foundation. As Lord McDonald stated in **Harper v National Coal Board** [1980] IRLR 260:

> "Obviously an employer cannot claim that a reason for dismissal is substantial if it is a whimsical or capricious reason which no person of ordinary sense would entertain. But if the employer can show that he had a fair reason in his mind at the time when he decided on dismissal and that he genuinely believed it to be fair this would bring the case within the category of another substantial reason. Where the belief is one which is genuinely held, and particularly is one which most employers would be expected to adopt, it may be a substantial reason even where modern sophisticated opinion can be adduced to suggest that it has no scientific foundation (*Saunders v Scottish National Camps Association Ltd* [1980] IRLR 174)."

In *Harper* it was stated by the EAT that the reason for dismissal could have been incapability or SOSR. It should be noted that in **Murphy v Epsom College** [1983] ICR 715 it was stated that if SOSR is to be put forward as a reason, in the alternative, it should be pleaded or at least the matter should be 'expressly ventilated' at the hearing otherwise a respondent may have a finding against him based upon a reason for dismissal that it has not had an opportunity to challenge.

A to Z of SOSR

Absences

It has been seen from other Chapters that absences from work may lead to a fair dismissal on the ground of capability or conduct. It was stated by the EAT in **Wharfedale Loudspeakers v Paynton** [EAT 82/92] that absences from work that are due to a genuine illness may lead to a dismissal for SOSR (see pages 139).

Business Re-organisations

See the forthcoming book: *Re-organisations, Redundancies and Transfers.*

An SOSR reason may apply where an employee refuses to accept a business re-organisation even if the employer is in breach of contract, provided the employer acted reasonably.

Where the employee refuses to agree to a variation of contract upon a business re-organisation the employer may feel in these circumstances that it has no choice than to terminate the contract of employment. This may be because the financial extingencies of the business are such that it cannot continue without making drastic cuts in one form or another. Alternatively, some or most of the workforce may have agreed to changes to improve efficiency and the employer feels that the business cannot continue unless all employees are working on the same basis. If dismissals do not take place and some employees stand on their original contracts the employee is faced with the potentially messy situation of different employees working on different terms and conditions. It may therefore feel that he has little choice other than to give employees who will not go along with the re-organisation their notice. It has been held that dismissal of employees who refuse to accept a change in their terms and conditions upon a re-organisation may amount to 'SOSR' and be potentially fair. However, the employer must still act reasonably and must adopt a fair procedure in deciding to dismiss.

This was made clear by the Court of Appeal in the leading case of **Hollister v National Farmers Union** [1979] ICR 542. In this case the applicant had been primarily remunerated by a share of commission on insurances effected with the Cornwall Insurance

Group. When the Cornwall group secretaries complained that the remuneration was inadequate and compared unfavourably with the rest of the country the employers decided to end the connection with the Cornwall Insurance Group and bring the Cornwall group secretaries into line with the rest of the country. The applicant objected that his remuneration was still inadequate and there had not been any consultation with the group secretaries about the re-organisation. He claimed unfair dismissal after he was dismissed for refusing to sign the new contract. The Court of Appeal held that dismissal for refusal to accept the new terms was a substantial reason of a kind to justify dismissal. Lord Denning stated that a dismissal in these circumstances would be for SOSR if there was "some sound, good business reason for the re-organisation". The applicant had also complained that there had been no consultation prior to the change and the employers had therefore not acted reasonably. However, Lord Denning and Eveleigh LJ stated that lack of consultation was only a factor to be taken into account in deciding whether a dismissal was fair. This aspect of the case must be viewed with a certain amount of caution since the House of Lords decision in *Polkey* from which it is clear that consultation has assumed an increased importance (see Chapter 4).

There are numerous examples of cases where the Courts have held that dismissal for refusal to accept changed terms and conditions amounts to SOSR and may be fair even though the employer has no contractual right to insist on the changes. In **Bowater Containers Limited v McCormack** [1980] IRLR 50, Mr McCormack was dismissed for refusing to undertake additional duties as a supervisor, where he had been given an undertaking at the time of his promotion that he would not be given additional duties, and for refusing to transfer from his position as supervisor in the transport department to a job as stacker truck driver which was the job he had first been employed to do. The Tribunal found his dismissal was unfair as he had a contractual right not to undertake additional duties. The EAT held that the Tribunal had erred. Although the employee was not contractually obliged to undertake additional duties this was not sufficient to make the dismissal unfair. It was necessary to consider the circumstances of the dismissal. Mr Justice Talbot stated:

"There then came the re-organisation which was as found by the Industrial Tribunal to be beneficial to the efficient running of the company and one, moreover, agreed with the trade union...By finding that merely because of his contractual term, therefore it was unfair was not giving a proper consideration to the circumstances of the dismissal, the reason for it and then the inquiry as to whether the employer was reasonable in treating it as a sufficient reason."

In **Davidson and Maillou v Camparisons** [1980] IRLR 360 the respondents were dismissed when they refused to transfer to a different hairdressing salon. The employer had discovered that the respondents intended to set up in competition within one hundred yards of the salon where they currently worked. The EAT held that the employer was entitled to protect himself from unfair competition and that the respondents were unreasonable in refusing to accept the offer to go elsewhere. The dismissal was for SOSR and fair.

Whether the employer, having shown the reason for the dismissal as being SOSR will then be able to go on and show the dismissal to be fair depends upon factors such as consultation, the manner in which the change is implemented or proposed and the needs of the business weighed against the interests of the employee in retaining the terms and conditions he has originally agreed. The Tribunal will consider the fairness of the employer's action in dismissing in accordance with the test set out in section 98(4) as with the other potentially fair reasons for dismissal. A good example of a case where it was reasonable for an employer to dismiss an employee who refused to go along with change is **Robinson v Flitwick Frames Limited** [1975] IRLR 261. Compulsory overtime was unilaterally introduced to cover orders during a peak period. The workforce were prepared to go along with this apart from the applicant and when he refused, he was dismissed. The EAT considered his dismissal to be fair.

The employee may be dismissed for refusing to go along with the change or may resign and claim unfair constructive dismissal based upon the fact that the employer was in breach of contract in seeking to impose change and acted unreasonably in the manner in which change was imposed. The fact that there is no contractual power to insist on the change does not necessarily mean that the unilateral variation is unfair.

In **St John of God (Care Services) Limited v Brooks & Others** [1992] IRLR 546 the approach to be taken where there has been dismissals as a result of a re-organisation was set out by the EAT. A hospital was forced to re-organise when National Health Service Funding was drastically cut. They offered new, inferior, terms and conditions to the workforce. Out of 170 employees, 140 accepted the new terms, though 115 signed a petition making it clear that this was under protest. Of the remaining 30 who did not accept, dismissal letters were sent and 24 complained of unfair dismissal. In considering whether the dismissal was fair or unfair the Tribunal quoted *Harvey on Industrial Relations and Employment Law* that "the crucial question is whether the terms offered were those which a reasonable employer could offer. A majority of the EAT thought that this was a misdirection. Knox J stated:

> "There is in the view of the majority...a danger in promoting the nature of the offer made by the employer of new terms and conditions to the status of the sole or crucial test...because it involves a departure from the words of the statute....if the only thing that is looked at is the offer, this necessarily excludes from consideration everything that happened between the time when the offer was made and the dismissal. That must in principle be wrong because it is to the dismissal that section 98(4) points and whether it was fair or unfair must be judged in the light of the situation when it occurred and not when an earlier step was taken....in the present case, in that what seems to us to be a potentially significant fact is excluded if the offer is concentrated upon to the extent of all subsequent matters, namely the very large percentage of employees who did accept the offer. The decision to dismiss was taken after the acceptances."

In **Savoia v Chiltern Herb Farms Limited** [1982] IRLR 166, Mr Savoia was asked to transfer to another job as part of a re-organisation of the company. He refused and resigned. The employer argued at the Tribunal hearing that he was the best person for the new job and unsuitable for his old job, hence the change. The Tribunal found a constructive dismissal but that the dismissal was for SOSR and fair. The Court of Appeal upheld this decision. Waller LJ stated that:

> "Although it would be more difficult for an employer to say that a constructive dismissal was fair in my view there may well be circumstances where it is perfectly possible to do so."

There may be no right to a contractual change but the employee acts unreasonably so that the dismissal is fair. On the other hand the employer may have a contractual right to impose a change but a dismissal could still be unfair because of the way in which the employer went about varying the employee's contract. This is illustrated by **Express Lift Co Limited v F L Bowles** [1977] IRLR 99. The applicant was employed on terms that he would work anywhere in the United Kingdom. He terminated his employment when he was instructed to transfer from Nottingham to Scotland. A Tribunal considered that he had been unfairly dismissed. The EAT held that he could not be taken to have been unfairly dismissed. Although he had refused to transfer because his wife was ill there was no evidence of any contractual exception to the employee's obligations to transfer. Nor could a term be implied that there were reasonable exceptions or because it was reasonable to do so. Since he was under a contractual obligation to move there was no constructive dismissal. Kilner-Browne J considered what the employee could have done to protect himself:

> "If he had stuck to his guns he could easily have manoeuvred the employer onto the wrong leg. Either he could have asked for a variation or an amendment of his obligations or he could have said to the employer that the employer's attitude, although strictly correct left him with no option but to regard it as an end of employment, that is, the employer was virtually giving him the sack.."

A tribunal will not substitute its own view for that the employer took provided that the employer behaved reasonably and can show that a re-organisation, which involved a unilateral change in employees' terms and conditions, was necessary for the business within the terms of the approach set out in *Hollister* and that the means by which the employer sought to implement this change was reasonable. As was said in **Grundy (Teddington) Limited v Willis** [1976] ICR 323, the Tribunal "has to decide, not what it would have done had it been the management, but whether or not the dismissal was fair or unfair, which depends on whether the employer acted reasonably...".

The employee may behave reasonably in refusing change but the dismissal still be fair. Indeed it may be that the employee has perfectly good reasons for refusing to go along with a re-organisation, and is therefore behaving reasonably, but that does not make the employer's conduct unreasonable. In **Chubb Fire Security Limited v Harper** [1983] IRLR 311, as a result of a change in sales policy, Mr Harper was offered a new contract as a salesperson, in a different territory on a different salary structure. He refused as he took the view it would involve a very considerable diminution in his earnings. He was dismissed. A Tribunal found that he had a sufficient reason to refuse the new contract and the dismissal was therefore unfair. The EAT found that the tribunal were wrong in not considering the advantages to the employer of the re-organisation and the reasonableness of the manner in which it was being implemented. Balcombe J disagreed with the Tribunal's approach (disapproving **Evans v Elementa Holdings Limited** [1982] IRLR 143) and agreed with the sentence in *Harvey on Industrial Relations and Labour Law* that "It does not follow that if one party is acting reasonably the other is acting reasonably". In the present case there were sound reasons for the re-organisation and the dismissal was fair.

An interesting case concerning the reasonableness of an employer's behaviour on a re-organisation is **Wilson v Faccenda Chicken Limited** [EAT 98/86]. The business was re-organised in such manner to alleviate distress to chickens. Mr Wilson who was a chicken catcher had his terms and conditions altered as a result. He was not prepared to go along with the change since the different hours that were proposed would affect his home life. The EAT held that a sound reason had been shown for dismissing him when he refused to go along with change and that in all the circumstances his dismissal was fair.

Where the employer has secured the agreement of most of the workforce to the proposed change but an employee refuses to go along with the variation the employer may be able to show that any dismissal was fair because of the employee's intransigence. In these circumstances the reason for dismissal may be the conduct of the employee. In **Horrigan v Lewisham LBC** [1978] ICR 15 a driver decided that he would not longer go along with overtime that he had worked for almost ten years. The overtime had been agreed with the unions. The EAT held that a term could not be implied that he would carry out the overtime but the dismissal was fair because of the disruption caused to the employer's services. Arnold J stated that:

> "...it was reasonable to treat [the] refusal to cooperate as a sufficient reason for dismissal, whether it involved any breach of contract or not."

(See also **Robinson v Flitwick Frames Limited** [1975] IRLR 261.)

In **Ellis v Brighton Co-operative Society Limited** [1976] IRLR 419 the EAT held that a refusal on the part of the employee to work extra hours which were necessary for the business could constitute a substantial reason for dismissal. Phillips J stated:

"Where there has been a properly consulted-upon reorganisation which, if it is not done, is going to bring the whole business to a standstill, a failure to go along with the new arrangements may well...constitute some other substantial reason."

Hollister made it clear that the dismissal may be fair although the business may not come to a standstill but there are sound business reasons for the change.

Whether the dismissal is fair may depend on the position of the particular employee, the extent of the change that is being requested, the effect on the employee and the needs of the business. A certain level of co-operation will be expected from employees, which may depend on their position in the organisation and the extent of the change that is being proposed. In **Grigg v Daylay Eggs Limited** [EAT 426/79] a sales representative was asked to assist in the warehouse for one week to keep the business running during a transport strike and adverse weather. He did so, but complained about the conditions he had to work under and was dismissed when he refused to work another week. The dismissal was found to be fair. The EAT upheld the Tribunal's decision. Talbot J stated:

"This is not a case where an employer invites a person to undertake a different type of work, or work in different conditions, or work in an entirely different place from that where he was required to work. Those principles in our judgment do not help us, because what happened here, as is plain from the finding of fact, was an unexpected emergency in which the employers found themselves, and a temporary emergency. In those circumstances it was not a question of altering or varying the appellant's contract; he was invited to assist them by working for a short period in charge of his warehouse in London.

In our view, when the tribunal found that the employer was entitled to look for and receive help from senior staff in times of crisis, they rightly stated the kind of obligation that an employer can look to in an employee and ask him to fulfil."

(See also **Martin v Solus Schall** [1979] IRLR 7).

In **Bowater Containers Limited v McCormack** [1980] IRLR 50 a re-organisation occurred and Mr McCormack was asked to carry out extra duties. He had previously been assured that he would not have to carry out extra work. He was dismissed for refusal to carry out these duties. The EAT held that the agreement was not conclusive and a dismissal could be fair because of the re-organisation. Talbot J that it was an error of law for the Tribunal to find that the dismissal was unfair merely because of the contractual term since it was necessary to consider the circumstances of the dismissal, the reason for it and to inquire whether the employer was reasonable in treating it as a sufficient reason.

The employer must act fairly in requiring the employee to change his duties. So in **Dale v Lignacite Products Limited** [EAT 138/78] where an employee was singled out for extra hours which had previously been shared the dismissal was unfair. This was despite the fact that in this case the employee could be contractually required to work these hours.

In showing that he acted reasonably in attempting to implement changes, the court will particularly consider whether the employer properly consulted with his workforce, explained the reasons for the changes and their impact and gave his workforce an opportunity to state their views. The scope of these obligations may differ depending on the urgency or need of the re-organisation; an emergency may not allow an opportunity for extended discussion.

It is clear, however, that impetuous or peremptory behaviour on the part of an employer with little investigation is likely to lead to a result that any dismissal was not fair. In **Green v Barnes** [EAT 647/82] an employee was dismissed when he refused to work overtime, which was contractually required. The dismissal was unfair as there was no evidence of the need for it or proper consultation with the employee.

Where the employer proposes a re-organisation, in the ordinary course of events, as with other areas there should be consultation with the workforce about it. Although consultation has taken on a greater significance since *Polkey* insistence on the need for consultation is not a recent innovation. In **Wicks v Charles A Smethhurst Limited** [1973] IRLR 327 for example, the applicant was engaged as an organ builder on terms that he could be required to erect an organ on any site in the UK. He was asked to go to work on a job in Newry, Northern Ireland but refused because of the Troubles. He was later asked to go to work in Belfast but refused unless he was insured for injury or death. He was summarily dismissed. A Tribunal found that the dismissal was unfair as the employer had acted unreasonably in refusing his request and had not even made any enquiries about insurance. There should have been some consultation or discussion about the reasonable stance that was being taken by the employee.

In **Wilson v IDR Construction Limited** [1975] IRLR 260, Mr Wilson was dismissed from his job as a bricklayer because he refused to go to work on a site the following day. His refusal stemmed from the fact that his wife was ill and he had heard that bricklayers were not really required on the site. His refusal related only to the following day and he would have been prepared to go to the site a couple of days later. The Tribunal held that although the respondents had a contractual right to order the applicant to go to work on the site they acted unreasonably in dismissing him. The applicant had never before refused to work on a site and the Tribunal considered that if there had been consultation with the applicant and he had been given a chance to state his reasons there was a chance he would not have been dismissed.

The effect of lack of consultation making a dismissal unfair was re-iterated in **UCATT v Brain** [1981] ICR 542. The employee was employed as the publications officer of the trade union. Acting on the instructions of the General Secretary an article was placed in the union journal which was defamatory of the employers' association in the building industry. A writ was issued against the employee as the editor of the journal. The union took over the conduct of the action and agreed a settlement without consulting the employee. He was not prepared to sign an undertaking that had been agreed by the union and was dismissed. The Court of Appeal held that the union had no power to order him to sign the undertaking and having regard to the fact he had never been consulted about the settlement the employers had acted unreasonably.

In **Martin & Ors v Automobile Proprietary Limited** [1978] IRLR 64 the RAC re-organised its business due to an increase in call out demands, increasing the hours of work of emergency controllers. Negotiations lasted 18 months and a collective agreement was reached which most of the employees were happy to accept. The applicants were not happy with the result that the union had achieved and resigned from the union. They were then dismissed for refusing to comply with the new terms. The EAT took the view that a tribunal had adopted the wrong approach to the question of fairness and remitted the case to another tribunal. They also made some comments about the need for individual consultation in this situation. Kilner Brown J stated:

> "The vital question is whether or not the employer had acted fairly and reasonably with reference to the individual, not whether or not they had consulted the staff association. That is only part of the story. Plainly in some cases, the individual may, notwithstanding his personal attitude demonstrate himself to have acted unreasonably and to have been unnecessarily obstinate. He may be caught by a collective agreement. In these we can envisage the employer with comparative ease being able to satisfy the proposition that he acted reasonably and to justify the reason for dismissal and the, ultimately, if there was an allegation of unfair dismissal to say that in all the circumstances the dismissal was fair..."

Kilner Brown J set out the way in which he thought a tribunal should approach the issue of fairness when an employee has been dismissed for refusing to accept changed terms and conditions:

> "What should be done in the circumstances of the case, is for dismissal having already been admitted and dismissal having been correctly found, by reason of some other substantial reason, then to investigate in depth and with care the position arising out of the reorganisation as it affected the employer and these three employees. The first thing that has to be examined is the contract of employment. The second thing that has to be examined is whether of not there was a change in the original contract of employment which was being enforced unilaterally by the employer. The next thing to be examined is whether or not the enforcement of that unilateral variation in the contract was properly handled. We use loose terminology because it involves a certain number of factors. It involves a patient understanding by the employer of the strongly held views of the employee. It involves an obligation upon the employer to demonstrate to the individual that this is a reorganisation which is sensible and in the interests of thousands of employees; to listen to and weigh up the representation of the employee; to exercise the managerial judgment whether or not it may not be possible to make an exception in the case of the individual and not to force him into a collective agreement..."

The authority provides a succinct statement of the steps that should be taken when a unilateral change is being considered. The key to an employer successfully resisting a claim for unfair dismissal where an employee has been dismissed or resigned because he refused to go along with the change lies in the employer identifying the reason that the variation is needed for the business, explaining to employees the reason for change and considering whether there is any other alternative, listening to the employees' representations and giving such representations proper weight and consideration and, if all else fails, explaining to employees why such changes must take place. As was said in **White v Reflecting Roadstuds Limited** [1991] ICR at page 742: "..no reasonable employer will, on reflection, wish to reach a decision having a material effect on one of his employees whether it is redundancy, mobility, switch of jobs or something similar without discussion, explanation or consultation...the principle is one of discussion – communication...".

The courts will take a number of factors into account in deciding whether the employer has justified the reason for the changes as being fair, which may include the following:

(1) Whether the reason for the change is simply to improve profitability or in order the enable the business to continue to run. Where the employer is merely seeing to increase its profits then Tribunals will need to be persuaded that it is reasonable for employees to have the change imposed upon them. However, it was made clear in **Catamaran Cruisers Limited v Williams** [1994] IRLR 386 that an employer does not need to show that the survival of the business is threatened before the change may be regarded as reasonable.

(2) It was also stated in *Catamaran* that the fact that the variations have union agreement may be a factor in deciding whether the employer acted reasonably.

(3) Where the proposed changes do not adversely affect the employee in terms of remuneration or working conditions the employer may find it easier to justify its position as being fair.

Competition

> Where an employer is concerned that an employee may set up in competition or use confidential information that is the property of the employer a dismissal for this reason may amount to SOSR and be fair (It may also amount to a dismissal by reason of conduct, as to which see Chapter 6).

Moreover, there may be circumstances where an employee has an association with a competitor of the employer where the employer considers it necessary to take steps to protect its position (for example where the employee has a relation who works for the competitor). In **Simmons v SD Graphics Limited** [EAT 548/79] the EAT said that it is a question of fact whether a dismissal is fair in circumstances where two employees who are 'connected' work for competitors. The employee lived with a senior sales manager who moved to work for a competitor. It was held that she was dismissed for SOSR.

In some cases the employer has sought to protect its position by taking steps that fall short of dismissal, for example, by requiring the employee to sign a restrictive covenant or asking the employee to move to a position or place of work where he is unlikely to be able to cause any harm. In **R S Components Limited v Irwin** the employees were dismissed when they refused to sign a restrictive covenant.

Where the employee has access to confidential information then a dismissal may be fair if there is a risk that the information will be divulged to competitors. This is an issue which has arisen in cases where the employee is related to an individual who works for a competitor. In **Foot v Eastern Counties Timber Limited** [1972] IRLR 83 an employee with access to confidential information was dismissed for SOSR when her husband set up in competition with her employer. In **Skyrail Oceanic t/a Goodmans Tours v Coleman** [1980] IRLR 226 an employee was dismissed when she was intending to marry an employee in a rival firm with the agreement of the two firms. She had access to confidential information and the EAT held that the reason for dismissal was for SOSR.

However, the Courts did not think that it was sufficient to be a dismissal for SOSR merely that an employee who was under notice of dismissal sought employment with a rival firm (See **Harris & Russell Limited v Slingsby** [1973] 3 All ER 31 and **Laughton & Hawley v Bapp Industrial Supplies Limited** [1986] ICR 634). Working for a rival employer during spare time will not necessarily justify a dismissal for SOSR where there is no confidential information to protect (**Novas Plastics Limited v Froggatt** [1982] IRLR 146).

Conduct not work related

The behaviour of an employee out of work may justify dismissal by reason of conduct, for example where a criminal offence is committed that is incompatible with continued employment. There may be cases where the actions of the employee are not such that they can justify dismissal for **misconduct** but the employer considers the continued employment of the individual to be inappropriate in the circumstances and the dismissal may be for **SOSR.** In **Abiaefo v Enfield Community Care NHS Trust** [EAT 152/96] a health worker was dismissed for SOSR when it was discovered that she punished her son by way of corporal punishment.

Deceit on the Part of Employee

Where the employee lies to the employer at a recruitment interview about his qualifications or experience and the employer subsequently discovers the truth dismissal may, in those circumstances be for SOSR. This is illustrated by **O'Brien v The Prudential Assurance Co Limited** [1979] IRLR 140 where the employee did not disclose a history of mental illness when interviewed for a job as an insurance agent and the company had a policy of not employing such persons because they were required to visit clients houses (consider now, however, the impact of the DDA 1995) he was fairly dismissed after being employed for eight months. Failure to disclose previous convictions or lying about qualifications may make a dismissal for SOSR fair.

Family Businesses

Where the employer's business is run along family lines it may be a dismissal for SOSR to dismiss an employee in order that a member of the family can be introduced to the business. This was the position in **Priddle v Dibble** [1978] ICR 149 where the employee was dismissed as the employer wanted his son to take over the business and the employee had been made aware that this was the position from the outset of his employment.

Fixed Term and Temporary Contracts

By section 95(1)(b) of the ERA 1996 the expiry of a fixed term contract is treated as a dismissal. Such a dismissal may be a dismissal for SOSR where the employee has been made aware that he has been taken on under a contract of temporary duration. This was the position in **Terry v East Sussex County Council** [1976] ICR 536 where a fixed term contract as a lecturer was not renewed and the EAT held that the dismissal could be for SOSR where 'the case is a genuine one where the employee has to his own knowledge been employed for a particular period, or a particular job, on a temporary basis'. The Court of Appeal confirmed this approach in **Fay v North Yorkshire County Council** [1986] ICR 115 where it was held that the expiry of a fixed term does not in itself constitute SOSR but is capable of doing so if it is shown that the fixed term was adopted for a genuine purpose which was known to the employee and has cased to be applicable. Browne-Wilkinson LJ stated:

> "If it is shown that the fixed term contract was adopted for a genuine purpose and that fact was known to the employee, and it is also shown that the specific purpose for which the fixed term contract was adopted has ceased to be applicable, then, for the purposes of section 98 those facts are capable of constituting some other substantial reason."

(For the issue of whether there was a redundancy see page 46). In **West Midlands Regional Health Authority v Guirguis** [EAT 567/77] the employer failed to establish the reason as being SOSR where it argued that it had a policy against permanent locums but there was evidence of locums being employed for long periods in the past whilst in **Beard v St Joseph's School Governors** [1978], ICR 1234 a dismissal for SOSR was unfair on procedural grounds.

Imprisonment

Where an employee is sent to prison but the contract has not been frustrated it was stated in **Kingston v British Railways Board** [1984] IRLR 146 that the dismissal may be for SOSR.

Mistake and Genuine Belief in Substantial Reason

There may be cases where the dismissal is based upon a genuine but erroneous belief that the dismissal is fair on the facts or that it is necessary to dismiss as a matter of law. In these circumstances dismissal may be for SOSR. In **Taylor v Co-operative Retail Services Limited** [1981] ICR 172 and **Leyland Vehicles Limited v Jones** [1981] IRLR 269 this was the position in cases where there was a mistaken belief about the operation of a closed shop. In **Bouchaala v Trust Forte Hotels Limited** [1980] ICR 721 the employee was dismissed based upon the genuine but mistaken belief that he needed a work permit. Waterhouse J stated that:

"It appears to us that if an employer is genuinely of the view that it is impossible to continue the employment of an employee because he understands that there is an enactment prohibiting the lawful employment of that employee he is entitled to argue that the reason he dismisses him comes under that sub-section.'

Personality Clashes

In certain cases there may be such personality clash between the employer and employee or between co-workers that the continued employment of the employee is impossible. In such cases it may be for SOSR. In **Tregoanowan v Robert Knee & Co Limited** [1975] ICR 405 there was a personality clash in the office between the appellant and other employees for which she was to blame. She was fairly dismissed for SOSR. Similarly, in **Gorfin v Distressed Gentlefolk's Aid Association** [1973] IRLR 290 a domestic worker was dismissed after complaints from other members of staff. It has been held that it is necessary for the employer to show that any breakdown is irremedial so that steps should be taken to seek an improvement in the relationship before dismissal is considered if the dismissal is to be held to be fair (**Turner v Vestric Limited** [1980] ICR 528).

Sexual Inclinations

It has been held that, in certain circumstances, the dismissal of an employee because of his or her sexual orientation may amount to SOSR. This was the position in **Boychuk v HJ Symons Holdings Limited** [1977] IRLR where the employee flaunted her sexual orientation in a way that caused offence. The Court of Session took this further in **Saunders v National Camps Association Limited**

[1980] IRLR 1784. The employee was dismissed from his job as a maintenance handyman at a children's camp when the employer found out that he was homosexual and had been involved in an incident in the nearby town. There was psychiatric evidence that he was no danger to young persons but the Tribunal took into account that a considerable proportion of the public may consider that the employment of a homosexual should be restricted in relation to working in proximity to children. The Court thought that this was a case where the area of decision was indeterminate and that some employers may have decided not to dismiss whilst others would feel it in the interests of the children that this was only the safe course. The Court thought that neither decision could be said to be unreasonable.

Spouses

Where the employer has engaged a married couple and one spouse has left or been dismissed then the dismissal of the other spouse may amount to SOSR if that post was dependant upon the couple being employed together. In **Kelman v G J Oram** [1983] IRLR 432 where the married couple ran a public house, the dismissal of a wife was fair and for SOSR even though the dismissal of her husband for misconduct in relation to stock deficiencies was unfair. However, in **Scottish & Newcastle Retail Limited v Standton** [EAT 1126/96] it was held that where a dismissal for misconduct was unfair, and the dismissal of the spouse for SOSR was dependant upon the other spouse being dismissed, then the dismissals were linked so that both could be unfair. It should also be noted that if, in reality, there is no need for the employees to be employed as a couple, as one carried out all the main duties, dismissal of the main worker when the co-spouse departs may be unfair (**Great Mountain and Tumble Rugby Club v Howlett** [EAT 173/88]).

Third Party Pressure

Pressure placed by a third party on an employer to dismiss the employee may, in certain circumstances, amount to SOSR. Pressure may come from a valued customer or from other employees where there is an internal dispute.

In the case of customers, a threat to withdraw custom unless the employee is dismissed or moved may amount to SOSR where the employee is dismissed. In **Dobie v Burns International Security Services (UK) Limited** [1984] ICR 812, Merseyside County Council had the right to vet employees of the respondent which provided services to the Council and it refused to permit Mr Dobie to continue to work after a disagreement with a senior council employee,. There was no comparable employment and Mr Dobie was dismissed. It was held that this was for SOSR and fair. The Court of Appeal held that in such cases, it is possible to take account of the injustice to the employee in deciding whether the employer acted reasonably. Sir John Donaldson MR stated:

> "In deciding whether the employer acted reasonably or unreasonably, a very important factor of which he has to take account, on the facts known to him at that time, is whether there will or will not be injustice to the employee and the extent of that injustice. For example, he will clearly have to take account of the length of time during which the employee has been employed by him, the satisfactoriness or otherwise of the employee's service, the difficulties which may face the employee in obtaining other employment, and matters of that sort. None of these is decisive, but they are all matters of which he has to take account and they are all matters which affect the justice or injustice to the employee of being dismissed."

Where a major customer insists on the employee's dismissal the reason may be SOSR (**Scott Packaging and Warehousing Co Limited v Paterson** [1978] IRLR 166) though it will be necessary for the employer to produce evidence that the customers did so instruct or consult and in any event the mere fact that the customer so instructed will not of itself make the dismissal fair (**Grootcon (UK) Limited v Keld** [1984] IRLR 302 and *Dobie* above). Where the employer has merely dismissed as a result of fear or concern on the part of the employer as to how a third party *may* react, this without more will not justify a dismissal for SOSR (**Securicor Guarding Limited v R** [1994] IRLR 633 where dismissal took place prior to a prosecution for sexual offences against children because the employer was concerned about third party sensibilities but did not discuss with the third party). The employer must show that reasons for the decision by the third party to refuse to continue to use the employee where he seeks to rely on this as SOSR (**Pillinger v Manchester Area Health Authority** [1979] IRLR 430). Moreover, improper or illegal pressure from a third party cannot amount to a SOSR justifying a dismissal (**Lavelle v Alloa Brewery Co Limited** [EAT 655/85]).

Where the employee has been dismissed as a result of third party pressure it will not be necessary for the employer to agree with the third party or to prove that allegations made by the third party are true to show SOSR (**Edwards v Curtis t/a Arkive Computers** [EAT 845/95]).

Pressure to dismiss may also come from co-employees where there is a major personality clash (see above at page 209).

In addition to showing that the reasons is for SOSR it will be necessary for the tribunal to consider whether the employer acting reasonably in the decision to and the manner of dismissal. In **Rigblast Energy Services v Hogarth** [EAT 665/93] the operator of a rig had the right to ask for any employee to be removed from the rig. When it refused to allow Mr Hogarth onto the rig he was dismissed without any warning or discussion. The dismissal was unfair as he had not even been informed that the operator had such power and his employer had made no attempt to find out why the operator was excluding him from the rig. In *Dobie* it was pointed out that his is an area where the injustice to the employee may be considered. The employer should in any event consider whether alternative steps such as redeployment are possible. (See **Norwest Construction Limited v Higham** [EAT 278/82].)

Transfer of Undertakings

See Chapter 23.

CHAPTER NINE
STATUTORY BANS

Definition

By section 98(2)(d) of the ERA 1996 a dismissal may be potentially fair if the reason for it:

> "Is that the employee could not continue to work in the position which he held without contravention (either on his part or that of his employer) of a duty or restriction imposed by or under an enactment."

It is necessary for the employer to show that the continued employment of the employee does in fact contravene a statutory enactment and a genuine but mistaken belief that this is the position will not comply with this sub-section though it may amount to a SOSR reason for dismissal.

In **Bouchaala v Trust House Forte Hotels Limited** [1980] IRLR 382 the appellant, a Tunisian national, was initially employed as a trainee manager by the respondents with a view to being employed by them as a manager in Tunisia. He decided to stay in the United Kingdom and the Home Office stated that his further stay would not be sanctioned because he had ceased to be a student and did not qualify under the rules for work permits. The employer was wrongly advised that he could not stay. He was therefore dismissed. In fact, this wrong advice was corrected shortly thereafter. The EAT held that the reason for dismissal could not fall in section 98(2)(d). It was not possible to add words to the effect that a genuine but mistaken belief could fall within the subsection as this would involve reading words into the statute that were not there. However, the reason could be for a SOSR reason.

Examples of contravention of a statutory enactment that will come within this ground for dismissal include the following:

(1) Loss of a driving licence.

See the cases referred to below.

(2) Employment contrary to regulations which relate to suitability or competence.

In **Sandhu v Hillingdon London Borough** [1978] IRLR 208 the continued employment of a teacher was unlawful following a determination by the DES. (See also **Haseen v Walsall Metropolitan Council** [EAT 213/80].)

In **Taylor v Alidair Limited** [1978] ICR 445 a pilot who was considered incompetent under the Air Navigation Order 1974 was dismissed by reason of a statutory ban.

(3) Restrictions on working in the jurisdiction.

See *Bouchaala* above.

Where the continued employment of the employee will amount to the contravention of an enactment so that this is a potentially fair reason the Tribunal must then still go on to consider the question of reasonableness which may include the question of whether any modification could have been made to the employee's duties or whether there was any alternative employment which would have the effect that the statutory prohibition would no longer apply.

The Tribunal may take into account the following six matters in deciding whether it would have been reasonable to modify duties or offer alternative employment:

(1) Whether the post necessitated the particular requirement to which the statutory prohibition applied.

This may apply particularly in a case where the requirement of a driving licence is essential to the post, as in **Appleyard v**

Smith (Hull) Limited [1972] IRLR 19 and **Fearn v Tayford Motor Co Limited** [1975] IRLR 336. In *Appleyard* the complainant lost his licence but he maintained that he was only a driver temporarily and that he had worked for most of his service with the respondents as a maintenance fitter on marine engines. The respondents, however, required anyone in their employment to be able to drive and they did not hire employees who do not hold driving licences. It was held that the employer acted reasonably since it would not have been reasonable for them to alter their customary practice of having vehicles tested by someone other than the one who does the repairing.

In *Fearn* the complainant was dismissed from his job as Used Vehicle Supervisor with the respondents after he was disqualified from driving for a period of 12 months following a motor accident. His employers claimed that, as driving constituted an important part of his job, he would not be able to carry out his duties during his disqualification. The respondents acted reasonably in treating the applicant's disqualification from driving as a sufficient reason for dismissing him. Though the applicant had many duties, some of them involving driving and others not, the evidence was that 40% of his time was spent driving. The testing and valuation of cars was an important part of his duties.

The dismissal *may* be fair even if the employee offers to provide an alternative director where the contract stipulates that he must be able to drive (**Roberts v Toyota (GB) Limited** [EAT 614/80]).

Even where an unfair procedure has been followed there is likely to be contribution (**Nairne v Highland and Islands Fire Brigade** [1989] IRLR 366).

(2) The length of service of the employee.

If the employee is long serving then allowance may need to be made for the statutory ban if the job can be performed in some other way. A question of a reasonable adjustment may arise if the ban arises out of a disability.

(3) The cost of the modification or alternative employment.

If alternative employment can be offered or the employee can carry out his job with, for example, a slight modification to equipment it may be unreasonable for the employer not to take this course.

(4) Whether the job could have been carried out in a way that is satisfactory with slight modifications.

Where the ban only relates to a small part of the job a modification may be necessary if the employer is not to be regarded as acting unreasonably. (C.f. the driving cases and note the question of reasonable adjustments under the DDA 1995.)

(5) Whether the statutory prohibition in fact applied or was likely to apply.

In **Sutcliffe and Eaton Limited v Pinney** [1977] IRLR 349 The applicant was dismissed from his job as a trainee hearing aid dispenser after he failed to pass the examination of the Hearing Aid Council within the five year period that was allowed though the period could be extended. Due to his failure in the exam, Mr Pinney's name was removed from the register of hearing aid dispensers set up under the Hearing Aid Council Act 1968. This Act makes it an offence for anyone not on the register to act as a dispenser of hearing aids and to be employed by a registered employer. After his dismissal, Mr Pinney successfully applied for an extension to sit the exam again. The EAT upheld a finding that the dismissal was unfair. It stated that the fact that to continue to employ someone could be a breach of a statute is not of itself conclusive as to the reasonableness of dismissal. Whether it is reasonable to cease to employ someone in such circumstances is a matter to be decided by an Industrial Tribunal. In the present case, the Industrial Tribunal were entitled to find that had the employee been kept on and an extension of his training period applied for, there was little likelihood of any proceedings resulting in a penalty against the employer.

(6) Whether the employee only became subject to the statutory ban because of the way that he was treated by his employer.

In the *Sandhu* case it was alleged by the complainant that he failed because of the manner in which he had been treated. The EAT stated that:

"if it really were established that he never really had a chance of proving himself; that he was treated quite unreasonably during the probationary period; that there was an element of racial discrimination; that there was a total lack of co-operation by the Local Education Authority; and that really this was all being done as a device to get rid of him — something on those lines — then it seems to us that the Industrial Tribunal could have [considered whether the employer] had acted reasonably in dismissing him, and whether, for example, — this is not meant to be exhaustive — what a reasonable employer would have done would have been to discuss the matter with him, with the Department of Education and Science, and see whether what had gone wrong could be put right, so that he could have a fair trial and a fair opportunity to prove himself."

PART THREE
AUTOMATICALLY FAIR DISMISSALS

CHAPTER TEN
NATIONAL SECURITY

Where dismissal is for the purpose of safeguarding national security then dismissal will be automatically fair. Under section 10(4) of the Employment Tribunals Act 1996 a certificate was required from a Minister that national security interests were involved. However, Schedule 8 of the Employment Relations Act 1999 substantially amends the law in this area. It is anticipated that the provisions will come into force by Easter 2000. The right to bring proceedings for unfair dismissal, save for 'whistleblowing' is given to the Security Service, the Secret Intelligence Service and the Government Communications Headquarters by an amended Section 193 of the ERA 1996. Amendments have therefore been made to section 10 of the Employment Rights Act 1996. As with much of that Act, provision is made for Regulations to enact the intention behind the new section. The scheme of the section is as follows:

(1) By section 10(1) on a complaint of unfair dismissal *"if it shown that the action complained of was taken for the purpose of safeguarding national security the employment tribunal shall dismiss the complaint"*

(2) Employment Tribunal Regulations may make provision regarding the composition of the Tribunal (Section 10(2)).

(3) By section 10(3) a direction may be given by a Minster of the Crown if it relates to Crown employment proceedings and the Minister considers it expedient in the interests of national security. By 10(4) an order may be made by the President or a Regional Chairman if is considered expedient in the interests of national security. Crown employment proceedings are proceedings where the complaint is connected with Crown employment or the performance of functions on behalf of the Crown.

(4) There is provision in section 10(5) for regulations to be made so that a Minister of the Crown (or by section 10(6) a tribunal) may in relation to Crown employment proceedings:

- direct a tribunal to sit in private for all or part of particular proceedings
- direct a tribunal to exclude the application from all or part of particular proceedings
- direct a tribunal to exclude the applicant's representatives from all or part of particular proceedings
- direct a tribunal to take steps to conceal the identify of a particular witness in particular proceedings
- direct a tribunal to keep secret all of part of the reasons for its decision in particular proceedings.

(5) By section 10(7) where an applicant or representative has been excluded regulations may make provision:

- for the appointment of the Attorney General or the Advocate General to represent the Applicant's interests
- about the publication and registration of the reasons for the tribunal's decision
- permitting an excluded person to make a statement to the tribunal before the commencement of the proceedings or part from which he is excluded.

A new section 10A makes provision for regulations so that tribunals may sit in private to hear evidence from a person where the evidence is likely to consist of

- information which would breach a prohibition in an enactment if disclosed
- information communicated in confidence or obtained because of confidence reposed in him by another person
- information which may cause substantial injury to any undertaking of his or where he works. (This does not apply to information relating to collective agreements and bargaining under section 178 of TULR(C)A).

Section 10B makes it an offence to publish information where there has been a direction or determination that the identity of a witness or part or whole of the decision be kept secret.

CHAPTER ELEVEN
INDUSTRIAL ACTION

Definition

Industrial action will often constitute a breach of the contract of employment. Where employees wholly withdraw their labour, i.e. strike, this will be a repudiatory breach of contract since it goes to the heart of the contract of employment. However, there are many forms of action short of striking (i.e. go slow, working to rule) that may amount to a breach of contract if sufficiently fundamental. The employer is likely to have contractual rights and remedies against the employees in such circumstances. However, for the purposes of unfair dismissal there are statutory provisions that are fundamental to the employee's right to bring a claim if he is engaging in industrial action. The Employment Relations Act 1999 has relaxed the position in relation to 'protected official'. Nevertheless, the right to bring claims for unfair dismissal is still severely curtailed in this area. It is necessary to consider:

- Dismissals during 'non protected' official action under section 238 of the Trade Union and Labour Relations (Consolidation) Act 1992 (TULR(C)A);
- Dismissals during 'protected' official action under section 238A of TULR(C)A as inserted by the Employment Relations Act 1999;
- Dismissals during unofficial action.

Dismissals during 'Non Protected' Official Action under Section 238 of TULR(C)A

Where the employee comes within this section, the Tribunal does not have jurisdiction to hear the claim. It was said by Phillips J in **Gallagher v Wragg** [1977] ICR 174 that the section is expressed in this way as it was intended the law remain neutral where industrial disputes are in issue (but cf **Faust v Power Packing Casemakers Limited** [1983] IRLR 117 per Stephenson LJ).

> The section applies where at the date of the dismissal there was a lock-out, strike or other industrial action.

The provisions of section 238, by 238(1) are expressed to apply to a claimant who asserts he has been dismissed:

"where at the date of the dismissal-

(a) the employer was conducting or instituting a lock out or,
(b) the complainant was taking part in a strike or other industrial action."

Lock-out

There is no definition of a lock-out in relation to section 238 and the courts have repeatedly emphasised that it is a matter of fact. Definitions contained in the legislation for other purposes such as continuity may be helpful but the higher courts have stated that it is for the tribunals to decide the issue on the facts and they are not to be bound by such definitions. In **Express & Star Limited v Blunday & Ors** [1987] IRLR 422 there was a dispute over new technology. After protracted negotiations with the union, all access to the premises were closed by management with the exception of one door and employees were taken to a meeting room. They were asked whether they were prepared to work under their contracts of employment without restriction and told that if they replied "no", they would be immediately suspended without pay. Ultimately, over 50 employees were dismissed. A Tribunal held that the employer had not conducted a lock-out at the time of the dismissal but that there had been industrial action. In the Court of Appeal it was stated that whether there has been a lock-out or whether there has been a strike is a question to be decided on the facts and merits of each case by the Industrial Tribunal using its industrial relations expertise. The definition of the necessary elements of a lock-out or a strike is not a question of law.

The Court of Appeal expressly rejected the argument that definitions contained in the Act in relation to other areas should be applied. Moreover, the dictionary definition of a lock-out as a 'refusal on the part of the employer to furnish work to their operatives except on conditions to be accepted by them collectively' was a reliable indication but not to be applied as though it were expressly contained in statute. Whether there has been a breach of contract will be a material consideration though a lock out can be instituted without a breach of contract. However, Glidewell LJ stated:

> "The proper construction of words in a statute is a matter of law. Since there is no statutory definition of the word "lock-out" where it appears in [s.238], it must be given its ordinary meaning. The ordinary meaning of "lock-out" comprehends not merely the act of the employer in refusing to allow his employees to work, but the reason why he so refuses. In the present case, therefore, in deciding that there had not been a lock-out, the Industrial Tribunal were entitled as a matter of law to consider whether the adoption of new technology involved a change in the terms and conditions of the employees' contracts of employment. The EAT's conclusion that this was not a relevant consideration to whether or not there was a lock-out was wrong in law."

Where the employer seeks to ascertain whether employees will co-operate with new terms and conditions and requires them to submit to an interview in breach of contract, with a view to dismissing them if they do not agree, it was held in **Manifold Industries Limited v Sims** [EAT 223/91] that this could be a lock-out. Where the employees are able to work but not in compliance with their full terms and conditions then this is unlikely to be lock-out. Where the employer tells his workforce that they may only work for him provided they do within their contract of employment, it appears this will not be a 'lock-out'. Glidewell LJ stated in *Blunday* that

> "What is material is that in my view the ordinary meaning of the word 'lock-out' comprehends not merely the act of the employer in refusing to allow his employees to work, but the reason why he so refuses. Suppose that a manufacturer has an urgent order from a valued customer, and that some of the employees threaten that they will 'go slow' and not complete the order on time unless they receive double pay; if the employer refuses, and tells the employees that they may only continue to work for him provided that they work at the normal speed and for the agreed rate of pay, can he be said to lock out his employees? I do not accept that he can."

Strike

A strike may be defined as a 'concerted stoppage of work' but this is a matter of fact for the Tribunal to decide. Section 246 describes a strike in this way but only for the purpose of continuity and, as with a 'lock-out' the question of whether or not a strike is taking place will be a question of fact. In **Tramp Shipping Corporation v Greenwich Marine Inc** [1975] ICR 261 (in a different context) a strike was described by Lord Denning as:

> "A concerted stoppage of work by men done with a view to improving their wages or conditions, or giving vent to a grievance, or making a protest about something or other, or supporting or sympathising with other workmen in such endeavour."

This may include a political issue.

It was held in **Connex South Eastern Limited v RMI** [1999] IRLR 249 that strike can encompass a ban on overtime and rest day working as there was a concerted stoppage of work during those periods.

Other Industrial action

As with the definition of lock-out and strike it is a question of fact whether particular action amounts to 'other industrial action. Examples will include:

- A work to rule or go slow (**Drew v St Edmundsbury Borough Council** [1980] IRLR 459; ICR 513;
- Picketing activities;
- Refusal to work on new machinery;
- Preventing the employer from testing machinery (**Thompson v Eaton Limited** [1976] IRLR 308);
- Refusal to work voluntary overtime where the same is premeditated (**Glenrose (Fish Merchants) Limited v Chapman** [EAT 245/89]);
- In **Midland Plastics v Till & Ors** [1983] ICR 118 the EAT referred to "actions which, in normal contemplation, might be thought of as industrial action: walking out, going slow, working to rule, banning of overtime, picketing."

But is not likely to include

- sending a deputation to management to complain about conditions.
- refusal to carry out non contractual overtime when the reason is not to put any pressure on the employer.
- Insistence on working to terms and conditions where there is no dispute other than that the employee wants to abide by his contract.

(2) The purpose of the action will be of importance since if there is a concerted effort to put pressure on an employee this is likely to amount to industrial action.

The nature and effect of the action will be of relevance as to whether there was industrial action. In **Rasool v Hepworth Pipe Co Limited (No 2)** [1980] IRLR 137; ICR 494 the EAT considered that a meeting at the employer's premises during working hours to discuss wage negotiations did not amount to industrial action. It is the purpose of the action that may be critical. In *Rasool* the meeting was to consider the views of employees with regard to wage negotiations and, although there was a degree of disruption if was more properly regarded as trade union activity. If nature and effect are to be considered it will be in relation to concerted action.

However, the purpose of the action was considered more important in **Power Packing Casemakers Limited v Faust** [1983] ICR 292; IRLR 117. Three employees were dismissed because they refused to work overtime in circumstances where there was no provision for overtime in their contracts. The EAT held that, although there was no breach of contract in refusing to work overtime, there was other industrial action as the employees were in dispute about their wages. The Court of Appeal dismissed the appeal. Lord Justice Stephenson stated:

> "To constitute 'industrial action' in the natural meaning of those words on the part of an employee there must be action in breach of his contract of employment. If he merely refuses to do something which he is not contractually bound to do, he cannot be taking part in industrial action. I would agree that if he refuses because he has a private commitment to visit a sick friend, or a personal preference for a football match, he is not taking industrial action. But that is not this case. If he refuses because

he and others who refuse with him hope to extract an increase of wages out of his employers because their business will be disrupted if they do not grant it, that continued application of pressure is industrial action in the common sense of the words."

Thus the purpose of the action is highly relevant and the motive of the employer in dismissing becomes irrelevant once section 238 is applicable.

Because the issue is one of fact different tribunals may come to different conclusions (**Naylor v Orton & Smith Limited** [1983] ICR 665; **Coates and Venables v Modern Methods and Materials Limited** [1982] IRLR 318).

(3) An individual may take industrial action.

The wording 'taking part' would appear to suggest that there must be more than one person taking part in industrial action and this was the approach taken in **Bowater Containers Limited v Blake** [EAT 552/81]. However, in **Lewis and Britton v E Mason & Sons** [1994] IRLR 4 the EAT held that one person may take part in industrial action. Mr Britton was dismissed for refusing to take a lorry on an overnight trip from Wales to Edinburgh unless he was paid £5 as an overnight allowance. Another driver was dismissed for refusing to go to Scotland. The two drivers and staff were driven home in a works van by Mr Lewis and it was agreed he would intercede on their behalf. He spoke to the employer and said all those in the van would not come into work the next day unless the two were reinstated, whereupon they were dismissed. With regard to Mr Britton it was held by the Tribunal that he was engaged in industrial action by his refusal to take the van out. The EAT held that the Tribunal had correctly concluded that one person may be involved in industrial action where there is conduct designed to coerce the employer to improve terms and conditions and Mr Britton was so involved because he would only have been prepared to do so for an extra payment. The case raises the spectre of an individual being unable to bring unfair dismissal proceedings because he is dismissed when he disputes whether he can be required to carry out duties under his contract of employment and requires to be paid for what he regards as additional work.

(4) A threat to take industrial action will not normally amount to industrial action.

In the *Lewis* case, Mr Britton's fellow workers had threatened that they would not go into work the next day if Mr Britton and the other worker were not re-instated. The EAT held that it was open to the Tribunal to conclude that there was industrial action at the time of the dismissals where there was a definite threat that the dismissed workers and work colleagues were not coming in the next morning unless there was reinstatement, since further negotiation could not have been expected to take place and the work for the following day had been allocated. The EAT referred to the decisions that made it clear that this issue was a matter of fact and stated that they could not say that the Tribunal decision was perverse.

The Tribunal referred to the decisions of **Midland Plastics Limited v Till** and **Winnett v Seamarks Brothers Limited** [1978] ICR 1240. The former case had held that a threat was not sufficient whilst in the latter, although some employees had not come into work collective action had already begun. The latter case was therefore distinguishable, since, although not all individual had attended work, it was clear that the industrial action had commenced. Nevertheless, the *Lewis* case does pose considerable risks that a mere threat that action may take place will come within the meaning of other industrial action.

(5) There may be industrial action without there being a breach of contract.

The majority of types of protest are likely to involve breach of contract. However, there are two areas, in particular, of difficulty. Where there is a dispute about the terms and conditions of the contract of employment so that the employees are demanding additional payment for work which is considered additional to the work they are contracted to carry out, any action taken is likely to come within the meaning of other industrial action. Where the employees refuse to work voluntary overtime this may amount to other industrial action even though it does not constitute a breach of contract. This was the view taken by the Court of Appeal in **Faust v Power Packing Casemakers** [1983] IRLR 117; ICR 292. Stephenson LJ stated:

"once an Industrial Tribunal, in the exercise of its good sense, decides that an employee was, at the date of his dismissal, taking part in industrial action, whether in breach of his contract or not, with the object of applying pressure on his employer or of disrupting his business, the Tribunal must refuse to entertain the complaint or to go into the questions of the employer's motive or reasons for dismissing."

This case may be compared with **Knowles v Fire Brigades Union** [1996] IRLR 617 where the ban on spare time work was because of concerns about ability to carry out the full time job rather than to pout pressure on the employer.

(6) There is a distinction between industrial action and trade union activities.

There is an, often difficult to draw, distinction between industrial action and union activities (see Chapter 24). In the latter, any dismissal may be automatically unfair. It is not possible for the dismissal to be for both reasons (**Drew v St Edmundsbury Borough Council** [1980] IRLR 459). It is a question of fact (or mixed law and fact) as to which side the action falls upon. Where, for example, a meeting is called during working hours in defiance of the employer's instructions this may be for union reasons or industrial action. In **Rasool v Hepworth Pipe Co Limited** [1980] IRLR 88 the Tribunal found that it was for trade union activites since the meeting was to discuss wages and not to put pressure on the employer. In **Naylor v Orton & Smith Co Limited** [1983] ICR 665 a meeting at which a vote was taken for an overtime ban was held not to amount to industrial action.

At the date of dismissal

By section 238(5) date of dismissal means the date when notice was given if the contract was terminated by notice or the effective date of termination.

Where any action has ceased at the date of dismissal then the section will no longer be applicable to such dismissals. Action may cease by the employees making it clear that they intended to return to work (**Glenrose (Fish Merchants) Limited v Chapman** [EAT 245/89]), accepting an ultimatum to return to work (**South East Kent Health Authority v Gillis** [EAT 927/83]) or by otherwise making it clear to the employer that they are no longer taking part. However, note the difficulties in relation to 'lock-outs' where the employee has held a direct interest at some stage. The NIRC made it clear in **Heayth v J F Longman (Meat Salesman) Limited** [1973] IRLR 214; ICR 407 that it is the point in time when the employer is made aware that the employees are no longer participating in action that is crucial, so that 'day' means a fraction of a day.

The dismissal must actually be communicated to the employee or there must be some means by which the employee has received notice of dismissal. In **Hindle Gears Limited v McGinty** [1985] ICR 111 notice had not been given when the letters were in the post and the employees returned to work before the letters were received.

Relevant employees

> The Tribunal shall not determine whether the dismissal was fair or unfair unless the complainant can show that one or more relevant employees have not been dismissed or that a relevant employee has been offered re-engagement within three months from the date of dismissal of the relevant employee and the complainant has not been re-engaged.

By section 238(2) where 238(1) is applicable:

> "...an employment tribunal shall not determine whether the dismissal was fair or unfair unless it is shown-
>
> (a) that one or more relevant employees of the same employer have not been dismissed, or
> (b) that a relevant employee has before the expiry of the period of three months beginning with the date of his dismissal been offered re-engagement and that the complainant has not been offered re-engagement."

By section 238(2B) the section does not apply to maternity, health and safety, employee representative cases or redundancy selection for those reasons.

Relevant employees in relation to lock outs

By section 238(3)(a) a relevant employee is:

> "in relation to a lock out, employees who were directly interested in the dispute in contemplation or furtherance of which the lock out occurred."

In relation to lock outs relevant employees are those that are directly interested in the dispute at some time.

In **Fisher v York Trailer Co Limited** [1979] ICR 834; IRLR 385 'interest' was defined as being at some time interested in the dispute. There was a go slow in respect of a dispute about productivity bonuses and the employees were locked out and required to sign a letter which stated they would work normally. All but several signed the document and a further letter was sent to them stating they would be regarded as having repudiated their contract unless they signed. Six of them, who persisted, were dismissed. The EAT held that the letters constituted an acceptance of a repudiatory breach, alternatively a termination. However, it held that the Tribunal were wrong in considering that only the seven were directly interested rather than all 34 who were originally locked out. The lock out occurred when the 34 men were told they were not allowed to work so that all 34 were interested at some time in the trade dispute in respect of which the lock out occurred (See also **H Campey & Sons v Bellwood & Ors** [1987] ICR 311.)

Relevant employees in relation to strikes or other industrial action

By section 238(3)(b) a relevant employee is:

> "in relation to a strike or other industrial action, those employees at the establishment of the employer at or from which the complainant works who at the date of his dismissal were taking part in the action."

The crucial issue is whether they were taking part at the time of the dismissal as to which see next section.

Taking Part

> In relation to strikes or other industrial action the comparison is between relevant employees 'taking part' and the complainant 'taking part' at the time of dismissal.

The expression 'taking part' is of twofold relevance:

(a) The complainant must have been 'taking part' in a strike or other industrial action at the time of his dismissal
(b) Relevant employees will be those employees who were 'taking part' at the time of the complainant's dismissal.

It is a question of fact whether the employees are taking part in a strike or other industrial action

As with other definitions in this section, it is a question of fact as to whether or not employees are taking part in action. It was stated by Stephenson LJ in **Coates and Venables v Modern Methods and Materials Limited** [1982] IRLR 318; ICR 763 that this type of issue is just the sort of question that the industrial jury is best fitted to decide. Browne-Wilkinson J criticised the undesirable results that this may have on industrial relations in *Naylor* since the effect is that employers are faced with the dilemma of dismissing everyone or potentially going out of business if they face huge sums in compensation. Given that it is a matter of fact, it is very difficult to advise.

The employees' motives are irrelevant

The motive of the employee does not matter if, objectively viewed, as a matter of fact the employee was taking part in the action. An employee who refrains from attending work for fear of crossing a picket line may nevertheless be participating in industrial action. This was considered in *Coates and Venables* (above). In this case, two complainants alleged that section 238 did not apply because an employee had not been dismissed. The employee had attended a meeting at the outset but had not gone in because she feared abuse from other strikers and had later become unwell. She was allowed to resume work when fit to do so. The Tribunal held that she had been taking part in a strike. A majority of the Court of Appeal upheld the Tribunal decision, holding that whether an employee is taking part must be judged by what the employee does and not by what he thinks or why he does it. Stephenson LJ stated:

> "I have come to the conclusion that participation in a strike must be judged by what the employee does and not by what he thinks or why he does it. If he stops work when his workmates come out on strike and does not say or do anything to make plain his disagreement, or which could amount to a refusal to join them, he takes part in their strike. The line between unwilling participation and not taking part may be difficult to draw, but those who stay away from work with the strikers without protest for whatever reason are to be regarded as having crossed that line to take part in the strike. In the field of industrial action those who are not openly against it are presumably for it."

Kerr LJ stated:

> "The fact that they had to cross the picket line to go in, and thereby suffer some abuse at the time, and quite possibly some unpopularity – or worse – among their fellow employees thereafter, and that feelings of this kind, as in the case of Mrs Leith, may have deterred them from going in, does not appear to me to make any difference. Nor would it make any difference, in my view, that their reason for staying out was that they were in sympathy with the strike. As it seems to me, their reasons or motives cannot be regarded as relevant; nor would it be relevant to consider whether their utterances or actions, or silence or inaction, showed support, opposition or indifference in relation to the strike.
>
> When it is necessary to determine the question whether an employee does or does not take part in a strike which is admittedly in progress, but which does not prevent the employee from going to work in defiance of the manifold pressures which the existence of the strike is bound to exert, then it seems to me that this question can in practice only be answered on the basis of his or her action by either staying out or going in. Of course, if the employee does not go to work for reasons which have nothing to do with the strike, such as illness or being on holiday, then the position would be different. But when the employee's absence from work is due to the existence of the strike in some respect, because he or she chooses not to go to work during the strike, then I think that the employee should be regarded as taking part in the strike."

It was held in **Wood Group Engineering Contactors Limited v Byrne** [EAT 447/92] that an employee taking part in a strike as an undercover informant was still taking part as on an objective factual basis he was participating.

The knowledge of the employer is irrelevant

It does not matter whether or not the employer is aware that the employee is participating in a strike or other industrial action if as a matter of objective fact this was the position (**Bolton Roadways Limited v Edwards** [1987] IRLR 392; **Manifold Industries Limited v Sims** [1991] IRLR 242 and **Jenkins v P and O European Ferries (Dover) Limited** [1991] ICR 652.) It is clear from the latter two cases that an earlier authority that introduced the concept of reasonable belief was wrong.

An employee may be taking part even if absent for a legitimate reason such as sickness

Where an employee is absent from work for a reason that has nothing to do with the industrial action at the time of its commencement (for example sickness or holiday) he will not be acting in breach of his contract of employment and there is no nexus between the action and his absence. However, the employee may be regarded as taking part in the strike if he **associates** himself with the strike. In *Bolton Roadways Limited v Edwards*, Scott LJ stated that:

> "Whether an employee is taking part in strike action is, as we have said, a question of fact. Whether an employee's activity represents a breach of his obligation to attend work, may be relevant to the question whether he is taking part in a strike, but it is not in our view, an essential ingredient. We would take, as an example, the case of an employee who is for the time being on holiday or away sick. That employee by reason of his holiday entitlement or his sickness would not be in breach of his contractual obligation to work; but if he associated himself with the strike, attended at the picket line or took part in the other activities of the strikers with a view to furthering their aims, he would, in our view, be capable of being held to be taking part in the strike. Any other view would be to make nonsense of the plain language of the phrase 'taking part in the strike or other industrial action'. The phrase is not 'on strike'; a person on holiday is not 'on strike', he is on holiday. But he may nonetheless be taking part in strike action."

Where the employee becomes absent, because of sickness or other legitimate reason, during the industrial action in which he has participated he will still be regarded as being on strike unless there has been some form of intimation that he is no longer on strike. As was said in **Williams v Western Mail and Echo Limited** [1980] IRLR 222; ICR 366:

> If a man is away on strike and one day by chance has a cold which would have prevented him from going to work, he is not, in the view of the majority of this appeal tribunal, to be regarded as on that day no longer taking part in a strike...

This may be compared to **Hindle Gears Limited v McGinty** [1985] ICR 111 where the employee was off sick before the strike began and could not be regarded as taking part merely because he chatted to striking pickets on the picket line.

The complainant and relevant employees must be taking part in the same action for the section to apply

This is illustrated by **McCormick v Horsepower Limited** [1981] IRLR 217; ICR 535 where the Court of Appeal took the view that a person from another department who stayed away in sympathy with another group was not taking part in the same action but his actions were the voluntary action of an individual.

The employees must be at the same establishment

Where factories or departments constitute different establishments the employer may be able to treat them differently. The establishment will be the place from where the employee works.

Relevant employees and re-engagement

> Where a relevant employee has not been dismissed or has been offered re-engagement within three months from when the complainant was dismissed and the complainant has not been offered re-engagement then the tribunal has jurisdiction.

The protection is only lost if relevant employees who were participating at the time of the complainant's dismissal are not dismissed (or re-engaged see the next section).

It has already been seen that the reason for the dismissals does not matter so long as the employees were relevant employees within the meaning of the section. The fact that the employer may use the occasion to get rid of 'troublemakers' makes no difference. The precise wording of the section is important here, since it refers to relevant employees of the same employee that "have not been dismissed". The crucial question arises: by what time should the relevant employees have been dismissed? It was held by the Court of Appeal in **P & O European Ferries (Dover) Limited v Byrne** [1989] IRLR 254 that the relevant date by which the relevant employees must have been dismissed is the conclusion of the Tribunal proceedings. 1025 employees were dismissed whilst on strike. Mr Byrne's case was the first to come before a Tribunal. It was alleged that one relevant employee had not been dismissed. The employers asked for particulars, including the employee's identity which was refused on the ground that it would enable the employer to dismiss the employee prior to the application being determined. The Court of Appeal held that the particulars sought were to enable the employer to know the case that they had to meet and it was necessary and proper that the information be given.

The relevant time for deciding whether an Tribunal has jurisdiction was the conclusion of the hearing as to jurisdiction.

Where the relevant employee has left the employment of the employer before the complainant's case is heard it was held in **Manifold Industries v Sims** [1991] ICR 504 that these employees should be ignored for the purpose of deciding jurisdiction and only those still in the employ of the employer should be considered.

The relevant employee must not have been offered re-engagement within three months of their dismissal

The aim of this part of the section is to prevent the employer picking and choosing who it decides to keep in employment by offering re-engagement. Where the employer does not know that the relevant employee was dismissed in the first place there cannot be an offer of re-engagement. This scenario may occur in large organisations where a different manager offers the employee fresh employment. This was the position in **Bigham v GKN Kwikform Limited** [1992] ICR 113 where a relevant employee was engaged two months after his dismissal, in circumstances where the manager who engaged him did not know about the dismissal. Knowledge can mean constructive knowledge and the manager only had to make a call to find out the position so it was held that he should have known of the dismissal.

(i) An offer of re-engagement is sufficient even if refused provide it relates to the job the relevant employee was employed in before dismissal or a job that is reasonably suitable.

By section 238(4) an offer of re-engagement means an offer, made by the original employer, a successor or associated employer, to re-engage an employee either in the job he held immediately before his dismissal or a different job which was reasonably suitable. It is clear that the offer of re-engagement need not be in precisely the same terms as the job that the relevant employee previously held. In **Williams v National Theatre Board Limited** [1982] ICR 715; IRLR 377 the appellants were dismissed whilst on strike and later received a letter offering re-engagement.

They were told that they would be re-engaged without effect on their continuity of employment and in the same posts but with the condition that they would be treated as "being on second warning" under the respondents' disciplinary procedure. The appellants rejected the offer of re-engagement and claimed that they had been unfairly dismissed. The Court of Appeal held notwithstanding that the re-engagement offer was on the basis that the appellants were to be regarded as being on second warning for the purposes of the disciplinary procedure, the Industrial Tribunal and the EAT had correctly found that the "capacity" in which the appellants would have been employed was the same as before their dismissal so that the offer was not an offer of a different job. The section does not require that the re-engagement offered must be on the same terms and conditions in all respects as the previous employment. Fox LJ stated:

> "Now the capacity in which a man is employed is not just a matter of the name or rank which is given to it. To some extent it cannot be considered apart from the terms of employment which attach to it. The job which a dismissed employee is offered may have the same name and involve the same duties in the same place of work as previously but have conditions attached to it which are so disadvantageous as compared with the position before he was dismissed that it cannot realistically, in the context of this legislation, be said that he is being offered re-employment in the same

capacity as before. An example, mentioned in argument, is a large reduction in pay (whether the same would apply to any reduction in pay I need not consider). The present case seems to me to be very different. The capacity in which the appellants were offered re-engagement seems to me to be, in essentials, exactly the same as it was before dismissal. They were, in fact, offered their jobs back. They were offered re-engagement in the same rank with the same work at the same pay in the same place and without effect on continuity of employment."

(ii) There must have been an offer of re-engagement

The statute does not contain any requirements as to the manner of the offer, so that it may be made orally or in writing and may be express or tacit, it may be made by words or conduct. The following emerges from the case law:

(a) The offer need not be in writing provided that the employee is aware of the terms of the offer and beliefs it applies to him (**Marsden v Fairey Stainless Limited** [1979] IRLR 103).

(b) The offer need not have been made directly by the employer, as in *Marsden* where the employee was not sent a letter by an oversight but he knew of the offer through other strikers.

(c) The employee must understand the nature of the offer (**Tomcaynski v J K Millar Limited** (1967) ITR 127 where a deaf employee did not understand that an offer had been communicated).

(d) An offer may be tacit as where an employee 'slid back into employment (*Bolton Roadways*).

(e) To be an offer it must be directed at the employee so a mere advertising campaign will not be an offer (**Crosville Wales Limited v Tracey** [1993] IRLR 60).

(iii) Offers may be made to different relevant employees at different times

Provided that the employees are offered re-engagement within three months it does not matter that the offers are made in 'batches'. In **Highland Fabricators Limited v McClaughin** [1984] IRLR 482 it was said that:

"for a variety of reasons offers of re-engagement may be made to striking employees in differing numbers and at different times. It would wreck all chance of negotiation in what is frequently a delicate and tense industrial situation if a limited offer of re-engagement were to confer immediately on employees to whom the offer was not directed a vested right to complain of unfair dismissal. Certainly if at the date of the Tribunal hearing such an employee can show that the terms of [s 238] have been complied with, the Tribunal will have jurisdiction to entertain the application. We regard the three month period introduced by the 1982 Act as something of a 'cooling off' period, designed to achieve the very objective which was reached in the present case, viz settlement of a strike on terms acceptable to management and work force alike, on sensible and honourable terms. To interpret [s 238] in the manner in which the majority of the Tribunal have done would make it impossible to attain this objective and we do not consider it was the intention of Parliament that it should be construed in this way."

Reasonableness

If the jurisdiction of the Tribunal is not excluded by section 238 it will then go on to consider the question of whether or not the dismissal was fair in accordance with ordinary principles. Going on strike will almost certainly be a breach of contract but it was made clear in **McClaren v National Coal Board** [1988] IRLR 215 that the fact there was industrial warfare does not excuse the employer from adopting a fair procedure. (See also **Glenrose (Fish Merchants) Limited** above where the employer failed to investigate the employees' grievances.) Moreover, selective re-engagement may be fair if based upon reasonable and objective criteria (See **Laffin v Fashion Industries (Hartlepool) Limited** [1978] IRLR 448).

Contributory Conduct

It was held in **Courtaulds Northern Spinning v Moosa** [1994] IRLR 43 (EAT) and **Tracey v Crosville Wales Limited** [1997] ICR 862 that participation in industrial action could not be contributory conduct leading to a reduction in compensation. In the latter case, the House of Lords stated that in the case of collective action by a number of employees against their employer, it is impossible to allocate blame for the industrial action to any individual complainant, without reference to the conduct of the other employees concerned, including those who were re-engaged, and to that of the employer. However, individual blameworthy conduct additional to or separate from the mere act of participation in industrial action must in principle be capable of amounting to contributory fault.

It should be noted that the time limit for bringing a claim is six months (section 239(2)(a) TULR(C)A).

Dismissal During Protected Official Action

The Employment Relations Act 1999 introduces a new section into TULR(C)A which aims at providing some further protection for those engaged in industrial action. These provisions are expected to come into force by Easter 2000. When the new section comes into force it will have to be read in conjunction with section 238.

Protected industrial action

By section 238A of TULR(C)A (as inserted by schedule 5 to the 1999 Act):

> "(1) For the purposes of this section an employee takes protected industrial action if he commits an act which, or a series of acts each of which, he is induced to commit by an act which by virtue of section 219 is not actionable in tort."

Sections 219 sets out the circumstances in which the employee will not be liable in tort, which equates effectively to official action.

Automatically unfair dismissal

By section 238A(2) a dismissal will be automatically unfair if the reasons that the employee took protected industrial action in subsections (3), (4) or (5) apply.

(1) A dismissal will be unfair if it takes place within a period of eight weeks beginning with the day on which the employee started to take protected industrial action (238A(3)).
(2) A dismissal will be unfair if it takes place after the end of the eight week period and the employee had stopped taking protected industrial action before the end of that period (238A(4)).

(3) A dismissal will be unfair if it takes place after the end of the eight week period, the employee has not stopped taking protected industrial action before the end of the period and:

By 238A(5)
   The employer had not taken such procedural steps as would have been reasonable for the purposes of resolving the dispute to which the protected industrial action relates.

Procedural steps

The Act introduces a duty on the part of the employer to take procedural steps without regard to the merits of the dispute (section 238A(7)) or whether a union has repudiated any act under section 21 (238A(8)).

Section 238A(6) requires the following matters to be considered in determining whether the employer has taken such procedural steps as were reasonable:

(1) whether the employer or a union has complied with procedures established by any applicable collective or other agreement.
(2) whether the employer or a union offered or agreed to commence or resume negotiations after the start of the protected industrial action.
(3) whether the employer or a union unreasonably refused, after the start of the protected industrial action, a request that conciliation services be used.
(4) whether the employer or a union unreasonably refused, after the start of the protected industrial action, a request that mediation services be used in relation to procedures to be adopted for the purpose of resolving the dispute.

An application for reinstatement or re-engagement may be made if there is an unfair dismissal but this cannot be considered until after the end of the protected industrial action in relation to the dispute (239(4)(a)) and there is power to make regulations to control tribunal proceedings by way pre-hearing reviews or adjournments, which may be particularly relevant where the employer is challenging the lawfulness of the industrial action or of the union's organisation of the action.

Dismissal During Unofficial Action

By section 237(1) of TULR(C)A:

> An employee has no right to claim of unfair dismissal if at the time of dismissal he was taking part in an unofficial strike or other unofficial industrial action.

There are the usual exceptions in relation to maternity, paternity etc, health and safety, employee representatives, protected disclosures and assertions of statutory rights (237(1A)).

Unofficial action and dismissal

Section 237(2) provides that action will be unofficial unless:

(1) the individual is a member of a trade union and the action is authorised or endorsed by the union;
(2) he is not a member of a trade union but there are amongst those taking part members of a trade union by whom the action is endorsed or authorised.

Where there are no union members the action does not become unofficial. If there was an employee who was a union member at the time the action began he will be treated as a member for the purpose of deciding whether the action was official notwithstanding that he has ceased to be a member.

Endorsement or authorisation

By section 237(3) the provisions of section 20(2) apply for the purposes of deciding whether there has been authorisation or endorsement by the union. By section 20(2) action will be taken to be endorsed by the union if it was done, endorsed or authorised by any person empowered by the rules to do, authorised or endorse acts of the kind in question, by the principal executive committee or the president or general secretary or by any other committee of the union or any other official of the union.

Repudiation

The union may repudiate liability in which case the action will become unofficial. By section 21(2):

(1) written notice must be sent to the committee or official in question without delay of the repudiation.
(2) the union must do its best to give written individual notice without delay to every member of the union who the union has reason to believe is taking part or might otherwise take part and to the employer of every such member. The notice must contain the statement set out in section 21(3):

> Your union has repudiated the call (or calls) for industrial action to which this notice relates and will give no support to unofficial industrial action taken in response to it (or them). If you are dismissed while taking part in unofficial industrial action you will have no right to claim of unfair dismissal.

There are three grounds on which the repudiation becomes ineffective:

(i)   The notice requirements are not complied with.
(ii) The principal executive committee, president or general secretary behaves in a manner that is inconsistent.
(iii) The union does not confirm to a party to a commercial contract that may be interfered with that it is repudiated if a request is made within three months.

Where the action has become unofficial it will not be so treated until the next working day after the date on which the action was repudiated by the union.

Timing of dismissal

The timing of the dismissal is the time at which it is to be decided whether the action is or is not official and by section 237(5) this will be the date that notice terminates, the effective date of termination if there is no notice or the expiry of a fixed term contract without it being renewed.

PART FOUR
AUTOMATICALLY UNFAIR DISMISSALS

CHAPTER TWELVE
GENERAL APPROACH

This part of the book sets out those areas where dismissal will be regarded as automatically unfair. It can be seen that there is an increasing tendency on the part of Parliament to identify areas where a dismissal will be regarded as unfair and, in addition, to ensure that the employee will not be subjected to a detriment because he or she has sought to exercise rights in those areas. The 'family friendly' policies introduced by the Labour Government in the Employment Relations Act 1999 (See Chapter 18) represent a major shift in the way that working practices are viewed and, given that the potential for compensation is now £50,000, employers will need to consider these rights carefully and review their contracts of employment (See Duggan, *Contracts of Employment: Law, Practice and Precedents*).

Since this book is concerned with unfair dismissal, space only permits a summary of the relevant provisions of the legislation that set out the substantive rights in the various areas and the chapters will concentrate on setting out the basis on which the complainant may claim unfair dismissal.

Where the employee is dismissed for one of the reasons set out in this section, other than in relation to spent convictions and transfers of undertakings where the one year qualification applies, it is not necessary for the employee to show that he has the required continuity and there is no upper age limit. Where the employee does not have the required continuity of service it will be for the employee, on a balance of probabilities, to show that the reason for the dismissal was an automatically unfair reason (**Smith v Hayle Borough Council** [1978] ICR 996; **Tedeschi v Hosiden Besson Limited** [EAT 959/95]).

In the *Smith* case it was the majority who considered that the burden of proof lay upon the employee where he did not have the requisite service. This approach has been criticised by commentators on the ground that the employer is the only person who knows the true reason for the dismissal and the burden of proving the reason for dismissal is on the employer. Lord Denning MR dissented taking the view that the onus is on the employer. However, until the decision is overturned it remains the law that it is for the employee to show the reason for dismissal where he does not have the requisite service.

Where the dismissal is that of:

- a health and safety representative (sections 100(1)(a) and (b));
- a representative under the Working Time Regulations (section 101A(d) ERA inserted 1999);
- a trustee of an occupational pension scheme (section 102 ERA 1996);
- an employee representative (section 103 ERA 1996);
- or the dismissal is for trade union reasons (section 151 TULR(C)A), trade union recognition; or
- the employee is made redundant for any of these reasons

the dismissal will include an additional award where the employee has requested reinstatement or re-engagement and this has been refused. Prior to the Employment Relations Act 1999 a special award was payable but special awards have been repealed by section 33 of that Act in order to simplify the compensatory scheme (See Chapter 29 as to additional awards).

CHAPTER THIRTEEN
CONVICTIONS

By section 4(3)(b) of the Rehabilitation of Offenders Act 1974:

> "a conviction which has been spent or any circumstances
> ancillary thereto, or any failure to disclose a spent conviction or
> any such circumstances, shall not be a proper ground for
> dismissing or excluding a person from any office, profession,
> occupation or employment, or for prejudicing him in any way in
> any occupation or employment."

By section 1(1) a person who has been convicted of a sentence that is
not excluded from rehabilitation or a subsequent offence, after the end
of the rehabilitation period, the conviction is to be treated as spent.

The sentences that are excluded, include:

- a sentence of imprisonment, youth custody or detention for more
  than **thirty months;**
- sentences of preventive detention or at her Majesty's pleasure;
- sentences for life.

Tables A and B specify the periods that must elapse before
convictions become spent and they vary from 10 years for a sentence
that did not exceed thirty months, five years in respect of certain
fines to three years in respect of certain offences by young offenders.
Reference should be made to the table below for this purpose.

Rehabilitation periods for certain sentences confined to young offenders

Sentence	Rehabilitation period
A sentence of Borstal training.	Seven years
[A custodial order under Schedule 5A to the Army Act 1955 or the Air Force Act 1955, or under Schedule 4A to the Naval Discipline Act 1957, where the maximum period of detention specified in the order is more than six months.	Seven years]
[A custodial order under section 71AA of the Army Act 1955 or the Air Force Act 1955, or under section 43AA of the Naval Discipline Act 1957, where the maximum period of detention specified in the order is more than six months.	Seven years]
A sentence of detention for a term exceeding six months but not exceeding thirty months passed under section 53 of the said Act of 1933 or under section [206 of the Criminal Procedure (Scotland) Act 1975.]	Five years
A sentence of detention for a term not exceeding six months passed under either of those provisions.	Three years
An order for detention in a detention centre made under [section 4 of the Criminal Justice Act 1982,] section 4 of the Criminal Justice Act 1961...	Three years
[A custodial order under any of the Schedules to the said Acts of 1955 and 1957 mentioned above, where the maximum period of detention specified in the order is six months or less.	Three years]
[A custodial order under section 71AA of the said Acts of 1955, or section 43AA of the said Act of 1957, where the maximum period of detention specified in the order is six months or less.	Three years]

By section 4 a rehabilitated person shall be treated as if he had not committed or been charged with or convicted or sentenced.

There is provision for the exclusion of certain professions, offices and employments by Regulation. Under the Rehabilitation of Offenders (Exceptions) Order 1975 (SI 1975/1023) section 4(3)(b) also is excluded in respect of those occupations and reference should be made to the Regulations for the full list.

CHAPTER FOURTEEN
EMPLOYEE REPRESENTATIVES

By section 103 of the ERA 1996 an employee will be regarded as unfairly dismissed if the reason or principal reason for the dismissal is that being:

(a) an employee representative for the purposes of Chapter II of Part IV of the Trade Union and Labour Relations (Consolidation) Act 1992 (redundancies) or Regulations 10 and 11 of the Transfer of Undertaking (Protection of Employment) Regulations 1981, or

(b) a candidate in an election in which any person elected will, on being elected, be such an employee representative, he performed (or proposed to perform) any functions or activities as such an employee representative or candidate.

Points to note:

(1) There is no age restriction or continuous service necessary under section 103.

(2) An additional award may be payable (special awards are abolished by the 1999 Act).

(3) By section 120 of the ERA 1996 a minimum basic award is payable. £3100 from 1 Feb 2000.

(4) Employee representatives are representatives elected for the purpose of collective redundancy consultation under sections 188 to 198 TULR(C)A or TUPE. Under section 188(1B) of TULR(C)A they are elected by the employees or, if an independent trade union is recognised, representatives of that union, or where there is a union and representatives one or the other as the employer chooses.

(5) There is no provision as to how representatives be elected or as to numbers or as to the provisions that should be given for a ballot.

(6) The representatives do not have to be elected for the specific purpose of consultation (section 196(1)(b)) provided it is

appropriate, having regard to the purpose for which they were elected, for the employer to consult them about dismissals that are proposed. Moreover, there is no requirement about permanent elected representatives so that they could be elected purely for the express purpose of consultation.

CHAPTER FIFTEEN
HEALTH AND SAFETY CASES

By section 100 of the ERA 1996 an employee is regarded as unfairly dismissed if the reason for the dismissal (or if more than one reason the principal reason) is one of six reasons set out in the section. Sections 110(a) and (b) relate to designated health and safety representatives whilst section 100(ba), (c), (d) and (e) apply to employees generally.

The Scope of Section 100

(1) Section 100 only applies to employees.

(2) There is an entitlement to seek interim relief for safety representatives.

(3) Dismissal of a health and safety representative carries a minimum basic award (£3100) and an additional award. There is now no compensatory limit.

(4) Employees who are dismissed because of their own medical condition do not come within section 100.

(5) The matters set out in section 100 must be the reason or principal reason for dismissal if the dismissal is to be automatically unfair. The burden is on the employee to show that a section 100 reason was the reason or the principal reason for dismissal. The employee failed to do this in **Parks v The Lansdowne Club** [EAT 310/95] where there was a conflict as to whether the applicant had been dismissed for gross misconduct or for raising concerns about fire extinguishers and the Tribunal could not decide so that the employee had not discharged the burden of proof. In **Tedeschi v Hosiden Besson** [EAT 959/95] it was held that it was not acceptable for a Tribunal to find that it could not distinguish between health and safety reasons and complaints about poor performance since it is the duty of the Tribunal to consider the principal reason for dismissal and whether the burden of proof has been discharged.

(6) A claim can still be made under section 100 even if there was industrial action that would otherwise prevent the Tribunal from considering the application (sections 237(1A) and 238(2A) TULR(C)A).

Health and Safety Representatives

Dismissal will be unfair in the following circumstances:

(1) Where having been designated by the employer to carry out activities in connection with preventing or reducing risks to health and safety at work, the employee carried out or proposed to carry out such activities (100(a)).
(2) Where being a representative of workers on matters of health or safety or a member of a safety committee, in accordance with arrangements established under or by any enactment or by reason of being acknowledged as a representative or member of a committee by the employer, the employee performed or proposed to perform any functions as representative or committee member (100(b)).

Manner of carrying out duties

Where the employee performs or proposes to perform these functions the manner in which he carries out his duties may be of some relevance. In **Goodwin v Cabletel UK Limited** [1997] IRLR 665 the applicant was employed as a construction manager and it was part of his duties to ensure that sub-contractors complied with the requirements of health and safety and other relevant legislation. The safety record of one particular firm of subcontractors caused him some concern. He wanted to take a strong line against the firm but his employers favoured a more conciliatory approach. At no time did the employers question the genuineness of Mr Goodwin's complaints. The employers decided that Mr Goodwin should be removed from direct dealings with the firm and he was demoted. He resigned and claimed that he had been constructively dismissed and that his dismissal was automatically unfair. The Tribunal held that he had been dismissed because of the way in which he carried out his duties and this did not fall within section 100. The EAT held that the approach taken was wrong.

The way in which a designated employee carries out health and safety activities can fall within the protection afforded and this protection must not be diluted by too easily finding acts done for that purpose to be a justification for dismissal. On the other hand, not every act, however malicious and irrelevant to the task in hand, must necessarily be treated as a protected act in circumstances where dismissal would be justified on legitimate grounds. The EAT stated that the Industrial Tribunal should have considered whether the manner in which the employee approached his concerns about the safety record of a subcontractor took him outside the scope of health and safety activities. A similar approach should be taken to that in section 152 of TULR(C)A.

A more difficult case is where the representative is acting from mixed motives, as in **Shillito v Van Leer (UK) Limited** [1997] IRLR 495. The Appellant was the senior shop steward of the recognised trade union, the TGWU, and the union-appointed safety representative for the section of the factory known as "line 8". There were complaints about an odour given off by a solvent on line 6, not the Appellant's area for health and safety matters. The Appellant, however, took over and rather than following the agreed safety procedures, he went to see the first aider and insisted, in a belligerent way, that those concerned should be seen by the company doctor or sent to hospital. He was disciplined and alleged he had suffered a detriment under section 44 of the ERA. He complained to an Employment Tribunal who dismissed his claim as he was he was acting outside his duties as the line 8 health and safety representative. The Tribunal stated that "He was confusing his role as a senior shop steward with that as a safety representative and he was acting as a senior shop steward in trying to use these matters to embarrass the company over health and safety matters." On appeal, the EAT held that the Industrial Tribunal had correctly concluded that the appellant had not been subjected to a detriment by the employers because of his performance of his functions as a safety representative when he was disciplined for the action which he took in connection with a problem which arose in an area of the factory other than that for which he was acknowledged by the employers as the safety representative.

However, the EAT held that the Tribunal had wrongly imported into its considerations questions of the appellant's reasonableness. The protection afforded to a safety representative does not require that the safety representative must act reasonably. If the employee was subjected to a detriment by the employer on the ground that he was performing the functions of a safety representative, the complaint would be made out. The EAT stated that it is no defence that the representative intended to embarrass the company in front of external safety authorities, or that he performed those functions in an unreasonable way, unacceptable to the employer and that the position is analogous to the protection afforded to those taking part in trade union activities at an appropriate time. The tribunal was entitled to find that the appellant's activities as a safety representative were not the reason for his being disciplined because he was not the representative for the area in question, he had acted outside the agreed procedures and he had acted in bad faith, in that his purpose was not to pursue a genuine health and safety matter but to pursue a personal agenda to embarrass the company. There was therefore no protection under section 44 (being subjected to detriment). The position would clearly be the same in relation to section 100.

Employees

The ERA sets out four sets of circumstances where a dismissal of an employee will be automatically unfair. The specific wording of the subsections must he considered.

(1) Health and Safety (Consultation with Employee) Regulations 1986

By section 100(ba) a dismissal is unfair where:

> The employee took part (or proposed to take part) in consultation with the employer pursuant to the Health and Safety (Consultation with Employees) Regulations 1996 or in an election of representatives of employee safety within the meaning of those Regulations whether as a candidate or otherwise.

(2) Circumstances connected with work harmful or potentially harmful to health and safety

By section 100 a dismissal is unfair where:

"Being an employee at a place where-

(1) there was no such representative or safety committee; or
(2) there was such a representative or safety committee but it was not reasonably practicable to raise the matter by those means, he brought to his employer's attention,

> by reasonable means, circumstances connected with his work which he reasonably believed were harmful or potentially harmful to health or safety."

The requirements under this subsection are that:

(i) There was *no safety representative or safety committee*: This is self explanatory.

(ii) Alternatively if there was a safety representative or safety committee it was *not reasonably practicable to raise the matter by those means*. Where the employee takes matters into his own hands when he could have gone through a safety representative or committee he will not have the benefit of section 100 if he is dismissed because he has complained, though the employer will still have to act reasonably.

(iii) He brought the matter to the attention of the employer by reasonable means.

Where the employee behaves unreasonably in the manner in which the concern is brought to the employer (i.e. by belligerence (cf *Goodwin* and *Shillito* above) he will lose the protection of the section. See further *Brendon* at (viii) below.

(vii) *Circumstances connected with his work.* Whilst the circumstances must be connected with the employee's work they may relate to the health and safety of third parties, see (viii).

(vii) *Which he reasonably believed.* It is essential that the employee has a reasonable belief that there were circumstances harmful to health or safety. This can mean that a belief though absolutely genuinely held is not based upon reasonable grounds, as in **Kerr v Nathan's Wastesavers Limited** [EAT 91/95] where the employee refused to drive a van he considered unsafe and was dismissed in circumstances where the employee had not taken advantage of a procedure whereby it could be arranged for him to swap vehicles.

(viii) *Were harmful to health or safety.* It was held by the EAT in **Brendon v BNFL Flurochemicals Limited** [EAT 966/95] that an employee may have the benefit of section 100 in relation to dangers to health and safety of third parties outside the workplace, as where a harmful product is being exported. However, in this case the employee was dismissed because he was devoting so much time to researching his concerns about a chemical that his sales suffered and he was dismissed for poor performance. The section is concerned with drawing health and safety matters to the attention of the employer by reasonable means, not by pursuing the matter personally in this way.

(3) Serious and imminent danger

By section 100(d) a dismissal is unfair where:

> "In circumstances of danger which the employee reasonably believed to be serous and imminent and which he could not reasonably be expected to avert he left (or proposed to leave) or (while the danger persisted) refused to return to his place of work or any dangerous part of his place of work."

This section covers the position where the employee left, proposed to leave or refused to return to work because of circumstances of danger. Before he will be protected in having taken such a course he will have to show:

(1) The employee must reasonably believe there is danger that is serious and imminent. Examples (from tribunal cases) may include:

- a requirement to drive a vehicle that is dangerous and which may cause an accident at any time.
- a requirement for a young girl to go into an unlit public place late at night.
- a requirement to work in an environment where there is a risk of violence.
- a requirement to carry out a process without protective clothing where there is a risk of injury because of the nature of the product.

(2) He cannot reasonably be expected to avert such danger.

In **Harvest Press Limited v McCaffery** 1999 [IRLR] 778 it was held that an employee who was dismissed for leaving work because he was being bullied was covered by section 100(1)(d) as the word 'danger' covered every form of danger so that the dismissal was unfair.

(4) Appropriate steps to protect against serious and imminent danger

By section 100(e) a dismissal is unfair where:

> "In circumstances of danger which the employee reasonably believed to be serious and imminent he took (or proposed to take) appropriate steps to protect himself of other persons from the danger."

This subsection covers the situation where the employee seeks to protect himself or is concerned about the health and safety of others. It was applied in **Masiak v City Restaurants (UK) Limited** [EAT 683/97] where a chef refused to cook food he believed was unfit for human consumption.

He may take appropriate steps which by section 100(2):

> "For the purposes of subsection 1(e) whether steps which an employee took (or proposed to take) were appropriate is to be judged by reference to all the circumstances including, in particular, his knowledge and the facilities and advice available to him at the time."

However, it may be that steps or proposed steps were so negligent that a reasonable employer might have dismissed.

By section 100(3):

> "Where the reason (of if more than one, the principal reason) for the dismissal of the employee is that specified in subsection 1(e), he shall not be regarded as unfairly dismissed if the employer shows that it was (or would have been) so negligent for the employee to take the steps which he took (or proposed to take) that a reasonable employer might have dismissed him for taking (or proposing to take) them."

Constructive Dismissal

Before a claim can be made for constructive dismissal there must be a fundamental breach of contract on the part of the employer. Where the employer simply ignores the complaints nothing has been done to fundamentally breach the contract in response to the complaint so that on the face of it nothing has been done in relation to section 100. However, there have been a number of Employment Tribunal cases that have found the duty of trust and confidence has been broken and this was in relation to a complaint under section 100 so that there was an automatic unfair dismissal. Guidance is waited from the higher courts.

CHAPTER SIXTEEN
TRUSTEES OF OCCUPATIONAL
PENSION SCHEMES

By section 102(1) of the ERA 1996 an employee shall be regarded as unfairly dismissed if the reason or principal reason for the dismissal is that:

> "being a trustee of a relevant occupational pension scheme which relates to his employment, the employee performed (or proposed to perform) any functions as such trustee."

An occupational pension scheme is as defined in section 1 of the Pension Schemes Act 1993 and is a scheme or arrangement comprised in one or more instruments or agreement which has or is capable of having effect in relation to categories of employment to provide benefits in the form of pensions or otherwise and which are payable on death, retirement or termination of service where the employee has the requisite qualifying service.

The following points should be noted:

(1) There is no threshold requirement in respect of continuous employment.
(2) There is no upper age limit.
(3) The employee will be entitled to apply for interim relief.
(4) The employee will be entitled to an additional award where the employer refuses to reinstate or re-engage after an unfair dismissal finding.
(5) The minimum basic award (£3100) applies.

CHAPTER SEVENTEEN
THE NATIONAL MINIMUM WAGE

The National Minimum Wage Act 1998 (NMWA 1998) came into force on 1st April 1999. The Act is supplemented by the National Minimum Wage Regulations 1999 SI 1999/584 and detailed Guidance. The Guidance contains many examples of the applicability of the NMWA 1998.

By section 104A ERA an employee will be regarded as unfairly dismissed if the reason or principal reason for he dismissal is that:

> "(a) any action was taken, or was proposed to be taken, by or on behalf of the employee, with a view to enforcing, or otherwise securing the benefit of a right of the employee's to which this section applies, or
> (2) the employer was prosecuted for an offence under section 31 of the National Minimum Wage Act 1998 as a result of action taken by or on behalf of the employee for the purpose of enforcing or otherwise securing the benefit of, a right of the employee's to which this section applies,
> (3) the employee qualifies, or will or might qualify, for the national minimum wage or for a particular rate of national minimum wage."

The rights conferred under the section are:

(1) any right under the NMWA 1998 for which the remedy is by way of a complaint to an employment tribunal;
(2) any right conferred by section 17 of the NMWA 1998 (additional remuneration where worker is receiving less than the national minimum wage).

Immaterial whether right exists

It is provided by section 104A(2) that it is immaterial whether a right exists or whether it has been infringed but for the section to apply:

> "The claim to the right and, if applicable, the claim that it has been infringed must be made in good faith."

Summary

It is beyond the scope of this book to consider the NMWA 1998 in detail. However, by way of summary:

(1) The Act provides that workers are to be paid the National Minimum Wage (section 1(1)) provided that they have reached school age and work or ordinarily work in the United Kingdom (section 1(2)). The definition of 'worker' (section 54) also expressly covers agency workers and homeworkers (sections 34 and 35) but, at present, it is only employees who have the right to claim unfair dismissal.

(2) Section 3 provides that certain classes of persons are excluded or the provisions of the Act to be modified in relation to them. Under Regulation 12:

   • Workers who have not reached the age of 18 do not qualify for the National Minimum Wage.
   • Workers who have not reached the age of 26, are employed under a contract of apprenticeship and are within the first 12 months of that employment, or are under 19, do not qualify for the National Minimum Wage.
   • Workers under a training, work experience, or temporary scheme do not qualify unless engaged under a trial period of work under arrangements made by the Government.
   • Workers attending higher education courses that require a period of work experience not exceeding one year do not qualify.
   • Workers who are provided with shelter and other benefits in return for performing work do not qualify. This provision covers those who are homeless or residing in a hostel for homeless persons or are in receipt of an income based job seeker's allowance.

(3) The Act excludes other classes of workers such as share fishermen (section 43), voluntary workers (section 44) resident workers in religious communities (section 44A), prisoners (section 45) and

contains restrictions on contracting out save for compromise agreements that are similar to the ERA (section 49).

(4) Under the Regulations:

    1) the single hourly rate is £3.60.

    2) the rate for a worker between the ages of 18 and 22 is £3.00 (Reg 13(1)).

    3) the rate for a worker who is 22, in the first six months of employment and undergoing accredited training is £3.20 (Reg 13(2)).

(5) There are detailed regulations (see Regs 3–10 and Parts III and IV) to calculate the pay by reference to the pay reference period which will be one month or, where a worker is paid by reference to a shorter period, the period for which the worker is paid and reference should be made to the detail set out in the Regulations in this respect.

(6) There is no qualifying period needed and no upper age limit. An additional award may be made where the employer does not reinstate or re-engage after an order to this effect from the Tribunal.

CHAPTER EIGHTEEN
PREGNANCY, PATERNITY, DEPENDANTS AND FAMILY FRIENDLY POLICIES

The Employment Relations Act 1999 contains a number of important amendments to the existing maternity legislation as well as introducing new paternity rights and the right to time off to care for dependants. The Act is supplemented by the Maternity and Paternity Leave etc Regulations 1999 which come into force on 15th December 1999. The rights given by the Employment Relations Act 1999 are protected by it being an automatic unfair dismissal if an employee is dismissed for seeking to exercise rights under the new legislation. In addition it should be noted that section 104B of the Employment Rights Act 1966 (ERA 1996) provides for an automatic unfair dismissal where employees seek to exercise their rights under the Tax Credits Act 1999.

Automatically Unfair Dismissals

The new provisions are applicable to all employees whose babies are due on or after 30th April 2000. Employees whose babies are due before this time will be subject to the old regime. The new section 99 of the ERA 1996, as inserted by the Employment Relations Act 1999 provides as follows:

"(1) An employee who is dismissed shall be regarded for the purpose of this Part as unfairly dismissed if-
  (a) the reason or principal reason for the dismissal is of a prescribed kind, or
  (b) the dismissal takes place in prescribed circumstances.
(2) In this section "prescribed" means prescribed by regulations made by the Secretary of State.

(3) A reason or set of reasons prescribed under this section must relate to-
   (a) pregnancy, childbirth or maternity,
   (b) ordinary, compulsory or additional maternity leave,
   (c) parental leave, or
   (d) time off under section 57A;
and it may relate to redundancy or other factors."

Parental leave and time off are considered in the following sections. Regulation 20(1) provides that an employee who is dismissed will be regarded as unfairly dismissed if the reason or principal reason is one of those set out in Regulation 20(3). Regulation 20(2) contains provisions relating to unfair redundancy (See Chapter 20) that mirror the provisions contained in section 105 of the ERA 1996.

By Regulation 20(3) a dismissal will be unfair if the reason or principal reason relates to:

- the pregnancy of the employee.
- the employee having given birth to a child.
- suspension from work on maternity grounds under section 66 of the ERA 1996 because of the application of a relevant requirement or recommendation – that is a requirement that the employee be suspended imposed by an enactment or a recommendation in a Code of Practice under the Health and Safety at Work Act 1974.
- the employee taking or seeking to take ordinary maternity leave.
- the employee taking or seeking to take additional maternity leave.
- the employee taking or seeking to take paternity leave.
- the employee taking or seeking to take time off under section 57A of the ERA.
- the employee refusing to sign a Workforce Agreement under the Regulations.
- the employee being a representative for the purpose of a workforce agreement on parental leave or a candidate in an election where such functions would be performed.

Pregnancy

Section 7 of the Employment Relations Act 1999 substitutes a new Part VIII into the Employment Rights Act 1996. The provisions greatly simplify the complicated provisions of the previous legislation. The Regulations flesh out the detail of the rights:

Ordinary maternity leave

(1) The employee is entitled to be absent during an ordinary maternity leave period (section 71(1)).

(2) The ordinary maternity leave period will be not less than 18 weeks (section 71(3) and Regulation 7).

(3) Subject to redundancy or provisions in relation to additional maternity leave the employee is entitled to the benefit of the terms and conditions which would have applied if she had not been absent and is entitled to return to the job in which she was employed before her absence.

(4) In order to qualify for ordinary maternity leave the employee must, at least 21 days before the date on which she intends her ordinary maternity leave to start, or as soon as is reasonably practicable, notify the employer of her pregnancy, the expected week of childbirth and the date that she intends her ordinary maternity leave period to start. The last requirement must be in writing if the employer so requires (Regulation 4(1)).

(5) The employee must supply a certificate from a registered medical practitioner or midwife setting out the expected week of childbirth if the employer so requires.

(6) The earliest date of intended absence is the 11th week before the expected week of childbirth (Regulation 4(2)).

(7) Maternity leave will be 'triggered' when childbirth commences or where the employee is absent from work wholly or partly because of pregnancy or childbirth after the beginning of the sixth week of the expected week of childbirth. The notice provisions are modified in such cases so that notification must be given as soon as reasonably practicable and in writing, if the employer so requests.

(8) Where the employee wishes to return to work after the 18 week period she needs to simply return to work.

(9) Where the employee intends to return to work before the end of the ordinary maternity leave period or the additional maternity period 21 days notice must be given (Regulation 11).

Compulsory maternity leave

Under section 72 the compulsory maternity leave period must be not less than two weeks during the ordinary maternity leave period.

Additional maternity leave

(1) Section 73 of the ERA makes provision for an additional period of maternity leave to be set out the Regulations. If the conditions are satisfied the employee is entitled to be absent during the additional maternity leave period.

(2) Subject to redundancy the employee is entitled to the benefit of the terms and conditions which would have applied if she had not been absent and is entitled to return to the job in which she was employed before her absence. Section 74 of the ERA 1996 provides that Regulations may be made to make provision about redundancy in certain circumstances. By Regulation 10 of the Maternity and Parental Leave Regulations 1999 where a woman on ordinary or additional maternity leave is dismissed and there is a suitable alternative vacancy she is entitled to be offered that alterative employment.

(3) The employee must have been continuously employed for at least one year in order to qualify (Regulation 5).

(4) Additional maternity leave commences on the day after the last day of ordinary maternity leave and continues until the end of the period of 29 weeks beginning with childbirth (Regulation 6(3(3)).

(5) Where the employee wishes to return after the additional maternity period she does not need to give notice to her employer unless the employer asks her to confirm her intention to return. By Regulation 12, where the employer, not earlier than 21 days before the end of the ordinary maternity leave period, requests the employee to give notification in writing of the date on which childbirth occurred and whether she intends to return to work at the end of the additional maternity leave period, then notification must be given within 21 days of receipt of the request.

(6) If notification is not given by the employee, when requested, the employee will lose the benefit of Regulations 19 and 20.

(7) The protection given by Regulation 20 does not apply if the number of employees do not exceed five at the end of the additional maternity leave period and it is not reasonably practicable for the employer to permit the employee to return to a job which is suitable and appropriate for her to do in the circumstances (Regulation 20(6)).

(8) The Regulation 20 right does not apply where it is not reasonably practicable for reasons other than redundancy for the employer to permit the employee to return to a job which is both suitable for her and appropriate in the circumstances, and an associated

employer offers a job of that kind which is unreasonably refused (Regulation 20(7)).

Whilst the new section 99 and the associated Regulations simplify the maternity legislation the following case law remains relevant in considering whether the dismissal was by reason of pregnancy. In particular it should be noted that in cases where the employee has not given the proper notice relating to return to work after additional maternity leave she may still be able to claim unfair dismissal in the normal way. Where a woman is selected for redundancy because she is pregnant this will clearly be a dismissal on the ground of pregnancy (**Brown v Stockton on Trees Borough Council** [1988] IRLR 263, ICR 410 HL). Dismissal due to a sickness connected with pregnancy will also come within the section **Halfpenny v IGE Medical Systems Limited** [1999] IRLR 1777.

Paternity

Section 76 of the ERA 1996, as inserted by the Employment Relations Act 1999, sets out the enabling provisions relating to the right to parental leave, which by section 76(1) is defined as leave "for the purpose of caring for a child". The Regulations flesh out the details of when parental leave may be taken. By Regulation 13:

- the employee must have one year of continuous service.
- the employee must be the parent, named on the birth certificate, of a child born on or after 15th December 1999 who is under five years of age or have adopted a child under the age of 18 (in the latter case the right then lasts for five years or until the child is 18) or have acquired parental responsibility for a child who is under the age of 5.

Parental leave may be taken as follows:

- the employee is entitled to take 13 weeks leave for each child born after 15th December 1999.
- the employee is entitled to remain employed during the period of leave and the employer and employee remain bound by the implied duty of good faith and any express obligations under the contract.
- the employee is entitled to return to his job or a suitable alternative.

- the employee's seniority, pension rights and other similar rights are preserved.

The Model Scheme

There may be a workforce agreement which must be expressly incorporated into the contract of employment otherwise the model scheme contained in Schedule 2 to the regulations *will* apply. In summary, this model scheme provides that:

- the employee must produce evidence of the responsibility or expected responsibility for the child and the age of the child if this is requested.
- leave is to be taken on a weekly basis.
- at least 21 days notice must be given and only four weeks may be taken in any one year.
- the employer can postpone the period of leave or a maximum period of six months from the date that the employee wishes to take the leave.
- where fathers wish to take leave after the birth of their child they must have given at least 13 weeks notice before the expected week of childbirth and the employer cannot postpone this period of leave.

Dependants

Section 57A contains important new provision that give an employee the right to time off to care for dependants. By section 57A(1) an employee is entitled to reasonable time off during working hours to take action which is necessary:

(1) to provide assistance on an occasion when a dependant falls ill, gives birth or is injured or assaulted.
(2) to make arrangements for the provision of the care of a dependant who is ill or injured.
(3) in consequence of the death of a dependant.
(4) because of the unexpected disruption or termination of arrangements for the care or a dependant.
(5) to deal with an incident which involves the child of the employee and which occurs unexpectedly in a period during which an educational establishment is responsible for the child.

The employee must tell the employer of the reason for the absence as soon as reasonably practicable and how long he expects to be absent (57A(2)).

A dependant means a spouse, a child, a parent or a person who lives in the same household as the employee other than as an employee, tenant, lodger or boarder (57A(3)). In relation to the first two categories above it also includes a person who reasonably relies on the employee for assistance on an occasion when the dependant falls ill or is injured or assaulted or reasonably relies on the employee to make arrangements for the provision of care in the event of illness or injury (section 57A(4)). In relation to the fourth category, a dependant will include any person who reasonably relies on the employee to make arrangements for the provision of care.

Tax Credits

By section 104B of the ERA a dismissal will be automatically unfair if the reason or the principal reason was that action was taken or proposed to be taken by an employee with a view to enforcing or securing the benefit of any rights under regulations promulgated pursuant to the Tax Credits Act 1999, a penalty was imposed on the employer under the Act or the employee was or may be entitled to working families' tax credit or disabled person's tax credit. Under section 104B it is immaterial whether or not the employee had the right or it has been infringed, provided the claim to the right and (if applicable) the claim that it has been infringed is made in good faith. These provisions came into force on 5th October 1999.

CHAPTER NINETEEN
PROTECTED DISCLOSURES ('WHISTLEBLOWING')

By section 103A of the ERA 1996 an employee shall be regarded as unfairly dismissed if the reason or principal reason for the dismissal is that:

The employee made a protected disclosure.

In order to understand the basis of this provision it is necessary to turn to Part IVA of the ERA 1996 which was inserted by the Public Interest Disclosure Act 1998. The Act sets out six circumstances in which an employee is to be given protection where he has disclosed information. A protected disclosure means a qualifying disclosure, as defined in section 43B, and made in accordance with sections 43C to 43H (the six circumstances).

Qualifying Disclosure

By section 43B a qualifying disclosure means any disclosure of information which, in the reasonable belief of the worker making the disclosure, tends to show:

(1) that a criminal offence has been committed, is being committed or is likely to be committed.
(2) that a person has failed, is failing or is likely to fail to comply with any legal obligation to which he is subject.
(3) that a miscarriage of justice has occurred, is occurring or is likely to occur.
(4) that the health or safety of any individual has been, is being or is likely to be endangered.
(5) that the environment has been, is being or is likely to be damaged.

(6) that information tending to show any of the five matters set out before has been or is likely to be deliberately concealed.

The six circumstances and the requirements are set out below.

A disclosure of such information will not be a qualifying disclosure if a criminal offence is committed by disclosing such information (43B(3)) or if it relates to information that was disclosed in the course of taking legal advice (43B(4)).

(1)   Disclosure to employee or other responsible person

By section 43C a qualifying disclosure is made where the worker makes the disclosure in good faith:

- to his employer; or
- to another person where he believes that the failure relates solely or mainly to the conduct of a person other than the employer or a matter for which a person other than the employer has legal responsibility.

(2)   Disclosure to legal adviser

By section 43D a disclosure qualifies if it is made in the course of taking legal advice.

(3)   Disclosure to Minister of the Crown or relevant body

A disclosure will qualify if made to a Minster of the Crown in circumstances where the employer is an individual or a body appointed by a Minister of the Crown.

(4)   Disclosure to a prescribed person

The requirements of this section are threefold:

- the disclosure must be made in good faith;
- the disclosure must be made to a person prescribed by an order made by the Secretary of State for the purposes of the section;
- the worker must reasonably believe that the failure falls within any description of matters in relation to which the person is so prescribed;

- the worker must believe that the information disclosed and any allegation are substantially true.

The Public Interest Disclosure (Prescribed Persons) Order 1999 (SI 1999/1549) sets out in detail the prescribed persons to whom complaints should be made.

(5) Disclosure in other cases

A qualifying disclosure is made in accordance with section 43G where:

- the worker makes the disclosure in good faith;
- the worker reasonably believes that the information disclosed and any allegation are substantially true;
- the worker does not make the disclosure for personal gain;
- it is reasonable for him to make the disclosure, taking into account those matters set out in section 43F(3), being:
  - (a) the identity of the person to whom the disclosure is made;
  - (b) the seriousness of the relevant failure;
  - (c) whether the failure is continuing or likely to continue in the future;
  - (d) whether the disclosure is made in breach of a duty of confidentiality;
  - (e) what action was taken or could reasonably be expected to have been taken in relation to previous disclosures;
  - (f) whether the worker complied with procedures in relation to previous disclosures made to the employer.

and one of the following conditions is met:

(1) at the time that the disclosure is made the worker believes that he will be subjected to a detriment by his employer if he makes the disclosure to the employer or to a prescribed person in accordance with section 43F.

(2) where no person is prescribed under section 43F the worker reasonably believes that it is likely that the evidence relating to the relevant failure will be concealed or destroyed if he makes disclosure to the employer.

(3) that the worker has previously made a disclosure of substantially the same information to his employer or a prescribed person under section 43F (which may include information about action

taken or not taken by any person as a result of the previous disclosure (43G(4)).

(6)   Disclosure of exceptionally serious failure

A qualifying disclosure is made in accordance with section 43H where:

- the worker makes the disclosure in good faith;
- the worker reasonably believes that the information disclosed and any allegation are substantially true;
- the worker does not make the disclosure for personal gain;
- the relevant failure is of an exceptionally serious nature;
- it was reasonable in all the circumstances for him to make the disclosure and, in this respect, regard is to be had to the identify of the person to whom the disclosure was made (43H(2)).

There is no qualifying period to make a claim and no upper age limit. In addition a claim for interim relief may be made.

The Employment Relations Act 1999 provides that there is no compensatory ceiling in respect of claims under this section.

Note that there is no compensatory limit.

CHAPTER TWENTY
UNFAIR REDUNDANCIES

Section 105(1) of the ERA 1996 sets out a number of circumstances in which a dismissal on account of redundancy will be unfair if:

(a) the reason (or, if more than one, the principal reason) for the dismissal is that the employee was redundant,

(b) it is shown that the circumstances constituting the redundancy applied equally to one or more other employees in the same undertaking who held positions similar to that held by the employee and who have not been dismissed by the employer, and

one of those matters listed in section 105 applies (note that other provisions also make redundancies unfair as set out below).

There is no qualifying service period or upper age limit under section 105. However, as well as showing that the reason, or principal reason for selection, is one of those set out in section 105 it is also necessary to show that employees held similar positions in the same undertaking and were not dismissed. It was said in **MacAskill v John G McGregor (Stornoway) Limited** [EAT 705/79] that there must be a comparison with another employee who holds a similar position so that where the employee is in a job with which no comparison can be made section 105 cannot apply. Consideration may still be given to whether the dismissal is unfair under section 98.

Similar positions

The pool of comparison is those employees holding similar positions in the undertaking. It may therefore be unfair to restrict selection to employees in one department where there are employees in other departments who are carrying out the same job (**Copeman & Sons v Harris** [EAT 792/86] as this may be an undue restriction of the pool so that the dismissal is automatically unfair. By section 235 of the ERA 1996:

'Position', in relation to an employee, means the following matters taken as a whole-
(a) his status as an employee;
(b) the nature of his work, and
(c) his terms and conditions of employment.

It is a question of fact for the Tribunal as to whether or not employees are in a similar position. In **Powers and Villiers v A Clarke & Co (Smethwick) Limited** [1981] IRLR 483 a Tribunal found that Class 1 drivers, who drove articulated lorries and four wheel vehicles were in a different position from Class 3 drivers who drove only the latter. The EAT held that the Tribunal had not erred in treating them differently. It had to be shown that the circumstances constituting the redundancy applied equally to one or more other employees in the same undertaking who held positions similar to that held by the dismissed employee and who had not been dismissed by the employer. Class 3 drivers could not drive articulated vehicles. This distinction made it impossible to hold that Class 3 drivers employed in the respondents' undertaking held positions similar to that held by the appellants who were Class 1 drivers.

The *Powers* case was distinguished from *Heathcote v North Western Electricity Board* and *Thomas & Betts Manufacturing Co Ltd v Harding* which were both concerned with employment of an unskilled nature where a high degree of flexibility could be expected.

The Tribunal will look at the job functions actually carried out so the fact that employees have the same title will not necessarily mean that they are actually engaged in similar positions (**Simpson v Roneo Limited** [1972] IRLR 5).

Same Undertaking

It is necessary for the employee to be employed in the same undertakings, which is a wider test that of establishment and may include all of the employer's business provided that there is some degree of commonality. In **Kapur v Shields** [1976] ICR 26 Phillips J considered the concept of an undertaking in a different context as involving evidence of organisational unity, common accounting management, purchasing arrangements, insurance and so on.

Automatically unfair redundancies

The matters under section 105 that are relevant cover:

Maternity, Paternity and Dependants (see Chapter 18)

Subsection (2) applies to redundancy selection for a reason set out in section 99 of the ERA 1996 (as amended by the Employment Relations Act 1999).

Under the Maternity and Paternity Regulations an employee who is dismissed is entitled under section 99 of the ERA 1996 to be regarded as unfairly dismissed if the reasons or principal reason is dismissal of a kind set out in Regulation 20(3). Regulation 20(2) extends this to a redundancy where the circumstances apply to employees who held similar position to the employee and who have not been dismissed and Regulation 20(3) is applicable.

The reasons under Regulation 20(3) are:

- pregnancy
- the fact the employee has given birth to a child
- suspension on maternity grounds under section 66 of the ERA 1996
- the fact that she has sought to take or taken of availed herself of the benefits of ordinary maternity leave
- the fact that she had sought to take additional maternity leave, paternity leave or time off under section 57A of ERA
- the fact that she has declined to sign a workforce agreement
- the fact that she has acted as a representative or been a candidate for the purposes of a workforce agreement on parental l leave.

Selection for redundancy for any of these reasons will be unfair.

Health and Safety (see Chapter 15)

Subsection (3) applies to redundancy selection for a reason set out in section 100 of the ERA 1996.

Shop workers and betting workers (see Chapter 22)

Subsection (4) applies to redundancy selection where the employee was a shop worker or betting worker and was selected for a reason set out in section 101 of the ERA 1996.

Working time (see Chapter 25)

Subsection (4A) applies to redundancy selection where the employee has made a claim in relation to the Working Time Regulations and was selected for a reason set out in section 101A of the ERA 1996.

Trustees of occupational pension schemes (see Chapter 16)

Subsection (5) applies to redundancy selection where the employee was a trustee of an occupational pension scheme and was selected for a reason set out in section 102 of the ERA 1996.

Employee representatives (see Chapter 14)

Subsection (6) applies to redundancy selection where the employee was an employee representative and was selected for a reason set out in section 103 of the ERA 1996.

Public interest disclosure (see Chapter 19)

Subsection (6A) applies to redundancy selection where the employee was has made a protected disclosure and was selected for a reason set out in section 103A of the ERA 1996.

Assertion of a statutory right (see Chapter 21)

Subsection (7) applies to redundancy selection where the employee has asserted a statutory right and was selected for a reason set out in section 104 of the ERA 1996.

National minimum wage (see Chapter 17)

Subsection (7A) applies to redundancy selection where the employee has taken or proposed to take any action under the NMWA, the employer has been prosecuted or the employee has the right to the National Minimum Wage and was selected for a reason set out in section 104A of the ERA 1996.

Tax credits (see Chapter 18)

Subsection (7B) applies to redundancy selection where the employee has taken or proposed to take any action under the Tax Credits Act 1999, a penalty has been imposed on the employer or proceedings brought as a result of the employee or the employee is entitled or will or may be entitled to a tax credit and was selected for a reason set out in section 104B of the ERA 1996.

Participation in official industrial action (see Chapter 11)

Subsection (7C) applies to redundancy selection where the employee has participated in official industrial action and was selected for a reason set out in section 238A of TULR(C)A.

Selection for trade union reasons (see Chapter 24)

By section 153 of TULR(C)A selection for redundancy for a reason set out in section 152 (Dismissal for trade union reasons) will be automatically unfair. By section 154 there is no qualifying period to claim dismissal and no upper age limit.

Selection for redundancy on the ground that the employee has sought to exercise rights under Schedule 1A of TULR(C)A, as inserted by Schedule 1 of the Employment Relations Act 1999, will be unfair (see paragraph 162). There is no upper age limit of qualifying period (see paragraph 164). Paragraph 161 sets out the reasons that will be regarded as automatically unfair.

Transfer of Undertakings

In certain circumstances a dismissal relating to the transfer of an undertaking may be for an economic, technical or organisational reason and potentially fair. An issue arises whether this may cover a redundancy situation and is considered in Chapter 23.

CHAPTER TWENTY-ONE
STATUTORY RIGHTS

By section 104 of the ERA 1996:

> "(1) An employee who is dismissed shall be regarded for the purposes of this Part as unfairly dismissed if the reason for it (or, ir more than one, the principle reason) for the dismissal is that the employee-
>
> (a) brought proceedings against the employer to enforce a right of his which is a relevant statutory right, or
>
> (b) alleged that the employer had infringed a right of his which is a relevant statutory right."

The rights

By section 104(4) the rights that are applicable are-

- Any right conferred by the ERA 1996 for which the remedy for its infringement is by way of complaint or reference to an Employment Tribunal.
- the right to statutory minimum notice under section 86 of the ERA.
- the rights given by sections 68, 86, (deduction of union dues or political fund contribution), 146 (action short of dismissal on trade union grounds), 168, 169 and 170 of TULR(C)A (time off for trade union duties and trade union activities).
- rights under the Working Time Regulations.

> The reason or principal reason for the dismissal must be that the employee has brought proceedings or made an allegation that a statutory right has been infringed.

Even where the employee has asserted a breach of a statutory right the Tribunal will consider whether this was the reason for dismissal, as in **Papadakis v Mermaid Inn Limited** [EAT 759/94] where the Tribunal found the reason to be the employee's conduct towards co-workers and not the assertion that there had been an unlawful deduction from wages (see also **Park v Bridges Coaches** [EAT 1183/94]). Where there are mixed reasons, particularly where the employee has been guilty of misconduct, the principal reason may be asserting a statutory right but compensation may be reduced on the ground of the employee's conduct.

> It is immaterial whether the employee has the statutory right or whether or not it has been infringed provided that the claim to the right and that it has been infringed has been brought in good faith.

Subsection 104(2) makes it clear that the right does not have to exist for a claim under this section provided the assertion as to the existence of the right it brought in good faith. The right may be asserted by the employee making a complaint to a Tribunal or making an allegation that the employer has breached the relevant statutory right.

Section 104(3) states that it is sufficient for the employee without specifying the right to make it reasonably clear to the employer what the right infringed was.

The provisions of the section were considered by the Court of Appeal in **Mennell v Newell & Wright (Transport) Contractors) Limited** [1977] IRLR 519. Mr Mennell worked as a HGV driver. After having been employed for some time he was required to sign a contract that permitted his employer to make deductions from final salary or emoluments in respect of training costs. He refused to sign the new contract and was dismissed. He made a complaint for constructive dismissal which was amended to claim that he had been dismissed for assertion of a statutory right under the predecessor provision to section 104. In his originating application, he stated that he had told his employers that he would not sign the new contract because he did not agree to some of its contents but that he would sign it if amendments were made. He maintained that one of clauses in the new contract to which he had objected was that relating to the deduction of training costs from final salary, and that he was thereby asserting a right under the Wages Act 1986 (now Part II of the ERA 1996). It was argued that by the employer that, since no deduction had in fact been made from Mr Mennell's wages, there had been no infringement of any right under the Wages Act in respect of which a complaint could be made to an industrial tribunal and, therefore, no infringement of a relevant statutory right. The mere future possibility that such an event might take place was clearly not covered by the Wages Act 1986 and so could not be covered by section 104. Mr Mennell, submitted that, in accordance with section 104(2), it did not matter whether the employee had the right, or that it had been infringed; the only question was whether he had alleged that a right had been infringed and that such a claim was made in good faith.

The Tribunal accepted the employers' submission that section 104 did not apply and held that it had no jurisdiction to hear the case on its merits. The EAT allowed Mr Mennell's appeal against that decision and remitted the case to the industrial tribunal (see [1996] IRLR 385).

The Court of Appeal (Lord Justice Phillips, Lord Justice Waller, Lord Justice Mummery) allowed the appeal and restored the Tribunal's Decision. The Court held that the Tribunal had correctly concluded that the respondent employee's dismissal, following his refusal to sign a new contract which would allow the employers to make deductions from wages in order to recover training costs, was not on grounds of asserting a statutory right.

Right infringed or merely threatened

The industrial tribunal had erred, however, in reaching its decision on the basis that, since no deduction from wages had ever been made, there had been no breach of Part II of the ERA and therefore no infringement by the employers of a relevant statutory right. Section 104 is not confined to cases where a statutory right has actually been infringed. It is sufficient if the employee has alleged that the employer has infringed the statutory right and that the making of that allegation was the reason or principal reason for dismissal. The allegation need not be specific, provided it was made reasonably clear to the employer what right was claimed to have been infringed. The allegation need not be correct, either as to the entitlement to the right or as to its infringement, provided that the claim was made in good faith.

In *Mennell* the issue of a threatened infringement was considered, since it was the assertion of Mr Mennell that the employer had threatened to infringe a statutory right in the future; i.e. when and if it made a deduction from wages. The difficulty in this respect is that the section speaks of an allegation that the employer *had infringed* a right that is a relevant statutory right. At the time when the contract was proffered it could not be said that a right had been infringed. Similarly, there is no right to bring proceedings for an unlawful deduction unless one has been made. It is not entirely clear from the Court of Appeal's decision whether a proposal to infringe a statutory right at some time in the future will be sufficient.

No allegation that right has been infringed

The important point is that the employee must have made an allegation of the kind protected by s 104: if he did not, the making of the allegation could not have been the reason for dismissal.

In the present case, the employee was unable to identify when, where, to whom or in what terms he had alleged that the employers had infringed his statutory right in requiring him to sign a new contract of employment which included a provision allowing the employers to make a deduction from wages in respect of training costs. The most he was able to say was that he had informed the management that he would sign the contract if an amendment relating to the proposed provision for deduction from wages was made. Since he could not show that he had ever made an allegation that the employers were in breach of a statutory right, such an allegation could not have been the reason for his dismissal. Accordingly, although the industrial tribunal had erred in its reasoning on the construction of section 104 it was correct in law in declining jurisdiction to hear the employee's complaint on its merits.

This is of some importance because, although section 104(3) provides that the employee need not specify the right provided, he must make it clear what the right claimed to have been infringed was. Where the employee merely requests a Written Statement of Terms and Conditions or an itemised pay statement, for example, without any further assertion of breach, then that may not be a sufficient assertion of a right that has been infringed. This was the position in **Jimenez v Nelabrook Limited** [EAT 614/97] where the employee repeatedly asked for a tax code as she was concerned that tax was not being paid. She asserted that the statutory right to an itemised pay statement had been infringed when she was dismissed but the EAT held that there had been no occasion on which he had alleged that her rights had been infringed. She had merely asked for her tax code and not, in any way, asserted that her employer should have provided an itemised pay statement.

Assertion of a right as opposed to an infringement

Section 104(1)(b) refers to the employee alleging a right has been infringed. It was held in **Williams v Asda Stores** [EAT 306/96] that where an employee asserted he did not have to work on Sundays under his contract this did not bring the assertion within section 104 as he had not asserted that the employer was in breach for requiring him to work on Sundays.

Good Faith

The employee must act in good faith in making the allegation and, provided he does so it is immaterial that he does not have the right.

A genuine but mistaken belief that the right exists will be enough (c.f. the provisions in relation to public interest disclosure). This is apparent from *Mennell* where the Court of Appeal made it clear that it is sufficient if the employee believes that a right has been infringed. This was the case in **Philip Hodges & Co v Crush** [EAT 106/95] where the employee asserted that there had been unlawful deductions from wages, after receiving erroneous legal advice from a law centre adviser. The fact that the dismissal was because of the assertion of a statutory right brought the case within section 104 even though no right had been infringed.

CHAPTER TWENTY-TWO
SUNDAY WORKING

By section 101 of the ERA Act 1996:

(1) Where an employee who is-
  (a) a protected shop worker or an opted out shop worker, or
  (b) a protected betting where or an opted out betting worker,
  is dismissed he shall be regarded for the purposes of this Part
  as unfairly dismissed if the reason (or, if more than one, the
  principal reason) for the dismissal is that he refused (or
  proposed to refuse) to do shop work or betting work, on
  Sunday or on a particular Sunday.

Subsections 101(2) and 101(3) provide that:

* the automatic dismissal provision does not apply where the reason
  or the principal reason is that he refused, or proposed to refuse, to
  do shop work or betting work, on any Sundays falling **before** the
  end of the three month notice period from when an opting out
  notice was given;
* a shopping or betting worker who is dismissed shall be unfairly
  dismissed if the reason or the principal reason for the dismissal
  is that he gave or proposed to give an opting out notice to the
  employer.

As with other automatic unfair dismissals there is no qualifying period
and no upper age limit. It should also be noted that a dismissal for
asserting these statutory rights will be unfair under section 104 of the
ERA 1996. The ERA provides that where the employee was employed
as a shop or betting worker on the last day of her maternity leave
period she will continued to be so treated until she is dismissed.

It is necessary to consider the definitions of:

(1) "Shop worker" and "betting worker".
(2) "Notice period", "opted out notices", "opting in notices", "opting out notice" and "protected status".

Shop worker and betting worker

Section 232 of the ERA 1996 defines a shop worker as an employee who may under his contract be required to do shop work.

- Shop work means work in or about a shop on a day when the shop is open for the serving of customers. This means that if the Sunday work is utilised for purposes where the shop is not open for customers (i.e. shelf stacking, stock inventories) the provisions do not apply (See **Sands v Donlan** [ET case no 3226/95]).
- A shop includes any premises where any retail trade or business is carried on and retail trade or business is defined as including a barber or hairdresser, the business of hiring goods other than in the course of trade or business and retail sales by auction, but not catering or the sale of theatres and places of amusement of programmes, catalogues and similar items.
- Catering business covers the sale of meals refreshments, or intoxicating liquor for consumption on premises where they are sold and the sale of meals or refreshments prepared to order for the immediate consumption off the premises.
- Where the premises are used mainly for other than retail or business only such part as is used wholly or mainly for retail trade or business and for the purposes of wholesale (whether considered singly or together) will be regarded as a shop.

Section 233 defines a betting worker as an employee who under his contract of employment may be required to do betting work, being:

- work at a track in England and Wales for a bookmaker on a day on which the bookmaker acts at the track, which consists of or includes dealings with betting transactions and work in a licensed betting office on a day when the office is open for such transactions;
- a betting transaction includes the collection and payment of winnings on a bet and any transaction in which one or more of the parties is acting as a bookmaker;

- a bookmaker is a person who whether on his own account, or as a servant or agent to any other person carries on the business of receiving or negotiating bets or conducting pool betting operations, or by way of business holds himself out or permits himself to be a person who receives or negotiates bets or conducts such operations.

Protected status of shop and betting workers

By section 36(1) of the ERA 1996 a shop worker or betting worker is protected if 36(2) or (3) is applicable.

Section 36(2) applies where:
- in the case of a shop worker, he was employed before 26th August 1994 and in the case of a betting worker, before 3rd January 1995 but not to do work only on Sunday;
- he has been continuously employed between that date and the effective date of termination;
- throughout that period he was subject to a contract of employment as a shop worker or betting worker. Section 36(4) deems an employee to be a protected worker even if the employment had ceased before the relevant commencement date where continuity was preserved under sections 212(2) or 212(3) or section 219 and when the employment relationship ceased the employee was a shop or betting worker not employed to work only on Sunday.

Section 36(3) applies where the shop worker or betting worker cannot be required to work on Sunday and could not be so required even if the provisions of Part IV relating to shop and betting workers were disregarded.

Opting Out

Opted out status for shop and betting workers

Under section 40 of the ERA a shop or betting worker may at any time give his employer written notice, signed and dated that he objects to Sunday working where the contract requires him to work on Sunday and he is not employed to work only on Sunday. The shop or betting worker will be regarded as opted out where:

- he has given his employer an opting out notice;
- he has been continuously employed during the period beginning with the date when the opting out notice was given and the effective date of termination;
- three months have expired after the opting out notice was served.

Duty of employer

Where the shop or betting worker may be required to work on Sundays, and that is not the only day that he works, the employer is under a duty to give notice in the prescribed form in accordance with section 42 of the ERA 1996 which sets out the employee's right to serve an opting out notice. If the statement has not been given within a period of two months from the date that the employee became a shop or betting worker then the three month notice to be given in order to opt out is reduced to one month (section 42(2) ERA).

Effect of opting out notice

The effect of an opting out notice will be that the contract under which he was required to work on a Sunday will become unenforceable after a three month period and any agreement to the contrary will be unenforceable (section 43 ERA 1996).

Opting in Notice

The shop or betting worker ceases to be protected if an opting in notice is given and after giving the notice the employee expressly agrees to do shop or betting work on a Sunday or a particular Sunday (Section 36(5)). Such opting in notice must be in writing, signed and dated by the employee and stating the he wishes to work on Sunday and does not object to Sunday working. The contract of employment will then be regarded as varied to give effect to such agreement (section 37(3)).

CHAPTER TWENTY-THREE
TRANSFER OF UNDERTAKINGS

This chapter will consider the effect of the Transfer of Undertakings (Protection of Employment) Regulations 1981 ('the TUPE Regulations') on the law of unfair dismissal. It is beyond the scope of this book to consider all the facets of the Regulations in detail, though their impact is summarised at the end of the chapter. The Regulations will be covered by a book to be published late Summer, *Reorganisations, Redundancies and Transfers.* This chapter will concentrate on four matters:

(1) The circumstances in which the TUPE Regulations will apply so as to make a dismissal concerned with a transfer of an undertaking automatically unfair under Regulation 8(1) of the TUPE Regulations;
(2) The extent to which the employer may be able put forward a defence of 'SOSR' under Regulation 8(2) so as to be able to argue that the dismissal was fair;
(3) Specific issues that may affect reasonableness in relation to TUPE cases;
(4) The effect of the Regulations in transferring rights and liabilities relating to employees that are transferred.

The TUPE Regulations give effect to the Acquired Rights Directive 1977/187. The purpose of the Directive and Regulations is that, where there is a transfer of an undertaking or part of an undertaking, the employees working in the part transferred will be transferred to the transferee, who will inherit the rights and liabilities of the transferor (other than in relation to pensions). Much case law has built up as to the issue of when there is a relevant transfer.

Automatically Unfair Dismissals

By Regulation 8(1)

> Where either before or after a relevant transfer, any employee of
> the transferor or transferee is dismissed, that employee shall be
> treated...as unfairly dismissed if the transfer or a reason concerned
> with it is the reason or principal reason for the dismissal.

Regulation 8(1) creates an automatically unfair dismissal where it is
connected with the transfer of an undertaking as a going concern.
Regulation 8(3) provides that the provisions of the Regulation apply
*"whether or not the employee in question is employed in the undertaking
or part of the undertaking transferred or to be transferred."*

It is possible for a dismissal to be by reason of a transfer under
Regulation 8(1) but still be fair under Regulation 8(2) as was made
clear by the Court of Appeal in **Warner v Adnet Limited** [1998]
IRLR 394.

The dismissal of an employee for a reason or principal reason
connected with the transfer of an undertaking will be
automatically unfair unless the employer can show that it was for
an economic technical or organisational (ETO) reason in which
case the fairness of the dismissal will be considered upon general
principles of unfair dismissal.

Where there has been a transfer related dismissal the following
employees will be able to argue that their dismissal is automatically
unfair under Regulation 8(1):

(1) Employees who are dismissed by the transferor (or, as is often the
    position in the authorities) by a receiver, prior to the transfer of
    the undertaking for a reason connected with the transfer.
(2) Employees who are retained by the transferor but are then
    dismissed for a reason connected with the transfer.
(3) Employees who are transferred but are dismissed by the
    transferee for a reason connected with the transfer.
(4) Employees who were employed by the transferee but are
    dismissed after the transfer for a reason connected with the
    transfer.

Reason connected with the transfer

Where the dismissal would have occurred wholly independently of the transfer, the dismissal will not be automatically unfair and will be considered in accordance with normal principles. In order for Regulation 8(1) to apply the reason or principal reason for the dismissal must be connected with the transfer. This raises particular issues in the context of receivers dismissing employees in order to make the business a more attractive proposition to buyers where no transfer is as yet arranged, formalised or contractually agreed. The EAT considered the wording of Regulation 8(1) in **Morris v John Grose Group Limited** [1998] IRLR 499. Regulation 8(1) refers to a dismissal because of "the" transfer or a reason connected with it. In *Morris* employees were made redundant by a receiver in order to make the business a more attractive going concern. The transferees were introduced to the company after the dismissals and reached an agreement to purchase the business over one month later. The ET found that the dismissals were not for a reason connected with "the" transfer. The EAT allowed the appeal. It held that in order for Regulation 8(1) to apply there must have been a relevant transfer, which means that the identify of the transferee, the date of the transfer and the terms of the actual transfer have all been decided by the time that the matter comes before the ET. However, the words "the transfer" does not have to refer to a particular transfer that has actually taken place. A dismissal falls within Regulation 8(1) where it may be referable to a transferee who might appear. The EAT remitted the case to another tribunal stating that:

> "...the finding that 'the reasons for making him redundant were primarily to slim down the workforce, such that the company could keep trading, in order to make it more attractive as a going concern in due course' might well have led the tribunal to conclude that a possible transfer, indeed a hoped for transfer, was the reason or principle reason for Mr Morris's dismissal."

On the other hand a dismissal where the possibility of a transfer was "remote" would not come within Regulation 8(1). The EAT preferred the approach taken in **Harrison Bowden Limited v Bowden** [1994] ICR 186 to that in **Ibex Trading Limited v Walton** [1994] IRLR 564. In the latter case a more restrictive approach had been taken to Regulation 8(1) where employees had been dismissed to make the business more economic for a prospective purchaser. In *Harrison* the EAT took the view that reference to a transfer simply meant reference to a transfer that actually took place. (See also **Michael Peters Limited v Fairfield and Michael Peters Group PLC** [1995] IRLR 190).

It is apparent from the authorities (and in this respect, *Morris* seeks to reconcile the cases, both reported and unreported) that the approach to be adopted to the words 'connected with the transfer' is as follows:

(a) An actual transferee does not have to be identified at the time of dismissal. It will be sufficient if the identify of the transferee and the date of transfer is known by the time of the tribunal hearing.
(b) It does not matter that there were several potential transferees at the time of dismissal or if one transferee is substituted for another.
(c) Dismissals to make the business more attractive to a potential purchaser are likely to be connected to the transfer.
(d) It will only be if the dismissals are so remote to the transfer that they will not be connected. This may include the situation where dismissals are effected to keep the business afloat without any consideration as to a transfer in the course of time.

It will be a matter of fact for the Tribunal to decide whether or not the dismissal is concerned with the transfer. Pre transfer dismissals may be for reasons that have nothing to do with any transfer, for example in order to continue the business. Similarly, dismissal by the transferee may not occur until some time after the transfer. The Tribunal will have to decide whether they were transfer related or took effect independently of the transfer, for example because the transferee had to make economies in order to continue the business. The ECJ noted in **P Bork International A/S (in liquidation) v Foreningen af Arbjdsledere i Danmark** [1989] IRLR 41 that the length of time between transfer and dismissal will be a relevant factor.

The dismissal may not be by reason of the transfer, even though a purchaser has already been identified, as in **Longden v Ferrari and Kennedy International Limited** [1994] IRLR 157. During the course of negotiations with receivers the, transferee provided a list of those employees who should be retained. However, employees were dismissed because of financial constraints and pressure from the company's bank and not became of any instruction from the purchaser as to who should be retained. Although the purchaser had identified those employees who it was essential to retain, there was evidence on which the ET could find that the purchaser's request did not necessarily carry with it a request that the other employees should be dismissed.

Dismissals by the transferor prior to the transfer

Where dismissals are carried out prior to the transfer of the business the contracts of employment of the employees may still be transferred to the transferee. In **Litster v Forth Dry Dock & Engineering Co Limited** [1989] ICR 341; IRLR 161, the House of Lords held that where an employee has been unfairly dismissed for a reason connected with the transfer he is deemed to have been employed in the undertaking immediately before the transfer so that the employment is statutorily continued with the transferee and liability transfers.

This is of some significance where the transferor or receiver dismisses employees at the behest of the transferee. However, pre transfer dismissals that are made for an ETO reason will mean that the contracts of employment are not transferred. This was the result in **Secretary of State for Employment v Spence** [1986] IRLR 224 where the workforce was dismissed under pressure from the Company's bankers. A purchase was agreed some hours after the dismissals but the Court of Appeal held that there was no transfer as the employment had been terminated for a reason unconnected with the transfer. The decision was approved, on its facts, in *Litster*. This may be compared with the facts of *Litster* where there had been collusion between the receivers and intending purchaser to dismiss the workforce so as to avoid the effect of the regulations.

Dismissal of employees retained by the transferor

One possible device that may be adopted by a transferor in order to make the sale of a business more attractive is for the transferor to retain certain employees but then to dismiss them sometime after the transfer (for example, by transferring employees pursuant to a mobility clause to another department that is not being transferred). If the subsequent dismissal of the retained employee relates to the transfer the dismissal will come within Regulation 8(1).

Dismissal of transferred employees by transferee

Where the transferee dismisses transferred employees then the dismissal will be unfair if it is for a reason connected with the transfer.

It may be that the transferee dismisses employees and offers them new (and often inferior) terms and conditions in order to regularise the terms and conditions of its workforce. This position was considered in **Wilson v St Helens Borough Council, British Fuels Limited v Baxendale** [1998] IRLR 706 which concerned joined appeals. In the first, employees of British Fuels Group were given notice of dismissal when BFG merged with National Fuel Distributors to form British Fuels Limited and were offered employment on less favourable terms by BFL. In the second case employees of Lancashire County Council were dismissed by Lancashire and were offered new posts on different terms and conditions the following day by St Helens Council, which had taken over the running of a community home. The House of Lords held that a dismissal for a reason connected with the transfer is legally effective and not a nullity and that a dismissed employee cannot compel the transferee to employ him. Where the transferee does not take on the transferor's employees because they have already been dismissed by the transferor or because they are dismissed on the transfer, then the transferee must meet all of the transferor's contractual and statutory obligations unless the employee objects to the transfer or there was an economic, organisation or technical reason for the dismissal entailing changes in the workforce. The liability transferred under TUPE will be to pay damages for wrongful dismissal or to comply with any orders under the unfair dismissal legislation.

In **Whitehouse v Chas A Blatchford & Sons Limited** [1999] IRLR 492 a supply contract to a hospital was transferred to a new contractor on the basis that there would be a reduction in staffing costs by reducing the number of technicians by one. Mr Whitehouse was selected by the transferee for redundancy. The ET held that it was a condition that the new contractor would reduce the contract price by reducing the number of technicians and that the contractor would not have obtained the contact if it had not agreed to this. The dismissal was therefore for an ETO reason and the defence under Regulation 8(2) was made out (see below).

Dismissal of the transferee's existing employees

Where the transferee dismisses employees who were already employed at the date of the transfer then this will be a dismissal within the Regulations if the dismissal is by reason of the transfer (for example, because the employees of the transferor were on inferior terms and conditions and the transferee wishes to bring its existing workforce into line with these terms).

The 'ETO Gateway'

The intention behind TUPE was to make transfer related dismissals automatically unfair and thus give effect to Directive No 77/187 on the "approximation of the laws of the Member States relating to the safeguarding of employees' rights in the event of transfers of undertakings, businesses or parts of undertakings or businesses." The transfer in itself cannot constitute grounds for dismissal. However, by Article 4 this principle shall not "stand in the way of dismissals that may take place for economic, technical or organisational reasons entailing changes in the workforce."

The provision of the directive is given effect by Regulation 8(2):

> Where an economic, technical or organisational reason entailing changes in the workforce of either the transferor or the transferee before or after a relevant transfer is the reason or principal reason for dismissing an employee-
> (a) paragraph (1) above shall not apply to his dismissal; but
> (b) ...the dismissal shall...be regarded as having been for a substantial reason of a kind such as to justify the dismissal of an employee holding the position which that employee held.

The approach to be taken to Regulation 8(2) was recently considered in **Warner v Adnet Limited** [1998] ICR 1056; IRLR 394. Microsystems Centre (Slough) Limited had receivers appointed over the company on 22nd July 1994. On 27th July the receivers dismissed all staff with immediate effect but the staff were told of the possibility of future employment if negotiations to salvage the business were successful. On 3rd August the business was sold to Adnet Limited. All of the former staff were re-engaged with the exception of Mr Warner and three other employees. His duties were taken over by another member of staff. In the Court of Appeal it was argued that Regulations 8(1) and 8(2) were mutually exclusive so that, if the principal reason for the dismissal was the transfer, Regulation 8(2) could not be relied upon if Regulation 8(1) applied. The Court of Appeal held that Regulations 8(1) and (2) must be read as a whole and there would be no point in having regulation 8(2) if dismissal by reason of a transfer was determinative of the employee's claim for unfair dismissal. If the transfer is the reason for the dismissal then regulation 8(2) *may* apply. If it does, then regulation 8(1) is disapplied and the dismissal is not automatically unfair.

The Court of Appeal, in **Whitehouse v Chas A Blatchford & Sons Limited** [1999] IRLR 492 held that the wording of Regulation 8(2) means that the reason must be connected with the future conduct of the business as a going concern. This means that where a transferor who has no intention of continuing the business dismisses employees, the reason for dismissal cannot relate to the future conduct of the business. In the present case the ET was entitled to conclude that the transfer was not the reason for the dismissal and that it was for an economic or organisational reason. The demand for services under the contract was for one less technician so that, although the transfer was the occasion for the reduction in the requirements of technicians, it was not the cause of reason for the reduction. The reduction was directly connected with the provision of the services and the conduct of any business which provided them. The case was not therefore, analogous with that of a vendor who dismissed employees solely for the purpose of obtaining the best price for the business, but was for an ETO reason.

Where the dismissal is by reason of a transfer under Regulation 8(1) the dismissal may not be automatically unfair if it was for an economic, technical or organisational reason that entailed changes in the workforce, in which case the normal principles relating to unfair dismissal will be applied.

There is a four stage process that must be considered:

(1) The dismissal must be by reason of a transfer so that it comes within Regulation 8(1) and is therefore prima facie automatically unfair. If the dismissal was not connected to a transfer then the normal principles relating to unfair dismissal will in any event be applied.
(2) If the dismissal was by reason of a transfer the relevant employer (transferor or transferee) may be able to show that the dismissal was for an ETO reason.
(3) The ETO reason must have entailed changes in the workforce.
(4) If (2) and (3) are proven by the relevant employer then the reason for the dismissal may be regarded as for SOSR and the Tribunal

will consider whether the employee was fairly dismissed applying the general principles relating to unfair dismissal.

ETO reasons

The language of Regulation 8(2) is lifted from the Directive and is not the type of language that is commonly found in English legislation. There is no statutory definition of the meaning of ETO (though there has been guidance issued by the Department of Employment) and the wording of the Regulation has generated a considerable amount of case law. It is necessary to consider each of the three words in turn. To fall within an ETO reason the party dismissing must have actually dismissed with that reason in mind. Therefore, in **BSG Property Services v Tuck** [1996] IRLR, where the transferor dismissed in the belief that the Regulations did *not* apply, he was unable to rely upon the fact that the transferee might have had a valid ETO reason for the dismissal.

Economic

The wording of the 'escape clause' is on the face of it extremely wide and, on the face of it, may include almost any financial reason relating to the business. The transferor who dismisses employees because this is required by the purchaser could be said to be acting for an economic reason as it otherwise may not get the business sold.

A limitation was, however, implied into the wording by the EAT in **Wheeler v Patel & J Golding Group of Companies** [1987] ICR 631; IRLR 211. Mr Wheeler was dismissed prior to a transfer on the wishes of the purchaser, in order to facilitate a sale. The EAT held that an economic reason must relate to the *conduct of the business* and the desire to achieve an enhanced sale price or a sale was not sufficient. The EAT took the view that if this approach was not taken then the protection of the Regulations would be considerably lessened. The Vice Chancellor stated:

> The "economic" reasons apt to being the case within paragraph [8(2)] must, in our view, be reasons which relate to the conduct of the business. If the economic reason were no more than a desire to obtain an enhanced price, or no more than a desire to achieve a sale, it would not be a reason which related to the conduct of the business.

The case was followed in **Gateway Hotels Limited v Stewart** [1988] IRLR 287. The earlier case of **Anderson v Dalkeith Engineering Limited** [1985] ICR which had held that a dismissal at the request of the transferee was capable of being an economic reason was expressly disapproved. In **Michael Peters Limited v Fairfield and Michael Peters Group PLC** [1995] IRLR 190 dismissals to promote the sale of a business did not come within the ETO reason even though the business would have closed down if there had not been dismissals.

The approach taken in *Wheeler* is in accordance with the spirit and intention of the Regulations. It may, however, be difficult for the transferor to show that a dismissal relates to the conduct of the business as it is unlikely to know the intentions of the transferee. Where there is a genuine redundancy situation the dismissal is likely to be for an economic reason. However, if the dismissals merely pander to the wishes of the prospective transferee and are not driven by the economic necessity of implementing such dismissals in order to keep the business afloat (as in *Litster*) the reason is not likely to be regarded as an economic one within the Regulation. The approach in *Wheeler* was approved by the Court of Appeal in *Whitehouse*, above.

A transferee may dismiss for economic reasons where it has overcommitted itself and thereby has to make substantial economies. This was the position in **Meikle v McPhail (Charleston Arms)** [1983] IRLR 351.

Technical

The Department of Employment Guidance gave, by way of an example, the situation where an employer moves over to computerised equipment with the result that less employees are needed. Technical innovations or advancement are the most obvious area where dismissals are likely to be for a technical reason despite a transfer.

Organisational

The relocation of a business to a different area in circumstances where it is not considered feasible or practical to re-locate some staff is an example of an organisational reason. This was the position in **Crawford v Swinton Insurance Brokers Limited** [1990] ICR 85; IRLR 42 (see below).

Changes in the workforce

The potentially wide scope of ETO is reduced by the further requirement that the ETO reason must entail changes in the workforce. The Court of Appeal considered the meaning of this phrase in **Berriman v Delabole Slate Limited** [1985] ICR 546; IRLR 305. After a relevant transfer Mr Berriman's basic wage was reduced in order to bring him into line with the terms of the existing workforce, though he was paid a bonus that was intended to bring him back up to his original wage. The proposed change was refused and Mr Berriman resigned and claimed constructive dismissal. Another employee was engaged to carry out Mr Berriman's duties. The Court of Appeal held that there had been an unfair constructive dismissal and Regulation 8(1) was applicable since the dismissal was connected to the transfer. The fact that another employee had been engaged after Mr Berrmian's resignation did not mean that the economic reasons for the proposal entailed changes in the workforce. Browne-Wilkinson LJ stated:

> It is the company's reasons for its conduct and not the employee's reaction to that conduct which is important. In the present case the reason for the company's ultimatum was to produce the standard rates of pay – not in any way to reduce the number in its workforce.

> Then, in order to come within Regulation 8(2) it has to be shown that the reason is an economic, technical or organisational reason entailing changes in the workforce. The reason itself (i.e. to produce standardisation of pay) does not involve any change either in the number or the functions of the workforce.

If the reason for dismissal does not **entail** changes in the workforce but is merely to increase efficiency or harmonise terms and conditions then it will not come within regulation 8(2).

The wording is of some significance when one comes to consider changes in the functions of the workforce as opposed to a change in numbers. It was held in the ET case of **Lane v DynoRod PLC** [COIT 1709/196] that a change in job title from area manager to senior engineer that also entailed different duties could be a change in the workforce. In **Crawford v Swinton Insurance Brokers Limited** [1990] ICR 85; IRLR 42 a change from clerical work to selling insurance with a change in hours of work was a change in the workforce. The EAT took the view that there would be a change in the workforce where people were kept on but were given entirely different jobs. The more fundamental the proposed change to the job functions of an employee the more likely it is that the employer will be able to rely on the ETO defence as such a fundamental change may be a change in the workforce.

A dismissal for an ETO reason may also be a dismissal for redundancy

Where the transferee does not require the full workforce that were employed by the transferor, such employees may be dismissed before the transfer by the transferor or after the transfer by the transferee. In such circumstances there may be a diminution in the requirements of the business for employees and thus, a genuine redundancy situation. It is possible for this situation to amount to an ETO reason for dismissal. In **Meikle v McPhail (Charleston Arms)** [1983] IRLR 351 the transferee took over a public house and it was a condition of the agreement that he took on existing staff. However, after some time he realised that substantial economies would have to be made. The entire staff, except for one barmaid, were dismissed. Mrs Meikle claimed that her dismissal was unfair, although it was not suggested that she should have been retained in preference to the other barmaid. The EAT held that the ET had correctly held that Regulation 8(2) applied to the circumstances of the case in which the appellant was dismissed by the respondent as an economic necessity four days after he took over the public house in which she was employed so that the Tribunal were entitled to hold that the reason for dismissal was an economic one entailing changes to the workforce, within the meaning of Regulation 8(2). There was a genuine redundancy situation in this case and the dismissal was held to be fair on ordinary principles of unfair dismissal. The EAT stated that the case was clearly analogous with a redundancy situation and the steps that would be expected in such a situation should have been taken.

In **Gorictree Limited v Jenkinson** [1994] IRLR 391 the EAT held that the ET was correct in deciding that an employee who had been transferred was entitled to a redundancy payment but that the dismissal was for an ETO reason and fair when the transferee decided to operate its business with self employed mechanics. It stated that redundancy, as a matter of fact, is one of the most common of the ETO reasons to which Regulation 8(2) applies.

General Principles relating to unfair dismissal and transfers

Where it is shown that an ETO reason entailed changes in the workforce the Tribunal must then go on and consider the reasonableness of the dismissal. It was said in **McGrath v Rank Leisure** [1985] ICR 527 that failure to do so will be an error of law. This will involve consideration of the usual principles such as consultation etc.

Who is liable?

Where an ETO reason has been made out and the employee has been dismissed *prior* to the transfer, the decision of the Court of Appeal in *Spence* should have the logical effect that liability will remain with the transferor. However, in **UK Security Services (Midlands) Limited v Gibbons & Ors** [EAT 104/90] the EAT held that the transferee was liable whether the dismissal was unfair under Regulation 8(1) or section 98. The employees had been dismissed for redundancy and the Tribunal held that the dismissals were unfair under Regulation 8(1). The EAT agreed but also stated that the dismissals were unfair even if there had been an ETO reason and the transferee was liable for this alternative. It is submitted that the case is wrong as it is contrary to the reasoning of the Court of Appeal in *Spence* as approved by the House of Lords in *Litster*.

Where the transferor has compromised claims with the employees before a transfer has taken place then the transferee will be able to rely on such a compromise as such rights will be transferred. However, a compromise entered into by a transferor after the transfer has taken place cannot be relied upon (**Thompson v Walon Car Delivery and BRS Automotive Limited** [1997] IRLR 343).

However, the EAT took the view in **Cornwall County Care Limited v Brightman & Ors** [1998] IRLR 228 that the transferee could become liable for payments under Regulation 8(1) or 8(2).

Where the Tribunal considers that there was an ETO reason for the dismissal, entailing changes in the workforce, then the Tribunal must decide, having regard to equity and the substantial merits of the case including the size and administrative resources of the employer whether the employer acted reasonably in treating the reason as sufficient for dismissal (section 98 ERA 1996). The usual procedural requirements of warning and consultation are likely to be applicable.

This may create particular problems where the employees are dismissed by the transferor at the behest of the transferee. In such circumstances the transferor should be informed of the transferee's plans for employees employed in the business to be transferred as it may, otherwise, be more difficult to justify dismissals. (Note that the consultation provisions in the Regulations which do not encompass providing such information to transferors.)

Where the dismissal may be for reasons of redundancy, this is one area where the Tribunal may investigate the employer's assertion that business needs meant a reduction in the workforce since it can examine whether there was an economic reason that did entail changes in the workforce. Transferees in such a situation must therefore be prepared to justify their business plans but this will not obviate the requirement to warn and consult with the workforce.

Constructive dismissal

By Regulation 5(5) the transfer of the rights and liabilities of the employment contract to the transferee:

> ...is without prejudice to any right of an employee arising apart from these Regulations to terminate his contract of employment without notice if a substantial change is made in his working conditions to his detriment; but no such right shall arise by reason only that, under that paragraph the identify of his employer changes, unless the employee shows that, in all the circumstances, the change is a significant change and to his detriment.

This provision is intended to preserve the right of an employee to resign and claim constructive dismissal. The wording is identical to Article 4(2) of the Directive and does not sit well with the contractual approach taken to constructive dismissal in English law. The following points should be borne in mind:

(1) The phrase 'working conditions' may refer to physical conditions. However, in order to construe the Regulation in line with common law principles it is submitted that working conditions should be read as meaning the terms and conditions

of employment of the employee in question, that is, contractual conditions and any duties that arise thereunder.

(2) The Regulation requires a 'substantial' change to the working conditions. On the face of it, this is rather less than the fundamental breach of contract that is required before an employee may resign and claim constructive dismissal under common law or the ordinary unfair dismissal jurisdiction. The EAT noted in **Servicepoint Limited v Clynes** [EAT 154/88] that it is the express wording of the Regulations that one looks to, so it may be that the Regulation is wider than the common law principles relating to unfair dismissal. This was confirmed in **Dabell v Nofotec Co Limited** [EAT 149/90] where the EAT held that the Tribunal had confused the test under Regulation 5(5) with the common law test of fundamental breach. The question to be asked was, quite simply; whether there was a substantial breach to the detriment of the employee.

(3) Whereas the substantial change aspect of the Regulation may expand the right to claim unfair dismissal, the requirement that it be to the detriment of the employee may limit the scope of Regulation 5(5). For example, job functions may be changed in a way that would amount to a substantial change, or even a fundamental breach, but overall not be to the detriment of the employee as the terms and conditions taken as a whole are equally as favourable. In such a case the employee will be thrown back on his common law and/or ordinary rights to claim unfair dismissal.

(4) It was held in **Sita (GB) Limited v Burton** [1997] IRLR 501 that the concern of an employee about the possible conduct of a proposed transferee will not amount to a breach of trust and confidence between the employee and transferor since the Regulations provide an absolute answer to any attempt by the transferee to change terms and conditions. Such a concern would not therefore provide a right to claim constructive dismissal.

The Regulations: A Summary

The Regulations have engendered much case law and raise difficult issues which it is not possible to do justice to in this book which is only concerned with unfair dismissal. A complementary book *Business Re-organisations, Redundancies and Transfers* is planned. Reference should also be made to the excellent looseleaf work *Transfer of Undertakings* by John Bowers QC & Ors.

Transfer of an undertaking

By Regulation 3(1):

> ....these Regulations apply to a transfer from one person to another of an undertaking situated immediately before the transfer in the United Kingdom or a part of one which is so situated.

Under regulation 2 'undertaking' means any trade or business and, by regulation 3(3) a transfer may be effected by a series of two or more transactions.

(1) The requirement that the undertaking be in the nature of a commercial venture was removed with effect from 30th August 1993. (See **UK Waste Control Limited v Wren** [1995] ICR 974 for the previous approach to be adopted.)

(2) The Regulations cover part of an undertaking and will include a professional practice: **Jeetle v Elster** [1985] ICR 366.

(3) The undertaking may, by Regulation 3(2) be transferred by sale or by some other disposition or by operation of law and apply even if the transfer is governed by the law of a country outside the United Kingdom or the employee is ordinarily resident outside the United Kingdom (Reg 3(3)). Share transfers are not included even if the intention was to avoid the Regulations (**Brookes v Borough Care Services** [1998] IRLR 636).

(4) There will be a relevant transfer where a lessor runs a business on taking back a lease (**I Danmark v Ny Molle Kro** [1989] ICR 330; where a lease is taken back and granted to a third party (**Foreningen af Arbejdsledere i Danmark v Daddy's Dance Hall A/S** [1988] IRLR 315; **Litster, P Bork Internatioinal A/S v Foreningen af Arbejdsledere i Danmark** [1989] IRLR 41); where a company is dissolved and business run by the former directors (**Charlton v Charlton Thermosystems (Romsey) Limited** [1995] ICR 79; where there is a retransfer to the original transferor (**Berg and Busschers v Besselsen** [1990] ICR 396).

(5) In order for there to be a transfer of an undertaking one issue is whether the undertaking retains its identify when carried on by the transferee. There are a wide range of circumstances that will be taken into account including whether the business is carried on in the same manner, what assets were transferred, whether goodwill or customers were transferred and the extent to which the business is similar before and after the transfer (see **Rask v**

ISS Kanineservice A/S [1993] IRLR133; **Dr Sophie Redmond Stichting v Bartol** [1992] IRLR 366).

(6) In the context of contracting out of services there may be no tangible assets so that the only identifiable matter is the economic entity that is contracted out. In **Schmidt v Spar-und Leihkasses der Fruheren Amter Bordersholm, Kiel und Cronshagen** [1995] ICR 237 it was held that there was a transfer when cleaning services were contracted out even though the services were carried out by one employee and there were no tangible assets. However, in **Rygaard v Stro Moole Akustik** [1996] IRLR 51 the ECJ took the view that the transfer must be that of a stable economic entity so that a contract merely to finish off a task in the context of an insolvency would not be a relevant transfer. Moreover, it was held in **Suzen v Zehnacker Gebaurdereingung** [1997] IRLR 255 that an activity in itself does not constitute an economic entity so that the fact a similar activity is carried out before and after may not be a transfer if there are no assets and where the majority of the workforce are not taken on in labour intensive situation there may be no transfer. In **ECM (Vehicle Delivery Service) Limited v Cox** [1998], IRLR 416 it was held by the EAT that there is an economic entity as opposed to a mere activity when the employees concerned are dedicated to a particular contract and their employment is contingent upon the existence of the service contract. There is no transfer where the loss of a customer does not result in dedicated and identified staff losing their employment. Further, it would not be proper for a transferee to be able to control the extent of its obligations by refusing to take on the workforce as that the issue as to whether employees should have been taken on cannot be answered by asking if they were in fact taken on. The decision was upheld by the Court of Appeal [1999] IRLR 559 which stated that the Tribunal was entitled to conclude that the identity of the economic entity was retained in the hands of ECM where the customers were essentially the same, the work was essentially the same and having regarded to the reason why the employees of the transferor were not appointed by the transferee. The Court emphasised that the matter turns upon the facts of each case as determined according to National law.

Effect of transfer

Under Regulation 5(1):

> ...a relevant transfer shall not operate so as to terminate the contract of employment of any person employed by the transferor in the undertaking or part transferred but any such contract which would otherwise have been terminated by the transfer shall have effect as if originally made between the person so employed and the transferee.

Under Regulation 5(2), on the completion of a relevant transfer:

- all the transferor's rights, powers, duties and liabilities under or in connection with any such contract shall be transferred by virtue of this Regulation to the transferee;
- anything done before the transfer is completed by or in relation to the transferor in respect of that contract or a person employed in that undertaking or part shall be deemed to have been done by or in relation to the transferee.

(1) References to a person employed in the undertaking are to a person employed immediately before the transfer. However, the House of Lords in **Litster v Forth Dry Dock and Engineering Co Limited** [1989] ICR 341 adopted a purposive approach to the Regulations so that an employee will be regarded as employed immediately before the transfer if the reason for the dismissal was the transfer. The Regulation should therefore be read as if the words were 'or would have been so employed if he had not been unfairly dismissed in the circumstances described in Regulation 8(1)'.

(2) The employee may object to the transfer (Regulation 5(4A)) in which case his contract will terminate but will not be treated as having been a dismissal by the transferor (Regulation 5(4B)). This is without prejudice to the right to claim constructive dismissal under Regulation 5(5). Where the employee resigns prior to the transfer because the transferee will not guarantee his existing terms and conditions then this will be a dismissal (**Merckx v Ford Motors** [1997] ICR 352) and the transferee will be responsible (**P & O Property Holdings Limited v Allen** [1997] ICR 436). Where an employee merely takes a severance payment from the transferor and accepts employment with the transferee his contract of employment will not have

been terminated (**Senior Heat Treatment Limited v Bell** [1997] IRLR 614).

(3) Special rules apply in the case of hiving down arrangements. By Regulation 4 where the business is transferred to a wholly owned subsidiary the Regulations do not apply unless the subsidiary ceases to be wholly owned or is transferred from the subsidiary to a third party at which point there will be a deemed transfer.

(4) A transfer will take place, in the absence of an objection on the part of the employee even if the transferor and transferee intend or agree otherwise (**Rotsaart de Hertaing v J Benoidt SA** [1997] IRLR 127 or the employee is not aware that there has been a transfer (**Secretary of State for Trade and Industry v Cook** [1997] ICR 288).

(5) Regulation 5(1) refers to a contract that would otherwise have been terminated by the transfer. Where the employee does not work in the part of the undertaking transferred or a mobility clause means that the transferor can move him to another part before transfer then the Regulation will not bite. However, where the employee works in different parts of the business, including a part that is being transferred then the Courts may consider where the employee was predominantly employed (**Buchanan-Smith v Scheichler & Co International Limited** [1996] ICR 613; **Duncan Webb Offset (Maidstone) Limited v Cooper** [1995] IRLR 633; **Sunley Turriff Holdings Limited v Thomson** [1995] IRLR 184). Where the transferor gets an employee to move to that part of the undertaking which it knows will be transferred in order to get rid of him the Regulations will not apply if the conduct of the transferor was fraudulent (**Carisway Cleaning Consultants Limited v Richards** [EAT 629/97]).

(6) Under Regulation 5(2) the transferee inherits rights and liabilities in connection with the contract of employment which will include:

- common law and statutory rights;
- liability for negligence and breach of statutory duty (**Taylor v Serviceteam Limited** rm602374, Romford County Court);
- liability for sex discrimination (**DJM International Limited v Nicholas** [1996] IRLR 76);
- the benefit of restrictive covenants may be transferred (**Morris Angel & Son Limited v Hollande** [1993] ICR 71);
- Terms of a collective agreement incorporated into the contract of employment (**Whent v T Cartledge Limited** [1997] IRLR 153).

(7) The Regulations do not assign:
- criminal liabilities (Reg 5(4));
- rights and liabilities relating to the provision of occupational pension schemes that relate to benefit for old age, invalidity or survivors (Reg 7) and see **Frankling v BPS Public Sector Limited** [1999] ICR 347; IRLR 212);
- transfer of future pension rights (**Adams v Lancashire County Council** [1997] IRLR 436);
- Breaches of duties owed to a union such as failure to consult under TULR(C)A so that the benefit of a protective award will not be transferred (**Angus Jowett & Co v Tailors and Garment Workers Union** [1985] ICR 646).

(8) It was held in **Credit Suisse First Boston (Europe) Limited v Lister** [1988] IRLR 700 that a transferee could not enforce a restrictive covenant it had entered into with a transferred employee because it was a variation by reason of the transfer and it was irrelevant whether under the contract as a whole the employee was better off.

Consultation

Regulations 9, 10, 10A, 11 and 11A contain provisions relating to consultation with employees, recognition and consultation with trade union and employee representatives and the provision of information where a transfer is to take place. The provision are outside the scope of this book and reference should be made to the Regulations for the detail.

Contracting out and exclusions

By Regulation 12, any provision of any agreement (whether a contract of employment or not) shall be void in so far as it purports to exclude or limit the operation of Regulation 5, 8, or 10 or to preclude any person from presenting a complaint to a tribunal under Regulation 11.

CHAPTER TWENTY-FOUR
DISMISSAL RELATING TO
TRADE UNION MEMBERSHIP,
ACTIVITIES AND RECOGNITION

By section 152 of TULR(C)A the dismissal of an employee shall be regarded as unfair if the reason or principal reason for dismissal was that the employee:

(a) was, or proposed to become, a member of an independent trade union, or

(b) had taken part, or proposed to take part, in the activities of an independent trade union at an appropriate time, or

(c) was not a member of any trade union, or of a particular trade union, or of one of a number of particular trade unions, or had refused, or proposed to refuse to become or remain a member of a trade union.

> Where the dismissal is shown to be for a reason coming within section 152 the motive of the employer is irrelevant.

Where the dismissal is one coming within sections 152, or relates to union recognition under paragraph 161 of TULR(C)A Schedule A1 there is no qualifying period before a claim may be made and no upper age limit (section 154). Dismissals for these reasons also attract the right to make a claim for interim relief (see chapter 29).

The motive of the employer is irrelevant if the dismissal is shown to be on trade union grounds. In **Dundon v GPT Limited** [1995] IRLR 403 the complainant was dismissed for redundancy. He had been an active trade unionist for many years and spent most of this time on trade union activities despite the employer's attempts to reduce the time he spent. His timekeeping was also poor. On a redundancy selection, he was assessed as "very poor" under the heading "quantity of work" and this was confirmed when the assessment panel reconsidered the position taking into account the trade union activities. The EAT held that the Tribunal erred in deciding the dismissal was not unfair as the employers had not deliberately or maliciously selected him because of trade union activities. It stated that an employer does not have to be motivated by malice or a deliberate desire to be rid of a trade union activist in order to fall within the provisions now set out in ss.152(1)(b) and 153 of the Trade Union and Labour Relations (Consolidation) Act. The Tribunal's finding that the "feature" of the employee's working life that made the employers select him was that he was spending far too much time on trade union duties, was the same as saying that "the reason" they selected him was because he was spending too much time on trade union duties. Had the Tribunal approached the matter correctly and gone on to consider whether those activities had been carried out at an appropriate time, it would inevitably have concluded that the reason why the employee was selected for redundancy was because he had taken part in trade union activities at times at which, in accordance with consent given by the employers (albeit tacitly and reluctantly), it was permissible for him to do so.

However, in view of the finding that the employee's dismissal was unfair because it was on grounds of union activities, rather than under section 98, the question of contributory conduct had to be looked at afresh, since the relative culpability of the parties' conduct might be seen in a different light in a case involving an automatically unfair dismissal. In all the circumstances, the EAT held that the proper figure for the employee's contribution to his own dismissal was 33%.

Where union membership is a subsidiary reason then the employee does not bring himself in the section by merely showing that he would not have been dismissed if he had not been a trade union member. In **CGB Publishing v Killey** [1993] IRLR 520 the complainant, who had less than two years service, claimed he was dismissed because of trade union membership. The ET, by a majority, upheld the complaint on the basis that if he had not been a trade union member he would not have been dismissed and that the actions, manner and attitude at a meeting were the outward and visible manifestation of his trade union membership. The EAT held that the ET had misdirected itself in concluding that the appellant had been dismissed by reason of his trade union membership. The Tribunal had applied the wrong test in finding that was the principal reason for dismissal on the basis that if the appellant had not been a trade union member, he would not have been dismissed. The reason for dismissal is the set of beliefs held by the employer which causes him to dismiss. A "but for" test is wrong in principle because it does not introduce any question as to the state of mind of the employer and because it does not adequately approach the notion of causation.

The Tribunal is entitled to consider why alternative employment was not offered in a redundancy situation as in **Driver Cleveland Structural Engineering Co Limited** [1994] IRLR 636; ICR 372. The employee was made redundant and asserted that the reason for selection and the fact he had not been selected for alternative employment was union activity. There was evidence of other employees being re-deployed to near where Mr Driver lived. In dismissing Mr Driver's complaint, the Tribunal held that the fact that he was not selected for alternative employment within the organisation was irrelevant to his claim that he had been dismissed because of his union activities. The EAT allowed the appeal on the ground that the Tribunal had misdirected itself in holding that the fact that the appellant former shop steward had not been selected for alternative employment within the respondents' organisation when the contract on which he was working came to an end, although others with less service were transferred, was not relevant to his claim that he had been unfairly dismissed because of his trade union activities.

It stated that in determining whether dismissal was for an inadmissible reason, it is legally relevant to inquire why the employee was dismissed instead of being selected for another job. It is well established that, as a matter of good industrial relations practice, a reasonable employer, when considering the circumstances surrounding a proposed or possible redundancy, will consider the question of alternative employment before taking the decision to dismiss. Accordingly, it is relevant for the Tribunal to take into account that practice and the reasons why, in a particular case, the employee was not offered alternative employment. In the present case, therefore, by excluding consideration of whether or not the employers had decided against transferring the appellant to another site because of his union activities, the Industrial Tribunal had erroneously restricted the scope of its factual inquiry into the reason or principal reason for his dismissal.

Moreover, the Tribunal may take subsidiary reasons into account as a factor in deciding reasonableness under general principles (**Britool Limited v Roberts** [1993] IRLR 481).

It should however, be noted that an employee will not be given preferential treatment by reason of his involvement in trade union activities or any associated matters, such as acting as a health and safety representative (See **Smiths Industries Aerospace and Defence Systems v Rawlings** [1996] IRLR 656). In *Rawlings* Judge Peter Clarke stated that:

> "Just as it would be invidious to assess a shop steward on the way in which he carries out those duties on behalf of his trade union and its members, it would be equally wrong to carry out such an assessment on a part-time health and safety representative, either in his favour of against him."

Membership of an independent trade union

It will be unfair to dismiss an employee because he is or proposed to become a member of an independent trade union. The section covers proposed membership, which will include a contingent proposal (**Crosville Motor Services Limited v Ashfield** [1986] IRLR 475).

A number of issues arise under section 152(1)(a):

(a) The extent to which it is unfair to dismiss an employee for belonging to a particular trade union as opposed to unions in general (note that section 152(4) distinguishes between branches of a union);
(b) The employer's motive or purpose in dismissing;
(c) The distinction between trade union activities under section 152(1)(a) and activities under section 152(1)(b).

Membership of any union or a particular union

It is to be noted that section 152(1)(c) expressly refers to the right to refuse to join a particular union whereas section 152(1)(a) simply refers to being or proposing to become a member of an independent trade union. However, it was made clear by the Court of Appeal in **Ridgway and Fairbrother v National Coal Board** [1987] IRLR

80; ICR 641 that the section protects the employee's right to be a member of a particular union.

The motive of the employer in dismissing

The employer's purpose in dismissing is not relevant if the reason for the dismissal was union membership. In **Dundon v GPT Limited** [1995] IRLR 403 the EAT held that the dismissal was automatically unfair where the reason for selection for redundancy was that the employee was spending too much time on union business and thus scored less than he would have otherwise done on a performance assessment.

In **Therm A Star Limited v Atkins** [1983] IRLR 78; ICR 208 it was held that the section is concerned with the dismissal of an employee and provides that it shall be regarded as unfair if the reason was that the (i.e. "that") employee had done or proposed to do one or more specified things. In this case, the reason for the dismissals was retaliation to the union's plea for recognition and not because of redundancy or anything under section 152. The Court of Appeal stated that it could not be accepted, as argued on behalf of the respondents, that section 152 should be construed in such a way as to recognise its "collective dimension" so that, as the respondents were members of a wider group, the union, and the reason for the dismissals were the activities of that group, the reason for their dismissal was their union membership or activities, albeit with others. Such a purposive construction of the statute went beyond permissible limits.

The distinction between union membership and activities

Where an employee is dismissed for exercising his rights as a trade union member the issue may arise as to whether the dismissal is for trade union membership or trade union activities.

(1) Where the employee consults his trade union and is sacked for seeking assistance the dismissal may be because of trade union membership. In **Discount Tobacco and Confectionery Limited v Armitage** [1990] IRLR 15; [1995] ICR 431n, Mrs Armitage sought her union's help in seeking to obtain her statutory statement of terms from her employer and was dismissed. The employer alleged that she had been dismissed on the ground of capability. However, the EAT held that the ET had

not erred in deciding that she had been dismissed on grounds of union membership when she was dismissed after she had made use of her union membership by enlisting the help of a union official to elucidate and negotiate the terms and conditions of her employment.

It was held that for the purposes of section 152(1)(a) there is no genuine distinction between membership of a union on the one hand and making use of the essential services of a union officer on the other. The activity of a trade union officer in elucidating and negotiating terms of employment is an important incident of union membership and the outward and visible manifestation of it. To construe s. 152(1)(a) so narrowly as to apply only to the fact that a person was a member of the union without regard to the consequences of that membership would be to emasculate the provision altogether.

Membership therefore encompasses important *incidents* of union membership. However, in **Associated Newspapers Limited v Wilson** [1995] IRLR 258; ICR 406 there was no general consensus as to the scope of the meaning of the word 'membership'. Lord Slynn approved the former case, taking the view that membership was not limited to bare status while Lord Browne-Wilkinson reserved his position. The majority however, took the view that membership protected status, Lord Bridge stating that to say that the provision covered the essential services of the union distorted the meaning of the sub-section which protected "membership as such". However, membership as such can go beyond status and it is submitted that the better approach is that the subsection protects status and dismissal for exercising rights as a union member. Alternatively, if it protects bare status then a dismissal for exercising the right is evidence that the employee was dismissed because of union membership.

The position was summarised as follows in **Speciality Care PLC v Pachela** [1986] IRLR 248; ICR 633 by Judge Peter Clarke:

> "we regard it as important that we provide clear guidance to industrial tribunals as to the correct approach to be taken in cases such as the instant one. Our conclusions are as follows:
> (1) Armitage was and remains unquestionably correct on its facts. That was the unanimous judgment of the Court of Appeal, expressed by Dillon LJ, on an issue material to its

decision in the appeal before the court. The observations of their Lordships on appeal from that decision were obiter. Nevertheless, Lord Bridge, with whose speech Lord Keith entirely agreed, did not question the correctness of the decision on its facts. Lord Browne-Wilkinson declined to express a view on this issue. Nevertheless, his comment that he would not share the view expressed by Lord Bridge places him closer to Lord Slynn, who plainly approved the approach of Dillon LJ in the Court of Appeal. Finally, Lord Lloyd thought that Knox J had gone too far in Armitage, but allowed that the decision in that case may have been correct on its facts. In summary, Armitage remains undisturbed on its facts in our judgment.

(2) That means in practice that where a complaint of dismissal by reason of union membership is made, as in this case, it will be for the tribunal to find as a fact whether or not the reason or principal reason for dismissal related to the applicant's trade union membership not only by reference to whether he or she had simply joined a union, but also by reference to whether the introduction of union representation into the employment relationship had led the employer to dismiss the employee. Tribunals should answer that question robustly, based on their findings as to what really caused the dismissal in the mind of the employer.

(3) In so holding we have deliberately refrained from making any wider observations as to the correct approach in cases where the facts are more akin to those in *Palmer* and *Wilson*. To do otherwise may give rise to the dangers of expressing views beyond those necessary for deciding this appeal."

Activities of an independent trade union

Section 152(1)(b) makes a dismissal unfair if it relates to the activities of an independent trade union. This will cover such activities as attending union meetings, participating in union ballots or consulting with the union provide that the activities are carried out at an appropriate time. It is necessary to consider (a) what may be regarded as union activities and (b) the meaning of 'appropriate time' within section 152(1)(b).

Union activities

(1) It was stated in **Dixon & Shaw v West Ella Developments Limited** [1978] IRLR 151; ICR 856 that the definition of activities should not be construed too restrictively. Consulting the union will fall within the section though it is not a union-organised activity. The distinction between membership and activities has already been noted.

(2) An attempt to persuade fellow employees to join the union will be a union activity (**Brennan & Ging v Ellward (Lancs) Limited** [1976] IRLR 378).

(3) An attempt to 'sell' the union at an induction course will be a union activity (**Bass Taverns Limited v Burgess** [1995] IRLR 596) though not organised by the union and holding a meeting that is critical of the union may be a union activity if the intent is to seek to make the union more active as opposed to acting contrary to union policy (**British Airways Engine Overhaul Limited v Francis** [1981] IRLR 9; ICR 278).

(4) The section protects union activities and not activities that are unrelated even if the employee is a union official or member (See **Drew v St Edmundsbury Borough Council** [1980] IRLR 459; ICR 513 referred to in Chapter 15).

(5) Official activities of a union official will be covered, including the right to recruit and organise (**Post Office v Crouch** [1974] ICR 378).

(6) Where the employee has gained a reputation as a trade unionist then an issue arises whether if the employer dismisses because it has found out about the employee's past activities, this falls within the section. In **Fitzpatrick v British Railways Board** [1991] IRLR 376; [1992] ICR 221 the employee was dismissed by Ford because of bad references. This employment was concealed from British Railways when the employee obtained employment but he was dismissed after an article in a paper referred to him as a union activist with ultra left wing sympathies. The employer purported to dismiss for deceit. The true reason for dismissal was found to be his reputation as a trade union activist. The Court of Appeal held that the section could only apply to current employment but that the dismissal in this case was because it was believed that the employee proposed to take part in trade union activities; in other words an assumed predisposition was

enough to be regarded as a proposal for the purpose of the section. Lord Woolf LJ stated:

> "As long as the reason which motivated the employer falls within the words 'activities that the employee ... proposed to take part in', there is no reason to limit the language. The purpose of the subsection, in so far as (b) is concerned, is to protect those who engage in trade union activities and I can see no reason why that should not apply irrespective of whether the precise activities can be identified
>
> If an employer, having learnt of an employee's previous trade union activities, decides that he wishes to dismiss that employee, that is likely to be a situation where almost inevitably the employer is dismissing the employee because he feels that the employee will indulge in industrial activities of a trade union nature in his current employment. There is no reason for a rational and reasonable employer to object to the previous activities of an employee except in so far as they will impinge upon the employee's current employment."

(C.f. **Birmingham District Council v Beyer** [1977] IRLR 211 where the dismissal was found to be because of deceit.) The dismissal will be by reason of trade union activities if the employer is dismissed because of activities that have taken place in the past whilst in the employment of that employer (See **Port of London Authority v Payne** [1992] IRLR 447).

(7) Provided that the activity is in truth a trade union activity it should not matter that the employee is behaving unreasonably though this may put into question whether he is carrying out a genuine trade union activity. It was, however, held in **Lyon and Scherk v St James Press Limited** [1976] IRLR 215; ICR 413 that wholly unreasonable, malicious or extraneous acts might be a ground for dismissal that might not be unfair. In this case the fact that a union chapel had been secretly and slyly organised so that the employer felt betrayed did not prevent the activity being a trade union one. This may be contrasted with *Beyer* where the act of deceit of the employee concealing his identity to get a job could not be considered to be a trade union activity (Cf the *Bass Taverns'* case where the employee was engaged in trade union activities though he had gone over the top in criticising the employer at an induction course.

(8) It was stated in *Drew* that industrial action will not be a trade union activity (see Chapter 11) though on a true construction of section 152 and sections 237 and 238 there is no reason why the sections cannot operate in tandem since dismissals that do fall within the latter sections will remove the jurisdiction of the tribunal to bring a claim.

Appropriate time

By section 152(2) the appropriate time means:

> "(a) a time outside the employee's working hours, or
> (b) a time within his working hours at which, in accordance with arrangements agreed with or consent given by his employer, it is permissible for him to take part in the activities of a trade union."

The employee's working hours are those hours that the employee is required to work in accordance with his contract of employment.

The trade union activity must have been carried out at the times stated within section 152(2) in order for the dismissal to be unfair under section 152(1)(b).

(1) Section 152(2)(a) refers to a time outside the employee's working hours; that is, *in the employee's own time*. The employee's own time will include tea breaks and meal breaks and times before and after employment when the employee may be on the employer's premises but not working under his contract of employment (**Zucker v Astrid Jewels Limited** [1978] IRLR 385). The approach was stated by Lord Reid in **Post Office v Crouch** [1974] ICR 378 to be as follows:

> "The definition includes all times outside the worker's working hours and "working hours" is defined as meaning time when in accordance with his contract he is required to be at work. I do not think it was or can be disputed that "at work" means actually at work and does not include periods when in accordance with his contract of employment the worker is on his employer's premises but not actually working."

(2) The appropriate time may also be a time during the working hours where there is an agreed arrangement or the employer has

consented, so that, for example a union shop steward may be entitled to stop his normal work to deal with matters that contain a trade union element. The section is sufficiently wide to encompass employees talking about trade union matters where the employer does not object to employees chatting while they work (See *Zucker*). However:

(a) There must be an arrangement or consent, which may be express or implied. However, consent will not be implied from mere silence on the part of the employer (**Marley Tile Co Limited v Shaw** [1980] IRLR 25; ICR 72).

(b) Where the employer refuses consent then section 152 will not apply, the consent may be conditional (i.e. on a meeting lasting only a certain time) but once consent has been given the employer cannot censor the contents of any meeting or discussion (See **Bass Taverns Limited v Burgess** [1995] IRLR 596).

(c) The appropriate time can include time when the employee is on the employer's premises though there is no reason why the employer should foot the bill for any meeting. See **Carter v Wiltshire County Council** [1979] IRLR 331 where it was appropriate for a meeting to be held at the social club where all but one employee were union members.

Refusal to be a member of a trade union

An employee has an unfettered right under section 152(1)(c) not to be a member of a union or a particular union.

Deductions in lieu

Where the employee has refused to become a member of a trade union a dismissal relating to payments or deductions shall be treated as falling within section 152(1)(c). Under section 152(3), the dismissal shall be treated as a section 152(1)(c) dismissal where the reason for dismissal was:

"(a) the employee's refusal or proposed refusal, to comply with a requirement (whether or not imposed by his contract of employment or in writing) that, in the event of his not being a member of any trade union, or of a particular trade union, or of one of a number of particular trade unions, he must make one or more payments, or

(b) his objection, or proposed objection (howsoever expressed) to the operation of a provision (whether or not forming part of his contract of employment or in writing) under which, in the event mentioned in paragraph (a), his employer is entitled to deduct one or more sums from the remuneration payable to im in respect of his employment."

This section prevents an employer from being able to insist the an employee pay sums or has deductions made where he is not a member of a union (i.e. payments made to charity in lieu of subscriptions). If the employee is dismissed for this reason then the dismissal will be unfair.

Union Recognition

Under paragraph 161 of Schedule A1 of TULR(C)A a dismissal will be unfair if the reasons for it, or the main reason for it was that:

- the employee acted with a view to obtaining or preventing recognition with a union under A1;
- the employee indicated that he supported or did not support recognition under A1;
- the employee acted with a view to securing or preventing the ending under A1 of bargaining arrangements;
- the employee indicated that he supported or did not support the ending under A1 of bargaining arrangements;
- the employee influenced or sought to influence the way in which votes were to be cast by other workers in a ballot arranged under A1;
- the employee influenced or sought to influence other workers to vote or abstain from voting in such a ballot;
- the employee voted in such a ballot;
- the employee proposed to do, or failed or declined to do any of the aforesaid.

Where the act or omission on the part of the employee is unreasonable then it will not be regarded as falling within the aforesaid.

Branches of a union

By section 152(4) references to becoming or ceasing to remain a member of a trade union include references to a particular branch or section of the union or to one of a number of branches or sections of the union and reference to trade union activities is to be construed in this way.

Selection for Redundancy

Selection for redundancy because of one of the reasons set out in section 152 will be automatically unfair (section 153).

Compensation and Remedies

Sections 155 to 159 contain a number of provisions relating to assessment of compensation in the event that a Tribunal finds that the dismissal was for a reason set out in section 152.

(1) Section 156 provides that the minimum basic award before any reduction is made under section 122 of the ERA 1996 will be not less than £3,100 from 1 February 2000 (£2,900 before) where the dismissal was for section 152 or 153 reason but in relation to section 153 dismissals reduction for contributory fault under section 122(2) of the ERA 1996 may be applied.

(2) Prior to the Employment Relations Act 1999 a special award was payable under sections 157 to 159 of the ERA 1996. These provisions are repealed by section 33 of the 1999 Act on a date to be appointed. The intention is to simplify the compensatory awards so that special awards are replaced with additional awards.

(3) An additional award will be payable under section 17 of the ERA 1996.

(4) In considering the level of compensation to be awarded section 155 of TULR(C)A provides that, in deciding what amount it is just and equitable to award, the following conduct shall be disregarded in considering what reductions are appropriate:

- conduct or action that constitutes a breach of a requirement to be or become a member of a trade union or of a particular trade union or one of a number of particular trade unions.
- conduct or action that constitutes a breach of a requirement to cease to be, or refrain from becoming, a member of a trade union or of a particular trade union or one of a number of particular trade unions.

- conduct or action that constitutes a breach of a requirement not to take part in the activities of any trade union or of a particular trade union or one of a number of particular trade unions.
- Conduct or action that constitutes a refusal or objection under section 152(3).

The requirement may be imposed on the complainant by arrangement or contract of employment or other agreement.

(5) Under section 160 of TULR(C)A where the employer or the complainant complains that:

- the employer was induced to dismiss the complainant by pressure which a trade union or other person exercised on the employer by calling, organising, procuring or financing a strike or other industrial action, or by threatening to do so, and
- that pressure was exercised because the complainant was not a member of any trade union or of a particular trade union or of one of a number of particular trade unions,

then the employer of complainant may request the Tribunal to direct that the person who he claims exercised the pressure be joined or sisted as a party to the proceedings.

The Tribunal shall grant this request if it is made before the hearing but may be refused if it is made after that time and such a request may not be made after the Tribunal has made an award for compensation or an order for re-instatement or re-engagement. Where a party has been joined an award of compensation may be made fully or partly against that party.

Burden of proof

This is dealt with in Chapter 12.

Pressure to dismiss, interim relief and remedies

This is dealt with in Chapter 29.

CHAPTER TWENTY-FIVE
WORKING TIME

By section 101A of the ERA 1996 an employee shall be regarded as unfairly dismissed if the reason or principal reason for the dismissal is that the employee:

"(3) refused (or proposed to refuse) to comply with a requirement which the employer imposed (or proposed to impose) in contravention of the Working Time Regulations 1998,

(4) refused (or proposed to refuse) to forego a right conferred on him by those Regulations,

(5) failed to sign a workforce agreement for the purposes of those Regulations, or to enter into, or agree to vary or extend, any other agreement with his employer which is provided for in those Regulations, or

(6) being-

(1) a representative of members of the workforce for the purposes of Schedule 1 to those Regulations, or

(2) a candidate in an election in which any person elected will, on being elected, be such a representative,

performed (or proposed to perform) any functions or activities as such a representative or candidate."

As with other automatic unfair dismissals there is no qualifying period and no upper age limit. Moreover, a dismissal may also fall within section 104 ERA where it consists of the assertion of a statutory right under the Regulations. The parties may not contract out of the Regulations though claims under the Regulations may be compromised (See Regulation 35).

There is not space in this book to cover in detail the substantive content of the Regulations but, in summary they provide as follows:

Relevant agreement

It is to be noted that many of the provisions of the Regulations may be covered by a relevant agreement, which is defined as a workforce agreement, a provision of a collective agreement which applies to the worker or any other agreement in writing that is legally enforceable. A workforce agreement is an agreement between the employer and workers or their representatives in respect of which Schedule 1 of the Regulations is satisfied, namely:

- the agreement is in writing;
- it applies to all the relevant members of the workforce or a particular group;
- it is signed by the representatives of the workforce or group or in the case of fewer than 20 workers the workers' representatives or a majority of the workforce;
- the employer provided the workers with a copy of the agreement and guidance before it was signed.

The 48 hour week

By Regulation 4 a worker's working time, including overtime in any reference period which is applicable in his case shall not exceed an average of 48 hours for each seven days.

- 'Working time' means any period when the worker is working at his employer's disposal and carrying out duties or activities, receiving relevant training or and additional period that is to be regarded as working time. (Reg 2).
- 'The reference period' is each such period where a relevant agreement provides for the application of the regulation in relation to successive periods of 17 weeks or any period of 17 weeks in the course of employment (Reg 4(3)). The 17 week period may therefore be a rolling period or a fixed period.
- Where the worker has worked less than 17 weeks the period that has elapsed since he has started work (Reg 4(3)).
- Where certain classes of worker are excluded under Regulation 21 the reference period is 26 weeks. These include activities such as security services, care services, work at docks and airports, the media, gas, water and electrical industries, research, agriculture, tourism. Postal services and where the place of work and residence are distant from each other as well as certain emergencies. Moreover, under Regulation 23 a collective

agreement or workforce agreement may for objective or technical reasons concerning the organisation of work substitute a period up to 52 weeks.

- Working time is calculated in accordance with Regulation 4(6) as being the working hours plus the aggregate number of hours during the course of the period beginning immediately after the end of the reference period and ending when the number of days on which he worked equals the number of excluded days, divided by the reference period. Period of absence during the reference period for holiday, sickness, maternity etc do not therefore count in adding up the reference period of 17 weeks (Regs 4(6)(7).

Exclusion of the 48 hour week

By Regulation 5(1) the limit will not apply where the worker has agreed in writing that it should not apply in his case, provided that the employer has complied with certain requirements under 5(4).

- The agreement to exclude may relate to a certain period or be indefinite (Reg 5(2)) and shall be terminable by the worker giving seven days notice in writing unless a difference period is specified in the agreement which cannot be more than three months (Reg 5(3)).
- The requirements under Reg 5(4) are that:
    - the employer maintains up to date records;
    - the records identify each of the workers that have agreed the limit shall not apply;
    - the record sets out the terms on which the worker agreed that the limit will not apply;
    - the record specifies the number of hours worked by the worker during each reference period since the agreement came into effect;
    - a Health and Safety Inspector is permitted to inspect on request and is provided with such information as he may request regarding any case in which a worker has entered into such an agreement.

Right to limits with night work

Night work is defined in Regulation 2 as work during night time which means a period of not less than seven hours which includes the period between midnight and 5 am as determined by a relevant agreement, or in default of a relevant agreement the period between 11pm and 6 am. In relation to nightworkers:

- the normal hours of work in the reference period shall not exceed an average of 8 hours for each 24 hours and the employer shall take all steps in accordance with health and safety to seek to ensure that this is complied with (Reg 6(1)(2)).
- It is important to note that Regulation 23 provides that a collective or workforce agreement may exclude or modify the application of Regulation 6(1)(2)(3) and (7).
- The employer shall ensure that the worker does not work for more than 8 hours in any 24 hour period where the work involves special hazards or heavy physical or mental strain (see Regs 6(7)(8)).
- There are similar provisions to regulation 4 where a reference period has not been worked out and for calculating the hours (see Regs 6(4)(5)(6)).
- By Regulation 7 a health assessment must be carried out before a worker is assigned to night work and there should be free health assessments at regular intervals and this is particularly applicable in relation to a young worker (15 to 18 years of age).

Right to rest periods

The rest period provisions are fourfold:

- Where the pattern according to which an employer organises work is such as to put the health and safety of a worker employed at risk, in particular because the work is monotonous or the work rate is predetermined the employer shall ensure that the worker is given adequate rest breaks (Reg 8).
- An adult worker is entitled to a rest period of at least 11 consecutive hours in each 24 period during which he works for his employer and a young worker is entitled to 12 hours in each 24 hour period subject to the minimum rest period in the case of the latter, being interrupted in the case of activities that a split up of short duration (Regulation 10). It is important to note that Regulation 23 provides that a collective agreement or workforce agreement may modify or exclude the effect of Regulation 10(1) in relation to adult workers.
- An adult worker is entitled to a weekly rest period of not less than 24 hours in each seven day period during which he works for the employer, which the employer may determine as being:

- two uninterrupted periods of not less than 24 hours in each 14 day period or
- on period of 48 hours in each 14 day period (Reg 11). This does not include the 11 hour rest periods unless it is justified by objective technical or organisational reasons. It is important to note that Regulation 23 provides that a collective agreement or workforce agreement may modify or exclude the effect of Regulation 11(1) in relation to adult workers

- A young worker is entitled to 48 hours in each 7 day period which may be interrupted in the case of activities that a split up of short duration or in the case of technical or organisational reasons where the period may be not less than 36 hours.

- An adult worker is entitled to a rest break of not less than 20 minutes (which may be modified by a collective agreement or workforce agreement) where the working time is more than a 6 hour period (Reg 12) whilst a young worker is entitled to 30 minutes where the working time is more than four and a half hours. It is important to note that Regulation 23 provides that a collective agreement or workforce agreement may modify or exclude the effect of Regulation 12(1) in relation to adult workers.

Holidays

A worker is entitled to a period of leave in each leave year as follows (Reg 13):

- Three weeks in relation to any leave year beginning after 23rd November 1998 but before 23rd November 1999 and a proportion of a fourth week equivalent to the proportion of the year beginning on 23rd November 1998 which has elapsed at the start of that leave year.
- Four weeks in relation to any leave year after 23rd November 1999.

The leave year begins:

- on such date during the calender year as may be provided for in a relevant agreement;
- where there are no provisions in a relevant agreement 1st October 1998 or the date on which the employment began if after that date.

The entitlement does not arise until the worker has been employed for 13 weeks. When the 13 weeks has elapsed the worker becomes entitled to his full leave entitlement which must be taken in the leave year to which it relates and cannot be replaced by payment in lieu except where the worker's employment is terminated.

Where the worker's employment is terminated, under Regulation 14, if he has not taken the proportion of his leave to which he is entitled he shall be entitled to a payment in lieu based upon the proportion of leave he has not taken in the leave year that has expired before the termination date.

There are provisions in Regulation 15 for giving notice that leave is to be taken:

- The employee may take leave on such days as he elects by giving notice subject to any requirement imposed by the employer and the employer may impose a requirement by requiring the worker to take leave under regulation 13 or not to take leave on particular days by giving notice.
- Notice must be given as follows:
  - Where the employee gives notice that he wishes to take leave or the employer gives notice that leave is to be taken, the notice shall specify the days on which leave is to be taken and give notice twice as many days in advance of the earliest date specified in the notice;
  - where the employer gives notice that leave is not to be taken the notice shall be as many days in advance of the earliest day so specified as the number of days to which the notice relates;
  - These provisions may be modified or excluded by a relevant agreement.

Under Regulation 16 a worker is entitled to be paid in respect of periods of annual leave.

Exceptions

Part III of the Regulations contain a number of excluded sectors and other special cases and reference should be made to that part for the detail. However, it should be noted that:

- The daily rest provisions (Reg 10) and the weekly rest period does not apply to shift workers where he cannot take such a rest period between the end of one shift and the start of another (Reg 22(1)) and Regulation 10(1) does not apply where the work is split up over the day.
- Where there has been exclusions by collective agreements, workforce agreement or in relation to shift workers then the employer should allow an equivalent period of compensatory rest wherever possible.

PART FIVE
REMEDIES AND RECOUPMENT

CHAPTER TWENTY-SIX
REMEDIES: REINSTATEMENT
AND RE-ENGAGEMENT

Upon a finding of unfair dismissal the Tribunal must then consider which remedy is the appropriate one for the Applicant. Chapter II of Part X of the ERA 1996 sets out the remedies that are available to an Applicant and the procedure that the Tribunal should adopt. The three remedies available are an order for reinstatement, an order re-engagement or an order for compensation.

Explaining to the Applicant

> Where a Tribunal finds that a complaint of unfair dismissal is well founded it shall explain to the complainant what orders may be made by way of reinstatement or re-engagement and in what circumstances they may be made and ask the complainant whether he wishes the Tribunal to make such an order.

Under section 112(2) it is mandatory that the Tribunal explain to the complainant the remedies of reinstatement and re-engagement that may be made. By section 112(3) the Tribunal may made such an order if the complainant expresses such a wish. If no order is made the Tribunal shall make an award of compensation in accordance with the provisions of the Act. The Tribunal should consider the remedies in the order of re-instatement, re-engagement and compensation.

In **Pirelli General Cable Works Limited v Murray** [1979] IRLR 190 the EAT held that it was mandatory to explain and that any failure to do so is an error of law. However, a more relaxed view was taken in **Cowley v Manson Timber Limited** [1995] IRLR 153 where the Court of Appeal held that the fact that the Tribunal has not explained its powers to the complainant does not render any decision on compensation a nullity. The decision may however, be voidable if an injustice has occurred or the complainant has been prejudiced by lack of any explanation. There was no such injustice or prejudice in the *Cowley* case where the complainant had at all times been represented and his Application had stated that he only sought compensation. In **Richardson v Walker** [EAT 312/79] the EAT refused to allow an appeal on the ground that no explanation had been given in a case where the employee had already obtained and settled into new employment as they considered that it would be pointless sending the case back to the Tribunal.

Where an order is refused the Tribunal should give reasons for the refusal (**Plumley v AD International Limited** [EAT 592/82].

The importance of reinstatement or re-engagement

In **Telcon Metals Limited v Henry** [EAT 287/87] the EAT stressed that the remedies of reinstatement or re-engagement are the main remedies under the legislation and Tribunals should *not* be slow to consider such remedies. However, it is apparent from the statistics that these remedies are granted in very few cases.

The Remedy of Reinstatement

Reinstatement is the first remedy under the legislation that the Tribunal should consider. By section 114(1) of the ERA 1996:

An order for reinstatement is an order that the employer shall treat the complainant in all respects as if he had not been dismissed.

The effect of an order for reinstatement is that the employee is treated as though he has never been dismissed so that the Tribunal will make an order that the employee has all the rights and benefits as if he had remained in employment. In **Sedco Forex v Collie** [EAT 404/87] the EAT stated that a reinstatement order does not mean reinstatement in exactly the same position as before so that where the oil rig on which the employee had worked was closed down it was possible for him to reinstated at another rig. It is submitted that this decision confuses the distinction between reinstatement and re-engagement.

By section 114(2) the Tribunal is under a duty to specify:

(1) Any amounts payable by the employer in respect of any benefit which the complainant might reasonably have been expected to have had but for the dismissal *between the date of termination of employment and the date of reinstatement.*

A similar provision exists where re-engagement is ordered. It is necessary for tribunals to consider what the employee would have actually earned during the period in question (**Coakley v Hutchinson Coaches (Overtown) Limited** [EAT 247/85].

By section 114(4) the employer's liability may be reduced in respect of sums received from the date of termination to the date of dismissal by way of wages in lieu of notice or ex gratia payments from the employer, or in respect of remuneration obtained from another employer and such other benefits as the Tribunal considers appropriate in all the circumstances. However, the sums payable cannot be reduced on the basis that the employee has failed to mitigate his losses (**City & Hackney Health Authority v Crisp** [1990] IRLR 47).

(2) Any rights and privileges (including seniority and pension rights) which must be restored to the employee. In **Whitbread West Pennines Limited v Reedy** [1988] ICR 807 the Court of Appeal held that it was proper for the employer to obtain possession of tied accommodation even though the employee was seeking reinstatement. They were entitled to adopt the position that they would not reinstate under any circumstances and an order for possession would not in any event affect practicability since the employer would have been able to dismiss the new manager.

Under section 114(3) if the complainant would have benefited from an improvement in his terms and conditions of employment the order for reinstatement will require him to be treated as if he had benefited from that improvement from the date on which he would have done but for the dismissal.

(3) the date by which the Order must be complied with.

The Remedy of Re-engagement

Where the Tribunal does not consider the remedy of reinstatement to be appropriate it will then go on to consider re-engagement. By section 115(1) of the ERA 1996:

"An order for re-engagement is an order, on such terms and the tribunal may decide, that the complainant be engaged by the employer, or by a successor or the employer or by an associated employer, in employment comparable to that from which he was dismissed or other suitable employment."

The effect of an order of re-engagement is that the complainant is placed so far as possible in employment that was the same as the job from which he was dismissed. Section 115(2) states that the Tribunal must specify the terms on which re-engagement is to take place, which includes six matters that are set out in the section:

(1) The identity of the employer.
     An order for re-engagement is not limited to the employer but may be made against a successor or an associated company (See **Department of Health v Bruce** [EAT 14/92].)

(2) The nature of the employment.
     It is not necessary for the order to specify the precise job so that identifying the nature of the job is likely to be sufficient (*Rank Xerox*) referred to below.

(3) The remuneration for the employment.

(4) Any amounts payable by the employer in respect of any benefit which the complainant might reasonably have been expected to have had but for the dismissal *between the date of termination of employment and the date of re-engagement.*

     By section 115(3) the employer's liability may be reduced in respect of sums received from the date of termination to the date of dismissal by way of wages in lieu of notice or ex gratia payments from the employer, or in respect of remuneration obtained from another employer and such other benefits as the Tribunal considers appropriate in all the circumstances. This and the following requirement are the same as that which is ordered on reinstatement.

     A re-engagement order may be made on different terms from that which the dismissed employee enjoyed before his dismissal but any assessment of earnings between dismissal and re-engagement will be based upon the remuneration that the employee would have based upon the salary before dismissal (**Electronic Data Processing v Wright** [1986] IRLR 8).

(5) Any rights and privileges (including seniority and pension rights) which must be restored to the employee.

(6) The date by which the Order must be complied with. It is necessary that a date be specified. In **British Telecommunications PLC v Thompson** [EAT 884/95] the EAT held an order that the employee must be re-engaged within 14 days from being certified as fit for work to be invalid, as a date was not specified.

It is important that the Tribunal make an order in the terms of section 115(2) by setting out the heads under that section. An order that does not comply will be invalid. In **Pirelli General Cable Works Limited v Murray** [1979] IRLR 190 an order that left the terms to be agreed between the parties was invalid. Moreover, an order that stated that the employee be re-engaged in employment comparable to that from which he was dismissed or other suitable employment as agreed between the parties on terms agreed between the parties was held in **Stena Houlder Limited v Keenan** [EAT 543/03] to be invalid.

There are no limits on the amount of compensation that can be awarded under an order of reinstatement or re-engagement (see **Foster Wheeler (GB) Limited v Chiarella** [EAT 111/82]).

Reinstatement or Re-engagement

Section 116 sets out the procedure that the Tribunal must adopt in deciding whether to order reinstatement or re-engagement.

Reinstatement?

By section 116(1) the Tribunal must first consider whether to make an order for reinstatement and in doing so shall take into account three matters:

(1) Whether the complainant wishes to be reinstated.
(2) Whether it is practicable for the employer to comply with an order for reinstatement.
(3) Where the complainant caused or contributed to some extent to the dismissal whether it would be just to order his reinstatement.

Re-engagement?

If the Tribunal decide not to make an order for reinstatement, by section 116(2) it shall then consider whether to make an order for re-engagement and, if so, on what terms. By section 116(3) it shall take into account three matters:

(1) Any wish expressed by the complainant as to the nature of the order to be made.
(2) Whether it is practicable for the employer (or a successor or an associated company) to comply with an order for re-engagement.
(3) Where the complainant caused or contributed to some extent to the dismissal whether it would be just to order his re-engagement and, if so, on what terms.

Except where contributory fault is taken into account any re-engagement shall be on terms that are, so far as practicable, as favourable as an order for reinstatement (116(4)). It was held by the EAT in **Rank Xerox (UK) Limited v Stryczek** [1995] IRLR 568 that it is not permissible for an order to be made for re-engagement on terms that are more favourable than could be made on an order for reinstatement and which in effect amounted to a promotion.

Practicability

In deciding whether an order for reinstatement or re-engagement should be ordered the Tribunal must consider whether it is practicable for the employer to comply with an order for reinstatement or an order for re-engagement. The EAT have stated that broad commonsense approach should be taken to the issue of practicability (**Meridian Limited v Gomershall & Anor** [1977] ICR 597). Reinstatement may not be practicable when the employee's job has disappeared because of a re-organisation. This was the position in **Thamesdown Borough Council v Turrell** [EAT 459/97] where it was also considered to be relevant that the employee's co-workers had threatened industrial action if the employee returned.

It is to be noted that where the employer has engaged a permanent replacement this is to be ignored in considering practicability unless the employer shows that either that it was not practicable for the dismissed employer's work to be carried out without engaging a permanent replacement, or he engaged the replacement after a reasonable period without having heard from the dismissed employee that he wished to be reinstated or re-engaged and when the replacement was engaged it was no longer reasonable for him to arrange the work to be done except by a permanent replacement (sections 116(5)–(6)). (See **Safeway Food Stores Limited v Cookson** [EAT 129/80].)

The issue of practicability arises at two distinct stages: when the Tribunal is deciding whether or not to make an order and when the employer has refused to comply with an order. It was held in **Port of London Authority v Payne** [1994] IRLR 9 by the Court of Appeal that at the first stage the Tribunal must make a provisional determination or assessment, which is not a final determination in the sense that it creates an estoppel or limits the employer to reliance upon facts after the order has been made. At the second stage the Tribunal must make a final determination as to practicability. The Tribunal must not apply too high a standard but must have regard to the commercial judgment of the employer who is not required to show that compliance is impossible.

The Court of Appeal approved **Timex Corporation v Thomson** [1981] IRLR 522. Mr Thomson was dismissed in circumstances where the Tribunal found that there was no admissible reason for dismissal and re-engagement was ordered. The EAT dismissed the employer's contention that re-engagement was impracticable. It commented that:

> "At the stage when the order to re-engage is being made, it is not in our judgment necessary for the Industrial Tribunal, looking at future possible events, to make a definite finding that the order for re-engagement was practicable. They must have regard to the question of practicability and if they are satisfied that it is unlikely to be effective, they will no doubt not make an order. The only strict requirement is that they should have regard to practicability."

This distinction was emphased in **Freemans Plc v Flynn** [1984] ICR 874. The employer did not initially object to an order for re-engagement being made but later asserted that compliance with the order was impracticable having been unable to find another job for the employee. The Tribunal stated that having found at the earlier stage that it was practicable this was settled once and for all. The EAT held that this was wrong and there is a very clear distinction between the two stages. At the earlier stage practicability was only a consideration whilst at the second stage the duty was on the employer to satisfy the Tribunal.

Where relations have broken down between the employee and his employer, or the employee and his work colleagues, an order may not be practicable. In **Intercity East Coast Limited v McGregor** [EAT 473/96] an order was not made where, in the words of the EAT 'war had broken out' between the employee's supervisor and the applicant. An order for reinstatement was considered to be impracticable in **Meridian Limited v Gomershall** [1977] ICR 597 where there had been a deterioration in working relations between co-employees. Similarly in **Nothman v London Borough of Barnet** [1980] IRLR 65 where the applicant alleged a long standing conspiracy by her work colleagues against her it was 'impossible' to make a reinstatement order. (See also **Miller v Liquidator for Matthew Primrose & Co Limited** [EAT 17/77].)

Where there has been a breakdown in trust and confidence it may not be practicable to make an order for reinstatement or re-engagement. (**Nothman v London Borough of Barnet** [1980] IRLR 65). In **SMT Sales & Service Co Limited v Irwin** [EAT 485/79] where the employee was dismissed on the grounds of capability the EAT stated that it would be unrealistic to expect the employer to continue to employ a senior manger in whom they had lost confidence, even if this was not with good reason. Indeed it was stated in **Wood Group Heavy Industrial Turbines Limited v Crossan** [1999] IRLR 680 that it will only be in the rarest of cases that an order for reinstatement or re-engagement will be ordered if there has been a breakdown in trust and confidence. Where the employer has a genuine, even if erroneous, belief in the misconduct of the employee such an order will not be practicable.

Where there are capability or ill health matters it may not be practicable to order reinstatement or re-engagement. (**British Telecommunications Limited v Thompson** [EAT 884/95]).

Contributory conduct

The Tribunal must consider the question of conduct and it will be a mistake of law for it to fail to do so (**Kelvin International Services v Stephenson** [EAT 1057/95]). Tribunals may make an order even though there has been significant contributory conduct as in **Automatic Cooling Engineers Limited v Scott** [EAT 545/81] where there was contribution of 75% or even where the employer believes that the employee is guilty of dishonesty, as in **Boots Co PLC v Lees Collier** [1986] IRLR 485 though such an order was refused where there was admitted dishonesty in **United Distillers Limited v Harrower** [EAT 115/96].

Other factors

As well as considering the employee's wishes, practicability and contributory conduct the Tribunal is entitled to take into account other factors that it considers relevant. In **Port of London Authority v Payne** [1994] IRLR 9 this included industrial relations consequences. An order for re-engagement was refused in **Coleman & Anor v Magnet Joinery Limited** [1974] ICR 46 where such an order would have immediately led to industrial action. Stephenson LJ stated:

> """Practicable", in the context in which it is used in s.106(4)(b), is not to be equated with "possible", which would oblige a Tribunal to make a recommendation for re-engagement provided the job was still open. It is the duty of the Tribunal to consider the industrial relations realities of the situation and, if the evidence points overwhelmingly to the conclusion that the consequences of any attempt to re-engage the employee will result in serious industrial strife, it will be neither practicable nor in accordance with equity to make such a recommendation."

In **Securicor Limited v Smith** [EAT 302/87] the treatment meted out to a third party employee who had been reinstated was to be a relevant factor in considering practicability.

It was stated in **Atlantic Steam Navigation Co Limited v Murdoch** [EAT 234/83] that it will rarely be a practicable proposition to order re-engagement in a subordinate capacity in general terms as to the place of employment and the rate of remuneration available.

Enforcement of Order

By section 117(1) where an order has been made for reinstatement or re-engagement and it has not been fully complied with an award of compensation may be made as calculated by section 117(2). Where there has been a total failure to comply, compensation is assessed in accordance with section 117(3).

Non compliance

It is for the tribunal to decide as a matter of fact whether the order has been complied with. In **Electronic Data Processing v Wright** [1986] IRLR 8 it was held by the EAT that the Industrial Tribunal was entitled to conclude that their order for re-engagement had not been complied with by an offer of re-engagement in Manchester rather than Sheffield where the respondent employee was previously employed, notwithstanding that the place of the respondent's work had not been specified in the re-engagement order. The Industrial Tribunal was entitled to interpret their own decision and to give effect to what they intended to say by holding that Manchester was not the place of work where re-engagement was to take place under their order.

The distinction between partial and total non compliance was considered in **Artisan Press v Srawley and Parker** [1986] IRLR 126. Two security staff were reinstated in circumstances where their jobs were radically altered as the employer had engaged outside contractors so that their job functions became predominately cleaning rather than security. The EAT held that there was total failure to comply with the order when an employee has been 'reinstated' in a different job on different terms.

Amount of compensation

Failure to comply may attract an additional award of between 26 to 52 weeks with a weekly ceiling from Ist February 2000 of £230 (£220 before that date) so that the award may be between £5,980 to £11,960.

By section 117(2) the amount of compensation will be such as the Tribunal thinks fit having regard to the loss sustained by the complainant in consequence of the failure to fully comply with the terms of the order.

Under section 117(3) an award will be made for unfair dismissal and an additional award may be made where the complainant is not reinstated or re-engaged in accordance with the terms of the order. By sections 117(5) and (6) the additional award is calculated as follows:

(1) Where the dismissal is an act of discrimination within the SDA 1975, RRA 1976 or DDA 1995 the award will be not less than 26 weeks nor more than 52 weeks pay.

(2) In any other case it shall be not less than 13 weeks or more than 26 weeks pay.

However, in a case of discrimination where it is shown not to be practicable to reinstate a tribunal is not then entitled to increase the damages that it awarded for race discrimination because it cannot award compensation under section 117(3): **London Borough of Lambeth v D'Souza** [1999] IRLR 240.

However, the Tribunal may take into account the fact that the complainant has unreasonably prevented an order under section 113 from being complied with in making an award as being a failure on the part of the complainant to mitigate his loss (section 117(8)).

Exceptions where no additional award will be made

Since the employee has been unfairly dismissed he is entitled to the normal award for unfair dismissal. Where the employer has not complied with the order for reinstatement or re-engagement an additional award may be given. Section 117(4) sets out two circumstances in which an additional award will not be ordered:

Practicability

Where the employer satisfies the Tribunal that it was not reasonably practicable to comply with the order no additional award will be made.

We have already seen that the Tribunal considers the question of practicability when deciding if an order should be made in the first place. However, at that stage the Tribunal need only take into account considerations of practicability and it will only be at the stage where the employer asserts that it was not practicable to comply that full consideration will be given by the Tribunal. The test is practicability rather than possibility. In **Port of London v Payne** [1994] IRLR 9 this distinction was made clear. The Court of Appeal stated that at the second stage the Tribunal must make a final determination as to practicability. However, it must beware about setting too high a standard and give due weight to the commercial judgment of the employer. Neill LJ stated that the employer cannot be expected to explore every possible avenue which ingenuity might suggest and to show that reinstatement or re-engagement was impossible.

Reinstatement should not normally necessitate the employer having to dismiss staff or make redundancies. In (**Freemans PLC v Flynn** [1984] IRLR 874 the EAT stated that it would be putting it far to highly to expect an employer to search for and find a place in their ranks irrespective of vacancies that came up as, taking this to logical extremes, it would necessitate the employer dismissing other employees to create the necessary space for he or she who is re-engaged.

However, the Tribunal will be astute as to whether an assertion by the employer that a post no longer exists is really an attempt to frustrate any possibility of an order as in **Cruickshank v London Borough of Richmond** [EAT 483/97] where the employer stated that the position had been deleted one month before the hearing on liability.

The Tribunal will not take into account the fact that a permanent replacement was engaged unless the employer can show that it was not practicable for the dismissed person's work to be done other than with a permanent replacement (section 117(7)).

CHAPTER TWENTY-SEVEN
THE BASIC AWARD

By section 118(1)(a) of the ERA 1996 a basic award shall be awarded where a tribunal makes an award of compensation for unfair dismissal. The basic award is intended to compensate loss of job security so the fact that the employee has suffered no financial loss is not relevant (**Cadbury Limited v Doddington** [1977] ICR 982).

Calculation

Under section 119(1) the basic award is calculated by:

(1) determining the period ending with the effective date of termination during which the employee has been continuously employed;
(2) reckoning backwards from the end of that period the number of years of employment falling within the period;
(3) awarding the appropriate amount for each year of employment.

Appropriate amount

By section 119(2) the appropriate amount is:

(1) one and a half weeks pay for each year that the employee was not below the age of forty one.
(2) one weeks pay for a year of employment in which he was not below the age of twenty two.
(3) half a weeks pay for a year of employment where (1) and (2) do not apply.

Where twenty years employment has been reckoned under (1) then no account is to be taken of any year of employment earlier than those twenty years (119(3)).

Age Limits

Where the termination is after the sixty fourth anniversary the amount is to be reduced by one twelfth for each month from the sixty fourth birthday (119(5)).

Minimum basic awards

By section 120 the minimum basic award shall be a prescribed amount (£3,100 from 1 Feb 2000 (£2,900 before)) if the reason or principal reason for dismissal or selection for redundancy is one of the reasons specified in sections 100(1)(a), (b), 101A(d), 102(1) or 103.

The minimum basic award applies in relation to dismissal for trade union membership or activities, carrying out duties as a health and safety representative, as a trustee of an occupational pension fund or as an employee representative (see the relevant Chapters). Otherwise the maximum level of award is £230 for each full year worked with a current maximum of £6,900.

By section 121 the basic award shall be two weeks pay where the reason or principal reason for the dismissal is that the employee was redundant and the employee is not entitled to a redundancy payment because he has unreasonably refused an offer or has unreasonably left during a trial period under sections 138 or 141 of the ERA.

Level of Basic Award

Under section 34 of the Employment Relations Act 1999 the basic award is index linked to the retail price act and will be increased or decreased by the same percentage of the amoount of increase or decrease in the same. In making such a calculation the Secretary of State will round up the sum to the nearest £100. The award from 1 February 2000 is £230.

Reductions

Section 122 specifies a number of grounds upon which the basic award may be reduced.

Refusal of reinstatement

By section 122(1) where the employee unreasonably refuses an offer that would have the effect of reinstating the complainant in all respects as if he had not been dismissed the Tribunal shall reduce or further reduce the amount for the basic award to such extent as it considers just and equitable having regard to that finding. The offer must have the effect of reinstating the employee *in all respects as though he had not been dismissed*. An offer that is made on different terms will not affect the basic award even if the offer was entirely reasonable and there is no ground to refuse the offer. However, such a refusal may amount to a failure to mitigate for the purposes of the compensatory award. The approach to be taken to this section was set out by Mummery J in **Parkes v Banham Locks Limited** [EAT 207/96]. The EAT considered that the wording of the section should be followed so that the Tribunal should ask: Has an offer been made? If an offer has been made would it have the effect of reinstating the employee as if he or she had not been dismissed? Did the employee refuse that offer? If the offer was refused did the employee behave unreasonably in refusing? Where the offer has been unreasonably refused the Tribunal is then at liberty to reduce the compensation by such amount as it considers just and equitable.

It should be noted that an offer must have been made so that an invitation to merely discuss the possibility of re-employment will not be sufficient (**McDonald v Capital Coaches Limited** [EAT 140/94].

Conduct

By section 122(2) where the Tribunal may consider that any conduct of the complainant before dismissal, or before notice was given, was such that it would be just and equitable to reduce or further reduce the amount of the basic award to any extent it may reduce the award accordingly. This provision is not to apply in a redundancy case unless an award is made under section 120 in which case it only applies to so much of the award as has been paid under section 120 (122(3)).

The Tribunal will consider the conduct of the complainant before the dismissal or before notice to dismissal was given though it is not necessary for the conduct to have caused or contributed to the dismissal. An award cannot be reduced on the ground because of conduct occurring during the notice period after notice had been given, though the compensatory award may be reduced on the grounds of the just and equitable principle. Moreover, the Tribunal will only reduce the award if they have evidence of misconduct. In **Western Leisure v Flynn and Ambridge** [EAT 375/92] the compensatory award was reduced to nil on the ground that the employees would have been dismissed but no reduction was made to the basic award as there was no evidence as to which employee was guilty of misconduct.

Where the applicant's conduct results in a reduction of the basic and the compensatory award an issue arises as to whether or not the compensation should be reduced in similar percentages for both types of awards. Two different situations arise:

(1) The compensatory award may have been reduced because of contributory conduct which caused or contributed to the dismissal (123(6)). The provision is different from that under section 122(2) which does not contain an element of causation. In these circumstances the EAT has held that it is not essential that the reductions be the same though it will only be in exceptional circumstances that the awards should be treated differently. In **RSPCA v Cruden** [1986] ICR 205 a full basic award was given whilst the compensatory award was reduced to nil. The EAT took the view that a proper exercise of discretion required the same deduction to be made. A different reduction was made in **Charles Roberts Developments Limited v (1) White (2) Hobbs** [EAT 450/93] where the compensatory award was reduced to nil whilst the basic award was reduced by 50%. This was justified on the ground that it would not be just and equitable to reduce the award to nil as the complainant had not been given a fair hearing. The position was considered again recently in **Optikinetics Limited v Whooley** [1999] ICR 984. The complainant was dismissed because he was using the employer's facilities for private work despite being warned against this. The ET found that dismissal was a grossly disproportionate sanction and made no reduction for contribution. This part of the decision was overturned by the EAT which made six points:

• The employee must be guilty of culpable conduct before a finding of contribution can be made.
• The employee's conduct must be known to the employer at the time of the dismissal and have been causative of it.

- If the first two points are made out the Tribunal should reduce the *compensatory* award by such amount as it considers just and equitable.
- There is no necessity for causation in respect of the reduction of the basic award as section 122(2) gives the Tribunal a wide discretion to reduce the basic award.
- Different proportionate reductions may therefore be made in respect of the basic and compensatory awards.
- It will be a rare occurrence for the Appellate Court to interfere with the percentage reductions.

The EAT considered that the compensatory award should have been reduced by 20%.

(2) The compensatory award may be reduced because of contributory conduct *and* because the Tribunal take the view that it would be just and equitable, under section 123(1) to reduce the award on the ground that the employee would have been dismissed even if a fair procedure had been followed. In **Rao v Civil Aviation Authority** [1994] IRLR 240 the Court of Appeal considered it permissible to reduce the basic award by a greater percentage in such a case to reflect the fact that the reduction of the compensatory award for contributory conduct may not be as great because the tribunal may take into account the fact that they had already reduced the award on the ground that it was just and equitable to do so. Such a situation is likely to occur, in particular, where the compensatory award is reduced on the just and equitable basis because the Tribunal take the view that the complainant would have been dismissed in any event or a fair procedure would have resulted in the chance of dismissal in any event.

Designated dismissals procedure agreement

By section 122(3A) where the complainant has been awarded any amount in respect of a designated dismissals procedures agreement the tribunal shall reduce or further reduce the amount as it considers it just and equitable having regard to that award.

Redundancy payments

By section 122(4) the basic award is to be further reduced by any redundancy payment made under Part XI of the ERA 1996 or any payment made by the employer on the ground that the employee was redundant. It was held in **Taylor v John Webster Buildings Civil Engineering** [1999] ICR 561 that there is no basis on which the basic award may be reduced to reflect the chance that the employee may have been dismissed in any event for redundancy as a redundancy payment would then have been paid in any event.

Ex gratia payments

Ex gratia payments will usually reduce any compensatory award that is made by the tribunal and may, in certain circumstances reduce the basic award. In **Chelsea Football Club Limited v Heath** [1981] ICR 323 an ex gratia payment was made which exceeded the maximum compensatory award and the employer argued that the balance should be applied to the basic award. The Tribunal however, gave a full basic award. The EAT set this aside on the ground that the employer had described the sum as 'ex gratia compensation'. It stated that:

> "where a general payment is made and in each individual case it is a question of construction as to whether the payment made is to be taken to have included any rights which the employee might have under the provisions of the statute. If the employer makes a general payment – particularly if it is made ex-gratia – he will risk the argument that he has not paid something which is referable to the liability for the basic award should he be held to have dismissed unfairly. But it seems to us that there can be cases in which a payment is made and which is, as a matter of construction or of fact, to be taken as including such rights as the employee may have under the statute, even if entitlement to the monies is initially denied by the employer."

It is therefore important that employers specify what any ex gratia payment is referable to if they wish to exclude the possibility of a basic award. For example, in **Pomphrey of Sittingbourne Limited v Reed** [EAT 457/94] a payment described as 'payment in lieu' was not a payment which was referable to the basic award and any reduction was refused. Similarly, in **Boorman v Allmakes Limited** [1995] ICR 842 the Court of Appeal rejected the argument that a payment described as 'statutory redundancy entitlement' could extinguish the basic award when the employee was found not to have been dismissed for redundancy. Section 122(4) only applies to reduce the basic award by an redundancy payment made in respect of the 'same dismissal'. Since the dismissal was not for redundancy it could not be said to be the same dismissal as the basic award only became payable when the Tribunal had found an unfair dismissal.

It should be noted that where there has been a compromise agreement this may be effective, in certain circumstances to prevent the employee from pursuing any claim.

CHAPTER TWENTY-EIGHT
THE COMPENSATORY AWARD

Principle of the Award

Where a complainant has been unfairly dismissed and is entitled to a compensatory award then by section 123(1) of the ERA 1996:

> "...the amount of the compensatory award shall be such amount as the tribunal considers just and equitable in all the circumstances having regard to the loss sustained by the complainant in consequence of the dismissal in so far as that loss is attributable to action taken by the employer."

> The aim of the compensatory award is to compensate the employee for the loss he has actually suffered as a result of the dismissal. The Tribunal therefore looks at the net remuneration that the employee actually received whilst he was employed. The award is not intended to express the Tribunal's disapproval of the manner in which the employer has conducted itself or to take into account the manner of the dismissal but is intended to compensation purely for financial loss.

It was made clear by Phillips J in **Lifeguard Assurance Co Limited v Zadrozny** [1977] IRLR 56 that the award is not intended to penalise employers. In **Norton Tool Co Limited v Tewson** [1972] 501 the NIRC stated that loss does not include injury to pride or feelings but is to be calculated on the basis of financial loss.

However, the Tribunal is to award compensation in accordance with what it considers to be just and equitable so that there is an element of discretion, in particular, where the Tribunal has to consider speculative matters such as whether the complainant will obtain comparable employment in the future or how long it will take him to get to the same salary level. This was made clear many years ago by Sir John Donaldson in *Tewson* where he stated that:

> "The Court or tribunal is enjoined to assess compensation in an amount which is just and equitable in all the circumstances and there is neither justice nor equity in a failure to act in accordance with principle. The principles to be adopted emerge from the section. First the object is to compensate and compensate fully but not to award a bonus, save possibly in the special case of a refusal by an employer to make an offer of employment in accordance with the recommendation of the Court or a tribunal. Second the amount to be awarded is that which is just and equitable in all the circumstances having regard to the loss sustained by the complainant. "Loss" in the context of the section does not include injury to pride or feelings. In its natural meaning the word is to be so construed, and that this meaning is intended seems to us to be clear from the elaboration contained in subsection (2). The discretionary element is introduced by the words having regard to the loss. This does not mean that the Court or tribunal can have regard to other matters, but rather that the amount of the compensation is not precisely and arithmetically related to the proved loss. Such a provision will be seen to be natural and possibly essential, when it is remembered that the claims with which the Court and tribunals are concerned are more often than not presented by claimants in person and in conditions of informality. It is not therefore to be expected that precise and detailed proof of every item of loss will be presented, although, after making due allowance for the skills of the persons presenting the claims, the statutory requirement for informality of procedure and the undesirability of burdening the parties with the expense of adducing evidence of an elaboration which is disproportionate to the sums in issue, the burden of proof lies squarely upon the complainant."

Minor mistakes in calculation may therefore be disregarded by the higher courts as in **Fougiere v Phoenix Motor Co Limited** [1976] ICR 495. Since the Tribunal has a discretion under the section to award what they consider to be just and equitable they may adopt a rather more broad brush approach than would be adopted in relation to common law claims (**Garagra Equipment Maintenance Co Limited v Hollaway** [EAT 582/94]) though the onus remains on the employee to prove each head of loss and the Tribunal should consider each head (**Tidman v Aveling Marshal Limited** [1977] IRLR 218.)

The £50,000 Ceiling

In assessing loss the Tribunal is not subject to the weekly pay limit as with the basic award but takes account of the net earnings of the employee. By section 34(4) of the Employment Relations Act 1999 the compensatory limit was increased to £50,000. This came into effect on 25th October 1999. The compensatory award has also been index linked and may be increased or decreased **proportionately** depending on the movement of the retail price index. In such case the Secretary of State will round up the figure to the nearest £100.

Stage 1: Assessing the Loss

It is necessary to first assess the loss that has been suffered by the complainant between the date of the dismissal and the tribunal hearing and to assess future loss and then to apply such deductions as are appropriate to the loss that has been suffered. The usual heads of loss and deductions that apply are as follows:

Assess the loss based upon:

(A) Immediate Loss
(B) Statutory Protection
(C) Future Loss
(D) Pensions

After taking into account what payments have been made the Tribunal will then consider whether any deductions should be made based upon:

(E) Failure to mitigate
(F) It being 'just and equitable' to make a deduction on the premise that the employee would have been dismissed in any event.
(G) Contributory fault

Each of these head must be considered in turn.

A. Immediate Loss

(1) *The principle*

The immediate loss is the financial loss that has been suffered between the effective date of termination and the date of the Tribunal hearing on remedies when the loss is assessed. It was stated in **Gilham v Kent County Council** (No 3) [1986] ICR 52 that this is the appropriate period even if there has been considerable delay in deciding the question of liability. The loss is to be assessed based upon the remuneration that the employee would have received if he had not been dismissed taking into account any sums that must be given by way of credit in order to ensure that the employee is placed in the same position. If the employee has obtained alternative employment in the interim period or received ex gratia payments or certain benefits then he must give credit for these otherwise he will be overcompensated. The heads of loss will first be considered then those items for which the employee should give credit will be considered. (See also **Davenport Vernon Milton Keynes Limited v Jones** [EAT 535/82] on the means of assessment.)

(2) *Calculating the Loss: Heads of Loss*

Remuneration

The main head of loss will be the net remuneration that the employee would have otherwise received from the employment if he had not been dismissed, which will include overtime, pay increases that could have been expected and other financial remuneration such as tips. The calculation of remuneration will include the following:

(a) Basic pay

In **Brownson v Hire Services Shops Limited** [1978] IRLR 73 the EAT stated that, all things being equal, what the employee loses as a consequence of being dismissed is what he got in his pay packet. This may include profit related pay or sums due under a profit share scheme (**Glen Henderson Limited v Nisbet** [EAT 34/90] and will include sums that the employee should have got under the NMWA 1998 if the employer has not paid the proper sums that are due.

(b) Pay rises and backdated pay increases

The employee will be entitled to pay rises that he would have received even if there is no contractual entitlement. In **Leske v Rogers of Saltcoats (ES) Limited** [EAT 520/82] it was held that a backdated pay increase may be included as part of the compensatory award if it was probable that such an award would be made. The Tribunal is entitled to consider the likelihood of such an award being made so that the award may be subject to a deduction to reflect the chance (**York Trailers Co Limited v Sparkes** [1973] ICR 518).

(c) Overtime

Payment for overtime will be included where it is expected that it would have been worked even if it is not a contractual entitlement. In **Mullet v British Electrical Machines Limited** [1977] ICR 829 the EAT said that if the evidence showed that up until dismissal the complainant was regularly in receipt of overtime a tribunal would be entitled to conclude that, had he not been dismissed, he would have received overtime.

(e) Expenses

Where the employee receives expenses that are not purely referable to what is spent on the employer's behalf this may amount to a profit in the hand of the employee (**S & U Stores Limited v Wilkes** [1974] ICR 645).

(f) Tips

In some cases tips may form an important part of the employee's remuneration and this will be a valid head of claim where tips are paid to the employee, though tax should be deducted (See **Palmanor Limited v Cedron** [1978] IRLR 303).

(g) Holiday pay

Where the complainant has lost paid holiday that is service related this will be a valid head of claim (**Tradewinds Airways Limited v Fletcher** [1981] IRLR 272).

(h) Notice pay

A claim for unpaid notice may be included as a head of immediate loss (**TBA Products Limited v Locke** [1984] IRLR 48).

(i) Redundancy payments

Where there is a contractual redundancy scheme that is more generous than the statutory scheme this may be a valid head of loss even where the claim is based upon an expectation rather than a contractual right. (**Lee v IPC Business Press Limited** [1984] ICR 306). See section 123(3) of the ERA 1996.

(j) National insurance contributions

When an employee has been dismissed there will be a break in contributions whilst the individual is unemployed. It was held in **Allen v Key Markets Limited** [ET case no 10088/83] that an award may be made where there is a risk of the complainant's future entitlement to benefits being affected and it was suggested that compensation for lost credits be awarded where the period is in excess of 8 weeks by reference to the weekly class 3 contribution (in this case a sum of £4.30 was awarded for each of 52 weeks of the break in contributions).

Benefits

By section 123(2) of the ERA the losses under section 123(1) are to be taken to include:

"(a) any expenses reasonably incurred by the complainant in consequence of the dismissal;

(b) ...loss of benefit which he might reasonably be expected to have had but for the dismissal."

The question of expenses are dealt with in the next section. Section 123(2)(b) makes it clear that the complainant will be entitled to recover damages for benefits that are not contractual in nature but which he reasonably expected to have received, for example regular overtime payments as in **Mullett v British Electrical Machines Limited** [1977] ICR 829. Since a particular value is unlikely to have been assigned to the benefit by the parties it is often necessary for the Tribunal to form its own view and there may be different ways in which a benefit can be valued. It has been said by the EAT that unless the assessment is obviously incorrect or unreasonable the tribunal's view will not be interfered with (**UBAF Bank Limited v Davis** [1978] IRLR 442). Indeed the EAT have stated that tribunals must make an assessment where there was a benefit and it would be wrong to decline to do so on the basis that the matter is too speculative and indefinite. In **Casey v Texas Homecase Limited** [EAT 632/87] the

EAT held that the Tribunal was wrong to refuse to value a share option scheme on this basis and assessed a figure of £1000.

The benefits that tribunals are commonly asked to assess include:

(a) Accommodation

Where the complainant had rent free or subsidised accommodation the loss of this will fall to be assessed. Where the employee was paying a market rent there will have been no loss (**Nohar v Granistone (Galloway) Limited** [1974] ICR 273). There are several methods by which the loss of accommodation may be assessed.

- An assessment may be made based upon the open market value of the accommodation. In **Butler v JJ Wendon & Son** [1972] IRLR 15 the value of a tied cottage was assessed on the basis of open market rent. It will be necessary to give evidence about open market values if this approach is to be adopted.
- An assessment may be based upon the cost of suitable alternative accommodation as in **Lloyd v Scottish Co-operative Wholesale Society** [1973] IRLR 93 where the difference between the rent paid in a council flat and the let accommodation previously paid was awarded. This approach was taken in **Dandy v Lacy** [EAT 450/77] though the complainant had not yet obtained a council flat.
- Another alternative where the complainant has purchased a property is to assess the loss based upon a proportion of the mortgage payments during the period of assessment, though there does not appear to have been any authority where this approach was taken.

It should be noted that if the complainant stays in the rent free or subsidised accommodation after dismissal this value may be offset against the losses suffered.

(b) Vehicles

By far the most contentious benefit in the reported cases is the loss of a vehicle and this has given rise to a number of approaches for the purpose of assessment of loss. It is only the loss of the private use of the car that is being compensated (**Texet Limited v Greenhough** [EAT 410/82]) and this may vary enormously depending on the type of vehicle and the basis on which it is supplied. The tribunals tend to take a broad brush approach to the assessment of this benefit but five possible alternative means of assessment appear from the authorities.

(1) Assessment based upon value of use

There have been a number of tribunal cases where the award has been based upon the loss of use of the vehicle, though it is hard to discern the reasoning whereby the tribunal arrived at a particular figure. In **Gotts v Hoffman Balancing Techniques Limited 1979** [COIT 951/115] a tribunal awarded £20 per week for loss of use as being a fair sum. Research by Income Data Services has indicated that tribunals award between £30 and £100 per week depending on the nature of the vehicle and the extent of private use. However, it is submitted that this rough and ready approach is undesirable given the other, more scientific, methods that can be adopted as set out below.

(2) Inland Revenue assessments

The Inland Revenue draw up car benefit assessments for tax purposes, based upon size, value, age and mileage of the vehicle. These assessments are regarded as generous and do not reflect the true value of the benefit. Their use was rejected in **Shove v Downs Surgical PLC** [1984] ICR 532 as they relate to value for tax purposes and not an assessment of the benefit to the employee. The same view was taken in **Kennedy v Brayan** [1984] Times 3rd May 1984.

(3) Sale of the vehicle

In **Nohar v Granistone (Galloway) Limited** [1974] ICR 273 the complainant purchased a vehicle which he resold when he found a new job at a loss of £80. He also claimed £38 for tax and insurance. The NIRC allowed £100 taking the view that this was a fair and reasonable award.

(4) Hiring a vehicle

In some cases the tribunal has allowed the cost of hiring a vehicle as being a reasonable assessment. However, given hire costs this is probably only a fair assessment if the period of time is short. Where the car is bought on hire purchase the employee will become the eventual owner of the vehicle so that an award of the full hire purchase cost may be excessive. In **S & U Stores v Wormleighton** [EAT 477/77] a Tribunal awarded half the hire purchase cost which the

EAT allowed as reasonable, though they did state that the method of assessment was unscientific.

(5) AA and RAC Guidelines

One method which has found favour is to use the AA or RAC guides that set out the value and running costs of vehicles. This was the approach adopted in **Shove v Downs Surgical PLC** [1984] ICR 532 and has the value of certainty. In *Shove* £10,000 was awarded for the loss of a Daimler vehicle for an 18 month period. Alternatively, where employers have their own allowances for running costs these may be adopted if they are more generous than the AA or RAC guidelines.

(c) Company loans and subsidised mortgages

Some employers offer preferential loans or subsidised mortgages which may be lost on termination of employment. Such loss can be assessed on the scientific basis of the difference between the preferential loan or mortgage and the market rate. However, it is apparent that tribunals take a broad brush approach to this head of loss, as in **UBAF Bank Limited v Davis** [1978] IRLR 442 where the Tribunal simply ordered a lump sum for all loss of benefits.

(d) Share options or ownership

An award may be made for loss of a share option if the tribunal consider that an option would have been granted as in **O'Laoire v Jackel International Limited** [1991] IRLR 170. However, where the scheme contains an exemption clause or provides that it is to lapse on termination of employment for whatever reason the benefit may not be claimable (**Micklefield v SAC Technology Limited** [1991] 1 All ER 275), though query whether section 203 of the ERA 1996 renders an exemption clause ineffective.

(e) Other benefits

Loss of subsidised meals, travel allowances medical insurance and use of telephone are all benefits that may attract an award where the use is private, even though the benefits are not contractual.

Expenses

Section 123(2)(a) of the ERA 1996 provides that a complainant may recover expenses reasonably incurred by reason of the dismissal. Such expenses will include the cost of finding a new job, which will include postage, telephone calls, the cost of attending interviews (**Leech v Berger, Jensen and Nicholson Limited** [1972] IRLR 58) and may include removal expenses where the complainant has had to move out of tied accommodation (**Lloyd v Scottish Co-operative Wholesale Society Limited** [1973] IRLR 93) or moving in order to take up a new job. Conveyancing costs and estate agents fees may be claimed (**Daykn v IHW Engineering Limited** [ET case 01838/83]) and the cost of selling a property may be included (**United Freight Distribution v McDougall** [EAT 218/94]).

Where a complainant cannot obtain comparable employment it may be perfectly reasonable to commence business on his own account and it has been held by the EAT in **Gardiner-Hill v Roland Berger Technics Limited** [1982] IRLR 498 that the expenses incurred in setting up a business may be recovered. In that case £500 was awarded as the cost of setting up a consultancy.

It should be noted that legal costs of bringing a claim are not recoverable unless they are awarded under the Industrial Tribunals (Constitution and Rules of Procedure) Regulations 1993 (see **Nohar v Granistone (Galloway) Limited** [1974] ICR 273 and **Raynor v Remploy Limited** [1973] IRLR 3 to this effect).

(3) Offsetting the Loss

The principle

Since the object of the compensatory award is to place the complainant in the position that he would have been if he had not been dismissed it is necessary for the complainant to give credit for sums earned in alternative employment and certain benefits and ex gratia payments from the employer otherwise the complainant will receive an unjustified windfall. The heads whereby the complainant must give credit will be considered in turn.

Fresh Employment

Where the complainant has obtained alternative employment between the date of dismissal and the tribunal hearing, credit must be given for sums earned in such employment. It was stated by the EAT in **Ging v Ellward Lancs Limited** [1978] ITR 265 that the Tribunal should offset the new earnings against the loss to arrive at an overall figure. This may work to the complainant's disadvantage where the new employment is substantially better paid as it may extinguish all liability. This may cause particular hardship where the new employment is temporary and will cease at some point after the tribunal hearing so that the complainant will be again unemployed at some stage. Mindful of this problem the EAT in **Courtaulds Northern Spinning v Moosa** [1984] IRLR 43 took the approach that compensation should cease when the employee has entered new permanent employment. The applicant had worked for 18 months of the three year period that it took for the tribunal case to be heard. The EAT held that the applicant's earnings after he entered into employment should be disregarded on the ground that the new employment was deemed to be permanent so that compensation was awarded up to the date that the employment was entered into and credit did not have to be given for the sums earned. The corollary to this was that damages were not awarded when the complainant was made redundant from this employment before the Tribunal hearing date.

The approach in *Moosa* gets round the undesirable effects of the *Ging* approach and has been applied in **Lytlarch Limited t/a The Viceroy Restaurant v Reid** [EAT 269/90] and **Fentiman v Fluid Engineering Products Limited** [1991] IRLR 150. In the latter case the complainant had worked for thirty nine weeks in new employment before the Tribunal hearing which took place 68 weeks after dismissal and it was held that these earnings should be disregarded from the date he took up employment.

The difficulty facing applicants is that it cannot be predicted whether a tribunal will adopt the approach in *Ging* or in *Moosa* which may lead to an all or nothing situation so far as loss of earnings is concerned. This was recognised in **Whelan & Anor r/a Cheers Off Licence v Richardson** [1998] IRLR 114. The complainant was dismissed from her job which paid £52 a week. The assessment of compensation was 15 months after dismissal. The complainant had worked in a job that paid £52 a week for 18 weeks and then obtained a job that paid £96. The Tribunal regarded the cut off date as the time she started in the higher paid employment and deduced the salary for the 18 weeks' employment. The EAT held that this was correct on the ground that the earlier employment was temporary.

Where the complainant has become self employed then monies earned will have to be offset in the usual way.

Benefits and early retirement schemes

Where the complainant has received state benefits an issue arises as to whether these need to be offset. It is apparent that the approach will differ depending on the nature of the benefit.

- Benefits relating to unemployment will not be offset but will be subject to the recoupment procedures.
- It is unclear whether invalidity benefits will have to be offset as the EAT has differed in its approach. In **Hilton International Hotels (UK) Limited v Faraji** [1994] ICR 259 it was held that such benefits will not be offset even if this means that the complainant receives more than if he had remained in employment. The benefit was dependent upon national insurance contributions and was therefore the proceeds of insurance. However, this decision was not followed in **Puglia v C James & Sons** [1996] IRLR 70 on the ground that earlier cases had not been cited, which showed that the amount of any sickness benefit should be deducted unless there was a provision in the contract that entitled the employee to full wages as well as sickness benefit. Both these approaches were rejected in **Rubenstein & Anor t/a McGuffies Dispensing Chemists v McGloughlin** [1996] ICR 318 in which the EAT held that, since section 123(1) allows the tribunal to award what it considers to be just and equitable, there is a degree of flexibility and the Tribunal could treat the parties equally by awarding one half of the benefit. The EAT had regard to the fact that one half benefit is awarded in personal injury cases and also to the fact that section 123(1) is 'autonomous' so that the tribunal can award what it considers to be just and equitable.
- It was held in **Savage v Saxena** [1998] IRLR 182 that housing benefit is not deductible as it was not sufficiently proximate to the loss sustained. The EAT noted that there was a power to clawback housing benefit when an award for unfair dismissal was made and this was applicable even if the tribunal had taken the benefit into account in arriving at its award so that an employee could be doubly penalised.
- Sums paid under early retirement schemes should not be deducted as they relate to money sets aside in respect of past work (**Smoker v London Fire and Civil Defence Authority** [1991] ICR 449).

Ex gratia and redundancy payments

Where a redundancy payment is made that exceeds the basic award, by section 123(7) it can be set off against the compensatory award.

Similarly, ex gratia payments will normally be offset against any award (see **Horizon Holidays Limited v Grassi** [1987] ICR 851). *Grassi* distinguished **Babcock FATA Limited v Addison** where it was found that the ex gratia payment would have been made in any event when the employee was made redundant and would therefore have formed part of his loss, so that it should not be offset.

The Tribunal should ensure that it assesses the complainant's losses and offsets any payment against those losses (**Darr v LRC Products Limited** [1993] IRLR 257) in order to arrive at the fairest calculation.

Where the ex gratia payment would be made on dismissal in any event it has been held that it may not be deductible (**Babcock FATA Limited v Addison** [1987] IRLR 173 and **Roadchef Limited v Hastings** [EAT 593/87]). In the latter case the Tribunal found that the dismissal would have taken place four weeks later than it had and there was no reason to believe that an ex gratia payment would not have been given then. However, in **Rushton v Harcro Timber & Building Supplies Limited** [1993] ICR 230 these cases were not followed. Judge Hague QC relied upon section 123(7) in stating that severance payments should always be deducted. It is submitted that the reasoning is incorrect since, if the tribunal find that the payment would have been made in any event, the employer will receive a double credit if it is deducted. The question that the tribunal should consider is whether the ex gratia payment would have been paid regardless, in which case it should not be deducted.

The notice period

The complainant is entitled to notice pay during the period of notice regardless of whether another job has been obtained (**Norton Tool Co Limited v Tewson** [1972] ICR 501 and **TBA Industrial Products Limited v Locke** [1984] IRLR 48) though this principle is likely only to apply to the statutory notice period and not to any longer contractual period (**Vaughan v Weightpack Limited** [1974] ICR 261). However, where the notice period is very long or the contract is for a fixed term it may be that any earnings will have to be offset. It was held in **Isleworth Studio Limited v Rickard** [1988] ICR 432 that earnings from new employment had to be offset where there was a lengthy period of the fixed term to run. Although in *Babcock FATA Limited v Addison* the Court of Appeal held that a payment in lieu must be taken into account, the EAT in Scotland have taken the view that it should be ignored (**Finnie v Top Hat Frozen Foods** [1985] IRLR 365). Where the employee waives the right to statutory notice there is no entitlement to a payment in lieu of notice (**Trotter v Forth Ports Authority** [1991] IRLR 419).

Remoteness

Compensation is only awarded under section 123(1) in so far as it is attributable to action taken by the employer so that after a certain point the losses may not be claimable on the ground that they are too remote (See below at 442).

B.   Loss of Statutory Rights

An employee who is unfairly dismissed will lose a number of statutory rights that require a period of continuous employment before they can be asserted. The Tribunal is therefore entitled to make an award for the loss of these statutory rights. It was said in **Hilti (Great Britain) Limited v Windridge** [1974] ICR 53 that the loss of a statutory right is permissible as a head of damage though it could not be expected to attract other than a very small award in the average case, whilst in **SH Muffett Limited v Head** [1987] ICR1 (in 1986) the EAT considered that the conventional sum should be £100. In **Daley v A E Dorset (Almar Dolls Ltd)** [1981] IRLR 385 compensation was awarded for half the statutory notice period where the employee had accrued twelve years' statutory notice. However, the EAT in *Muffett* stated that this should be awarded only in exceptional cases and in **Arthur Guiness Son & Co (GB) Limited v Green** [1989] IRLR 288 where the employee had 28 years' service the EAT nevertheless, reduced the award from 10 to 4 weeks. In **Puglia C James & Sons** [1996] IRLR 70 is was stated that no award should be made if the employee would have been dismissed in any event.

C.   Future Loss

Calculating Future Loss

Whilst tribunals may be able to assess immediate loss on a scientific basis any calculation of future loss will, by its very nature, be speculative since it will have to take into account a number of contingencies that may or may not happen, most particularly when the complainant will achieve other comparable employment. Whilst a tribunal will have to make an assessment based upon informed guesswork there should be some basis for them to arrive at their conclusion. In **Sandown Pier Limited v Moonan** [EAT 399/93] the Tribunal took the view that the complainant was likely to remain unemployed for fifteen years. The EAT held that the Tribunal was entitled to arrive at the conclusion which they had based upon the fact that the employee was fifty years old, had already made unsuccessful attempts to obtain another job and lived in an area of high unemployment. However, where the Tribunal bases its decision upon the Member's knowledge of job vacancies in the area or particular trade it should draw this to the parties attention so that they can deal with it. In **Hammington v Berker Sportscraft Limited** [EAT 344/79] the EAT said that it was wrong for a tribunal to form the view that the complainant's chances of re-employment were greater than asserted, based upon one of the Member's expert knowledge, without allowing the Respondent to deal with this view.

Where the tribunal has to rule on future loss there are a number possibilities with regard to employment:

(1) The complainant has obtained a *permanent* job that is as well or better paid than the job that he was in.
(2) The complainant has obtained a temporary job that is as well or better paid than the job that he was in.
(3) The complainant has obtained an job that is not as well paid and is likely never to match up to the employment which the employee was in.
(4) The complainant has obtained a job that is currently not as well paid but will increase to the level of employment that the employee was in at some foreseeable point in the future.
(5) The complainant has not obtained new employment. It is open to a tribunal to form the view that the complainant will never obtain another job. In **Morganite Electrical Carbon Limited v Donne** [1987] IRLR 363 an award for a period of 82 weeks was upheld.

Factors to take into account

The employer must take the employee as it finds it so that if there are particular characteristics that render it more difficult for the employee to obtain employment this will not count against the complainant. Particular matters that may be relevant include:

- **The abilities of the employee**
  Where the complainant lacks qualifications and will have difficulty in obtaining employment these are factors that the

tribunal is entitled to take into account in awarding compensation for future loss.

- **Ill Health**

  It was held in **Fougiere v Phoenix Motor Co Limited** [1976] ICR 495 by the EAT that the Tribunal should have taken into account the fact that the complainant suffered from a hernia and bronchitis and was aged 58. The fact that the complainant was of ill health meant that he would find it more difficult to obtain employment. On the other hand his incapacity due to sickness could have justified the employer dismissing him. These were matters that the Tribunal had failed to take into account in deciding future loss. Damages were reduced in **Curtis v James Paterson (Darlington) Limited** [1973] ICR 496 to take into account the fact that the employee would have been absent from work due to ill health. Where the employee's incapacity arises because of the dismissal the Tribunal is entitled to find that this is attributable to the acts of the employer. This was the position in **Devine v Designer Flowers Wholesale Florist Sundries Limited** [1993] IRLR 517. Damages will not, however, be awarded due to the *manner* of the dismissal.

- **Self employment**

  Earnings arising from self employment will be offset. The tribunal is entitled to arrive at a conclusion as to the likely future earnings from self employment and whether or not becoming self employment was reasonable mitigation in the circumstances. The decision to become self employed may on the other hand, break the chain of causation as the losses may no longer be attributable to the employer. These issues are considered under 'remoteness of loss' at (4) below. It is important to note that the conduct of the employee in deciding to pursue an alternative career path may make the losses too remote.

Tax

The complainant who has been dismissed in circumstances where he remains unemployed for a period of time may become entitled to a tax rebate. The general principle is that tax rebates will not be taken into account in assessing compensation (**Adda International Limited v Curcio** [1976] IRLR 425). The approach to take was set out by the EAT in **MBS Limited v Calo** [1983] IRLR 189 where it was stated that in cases involving high earners where the sums involved may be very substantial, it may be appropriate for a Tribunal to go into the tax repercussions of the dismissal. Where the sums are the 'usual' amounts awarded by the Tribunals tax may be ignored. It remains to be seen whether the increase in the compensatory limit will change the Tribunal's approach in this regard.

Remoteness of Loss

By section 123(1) of the ERA 1996 the losses suffered by the complainant must be attributable to the actions of the employer. Where the complainant embarks upon a course of training or becomes self employed the losses may still be regarded as attributable to the employer. This was the position in **Glen Henderson Limited v Nisbet** [EAT 34/90] where the complainant embarked upon a five week business course and thereafter became self employed. The decision to award her compensation for the time she was on the course and for one year after she entered into self employment was upheld by the EAT. However, there are cases which have decided that the chain of causation is broken by the decision to embark upon a training course. In **Simrad Limited v Scott** [1997] IRLR 147 the EAT took the view that any losses arising after the decision to retrain as a nurse were not attributable to the actions of the employer in dismissing. The EAT set out the test as follows:

> The process is a three-stage one, requiring, initially, factual quantification of losses claimed; secondly, but equally importantly, the extent to which any or all of those losses are attributable to the dismissal or action taken by the employer, which is usually the same thing, the word 'attributable' implying that there has to be a direct and natural link between the losses claimed and the conduct of the employer in dismissing, on the basis that the dismissal is the causa causans of the particular loss and not that it simply arises by reason of a causa sine qua non, i.e. but for the dismissal the loss would not have arisen. If that is the only connection, the loss is too remote. The third part of the assessment in terms of the reference to the phrase 'just and equitable' requires a tribunal to look at the conclusions they draw from the first two questions and determine whether, in all the circumstances, it remains reasonable to make the relevant award. It must again be emphasised, however, that what is to be considered under the third test already has to have passed the second. Finally, it has to be observed that while the facts relating to a question of mitigation will frequently bear upon the question of causative link, mitigation is essentially an equitable plea to be judged in the context of reasonableness at common

law and thus on not too fine a balance. Accordingly, the issue of mitigation will feature in the application of the third test rather than the second, and subsection (4) of the section merely directs the tribunal as to the proper approach to mitigation if that is what is being considered.

The EAT considered that whilst the decision to retrain was a reasonable one it was too remote in time and content to be directly linked to the dismissal. This was so even though the employee would not have sought different employment but for the dismissal. However, a less technical approach was taken in **Leonard v Strathclyde Buses Limited** [1998] IRLR 693 by the Court of Session. It was stated by Lord Coulsfield that the legislation in the field of unfair dismissal was not intended to be dealt with in the same manner as other areas with principles of foreseeability or remoteness in the technical sense. Precise arithmetical proof of every item of compensation could not be expected. Judge Peter Clarke was influenced by the Scottish decision in **Larkin v Korean Airlines** [EAT 1241/98] and decided that the decision to undertake a course and a new career direction could not be said to be too remote. There does appear to be a change of attitude on the part of the Courts since the *Leonard* decision so that Tribunals may be more willing to accept that a change in career or training still does not make any claim too remote.

In **Khanum v IBC Vehicles Limited** [EAT 685/98] the EAT held that where an employee enrolled for a degree course after being unfairly dismissed she was entitled to be compensated for her losses beyond the date of enrolment as her losses arose from a direct result of her dismissal since she would still have been working rather than studying.

Losses not attributable

> There are a number of factual areas where the higher courts have had to consider whether the losses suffered are not attributable to the action of the employer:

Dismissal from new employment

Where the complainant obtains new employment but is dismissed prior to the tribunal hearing the losses suffered thereafter may no longer be attributable to the original dismissal (**Courtaulds Northern Spinning Limited v Moosa** [1984] IRLR 43). This will be the case where the complainant obtains what was potentially permanent employment and is dismissed for reasons unrelated to the original dismissal (**Mabey Plant Hire v Richens** [Court of Appeal, unreported) though an attempt to mitigate loss by taking up employment which proves to be unsuitable is unlikely to break the chain of causation (**Witham Weld v Hedley** [EAT 176/95] and **Dundee Plant Co v Riddler** [EAT 377/88]). Even if the employee obtains employment which he believes to be permanent the chain of causation may not be broken where the employment ceases after a short period of time (**Dench v Flyhnn & Partners** [1998] IRLR 653) since employees should not be discouraged from seeking to mitigate by finding new employment (**Whelan v Richardson** [1998] IRLR 318).

Training

It has already been noted that a decision to retrain may render any further losses too remote as not being attributable to the actions of the employer, as in **Simrad Limited v Scott** [1997] IRLR 147 though there has recently been a change of approach by the Courts.

Other contingencies

If other contingencies would have intervened to render the losses no longer attributable to the actions of the employer in dismissing, for example, where dismissal would have occurred at some point in any event then losses suffered thereafter may be too remote. This was the position in **James W Cook & Co (Wivenhoe) Limited v Tipper** [1990] ICR 716 where the employees would have been dismissed in any event at a time when their work premises closed down. It was held in **Balfour Beatty Power Construction Limited v Williams** [EAT 112/83] that the fact that the employee would have been dismissed within six weeks after the Tribunal hearing should have been taken into account as there could be no loss after that date.

Pensions

An employee who is a member of an occupational pension scheme may claim for the losses arising upon dismissal. The calculation of such losses may involve complicated actuarial calculations which are likely to take on greater significance given the increase in the compensatory limit. Since 1990 there has existed a set of guidelines prepared by three tribunal chairmen, entitled 'Industrial Tribunals – Compensation for Loss of Pension Rights' which have been approved by the EAT in **Benson v Dairy Crest Limited** [EAT 192/89] though it has been stressed that the booklet does only provide guidelines and tribunals are entitled to depart from it if they consider it to be appropriate. In **Bingham v Hobourn Engineering Limited** [1992] IRLR 298 the Tribunal declined to follow the guidelines where the employee had transferred his pension rights to a new scheme and was therefore unlikely to suffer any loss whereas if the guidelines had been followed he would have been awarded a sum of £20,366. The EAT also noted that the assumptions contained in the guidelines about salary rises was not appropriate since the prospects in the old employment were poor.

It is for the complainant to prove his pension losses though the tribunal are under a duty to consider each head of compensation and should assist the unrepresented applicant in this respect (**Tidman v Aveling Marshall Limited** [1997] IRLR 218) though the burden remains on the complainant, particularly if represented (**Cawthorn & Sinclair Limited v Hedger** [1974] ICR 146).

Pensions

The State pension scheme provides a basic pension to all who reach pensionable age whilst the State Earnings Related Pension Scheme (SERPS) is dependant on earnings paid by the employee from April 1978. It is possible to contract out of SERPS where there is a guaranteed minimum pension or where employees operate their own pension scheme. There are two types of pension schemes:

- **Final salary**
  The final salary scheme is also known as the defined benefit scheme. The pension is based upon a proportion of pensionable pay at retirement multiplied by years of pensionable service (i.e. $1/60$th of salary after 25 years on a salary of £30,000 is equivalent to $25/60$ of £30,000 = £12,500). Contributions to this scheme vary in order to provide the final benefits.
- **Money purchase**
  The money purchase scheme is also known as the defined contribution scheme and is based up on predetermined contributions for the individual employee. The loss suffered by the complainant will therefore be based upon the value of contributions to be made to the scheme and any penalty for early departure from the scheme.

Losses

There are three potential heads of loss:

Loss of rights from the date of dismissal to the date of hearing

In the case of a money purchase scheme the loss will be based upon the contributions that would have been made. In the case of a final salary scheme the Guidelines recommend that the compensation be based upon notional contributions that the employer would have made.

Loss of future pension rights between the date of dismissal and retirement

Again, the guidelines recommend that the calculation is based upon the employer's contributions or, in the case of a final salary scheme, the notional contributions. Compensation will be dependent upon whether the complainant has obtained employment that has a pension scheme.

- **No employment**

  Where the complainant has not yet obtained employment the tribunal will have to attempt the exercise of predicting what employment he is likely to obtain and what impact that will have on any pension.

- **Employment with no scheme**

  Where there is no occupational pension scheme the employee will nevertheless be entitled to SERPS which the Guidelines state should be regarded as 3% of gross pay. In a case where the employer contributed 15% the loss will then be taken as 12%. However, where the employee has obtained employment at a salary that is greater than the old job this may be offset against the pension claim. It is also possible for a claim to be based upon the loss of an opportunity to enter into a pension scheme as in **Samuels v Clifford Chance** [EAT 559/90] where the complainant was not entitled to enter into the scheme until he had completed five years of employment. However, in that case the Tribunal found that the complainant would not have stayed in employment for a period of five years based upon her previous employment record.

Loss of the enhancement of accrued pension rights

The complainant may also be entitled to compensation for loss of enhancement of accrued rights based upon the fact that the deferred pension which is receivable is considerably less than it would have been if the complainant had remained in employment. The Guidelines set out three possible approaches:

- no compensation may be payable if the employee has been a member of an inflation proof scheme, where the employee is a member of a private scheme within five years of normal retiring age or where the employment would have ended within a year.
- The second method is to carry out an actuarial assessment based upon the methods set out in the Guidelines which will be subject to deductions to take into account the likelihood of withdrawal from the scheme (**TBA Industrial Products Limited v Locke** [1984] IRLR 48).
- The third method is to assess the contributions made by the employer and employee which may be difficult where the employment is not lengthy and contributions have varied.

Stage 2: Applying Deductions

Having assessed the employee's losses the Tribunal must then consider what deductions should be made in the following order:

(1) Deduction of contractual or ex gratia payments as appropriate.
(2) Deduction to take into account failure to mitigate.
(3) Reductions to take into account the fact that the employee would or may have been dismissed in any event.
(4) Reduction for contributory conduct.
(5) Recoupment.

The order in which these directions may be made can be of considerable importance and Tribunals have had considerable difficulty in deciding what approach to adopt. In **Digital Equipment Co Limited v Clements (No 2)** [1997] IRLR 237, 1998 ICR 258 the President therefore gave the following guidelines:

(1) Any contractual or ex gratia payments should first be deducted to arrive at the net loss of the complainant.
(2) Any appropriate deduction to take into account failure to mitigate should then be made.

(3) Any proportionate reduction should then be made to take into account fact that the complainant would have been dismissed in any event.

(4) A reduction may then be made for contributory conduct (**Rao v Civil Aviation Authority** [1994] IRLR 240). It was noted in *Rao* that the size of the reduction on the ground that the complainant would have been dismissed in any event can have an effect upon the reduction for contributory conduct.

(5) Where there has been a contractual redundancy payment this should be deducted last to give full credit for the same.

In **Ministry of Defence v Wheeler** [1998] IRLR 23 the Court of Appeal considered that other payments should first be deducted. However, the EAT in **Heggie v Uniroyal Englebert Tyres Limited** [1998] IRLR 425 applied the percentage reductions before pay in lieu of notice was deducted. This does appear to go against *Digital* and *Wheeler* and should be treated with caution.

Where a redundancy payment has been made that is in excess of the basic award this reduction will be made once the compensatory award has been assessed as section 127(7) of the ERA provides that this deduction should be made from the compensatory award (**Digital Equipment Co Limited v Clements (No 2)** [1998] IRLR 134).

Failure to Mitigate

Under section 123(4) of the ERA 1996 in ascertaining the compensatory losses the Tribunal

> "shall apply the see rule concerning the duty of a person to mitigate his loss as applies to damages recoverable under the common law of England and Wales or (as the case may be) Scotland."

The test is whether the employee has acted reasonably in all the circumstances in seeking, taking or refusing new employment (see the common law test set out in **Yetton v Eastwoods Froy Limited** [1966] 3 All ER 353 and see Duggan on *Wrongful Dismissal: Law Practice and Precedents*). The test was stated in **Archbold Freightage Limited v Wilson** [1974] IRLR 10 as follows:

> It is the duty of an employee who has been dismissed to act reasonably and to act as a reasonable man would do if he had no

hope of seeking compensation from his previous employer. It follows from that, he should accept alternative employment if, taking account of the pay and other conditions of that employment, it is reasonable so to do.

The Tribunal will assess the loss on the basis of the date when it considers the employee should have found new work (**Peara v Enderlin Limited** [1979] ICR 804).

The following principles apply in considering the issue of failure to mitigate:

(1) The burden of proof is on the employer who is alleging that there has been a failure to mitigate (**Fyfe Scientific Publishing Limited** [1989] ICR 648)

(2) The standard of reasonableness is not high given that it is the employer who is in breach and the issue will be whether:
    "The applicant has acted reasonably...When approaching the issue of reasonableness it is important to look at the surrounding circumstances, and the reaction of the application to any offer made to him must depend upon the circumstances in which that offer was made, the attitude of the employers and the way he hd been treated, indeed upon all the surrounding circumstances (*Fyfe*)."

(3) The Tribunal will consider the individual circumstances of the employee, including the area of employment and local circumstances, the circumstances of the individual including any difficulties that he or she may have in obtaining employment. For example, in **Bennett v Tippins** [EAT 361/89] the Tribunal took into account the fact that the employee had difficulty in obtaining another job because of her pregnancy in deciding that there had not been a failure to mitigate.

There are a number of factual situations where the Tribunals have considered whether there has been a failure to mitigate.

Alternative employment
The employee must take reasonable steps to seek alternative employment. This will mean taking active steps to seek employment (**Burns v George Boyd (Engineering) Limited** [EAT 458/84]; **Bristol Garage (Brighton) Limited v Lowen** [1979] IRLR 86).

Failure to appeal against dismissal

The Courts have held that a failure to internally appeal against dismissal will probably not amount to a failure to mitigate (**Lock v Connell Estate Agents** [1994] IRLR 444). However, section 127 ERA 1996, as inserted by the Employment Rights (Dispute Resolution) Act 1998 provides that compensation may be reduced where there is an appeal procedure and the employee fails to make use of the procedure. The approach to be taken is as follows:

- The employer must have provided a procedure for appealing against dismissal of which the complainant was, at the time of dismissal or a reasonable period thereafter, given notice in writing of the procedure and details.
- The complainant did not appeal against the dismissal.
- The Tribunal shall have regard to all the circumstances of the case, including in particular the chances that an appeal under the procedure provided by the employer would have been successful.
- The amount of the reduction is subject to a maximum of two weeks pay.

Leaving fresh employment

Where the employee obtains new employment but leaves because he cannot cope with the work it will be wrong to treat such resignation as a failure to mitigate (**Wilson v Gleneagles Bakery Limited** [EAT 40/88]).

Offers of re-employment

Where the employer is prepared to take the employee back on *after dismissal* a refusal to accept such re-employment may amount to a failure to mitigate, though the duty to mitigate cannot arise before the actual dismissal (**Savoia v Chiltern Herb Farms Limited** [1982] IRLR 166). However, where the conduct of the employer is such that a continuing relationship cannot be maintained because of the manner in which the employee has been treated or a breakdown in trust and confidence it may be reasonable to reject any offer, as in *Fyfe* where the employee had been summarily dismissed. An offer of employment on terms that are less advantageous may be reasonable (**Baillie Brothers v Pritchard** [EAT 59/89] though the employee may fail to mitigate if he is not prepared to accept re-employment on terms that are clearly appropriate.

Setting up in business

Where the complainant sets up in business on his own account and this is considered to be a reasonable course to adopt then he may claim for loss of earnings during the time spent setting up the business (**Gardiner-Hill v Roland Berger Technics Limited** [1982] IRLR 498) and any claim can include the expenses of setting up the new business (**United Freight Distribution Limited v McDougall** [EAT 218/94]). Where the employee sets up in business an award will not be made for loss of unfair dismissal rights (**York Trailers Co Limited v Sparkes** [1973] IRLR 346; ICR 518).

Training

The dismissed employee may decide to embark upon a course of study in order to retrain and undertake another career. It has already been noted that this decision may render any further losses too remote. Where the decision to undertake new training is unreasonable this may amount to a failure to mitigate, but if the complaint's decision is reasonable and the course would not have been taken but for the dismissal, as in **Mullarky v Up The Creek Limited** [EAT 263/95], then it should not amount to a failure to mitigate. (See the cases on remoteness in this respect).

The 'Just and Equitable' Principle

By section 123(1) of the ERA:

> "...the amount of the compensatory award shall be such amount at the tribunal considers just and equitable in all the circumstances having regard to the loss sustained by the complainant in consequence of the dismissal...."

There are two grounds on which a Tribunal may consider it appropriate to reduce compensation on the basis of it being 'just and equitable'.

(i) Just and Equitable Principle 1:

Where the employer can show that there are facts that merit dismissal in any event but which did not come to light until after the dismissal.

The leading case is **Devis (W) & Sons Limited v Atkins** [1977] ICR 662 in which the House of Lords held that it was just and equitable not to make any award where it had become apparent after dismissal that the complainant was guilty of conduct that would have justified his summary dismissal. However, acts that are carried out after dismissal are not relevant to reducing compensation on this ground (**Soros v Davison** [1994] ICR 590) and the tribunal must base its award on the losses arising out of the dismissal so that a reduction to reflect disapproval of the way in which the employee has conducted his case is not appropriate (**Abbey Motors (Hemel Hempstead) Limited v Carta** [EAT 403/95]). However, where the employer is aware of facts at the time of dismissal but chooses not to rely on them the Court of Appeal was of the view in **Devonshire v Trico-Folberth Limited** [1989] ICR 747 that compensation cannot be reduced under the just and equitable principle. A different approach was adopted by the EAT in **McNee v Charles Tennant & Co Limited** [EAT 338/90] where the reason for dismissal was changed on appeal but the EAT took the view that the original reason could have justified the dismissal.

(ii) Just and Equitable Principle 2:

Where the employer can show that proper procedure would have led to a fair dismissal at some stage.

Since **Polkey v A E Dayton Services Limited** [1998] ICR 142 the importance of employers complying with a proper procedure has been apparent. The House of Lords rejected the approach that had been followed for a number of years that a dismissal would be regarded as fair if the employer could show that a procedural irregularity would have made no difference. It would only be in cases where it would be 'utterly useless' to follow a proper procedure that the dismissal may be fair. Where there has been procedural impropriety the dismissal will be unfair but Tribunals are entitled to consider what would have happened if a proper procedure had been followed. The effect of this will be that, although an employer may be found to have unfairly dismissed the complainant, compensation may be reduced despite the employer's conduct. The EAT have emphasised that the *Polkey* principle only applies to procedural matters so that if the dismissal is substantively unfair a reduction will not be made. In **Steel Stockholders (Birmingham) Limited v Kirkwood** [1993] IRLR 515 it was held to be a substantive matter where the wrong pool was adopted for selection for redundancy with the result that there was no basis for assessing what would have happened if the right pool had been selected. However, this approach was disapproved of by the Court of Appeal in **O'Dea v**

ISCV Chemicals Limited t/a Rhone Poulenc Chemicals [1995] IRLR 599. Nevertheless, in **Chloride Limited v Cain** [EAT 564/94] the EAT refused to reduce compensation to reflect the percentage chance of dismissal if a fair procedure had been followed where there had been no objective criteria for redundancy and no procedure had been followed.

The Tribunal should ask itself what the result would have been if a fair procedure had been followed. In **Hunter Timber Group Limited t/a Hunter Timber Hardwood v Newcombe** [EAT 294/92] the EAT thought that a Tribunal was wrong to reduce compensation by 50% in a case where there was no proper consultation for redundancy. Given the complainant's assessment he would not have been retained in any event so that there should have been a full reduction. Furthermore, the Tribunal is not under a duty of its own motion to consider what would have happened in the absence of any evidenec of what might have happened if a fair section procedure for redundancy had been followed **Bolton & Paul Limited v Arnold** [1994] IRLR 532). More recently, in **King v Eaton Limited (No 2)** [1998] IRLR 686 the Court of Session stated that the employer may in fact not be allowed to lead such evidence where the failure on the part of the employer is so fundamental that it is not appropriate for the Tribunal to embark on speculation as to what may have happened. Lord Prosser stated:

> ...while in many cases it may be inappropriate to allocate the particular facts to either category, or to do so without enquiry, it seems to us that a distinction between the 'merely' procedural, and the more genuinely 'substantive' will often be of some practical use, in considering whether it is realistic, or practicable, or indeed 'just and equitable' to embark upon an attempt to construct a hypothesis, enabling one to assess what would have happened, if only it had. If there has been a 'merely' procedural lapse or omission, it may be relatively straightforward to envisage what the course of events would have been if procedures had stayed on track, rather than briefly leaving the track in this way. If, on the other hand, what went wrong was more fundamental, or 'substantive', and seems to have gone 'to the heart of the matter', it may well be difficult to envisage what track one would be on, in the hypothetical situation of the unfairness not having occurred. It seems to us that the matter will be one of impression and judgment, so that a tribunal will have to decide whether the unfair departure from what should

have happened was of a kind which makes it possible to say, with more or less confidence, that the failure made no difference, or whether the failure was such that one simply cannot sensibly reconstruct the world as it might have been. It does not seem to us that there is anything very wrong in using the word 'substantive' in connection with this latter situation.

There are several alternative outcomes which may have occurred if a proper procedure had been followed.

(1) The employee would not have been dismissed if a proper procedure had been followed.

(2) There remained a chance that the employee would have been dismissed if a proper procedure had been followed.

Where the Tribunal is satisfied that the dismissal is unfair, although the burden of proving loss is on the complainant, he will have to do very little to shift the burden of proof that he has suffered loss (**Britool Limited v Roberts & Ors** [1993] IRLR 481). However, if the tribunal think that the employee may have still been dismissed if a proper procedure had been followed then it may reduce compensation to reflect the percentage chance of dismissal as was stated by Browne-Wilkinson J in **Sillifant v Powell Duffryn Timber Limited** [1983] IRLR 91. There are a large number of authorities in which compensation has been reduced to reflect this percentage chance as in **Church of England Board of Social Responsibility v Forsyth** [EAT 699/87]. Compensation was reduced by 35% to reflect the chance that the complainant would still have been dismissed for disobedience if a proper procedure had been followed.

(3) The employee would still have been dismissed if a proper procedure had been followed.

Where a proper procedure would still have led to dismissal the compensation will be based upon the time that it would have taken for the procedure to be carried out. In **Mining Supplies (Longwall) Limited v Baker** [1988] ICR 676 compensation was awarded for the two weeks that it was considered it would have taken for redundancy consultation to be carried out. (See also **Abbotts & Standley v Wesson-Glynwed Steels Limited**.) Full compensation will be awarded for the period that consultation would have taken and a percentage reduction may thereafter be made based upon the Tribunal's view of whether dismissal would have occurred in any event (**Walker v Dysch Rosen Shores Limited** [EAT 341/90]). In **Slaughter v C Brewer & Sons Limited** [1990] ICR 730 the EAT took the view that in a capability case a dismissal may be unfair for lack of following a proper procedure but a tribunal could take the view that the complainant may have been dismissed on the medical evidence in any event. The onus is on the employer to show that dismissal would have occurred if a fair procedure had been followed and the employer will have to present material to the tribunal to justify its argument that dismissal would have followed in any event (**Britool Limited v Roberts** [1991] IRLR 481; **Schlumberger Evaluation and Production Services (UK) Limited v McDonald** [EAT 678/93]. In **Cormack v Saltfire Vehicles Limited** [EAT 209/90] no compensation was awarded despite the fact that the employee was not allowed to follow the contractual appeal procedure because the Tribunal found that a fuller appeal procedure would not have made any difference.

Even where the employee would have been dismissed in any event compensation may be substantial if the consultation period would have been lengthy. This was the case in **Walker v (1) Dysch Rosen Shoes Limited (2) Secretary of State for Employment** [EAT 341&342/90] where there was a dismissal after a transfer of an undertaking which was found to be for an ETO reason. The Tribunal had reduced the compensatory award by 90% on the basis that the employer would have dismissed in any event. However, the EAT held that a full award should have been made to reflect the period of consultation if there had been a fair procedure and it is only after the process has been gone through that a reduction may be made to reflect the fact that dismissal may have occurred in any event.

(4) In a redundancy case a proper procedure may have led to the offer of another job.

Where consultation is likely to lead to another job which the complainant would have accepted then the compensation should be based upon the rate of pay in the alternative position (**Thompson Wholesale Foods v Norris** [EAT 800/92]).

(5) It was futile to follow a proper procedure as the employee would have been dismissed in any event.

This is the exception referred to by he House of Lords in the *Polkey* case.

Whilst the emphasis in the case law is on proceduralism the Tribunal is entitled to reduce any award under the just and equitable principle on the ground that dismissal would have taken place in any event at a particular point in time. This was the position in **Young's of Gosport Limited v Kendell** [1977] IRLR 433 where it was found that the complainant would have been made redundant within a period of nine months.

Contributory Fault

Having made a deduction, if appropriate, based upon the chance that the complainant would have been dismissed the Tribunal will then go on to consider contributory fault under section 123(6) of the ERA 1996, though the Court of Appeal stated in **Rao v Civil Aviation Authority** [1994] IRLR 240 that the tribunal should bear in mind that it has already made a deduction under section 123(1) when considering contribution. *A reduction may be* made for contribution even though the employer has not shown a reason for dismissal (**Chauhan & Wood v Man Truck & Bus UK Limited** [EAT 931/94)] though the employee's conduct must be a material factor that contributed to the dismissal (**Robert Whiting Designs Limited v Lamb** [1978] ICR 89).

The Court of Appeal considered the test to be applied in **Nelson v BBC (No 2)** [1979] ICR 110 where it identified the factors that must be present if the damages are to be reduced on the ground of contributory conduct as follows:

"An award of compensation to a successful complainant can only be reduced on the ground that he contributed to his dismissal by his own conduct if the conduct on his part relied on for this purpose was culpable or blameworthy...It is necessary, however, to consider what is included in the concept of culpability or blameworthy conduct in this connection. The concept does not, in my view, necessarily involve any conduct of the complainant amounting to a breach of contract or a tort. It includes, no doubt, conduct of that kind. But it also includes conduct which, while not amounting to a breach of contract or a tort is nevertheless perverse or foolish or, if I may use the colloquialism, bloody minded. It may also include action which, though not meriting any of those more prerogative epithets, is nevertheless unreasonable in all the circumstances."

Not all unreasonable behaviour will be regarded as culpable or blameworthy; it must depend on the unreasonableness involved. Brandon LJ identified three factors that should be taken into account:

"It follows from what I have said that it was necessary for the industrial tribunal in this case, in order to justify the reduction of N's compensation which they made, to make three findings as follows. First, a finding that there was conduct of N in connection with his unfair dismissal which was culpable or blameworthy in the sense which I have explained. Secondly, that the unfair dismissal was caused or contributed to some extent by that conduct. Thirdly, that it was just and equitable, having regard to the first and second findings to reduce the assessment of N's loss by 60%."

Culpable or blameworthy actions

The Court of Appeal made it clear in the *Nelson* case that it is not necessary that there be illegality for the conduct to be regarded as culpable or blameworthy. Bloody minded behaviour such as refusal to attend a disciplinary hearing (**London Dungeon Limited v Belacal** [EAT 52/89]) or walking out of a meeting (**Wall v Brookside Metal Co Limited** [EAT 579/89]) may fall into this category. Since the conduct must be culpable or blameworthy it will be a rare case where any reduction is made because of a dismissal due to incapacity or ill health. (In **Slaughter v C Brewer & Sons Limited** [1990] IRLR 426.)

Similarly, in **Kraft Foods Limited v Fox** [1978] ICR the EAT were of the view that incompetence or incapability per se does not justify a reduction. However, if the employee is not up to the job because of lack of effort this may justify a reduction (**Chauhan v Man Truck & Bus Co UK** [EAT 931/94]). Conduct may be regarded as blameworthy, however, where the employee thinks that he is acting properly, as in **Alan v Hammett** [EAT 245/81] where an employee was dismissed for refusing, on legal advice, to pay back monies that had been paid to him by mistake and the damages were reduced by 60%.

Conduct caused or contributing to unfair dismissal

Where the employee refuses to give an explanation for his conduct that, if proffered, may have amounted to a good defence he may be regarded as having contributed to his dismissal, as in **Kwik Save Stores Limited v Clerkin** [EAT 295/96] where the employee was dismissed for clocking offences and failed to state that he thought it was normal company practice to clock out co-workers. The contributory conduct must be that of the complainant (**Parker Foundry Limited v Slack** [1992] IRLR 11) so the fact that other employees were treated differently will make no difference (**Salmon v Ribble Motor Services Limited** [EAT 51/91]).

Because the conduct must have caused or contributed to the dismissal only conduct that takes place prior to the dismissal and is known to the employer will be taken into account and the conduct must have contributed to the dismissal. In **Hutchinson v Enfield Rolling Mills** [1981] IRLR 318 the complainant was dismissed because he was seen at a demonstration whilst purportedly off sick. While the dismissal was held to be unfair compensation was assessed at 100% because of the complainant's attitude. The EAT held that this had no relevance to his dismissal so that compensation could not be reduced for this reason, though it could have been reduced because of his misbehaviour. However, it was stated in **Robert Whiting Designs Limited v Lamb** [1978] ICR 89 that Tribunals may take a broad view of conduct contributing to dismissal so that this may include conduct that is not the main reason for dismissal.

Extent to which it is just and equitable to reduce the award

Tribunals have been urged to a broad brush approach to the question of contributory fault and it has been stated that the issue is a question of fact with which the appellate courts will rarely interfere (**Hollier v Plysu Limited** [EAT 431/81]. In that case bands of 25% (slightly to blame); 50% (equally to blame); 75% (largely to blame) and 100% (wholly to blame were suggested) though tribunals have a large discretion to award other percentages. In **Yorke v Brown** [EAT 262/82] it was stated that an assessment of 10% was de minimis and it should be assessed on a broader basis or not at all.

Some examples, in descending order of size of reduction, include:

- **Smith v Lodge Bros (Funerals) Limited** [EAT 92/88]. The EAT considered it to be proper to reduce compensation by 100% where the employee wholly contributed to his dismissal by being absent from work, even though there had been no procedure.
- **Nairne v Highland & Islands Fire Brigade** [1989] IRLR 366. Compensation was increased by the EAT to 75% when an officer who needed to drive as part of his job was disqualified a second time for drink driving.
- **Coalter v Walter Craven Limited** [EAT 314/79]. Compensation was assessed at 25% by the EAT when the employee was dismissed for a first, but serious mistake, and she had not been given clear instructions.
- **Cornelius v London Borough of Hackney** [EAT 1061/94]. The EAT considered it to be wrong to reduce compensation by 50% in a case where an employee disclosed confidential information that revealed corruption. (See now the Public Interest Disclosure Act 1998 and Chapter 19).

Where the employee is dismissed by one employer and obtains employment with a second, but is dismissed by the second for culpable behaviour that dismissal cannot be regarded as contributing to the first dismissal (**Mabey Plant Hire Limited v Richens** (CA, Unreported)).

How has contributory fault been applied?

Constructive Dismissal

Where the employer's conduct has amounted to a repudiatory breach of contract it would, on the face of it, be illogical for there to be a finding of contribution and this led the EAT in **Holroyd v Gravure Cylinders Limited** [1984] IRLR 259 to state that such a finding could only be made in exceptional cases. However, the Courts have backtracked from this and there have been a number of cases in which contribution has been applied.

- In **Morrision v Amalgamated Transport & General Workers' Union** [1989] IRLR 361 compensation was reduced by 40% in a case where the complainant had been suspended, in breach of contract, because her conduct had caused the employer to react in this way. Two points were made. The *Holroyd* decision is not authority that there cannot be a finding of contribution in a constructive dismissal case. Since a constructive dismissal may be fair there is no reason why a finding of contribution cannot be made in any event.

• In **Polentarutti v Autokraft Limited** [1991] ICR 757 the employer was dissatisfied with the standard of the complainant's work and, in breach of contract, refused to pay for overtime. Although the dismissal was unfair there was a sufficient link to justify a finding of contribution and a finding of 2/3rd contribution was upheld by the EAT.

Where there has been a course of conduct over a period of time then the Tribunal may take this into account and does not have to rely upon the culminating incident (**Garner v Grange Furnishings Limited** [1977] IRLR 206).

Industrial pressure to dismiss and industrial action

By section 123(5) of the ERA 1996 the Tribunal:

> In determining for the purposes of *[assessing the compensatory award]*...no account shall be taken of any pressure which by-
> (a) calling, organising, procuring or financing a strike or other industrial action or
> (b) threatening to do so, was exercised on the employer to dismiss the employee; and that question shall be determined as if no such pressure had been exercised.

There is a distinction between industrial pressure to dismiss and other factors so that where there are reasons other than industrial pressure compensation may be reduced. In **Colwyn Borough Council v Dutton** [1980] IRLR 420 compensation was reduced where co-workers refused to work with a driver because of a number of driving incidents. Although industrial pressure was brought to bear, the careless driving was a factor that contributed to the dismissal. (See also **Sulemanji v Toughened Glass Limited** [1979] ICR 799).

In the case of industrial action, there are specific provisions relating to the fairness of dismissals (see Chapter 11). For the purpose of contribution the Courts have made it clear that they will not go into the rights and wrongs of a strike so that actual participation in industrial action is not a factor that will be taken into account (See **Courtaulds Northern Spinning Limited v Moosa** [1994] IRLR 43). However, there may be a distinction between the mere participation in industrial action; as to which it may be impossible to allocate blame, and the actual conduct of an individual during such action. This distinction was noted by the House of Lords in **Crosville Wales Limited v Tracey & Ors** [1997] IRLR 691. The House of Lords agreed with the Court of Appeal's view that any compensation due to the complainants in respect of their unfair dismissals, which arose from the employers' selective re-engagement of those dismissed while taking part in industrial action, did not fall to be reduced because of their conduct in participating in the industrial action. It stated that when an employment tribunal has jurisdiction to hear unfair dismissal claims by employees dismissed while taking part in industrial action because some of those involved have been offered re-engagement, participation in the industrial action itself cannot amount to "conduct" or "action" of the complainant justifying a reduction in compensation. In the case of collective action by a number of employees against their employer, it is impossible to allocate blame for the industrial action to any individual complainant, without reference to the conduct of the other employees concerned, including those who were re-engaged, and to that of the employer. However, individual blameworthy conduct additional to or separate from the mere act of participation in industrial action must in principle be capable of amounting to contributory fault.

2. Interest

Interest begins to accrue 42 days after the promulgation of the award by the Tribunal at the Judgments Rate (Industrial Tribunals (Interest) Order 1990 SI 1990/479.

CHAPTER TWENTY-NINE
INTERIM RELIEF AND ADDITIONAL AWARDS

Interim Relief

A Tribunal may grant interim relief in the following situations:

(1) Where a complaint of unfair dismissal has been presented under section 152 of the Trade Union and Labour Relations (Consolidation) Act (TULR(C)A).

(2) Where a complaint of unfair dismissal has been presented under:
- 100(1)(a) and (b) ERA (representative in Health and Safety cases).
- 101A(d) (representative under the Working Time Regulations)
- 102(1) (Trustee of occupational pension scheme)
- 103 (Employee representatives).
- Paragraph 161(2) of Schedule A1 to the TULR(C)A (Dismissals relating to recognition)
- 103A (Protected disclosures)

Sections 161 to 167 of TULR(C)A set out the approach to be taken in interim relief cases in relation to section 152 dismissals. Sections 128 to 132 of the Employment Rights Act (ERA) 1996 contains a similar approach in respect of the other dismissals for which interim relief may be granted.

By TULR(C)A, section 161(2) and ERA section 128(2) an application for interim relief must be presented before the end of the period of seven days immediately following the effective date of termination or the application may not be entertained. The essence of this remedy is that applications must be dealt with speedily so the employee must present an application with all due speed. The application should set out the reason for the dismissal It was held in **Barley & Ors v Amey Roadstone Corporation Limited** [1977]

ICR; IRLR 299 that an application for interim relief does not have to refer to the Act and will not be a nullity if it refers to unfair dismissal and interim relief even if it does not set out the reasons for seeking interim relief so that an amendment may be made after the seven day period ha elapsed.

Where the employee relies upon TULR(C)A, sections 152(1)(a) or (b) (union membership or activities), the Tribunal shall not entertain an application for interim relief unless within the seven day period there is also presented a certificate in writing signed by an authorised official of the independent trade union of which the employee was or proposed to become a member stating:

- that on the date of the dismissal the employee was or proposed to become a member of the union;
- that there appear to be reasonable grounds for supposing that the reason for the dismissal, or the principal reason, was one alleged in the complaint.

An authorised official is an official authorised by the trade union to act for this purpose and any document which purports to give such authorisation will be taken as such unless the contrary is proven as will any document purporting to be a certificate. In **Farmeary v Veterinary Drug Co Limited** [1976] IRLR 322 a GMWU recruitment officer signed his own certificate which stated "For the purposes of the Act, P Parmeary, Authorised District Officer". The application for interim relief was misconceived as the complaint was about selection for redundancy. However, the Tribunal made a number of comments about applications of this nature. It stated that the application for interim relief was defective in a number of respects. It was not clear whether the union official was an "authorised official". The Tribunal noted that an authorised official is not just any official validly appointed to his office but must be authorised to act for the purposes of the section. Whilst in the present case the official relied on the rules of the union which provide that within a district an officer for that district can do any act on behalf of the union, whether this was the case would depend on the scope of his authority and no certificate had been produced from the inion that he was so authorised. The certificate should in substance follow the wording of the Act and stipulate that the employee in question was a member of the union on the date of dismissal and that there appear to be reasonable grounds for supposing that the reason for dismissal was the one alleged in the complaint.

The EAT stated in **Sulemany v Habib Bank Limited** [1983] ICR 60 that it is not mandatory that the certificate should state on its face that the signatory is an authorised official. Authorisation may be express or implied but if it is challenged the burden is on the union to show that the signatory had the necessary authority. If no evidence is produced to this effect then the case will fail. It was also stated in *Sulemany* that the certificate may be read in conjunction with the Originating Application and that the fact it did not refer to reasonable grounds would not render it a nullity (See also **Bradley v Edward Ryde & Sons** [1979] ICR 488).

An application for interim relief will be heard as soon as practicable after receiving the application and certificate (TULR(C)A, 162(1)) or in the other cases after receiving the application (ERA 1996, 128(3)). The employer shall be given a copy of the application (and in section 152 dismissals copies of any certificate) not later than seven days before the hearing (TULR(C)A, 162(2), ERA 1996, 128(4)) together with notice of the date, time and place of the hearing.

Where the complainant has made a request that a third party be joined under section 160 of TULR(C)A three days or more before the date of the hearing that person shall be given a copy of the application and of any certificate not later than seven days before the hearing (TULR(C)A, 162(3)) together with notice of the date, time and place of the hearing.

A Tribunal shall not exercise any power of postponement that it may have in relation to an interim relief application unless it is satisfied that there are special circumstances which justify it in doing so (TULR(C)A, 162(4), ERA 1996, 128(5)).

By section 163(1) of TULR(C)A if, on the hearing of an application for interim relief, it appears to the Tribunal that:

> ...it is likely that on determining the complaint to which the application relates that it will find that, by virtue of section 152, the complainant has been unfairly dismissed...

then the provisions contained in TULR(C)A, sections 163(2) to (6) apply, as follows:

The Tribunal shall announce its findings to both parties, if present, and shall explain its powers and the circumstances in which it will exercise these powers. The employer shall be asked whether he is willing, pending the determination or settlement of the complaint

- to reinstate the employee, that is to say, to treat him as if he had not been dismissed, or
- if not, to re-engage him in another job on terms and conditions not less favourable than those which would have been applicable to him if he had not been dismissed. The period prior to the dismissal will be regarded as continuous following the dismissal.

A similar procedure is contained in section 129 of the ERA 1996.

Likelihood of success

Central to the Tribunal exercising its powers under the interim relief provisions is the necessity for a finding that the complainant is likely to succeed at the full hearing in making out the inadmissible ground for dismissal. The test to be applied was considered in **Taplin v C Shippam Limited** [1978] IRLR 450 the EAT stated that in order to determine for the purposes of an application for interim relief whether it is "likely" that an applicant will be found to have been dismissed on grounds of trade union membership or activities, the correct approach is for the Industrial Tribunal to ask itself whether the applicant has established that he has a "pretty good" chance of succeeding in the final application to the Tribunal. In order to obtain such an order under an applicant must achieve a higher degree of certainty in the mind of the Tribunal than that of showing that he just had a "reasonable" prospect of success. The EAT stated that alternative tests such as real possibility, reasonable prospect or 51% or better were not appropriate.

Where the employer states that he is willing to re-instate the employee the tribunal shall make an order to that effect (TULR(C)A, 163(4); ERA 1996, 129(5)).

Where the employer is willing to re-engage the employee and specifies the terms and conditions then the employee will be asked if he is willing to be re-engaged on these terms (TULR(C)A, 163(5); ERA 1996, 129(6)). Where the employee's refusal is, in the opinion of the Tribunal reasonable, then an order shall be made for continuation of the contract of employment. If the refusal is not reasonable no order shall be made.

Where, on the hearing of an interim relief application, the employer fails to attend or states that he is unwilling to reinstate or re-engage the employee the Tribunal shall make an order for the continuation of the employment (TULR(C)A, 163(6); ERA 1996, 129(9)).

By TULR(C)A, section 164(1) or ERA 1996, 130(1) an order for the continuation of employment is an order that the contract of employment shall remain in force from the date of termination until the determination or settlement of the complaint:

- for the purpose of pay or any other benefit derived from the employment, seniority, pension rights and other similar matters, and
- for the purpose of determining for any purpose the period for which the employee has been continuously employed.

The Order will not lapse until the determination of settlement of the complaint (**Zucker v Astrid Jewels Limited** [1978] IRLR 38).

Where an order is made the Tribunal shall specify the amount to be paid by the employer by way of pay in respect of each normal pay period or part of any period falling between the date of termination and the determination or settlement of the complaint (TULR(C)A, 164(2); ERA 1996, 130(2)). The amount specified shall be that which the employee could reasonably have been expected to earn during the period or part and shall be paid on the normal day for the period or as so ordered (TULR(C)A, 164(3); ERA 1996, 130(3)) and shall be determined as if he had not been dismissed (TULR(C)A, 164(7); ERA 1996, 130(7)). The Tribunal should take into account payments that have been made to the employee under the contract of employment, as damages for breach of contract or as a lump sum payment in calculating liability (TULR(C)A, 164(5), (6); ERA 1996, 130(5), (6)). Payments made under a continuation of contract order are not repayable and the Courts will not stay such an order in anticipation of an appeal (**Initial Textile Services v Rendell** [EAT 383/91]) even though the money may not be repaid.

The employer may apply at any time between the making of the order and the determination or settlement of the complaint for the order to be varied or revoked on the ground of a change in circumstances since the making of the order (TULR(C)A, 165(1), ERA 1996, 131). It was held in **British Coal Corporation v McGinty** [1988] IRLR 7 that a different tribunal from that which made the interim relief order has power to hear an application to revoke or vary. In that case is was also stated that it was undesirable that the tribunal who made the order should hear the full matter as it may appear to have already prejudged the issue by the interim relief order.

Where the employer does not comply with an order for reinstatement or re-engagement the employee may apply to the Tribunal, which may make an order for the continuation of the employment and order such compensation to be paid as is just and equitable having regard to the infringement of the employer's right to reinstated or re-engaged and any loss suffered by the employee in consequence of non compliance (TULR(C)A, 166(1); ERA 1996, 132(1)).

Where the employer has failed to comply with the terms of an order for the continuation of the contract of employment and this consists of non compliance with an order to pay an amount specified the Tribunal may determine the amount owed by the employer on the date of the determination (TULR(C)A, 166(4), ERA 1996, 132(5)) and, in any other case, order compensation as is considered just and equitable having regard to the loss suffered by the employee (TULR(C)A, 166(5); ERA 132(6)).

Additional Awards

Prior to the Employment Relations Act 1999 there was a dual scheme in respect of awards over and above the normal unfair dismissal awards. There was power to make a special award in respect of certain inadmissible reasons for dismissal. By section 33 of that Act the provisions relating to special awards have been repealed. The scheme that is now in place is therefore simplified and the Tribunals have power to make an additional award in all cases.

By section 117(3) of the ERA 1996 where an order is made for reinstatement or reengagement and the complainant is not reinstated or re-engaged then an additional award may be made of not less than 26 or more than 52 weeks pay unless it can be shown that it was not practicable to comply with the order (117(4(a)) though for this purpose engagement of a permanent replacement is not to be taken into account unless the employer can show that it was not practicable for the employee's work to be done without engaging a permanent replacement. The provision as to the amount to be awarded was inserted by section 33(2) of the ERA 1999.

Where the complainant has unreasonably prevented an order for reinstatement or re-engagement from being complied with that conduct may be taken into account as part of the complainant's failure to mitigate his loss (117(8)) ERA 1996.

It is to be noted that section 117(5) and (6) which provided for an additional award of between 26 and 52 weeks in the case of discriminatory dismissals where reinstatement or re-engagement were refused are also repealed. This does not have any effect as those sums can now be awarded under the new section 117(3). The following guidance may be taken from the case law:

(1) A proper assessment must take place and the Tribunal should provide reasons for the award (**Morganite Electrical Carbon Limited v Donne** [1987] IRLR 363). The conduct of the employer and the losses suffered by the complainant may be taken into account.

(2) It was stated in **George v Beecham Group** [1977] IRLR 43 that an award may be made to mark the Tribunal's disapproval of the employer's refusal to reinstate.

(3) A blatant refusal to reinstatement is likely to mean that something above the minimum additional award is appropriate even if the employee has become incapacitated by illness (**Motherwell Railway Club v McQueen and McQueen** [EAT 652/88]).

(4) The amount of an award will also be fixed by taking into account the merits of the case including the failure of the employee to mitigate his losses (**Mabirizi v National Hospital for Nervous Diseases** [1990] IRLR 133.

(5) A full award may be made in a discrimination case, even if it is indirect discrimination, where the employer knew about it **Dick v University of Dundee** [COIT]

(6) Ex gratia payments may be set off against the additional award (**Darr v LRC Products Limited** [1993] IRLR 257).

CHAPTER THIRTY
RECOUPMENT

Where an employee is awarded compensation for future loss he will not be entitled to receive jobseekers allowance or income support as the compensatory award will have fully compensated him in respect of his anticipated losses. Other benefits may be taken into account as set out in Chapter 28.

The Regulations do not apply to statutory redundancy payments or to settlements reached between the parties.

Where the employee has been paid benefits between the date of the dismissal and the date of the Tribunal hearing then the Employment Protection (Recoupment of Jobseeker's Allowance and Income Support) Regulations 1996 [1996/2349] will be applicable. Key points are:

(1) The Tribunal will assess compensation without regard to the amount of the income support or Jobseeker's Allowance that has been paid to or claimed by the employee in the period that coincides with any part of a period to which the prescribed element is attributable (Reg 4(1)).

(2) The prescribed element are those payments set out in column 1 of the Regulations and to payments of a protective award. In an unfair dismissal case this is the compensation for loss of wages for a period before the conclusion of the Tribunal proceedings. (See the column at the end of this chapter which sets out the prescribed elements for the different claims). The conclusion of the hearing will be the date of the final hearing so that if there is an appeal and the case is remitted it will be this date (**Tipton v West Midlands Co-operative Society Limited** [EAT 859/86] – where after numerous appeals the period was five years).

(3) Where a reduction is made by the Tribunal for contribution, a proportionate reduction is made in arriving at the amount of the prescribed element (Reg 4(2)).

(4) The Tribunal must set out the monetary award, the prescribed element, the dates to which the prescribed element is applicable and the amount, if any, by which the monetary award exceeds the prescribed element (Reg 4(3)).

(5) The decision will be forwarded to the Secretary of State (Reg 4).

(6) Under Regulation 7 so much of the award as consists of the prescribed element shall be regarded as stayed as respects the relevant employee until a recoupment notice is served on the employer or notification has been given that a recoupment notice will not be served.

(7) Under Regulation 8 the Secretary of State may serve a recoupment notice claiming total or partial recoupment and:
   • the appropriate amount shall be the lesser of the amount of the prescribed element less tax or national insurance to be paid by the employer or the amount paid on account of Jobseeker's Allowance or Income Support which coincides with the period to which the prescribed element is attributable.
   • the recoupment notice shall be served on the employer and operate as an instruction to pay by way of deduction out of the sum due under the award the recoupable amount to the Secretary of State and the employer shall be under a duty to comply with the notice.

(8) There is provision in Regulation 10 for determination and review of the benefit which the Secretary of State seeks to recoup if the employer gives notice within 21 days or such further time as is allowed that he does not accept the amount specified as correct and this shall be determined by an adjudication officer.

CHAPTER THIRTY-ONE
INTERRELATIONSHIP WITH OTHER
AREAS: A FOOTNOTE

Since the increase of the compensatory award to £50,000 the significance of other parallel claims, particularly for discrimination, where there is no statutory ceiling, may diminish. When the statutory limit was £12,000 for compensatory awards an award for race, sex or disability discrimination may have attracted compensation that was many thousands above this limit. However, parallel claims in respect of discrimination may still be of significance both substantively and from the point of view of compensation. The following general points may be made:

(1) Under section 126 of the ERA there is not to be any double recovery in respect of unfair dismissal and discrimination claims.

(2) However, a claim under the discrimination legislation will attract interest on different principles from an unfair dismissal claim.

(3) Damages for injury to feelings may be awarded in discrimination cases.

(4) It is still possible that the £50,000 compensatory ceiling can be exceeded.

(5) Additional awards are now brought into line whether or not the refusal to reinstate or re-engage relates to discrimination or other reasons.

(6) Substantively, it may be difficult to show a fair dismissal for capacity where the tribunal finds the employer liable under the Disability Discrimination Act 1995.

(7) Similarly a finding of race or sex discrimination may make it difficult to show a fair dismissal. It should also be noted that in pregnancy cases there may be a wider power to make a claim for pregnancy related sicknesses than under the ERA.

(8) There are different procedural weapons available in discrimination cases i.e. the questionnaire procedures.

(9) There are different remedies, i.e. recommendations in discrimination cases.

(10) Similarly, there is no corresponding provision for reinstatement or re-engagement in the discrimination legislation.

INDEX